CHAOS, DISORDER, AND REVOLUTION

Prince

Jason Draper

Prince
CHAOS, DISORDER, AND REVOLUTION
Jason Draper

To my darling Nicky

A BACKBEAT BOOK
First edition 2011
Published by Backbeat Books (an imprint of Hal Leonard Corporation)
19 West 21st Street, New York, NY 10010, USA
www.backbeatbooks.com

Devised and produced for Backbeat Books by Outline Press Ltd
2A Union Court, 20-22 Union Road, London SW4 6JP, England

ISBN: 978-0-87930-961-9

Editor: Thomas Jerome Seabrook
Design: Paul Cooper Design

Printed by Regent Publishing Services Limited, China

11 12 13 14 15 5 4 3 2 1

CONTENTS

5 INTRODUCTION

CHAPTER 1
8 I WASN'T BORN LIKE MY BROTHER: HANDSOME AND TALL
CHAPTER 2
13 LET'S WORK
CHAPTER 3
24 PEOPLE CALL ME RUDE; I WISH WE ALL WERE NUDE
CHAPTER 4
35 ALL THE CRITICS LOVE U
CHAPTER 5
44 BABY I'M A STAR
CHAPTER 6
58 U GOT 2 TRY A NEW POSITION
CHAPTER 7
72 GOT ANY DREAMS YOU AIN'T USIN'?
CHAPTER 8
81 TALKIN' STUFF IN A VIOLENT ROOM
CHAPTER 9
93 I'VE SEEN THE FUTURE
CHAPTER 10
109 WE R THE NEW POWER GENERATION, WE WANT 2 CHANGE THE WORLD
CHAPTER 11
121 EYE HATE U
CHAPTER 12
134 THE EXODUS HAS BEGUN
CHAPTER 13
161 EMANCIPATION
CHAPTER 14
172 U EVER HAD A CRYSTAL BALL?
CHAPTER 15
185 THIS IS THE WORK WE MUST DO 4 REVOLUTION 2 COME 2 PASS
CHAPTER 16
198 DON'T U MISS THE FEELING MUSIC GAVE YA BACK IN THE DAY?
CHAPTER 17
210 U NEED 2 BE A SUPERSTAR OR GROW UP — BUT NOT BOTH
CHAPTER 18
224 PRINCE IS ALIVE! (AND HE LIVES IN MINNEAPOLIS)

TIMELINE 231
ENDNOTES 261
INDEX 265
ACKNOWLEDGEMENTS 272

INTRODUCTION

I make music because if I don't, I'd die. I record because it's in my blood. I hear sounds all the time. It's almost a curse: to know you can always make something new.

PRINCE

Prince Rogers Nelson first became fascinated with music at the age of six, when he saw his father's three-piece jazz band perform. Everything about it seemed amazing: the sounds that came out of his father's piano; the chorus girls that came out dancing at Nelson Sr's command; the emotive power the whole thing had over the people in the audience.

Prince became obsessed with music as an outlet for his innermost feelings. In the 80s, those feelings seemed to fall perfectly in tune with the zeitgeist. Twenty years after that epochal event in a tiny jazz club in his hometown of Minneapolis, Minnesota, Prince had become a global superstar. The most famous musician on the planet, the author and star of *Purple Rain*, had only just turned 26.

Commercial success is one thing. Being one of the most important and talented artists ever to have graced the earth is quite another. With the April 1978 release of his debut, *For You*, Prince began a ten-year run of albums on which he continued to push himself and his art further and further. In a decade widely remembered for its selfishness and soullessness, Prince redefined the concept of 'soulful' music.

Taking his lead from the flag-bearers of funk – Sly Stone, James Brown, and George Clinton – and artistic pioneers such as Miles Davis and Joni Mitchell, Prince imbued his art with his idiosyncratic view of life, turning out music from the mind of a sex-obsessed deviant (*Dirty Mind*); a bomb-fearing party-animal ('1999'); a God-fearing man searching for a ways to reconcile the spiritual with the sexual (*Lovesexy*); and so much more.

When Prince had finished redefining the music, he took his battle for individuality to the record business. During the 90s he waged war against his record label, Warner Bros, changed his name to an unpronounceable symbol, and pronounced himself a slave to the system. He might have faced derision from all corners then but now, a decade into the 21st century, it's become obvious that Prince's actions weren't just crucial for him, but for whole generations of musicians to come.

Many in the music business continue to suffer as a result of their initial failure to embrace the internet, but not Prince. He was the first artist to release a whole album online via his own self-financed record label, and has continued to seek out new ways to release and promote his music, even going so far as to give it away for free. His fight for artists' rights has shown future generations that they don't have to adhere to anyone else's rules, and shown how one man can stay relevant for more than 30 years on the strength of a passion to challenge the status quo and change the way things are done.

It should come as no surprise that an artist who wages war on staying still remains impossible to define. "I'm not a woman, I'm not a man," he sang on *Purple Rain*'s 'I Would Die 4 U.' "I am something you'll never understand." He has remained true to that expression ever since, whether by fusing masculine and feminine concepts, changing his name to an unpronounceable symbol (and back again), turning his back on his raunchy past and becoming a devout Jehovah's Witness, or breaking new ground on the internet and then seemingly removing himself from it entirely. Throughout it all he remains Prince: indefinable, contradictory, an enigma wholly committed to beating his own path.

This book is not a muckraker, it's not a gossip, and it's sure as hell not bent on setting one man up to knock him down. Prince has been ridiculous, Prince has been amusing, Prince has been astounding. He's been the envy of every musician on the planet. His peers might be stuck in an endless cycle of albums and tours, but Prince doesn't need to be seen unless he wants you to see him. *Prince: Chaos, Disorder, And Revolution* will simply tell you what happened and how, leaving it up to you to make your own conclusions about the man who has done it all, and yet continues to look for more ways in which to do it.

Jason Draper
London, England

7

I WASN'T BORN LIKE MY BROTHER: HANDSOME AND TALL

I went through a lot when I was a boy. They called me sissy, punk, freak, and faggot. See, the girls loved you, but the boys hated you. They called me Princess.

PRINCE

" I named my son Prince because I wanted him to do everything I wanted to do," Prince's father, John L. Nelson, told *A Current Affair* in 1991. Even though his son was only 33 at the time, Nelson Sr boasted: "He's done all of it."[2]

Much less could be said for John L., a gifted pianist and leader of The Prince Rogers Trio – a Minneapolis jazz combo that gave Prince Rogers Nelson his name. With both parents musicians (his mother, Mattie Shaw, was a former jazz singer), Prince was surrounded by music from the moment he was taken home. Apart from co-credits on his son's future compositions, however, John L. Nelson would struggle to break out of the small-time gigging scene. His son would go on to become the first artist since The Beatles to simultaneously land a Number One album, single, and film – all at the age of just 24.

Having struggled in Louisiana, Prince's parents had moved separately to Minnesota during the early 50s in search of work in a part of America that was known for its liberal race-relations. Prince would later use his parents' mixed heritage – his father was part Italian, while his mother had African American, Native American, and white roots – to confuse interviewers who refused to focus on his music alone. A much less mixed influence was, undoubtedly, John L.'s career as pianist in the Minneapolis clubs.

Prince was born on June 7 1958 at Mount Sinai Hospital, Minneapolis, and at the age of five was taken by his mother to see The Prince Rogers Trio play in a downtown Minneapolis club. The group's mix of jazz standards and original material wasn't earth shattering, but the experience seemed nonetheless to change Prince forever. He watched with interest as his father, decked out in the sharpest of suits, led the band through its repertoire and held sway over the crowd. When a line of dancing girls came out – seemingly also under Nelson's control – Prince had seen all he needed to see to know that the musician's life was for him.

There are similar echoes in Prince's recollections of seeing James Brown at the age of ten. "[My] stepdad put me on stage with him," he told MTV in 1985, "and I danced a bit until the bodyguard took me off."[3] Like Nelson Sr, Brown would have a lasting effect on the boy. "He inspired me because of the control he had over his band," Prince later revealed, "and because of the beautiful dancing girls he had. I wanted both."[4]

There was a piano in the front room of the Nelsons' house, and whenever he wasn't at school or at the local Seventh Day Adventist church, the young Prince – nicknamed Skipper by his mom – could be found playing it. The first pieces he learnt to play were the theme tunes to *Batman* and *The Man From U.N.C.L.E.*; by the age of seven, he had reportedly written his first song, 'Funkmachine.'

The city of Minneapolis itself was similarly influential on Prince's development. It was one of the few places in America's Midwest where white and black communities weren't so strictly divided, which meant that radio was also less segregated. Whereas big cities such as New York and Chicago had stations that played black music all day, KUXL would only broadcast contemporary funk and soul between 10am and 2pm before reverting to rock'n'roll later in the day, when more listeners would be tuned in. "Listening to white radio was a positive thing that gave [Prince] a real, rounded way of finding out what was going on in music," his first manager, Owen Husney, later recalled, noting that being forced to listen to white pop gave Prince "a real edge."[5]

Music and the radio became a means of escapism for the young Prince as he sought both a way to communicate his innermost thoughts and also a diversion from the physical abuse he suffered at the hands of his father. He has since downplayed this area of his upbringing, telling Larry King that his father was merely "a very strict disciplinarian," but the situation appears to have been rather more serious than that.[6] Prince has reportedly shared stories of abuse with a few close confidantes, notably Susan Rogers, his engineer from 1983 to 1988, who worked on his bestselling albums. "Prince told me there was abuse in his childhood," she later recalled. "He had a weird name, he was small. He was also extremely intelligent and sensitive."[7] Confirming such claims, Prince addressed family abuse in the semi-autobiographical *Purple Rain* movie and the song 'Papa,' on which he sings: "Don't abuse children, or else they turn out like me."

John L. Nelson and Mattie Shaw divorced in 1968, and their ten-year-old son soon began shuffling from home to home. Prince's father left his piano behind, giving the boy free reign to learn the instrument by himself. Mattie Shaw remarried a couple of years later, but Prince's relationship with his stepfather, Hayward Baker, was fraught. "I disliked him immediately," he recalled. "He would bring us lots of presents all the time, rather than sit down and talk with us and give us companionship."[8] One direct result of this was that it was left to Prince's mother to teach him about the birds and the bees – which Prince once claimed she did by providing him with an assortment of *Playboy* magazines and erotic literature.

Prince's parents' split had a lasting effect – and not only on his sex education. Noting Prince's later, well publicised quirks, Alan Leeds, his tour manager through most of the 80s, said: "His mother basically walked away from him, and his father struggled to raise him and threw in the towel. ... It certainly doesn't add up to a very secure, well-rounded individual."[9]

In 1970, Prince enrolled at Bryant Junior High and moved in with his father for a brief spell, during which time he hung out with his much taller and more athletic stepbrother, Duane. This too had quite an effect on the young Prince. "My older brother was a basketball star," he told the *Los Angeles Times* in 1981. "He always had girls around him. I think I must have been on a jealous trip, because I got out of sports."[10] (Prince later referenced Duane – "my brother, handsome and tall" – on

1999's 'Lady Cab Driver,' and subsequently hired him first as a bodyguard and then as head of security at Paisley Park in the 90s.)

Prince didn't stay with his father for very long. In 1972 he moved to Central High, where he began to come into his own. He was still a quiet, shy boy who walked around in denim flares, knitted tank tops, and an Afro, and spent his lunch breaks practicing alone in the music room – in part to avoid his schoolmates, who seemed happy making life difficult for the introverted teenager. "People would say something about our clothes or the way we looked or who we were with," Prince told *Rolling Stone* in 1981, "and we'd end up fighting. I was a very good fighter. I never lost. I don't know if I fight fair, but I go for it."[11] But he had also a natural teenage interest in girls, and was reportedly kicked out of his father's house after being caught in bed with one of them.

In 1985, while giving *Rolling Stone* journalist Neal Karlan a tour of Minneapolis in the wake of *Purple Rain*'s extraordinary success, Prince pointed out a phone booth as being the one from which "I called my dad and begged him to take me back … he said no, so I called my sister [Tyka] and begged her to ask him. So she did, and afterward told me all I had to do was call him back, tell him I was sorry, and he'd take me back. So I did, and he still said no. I sat crying at that phone booth for two hours. That's the last time I cried."[12]

Prince spent a brief period living with his aunt Olivia Nelson before moving in with a close school-friend, André Anderson, whose mother became a kind of surrogate mom to Prince, too. Prince initially shared a room with André, but soon grew frustrated at his friend's untidiness and moved into the basement. By then the boys had already formed a band together – Grand Central, with Prince on guitar, Anderson on bass, and cousin Charles Smith on drums, with André's sister Linda and neighborhood friend Terry Jason joining later – and now had somewhere to practice. Surrounded by musical instruments after rehearsals, Prince continued to practice on his own in the comfort of isolation. But that wasn't all that went on in the basement. Stories abound of more typical adolescent behavior taking place down there. "Prince and I made music and entertained various local girls," Anderson later recalled. "When I first met Prince he was a nice respectable boy. He didn't even cuss. I was the renegade."[13]

Charles Smith had a rather less romanticized view of his time in the basement. "[It] would flood all the time in the spring," he later said in an interview for the BBC documentary *Liquid Assets: Prince's Millions*. "[Prince] would always cry to me: 'I'm not gonna live like this anymore … . When I make it, I ain't ever gonna turn back.'"[14] Smith didn't stay in the group for long, with the other members soon deciding that he was devoting too much time to the school football team. He was replaced in 1974 by another of Prince's school friends, Morris Day, who later went on to front The Time.

The group then became Grand Central Corporation and picked up their first manager in the form of Day's mother, LaVonne Daugherty. She subsequently invited Prince's cousin by marriage, Pepé Willie, to help oversee the group. Willie had recently moved to Minneapolis from New York, where he had worked as a musician, and had often given Prince advice over the phone. His first job was to acquire studio time for the band at the local Cookhouse facility.

At first Willie wasn't sure who Grand Central Corporation's main star was. "Everybody was talented," he later recalled. "But I always, always noticed Prince going over to Linda, the keyboard player, and showing her: 'No, this is what you play.'"[15] Prince would then do the same with Anderson, picking up the bass and showing him what to do, too. Before long Willie had hired Prince as a session player in his own funk band, 94 East. (Several tapes of their collaborations exist, notably 2000's *Prince With 94 East: One Man Jam*.)

On February 13 1976, the *Central High Pioneer* ran Prince's first ever interview. The school paper marveled at his ability to play "several instruments, such as guitar, bass, all keyboards, and drums," noting that he had also started to sing but had given up on the saxophone. In the weeks prior to the interview, Prince had been working on a demo with Grand Central Corporation in Minneapolis's ASI Studio (paid for by Morris Day's mother). Prince told the *Pioneer* that they hoped to have an album out in the early summer, but conceded that, because of the lack of major studios and record companies, it would be "very hard for a band to make it in this state. ... I really feel that if we had lived in Los Angeles or New York or some other big city, we would have gotten over by now."[16] Little did he realize that, in ten years time, he would have turned Minneapolis into a new center of cool, and would be running his own label and hi-tech recording studio out of it.

By the middle of 1976, Grand Central Corporation had renamed themselves Champagne, partly because of the old name's similarity to Sly & The Family Stone bassist Larry Graham's new group, Graham Central Station, and partly because Charles Smith had begun to complain that he had come up with the original name. Champagne began recording at Moonsound Studio, a small recording facility owned by Chris Moon, a local concert promoter who wrote jingles for advertisements. Moon quickly took note of Prince's talent and invited him to collaborate on some songs he had started writing the lyrics to in exchange for as much free recording time as he wanted. Despite suggestions that Isaac Hayes might offer Champagne a recording contract, Prince accepted Moon's offer, and was given the keys to Moonsound just in time for his graduation from Central High on his 18th birthday. Under the Employment heading of his graduation book, Prince simply wrote the word 'music.'

CHAPTER 2

LET'S WORK

He was sort of what we would call an urban legend up in the Minneapolis area. There were these hushed conversations about … the next Stevie Wonder.

DEZ DICKERSON

Despite his precocious talents and free reign to write and record his own music around the clock at Moonsound Studios, Prince was still stuck in Minneapolis without access to major studios and record labels. Struggling to find success, he found himself a growing fish in an increasingly small-seeming pond. "I didn't have any money," he later told *Rolling Stone* magazine, "so I'd just stand outside [McDonald's] and smell stuff. Poverty makes people angry, brings out their worst side. I was very bitter when I was young." Realizing that, in Minneapolis, "we got all the new music and dances three months late," Prince decided to create something of his own. "Anyone who was around then knew what was happening. I was *working*. When they were sleeping, I was *jamming*. When they woke up, I had another groove."[2]

It was around this time that Prince asked Moonsound's owner, Chris Moon, to manage him. Moon wasn't interested in taking on the extra load, but did make one important suggestion: that Prince drop his surname and perform simply as Prince. In the autumn of 1976 he traveled to New York with a demo tape of four of the 14 songs he had completed at Moonsound. One of them, 'Baby,' was a Prince original that would later show up on his debut album, *For You*. 'Soft & Wet' would, too, but that was a Chris Moon co-write, as were the other two songs, 'Love Is Forever' and 'Aces.'

While staying in New York with his half-sister Sharon, Prince received an offer from Tiffany Entertainment to buy the publishing rights to the four songs but declined it, aware even at this early stage of the way the music business worked, and that Tiffany would subsequently make all the money from his work. Returning to Minneapolis, he was introduced by Moon to Owen Husney, the head of The Ad Company, an advertising agency that also marketed local musicians. "I thought this group was phenomenal," Husney recalled, "and I said to Chris: 'Who's the group?'"[3] Moon explained that it was just one kid, writing, playing, and singing everything.

Husney was stunned, and so enthused that he offered to manage Prince, gearing the $8 million per year that The Ad Company made from its existing clients toward promoting his new charge's interests. With the help of his lawyer, Gary Levinson, Husney raised $50,000 and founded American Artists Inc with the sole purpose of managing Prince. He gave the singer a rehearsal space in his offices, rented him a one-room apartment, and took over from where Chris Moon had left off. "I presented myself as the protector of creativity," Husney recalled. "He was young and a lot of people were going to come at him, and he was vulnerable at the time."[4]

In December 1976, Husney booked Prince – who was winding up recordings with his cousin Pepé Willie's 94 East – into Minneapolis's Sound 80 studios to record a new demo tape with local engineer David Rivkin. Sound 80 was much bigger than Moonsound. It gave Prince the opportunity to transfer all that he already knew into a bigger arena – and the chance to take advantage of a wealth of new technology, notably a range of synthesizers such as the Oberheim 4-Voice. To begin with, a group of string players were brought in, but Prince – keen as ever to dominate his own recordings – preferred to use synthesized sounds that he could control himself. He would later declare that this allowed him to inject the "joy" he felt "into all these 'players' [so that] the same exuberant soul speaks through all the instruments."[5]

By the following spring, Prince and Husney had completed work on a demo tape, and Husney printed up 15 press packs at a cost of $100 each. The two men had decided that the best way to market Prince was with an air of mystery. As such, the all-black press packs featured nothing but his name on the outside, with just the tape on the inside. The idea was that Prince could be marketed as a new Stevie Wonder – somebody who demanded total creative control, just as Wonder had.

"I lied my way in everywhere to get him in," Husney later admitted. "Jealously is what makes this business go round."[6] He called Warner Bros vice-president Russ Thyret and told him that CBS was planning to fly Prince out to LA for a meeting. This had the desired effect, as did a similar call to CBS. Soon, as well as securing meetings with the two biggest record labels in America, Husney had also managed to pique the interest of A&M, ABC/Dunhill, and RSO.

Husney's approach to the meetings was similarly clever. He would present the label representatives with the press kit and play them the tape while Prince sat outside in the hallway, in order to maintain an air of intrigue. But while securing the meetings had been easy, getting the right deal would prove rather more complicated. Neither RSO nor ABC was interested in signing Prince, while A&M wouldn't offer anything beyond a standard two-album deal. CBS's representatives were treated to a live, in-studio audition when they watched Prince record 'Just As Long As We're Together' at Village Recorders in Los Angeles on April 8 1977, but still only offered a three-album deal with the added stipulation that Earth Wind & Fire bassist Verdine White would come onboard as producer.

This, to Prince, was unacceptable, and left only Warners. Once again the offer was for a three-album deal, but at least this label had a reputation for being more artist-friendly. "While everybody was wining and dining," Husney recalled, "Russ [Thyret] took us back to his house, sat on the floor, and talked music with us."[7] Thyret wanted a debut album within six months, and two more by the end of the 70s.

The contract only guaranteed that Prince would be allowed to co-produce his albums, and gave Warners the option of renewing it at the end for either three more albums over two years or two more over one. But it was good enough. On June 25 1977, less than three weeks after his 19th birthday, Prince signed the deal. On his return to Minneapolis he headed straight for Studio 80 to record a new song, 'We Can Work It Out.' It was intended as a symbol of the understanding between label and artist, but the relationship would prove to be rather less harmonious than that.

The note on the back of *For You* says it all: "Produced, Composed, Arranged, And Performed By Prince." Barring a co-writing credit for Chris Moon ('Soft & Wet'), there was nothing more to say. He might be a 19-year-old boy from Minneapolis who had only signed to the label ten months before the album was released, but in that short time Prince had become the youngest producer Warners has ever had. He was also an accomplished multi-instrumentalist, credited with playing 23 different instruments in the album's liner notes. And, with his debut album, Prince was hotly tipped to become the 'new' Stevie Wonder.

Warner Bros knew from the start that Prince was a singular talent. The label had beaten three others to secure the signature of a man they all felt had the potential to become one of the most forward-thinking artists of the time. Even so, the hit-making mentality prevailed. Hit records were supposed to have hit producers behind them: a Sam Phillips or a Phil Spector. To the ears of the Warners executives, Prince should have been aspiring toward the disco sound of Giorgio Moroder, Nile Rodgers, and Earth Wind & Fire.

And so it was that the label made provisional arrangements for Earth Wind & Fire's Maurice White to produce Prince's debut. The trouble with this was that Prince had already turned down CBS partly because of the label's insistence that Maurice's brother, Verdine, should produce his debut. As far as Prince was concerned, the slick, metronomic sound of disco would soon be a thing of the past. Punk had already begun to tear up the rock'n'roll rulebook, and it was only a matter of time, he thought, before a similar change affected the club scene. Giving his debut album the Earth Wind & Fire treatment could potentially kill it before it even got into stores.

"He didn't want that sound placed on him – he wanted to go forward," Husney recalled. "Prince walked out of the room and said: 'Nobody's producing *my* first album.'"[8] Husney was then left with the unenviable task of convincing one of the world's biggest record labels that an unknown teenager with no previous track record should be allowed to produce his own album.

Warners put Prince to the test in much the same way that CBS had a year earlier. After booking him a weekend in Los Angeles's Amigo Studio, a series of top executives came in and out, surreptitiously, to watch as he recorded 'Just As Long As We're Together' from scratch, all by himself. Prince thought they were janitors and carried on as normal, but the executives were suitably impressed, and agreed to his wish to produce the whole album himself. There was just one catch: somebody more experienced would be brought in as the album's executive producer, just in case Prince ran into any difficulties.

The *For You* sessions began in September 1977 at Sound 80 studios in

Minneapolis, where Prince had recorded his first proper demo. It was suggested at one point that the engineer of those previous sessions, David Rivkin, might serve as *For You*'s executive producer. In the end, however, Warners settled on Tommy Vicari, who had previously worked with one of Prince's heroes, Carlos Santana.

Vicari wasn't impressed with the facilities at Studio 80 and suggested decamping to Los Angeles. This concerned Husney, who thought his young workaholic might find himself distracted by the city's abundance of sex, drugs, and rock'n'roll. Husney suggested a compromise – the Record Plant in nearby Sausalito – but needn't have worried. As soon as he settled into recording, all Prince wanted to do was work.

After moving out to California in October, Prince lodged in a spacious apartment in Mill Valley, overlooking the San Francisco Bay, with Vicari, Husney, and Husney's wife, Britt. Their home life was pleasant enough: Husney cooked Prince scrambled eggs, while his wife made the singer's lunch and washed his clothes. Recording was a different matter. Prince made it very clear that this was *his* show, and would roll his eyes whenever Vicari approached the mixing desk. If he ever did deign to ask the producer something, Prince would push him away as soon as he'd received enough information. By the time the sessions were finished, Husney said, Prince had "absorbed everything he needed out of Tommy Vicari's brain. ... Tommy was heartbroken, because he had just been treated like shit."[9]

Having completed work on the basic tracks by the end of December, the *For You* team moved to LA's Sound Labs studio in January 1978 to begin overdubbing. It was here that the pressure seemed to get to Prince. Pushing Vicari away, he spent over a month and a half piling up overdub upon overdub, gradually eroding the spontaneity of the original recordings in a self-conscious bid to prove that he was capable of making the kind of polished, commercial record that Warners wanted. He finally finished the record on February 28, eight months after he had started work on it. It had cost $170,500 – just $500 short of the planned budget for the first three Prince albums – and had turned its creator into a wreck.

Released on April 7 1978, *For You* received largely positive reviews, although most of them were concerned more with the fact that it was the work of a 19-year-old and had little to say about the actual musical content. Prince's local paper, the *St Paul Dispatch*, called the album "a technical marvel and a curiosity" most interesting "because one man did it."[10]

For You is a competent record, and the making of it proved to be a useful learning experience. Prince had got to grips with a wide range of synthesizers, notably the Oberheim, which would characterize much of his early work. He would not feel comfortable enough with the idea of using real brass instruments on record – in the way that James Brown and 70s funk pioneer George Clinton had before him – until the mid 80s. Anxious to avoid replicating the sound of contemporary disco, he went for something totally different, creating his own 'horn section' by multi-tracking synthesizer and guitar lines.

Another important characteristic of *For You* is Prince's reliance on high-pitched vocals on both the suggestive, up-tempo material ('Soft & Wet,' the album's only minor hit) and the lovelorn, acoustic ballads ('Crazy You'). The whole thing seemed to be aimed squarely at the young, female R&B market, right down to the softly airbrushed sleeve art of the Afro-haired singer. Only the final track seemed to suggest something else. With its frenzied, finger-tapping solos and similarly showy bass-playing, 'I'm Yours' sounded closer to the MOR rock of Journey than Santana, and a firm reminder of the fact that Prince wanted to reach beyond the black audience. Recalling such conscientious virtuosity, even 20 years later he was still reminding people that he had been brought up "in a black and white world. ... I want to be judged on the quality of my work, not on what I say, nor on what people claim I am, nor on the colour of my skin."[11]

Genuine mainstream success was still some way off, however. As impressive as *For You* might have been, it still bore the hallmarks of overproduction – the opening title track has over 40 layers of Prince's vocals – while too many of the songs simply repeat themselves without going anywhere, and aren't quite snappy or sharp enough for mass appeal.

For You did nonetheless reach Number 21 on *Billboard*'s R&B chart, while 'Soft & Wet' made it to Number 12 on the R&B chart and Number 92 on the Pop chart. Prince set off on a minor promotional jaunt, appearing at signings in cities where the records were selling well. After being confronted by 3,000 screaming fans on one such occasion in Charlotte, North Carolina, however, Prince was more than a little spooked, and soon began to shy away from personal appearances.

In the summer of 1978, Prince used his Warner Bros advance to move into a new home at 5215 France Avenue in the Edina area of Minneapolis. He then set about holding auditions for a band that he could take out on the road with him, choosing Del's Tire Mart as a rehearsal space. Bobby Rivkin – the brother of the Sound 80 demo engineer David Rivkin, and an employee of Owen Husney's – came in on drums, while Prince's old school-friend André Anderson (now calling himself André Cymone) played the bass, just as he had done years earlier in his mother's basement. The three of them had played together before, so it made sense to carry on with a well-rehearsed rhythm section.

With a mix of ethnicities already in place (Bobby Rivkin, or Bobby Z as he became known, was white; André Cymone was black), Prince was keen to mix up the band's sexuality as well – just as Sly & The Family Stone had done in the 60s. Prince had his eye on a similar boundary-crossing line-up when he brought

Gayle Chapman into the fold, telling her: "You're white, you're blonde, you have blue eyes, and you can play funky keyboards."[12] ("Everything he did had groove," Chapman would later remark. "You could tell a Prince piece when you heard it."[13])

Dez Dickerson was next to join. A veteran of the Minneapolis scene, with a punkier look than most black guitarists of the time, he was impressed by Prince's professionalism – despite the fact that the singer turned up two-and-a-half hours late for their scheduled rehearsal. "He was very clear that he wanted the band to be an amalgam of rock and R&B,"[14] Dickerson later recalled. The only guitarist who opted not to showboat in rehearsals, Dickerson quickly settled into a comfortable, complimentary role in the band.

The last member to join was keyboardist Matt Fink, who had been intrigued by Prince ever since Bobby Z played him a demo tape in 1977. He had asked Bobby to keep him in mind if Prince was ever on the lookout for a keyboard player, and now was the time.

Having assembled the band, Prince spent the rest of the year whipping them into shape while Owen Husney tried to focus his energies on putting together a tour. Since the release of *For You*, however, Prince had begun to see Husney as more of a runner than a manager, perhaps as a result of his frustration that the album hadn't been an instant smash hit.

Prince's demands eventually became too much. After having their equipment stolen from Del's Tire Mart, the band moved into Pepé Willie's basement. "Sometimes the basement was less than balmy," Dez Dickerson recalled. "Prince called Owen and told him to get a space heater and bring it to Pepé's."[15] Husney, however, was waiting on an important call, and didn't think it wise to leave the office. Prince demanded that the job be done there and then. An argument ensued that resulted in Husney quitting on the spot. Prince tried to convince him to return, but the three-page letter he had written detailing what he considered to be a manager's responsibilities didn't jive with what Husney thought the job should entail. Pepé Willie was willing to do the smaller jobs, but that served only to mask a bigger problem: having just released his debut album, and while still trying to get his band tight enough for a tour, Prince lacked a guiding force.

With *For You* already three-quarters of a year old, Prince had high hopes that 1979 would begin with a tour in support of it, but he would first have to convince Warners to back it financially. In the interim, Willie organized a pair of shows at Minneapolis's Capri Theater.

Prince made his live debut as a solo artist on January 5 1979. Given the circumstances, the show was neither here nor there. It wasn't a sell-out, but still drew a crowd of several hundred fans, friends, and family members, all intrigued to see the local-boy-made-good in action. But Prince was still a tentative live performer and often played with his back to the audience. All in all, the show – for which each of the band-members wore tight spandex, leg-warmers, and high heels – seemed more like a dress rehearsal than a proper concert.

Two nights later, a delegation of Warners officials came to watch Prince's second show and decide whether or not he was ready for a full tour. This was unfortunately the night that Dez Dickerson decided to try out a wireless pickup, which refused to work properly. ("There were some definite uncomfortable moments," he later recalled, "[which] caused a couple of delays.") None of this helped Prince, who was already nervous at the prospect of his second ever solo show being his most important to date. The constant breaks to fix Dickerson's equipment disrupted the flow, and when a "painfully shy" Prince plucked up the courage to address the audience, the guitarist recalled, he "barely spoke above a whisper."[16]

The concert was an unqualified failure. Having put so much effort into proving he could make a record entirely on his own terms, Prince was devastated that he couldn't do the same in a live setting. "I kept trying to speak to him and he wouldn't even talk," his cousin, Charles Smith, recalled. "He thought the show was shit."[17] So did the Warners officials, who vetoed any plans for Prince to tour. But this in itself posed another problem: what to do with an artist who had used up virtually all of his three-album budget on one record, wasn't ready to tour, and had just sacked his management?

Warners' main focus was on finding a new management team. The label opted for the Hollywood-based firm Cavallo & Ruffalo, a highly experienced agency run by a pair of Italians, Bob Cavallo and Joe Ruffalo, who had previously worked with Little Feat, Earth Wind & Fire, and Weather Report. Cavallo & Ruffalo sent runners down to handle Prince's day-to-day requests, and installed a senior employee, Steve Fargnoli, as his manager. Fargnoli proved so important to the Prince setup that he would soon be invited to become a partner in the company, which was renamed Cavallo, Ruffalo & Fargnoli.

Meanwhile, Prince busied himself working on songs for his next album. From late April to late May he recorded at Alpha Studio in Los Angeles with engineer Gary Brandt – Warners having decided, after the Tommy Vicari debacle (which made it clear that Prince wouldn't listen to anybody), that there was little point in insisting on another executive producer. Left to his own devices, and having decided that he now "knew how to write hits," Prince recorded his self-titled second album in 30 days, and needed only a couple more weeks to add overdubs and complete the final mix at Hollywood Sound Recorders – a far cry from the four months spent working on For You.[18]

Despite working so quickly, Prince was unable to enjoy his downtime. Soon after moving into his new house in Minneapolis during the summer of 1978, Prince met a local singer, Sue Ann Carwell, and began working on songs with her at home and at Sound 80. But while Prince would later become known for his ability to adapt to a different sound for each project, much of what he recorded with Carwell just sounded like his own material. Just one year into launching his own career, Prince clearly had eyes to becoming a svengali, but once Carwell signed to Warners (with the help of Owen Husney), she was assigned a different producer in order to differentiate her sound from that of the label's other young star.

Prince's interest in masterminding other acts didn't end there, of course. In June 1979, not long after completing work on *Prince*, he told Dez Dickerson of his plan to "record an entire record, with the band, under the nom de plume The Rebels." The band, according to Dickerson's memoir, *My Time With Prince*, "were being asked to come along for the ride and make him look good."[19]

This time around, instead of making something that sounded transparently like his R&B-orientated solo work, Prince decided to build on the rockier elements of songs such as 'I'm Yours' and 'Bambi.' He also intended for The Rebels to be more of a collaborative effort, even allowing Dickerson and André Cymone to write some of the material. But after working on nine songs at Ears Sound Studio, Colorado, in July 1979, Prince scrapped the project, deciding that the whole thing sounded too generic.

The idea was for The Rebels to be a kind of 'secret' side project, but what Prince learnt from the experience was that, if he was to successfully mastermind a new act such as this, he should be in control but not necessarily involved on a full-time basis. Similarly, after working with Sue Ann Carwell, he realized that there should be a link to his own sound, but not to the point where there was no differentiation between the two. Both experiences proved useful in the long run, however, in that they would inform Prince's plans for the launch of The Time in 1980.

Having proved that he could lead two other acts while improving on his own previous work, Prince began to trust himself more. One example of his growing confidence came with the recording of the single 'I Wanna Be Your Lover,' which, according to Gary Brandt, "didn't come together until we put the [live] drums on." Prince recorded the drums himself, playing along to what had already been taped. "[Drum machines] are kind of hard to play to," Brandt recalled, "because they're usually right on the meter." Prince, however, was "very synchronized," and had no trouble "fit[ting] himself into that track, knowing exactly what would come up."

Prince was released on October 19 1979. It was preceded by the single release of its opening track, 'I Wanna Be Your Lover,' which showed much more commercial promise than anything on *For You*, hitting Number One on *Billboard*'s R&B Chart and Number 11 on the Pop chart. Like much of *For You*, 'Lover' is a simple love song sung in what *Rolling Stone* called "the most thrilling R&B falsetto since Smokey Robinson."[20] (Hip-hop producer Timbaland would later describe it as "one of the most innovative songs ever released. ... It was the record that got me interested in music."[21]) It was also a lot tamer than the highly charged 'Soft & Wet,' and as such appealed to a much wider audience.

Taken as a whole, *Prince* sounds like the work of an artist who had learned from the mistakes of his previous album. Where *For You* meandered at times, the follow-up contains a wealth of more varied, interesting grooves. The songwriting is snappier and more hook-laden, as evidenced by 'Why You Wanna Treat Me So Bad?' and 'I Feel For You' (later a hit for Chaka Khan). There are still hints of Prince's love for MOR rock, notably on 'Bambi.' But while the music is fairly generic, the lyrics – in which Prince tries to convince a lesbian that "it's better with a man" – point toward the sort of taboo subjects that Prince would later mine to great success. The album's ballads, meanwhile, are tighter and more convincing, and helped by a more minimal production style, which made them much more club-friendly. Prince himself was very much aware of the difference this made. "I never saw Prince again," Gary Brandt later said, "but I got countless calls from his managers asking me how I recorded various parts of his album."[22]

Prince was still very much an R&B record aimed squarely at female listeners. On the front jacket Prince is pictured topless, with messy hair and thick moustache, against a baby-blue backdrop; on the back he is naked, riding a Pegasus (no explanation necessary); his name is inscribed in purple, with a heart dotting the 'i.' The album reached Number 22 on the *Billboard* Pop chart – a mere 141-point improvement on *For You* – and hit Number Three on the R&B chart. Now it was time, once again, to think about touring.

The Prince tour was certainly eventful. To begin with, two months of shows had to be cancelled after the singer caught pneumonia in early December. Then there was the small matter of an appearance on *American Bandstand*, for which Prince and his band were set to perform the album's first two singles, 'I Wanna Be Your Lover' and 'Why You Wanna Treat Me So Bad?' Backstage they met the host, Dick Clark, one of the most respected figures on American television. Everything was going well until Prince came up with a mischevious idea: he and his bandmates should refuse to answer any of Dick Clark's questions. The band was mortified, but the stunt worked. Prince became infamous almost overnight after answering Clark's questions with nothing more than series of hand gestures, such as holding up four fingers when asked how many years he had been playing. (Clark later called it the hardest interview he ever conducted.)

Another issue to resolve was the group's image. "We were all groping for images of how we wanted to look on stage," Matt Fink recalled. "Prince pretty much left it up to each individual member of the band to figure it out, of course, with his final approval."[23] For Fink this meant everything from prison chic to a doctor's gown and mask (which earned him the nickname Dr Fink). Prince, however, had an entirely different look in mind: "loud spandex and bright colors," as Dickerson put it. "I overheard Bob [Cavallo] talking to Prince about the fact that he could not scandalize the audience by wearing that spandex and no underwear." Prince took Cavallo's instructions literally. "That's all he wore: a pair of bikini briefs!"[24]

In February Prince was invited to join Rick James's Fire It Up tour as the supporting act in what was billed as the Battle Of Funk. Prince's young bucks did to James what Prince's future protégés The Time would threaten to do to their master a few years later: winning over the crowd with a short, snappy set that had a lot more going for it than the headliner's two hours of overindulgence. As Bobby Z later put it: "We were young and hungry and we started kicking his ass."[25] James found himself struggling to follow Prince's energetic, flamboyant performance, with large chunks of the audience leaving during his set.

The animosity between the two was further fueled by the fact that Prince and his band tended to avoid socializing with James and his party-hard entourage. James wasn't sure what to do with a group so far from his own sensibilities. "I felt sorry for him," he later recalled. "Here's this little dude wearing high heels, standing there in a trench coat. Then at the end of the set, he'd take off his trench coat and he'd be wearing little girl's bloomers. The guys in the audience would boo him to death."[26]

As the Prince tour wound down in April, further trouble emerged from within Prince's own traveling party. As a member of a religious sect called The Way, keyboardist Gayle Chapman found herself increasingly conflicted about her role in the group. "Prince was tired of the costumes that I was coming up with," she later recalled. "He sent his girlfriend down to the hotel room that I was in, she knocked on the door … dumped this bag of multicolored underwear on my bed, and said, 'Prince says wear this or you're fired.'"[27]

Chapman felt similarly uncomfortable about having to kiss her bandleader rather suggestively during the song 'Head' (which subsequently appeared on *Dirty Mind*). "There had been some tension between her beliefs and what she was being called upon to do in our live show," Dickerson recalled. "There was a developing role that she was given that involved the simulation of some pretty vulgar things on stage."[28]

Things came to a head when Chapman told Prince she planned to go on a trip with her Way group; Prince wanted her to commit to some short-notice rehearsals instead. An argument broke out that resulted in her leaving the group, leaving Prince with another round of personnel issues to deal with. All of this paled in comparison, however, to the kind of shake-up he already had in mind.

CHAPTER 3

PEOPLE CALL ME RUDE; I WISH WE ALL WERE NUDE

I was horrible. ... A lot had to do with me not being quite sure exactly which direction I wanted to go in. Later on, toward the *Controversy* period, I got a better grip on that.

PRINCE

Prince's first full tour saw him usurp the headlining act and win popularity contests against his new funk rival, even if he lost friends within his own group. Undeterred, he barricaded himself inside the makeshift studio in the basement of his new house on Lake Minnetonka to start work on his next record. *For You* and *Prince* had built him a strong black following, but he now had his sights set on a wider market.

His next move might risk losing an established audience, but would potentially open up a much bigger one. "Nobody knew what was going on," he said, "and I became totally engulfed in it."[2]

For several years a new form of music had been slowly gaining ground in Britain and America. From The Ramones to The Clash, punk had begun to take over the white rock market, which had been dominated for most of the 70s by overblown bands such as Pink Floyd and Led Zeppelin. By the dawn of the 80s the likes of Blondie had begun to add keyboards and a pop sensibility to punk's stripped-down template, creating a sound that was christened 'new wave.'

Prince had noted a similar sea change on the horizon in the disco market, having refused to allow Earth Wind & Fire's Maurice White to produce his debut on the grounds that it would immediately sound dated. Two years later, he hit upon a new sound that shared a number of stylistic similarities with new wave.

Live and in the recording studio, Prince had already developed a reputation for being interested in all things carnal, thanks to his stage outfits and the brazen sexuality of songs such as 'Soft & Wet.' The new music he presented to Warner Bros took things a step further, however. Not only were these stripped-down recordings rough and punky, with an urgent physicality lacking in his earlier work, they were also obscene – and Prince wanted them to stay that way. "It really felt like me for once," he told *Rolling Stone*. "When I brought it to the record company it shocked a lot of people. But they didn't ask me to go back and change anything, and I'm really grateful."[3]

It wasn't quite so easy a sell as Prince might have made it out to be. "The record company, understandably, was very nervous about this sudden change," Dez Dickerson recalled.[4] It wasn't only the lyrical content that bothered Warners, but the blatant shift in musical style. According to Dickerson, the label's attitude was: "We've signed Stevie Wonder and now we've got Ric Ocasek. What happened?" It took quite a lot of smoothing over on the part of Bob Cavallo and Steve Fargnoli before Warners gave the project the green light, Cavallo noting that, "*Dirty Mind* was a risky record. Some thought we were losing our minds."[5]

"Mo Ostin did what any 'artist friendly' 80s label head would have done with an artist as gifted as Prince: nurture and support him," Alan Leeds, Prince's future tour manager and record label boss, recalled.[6] Prince did agree to give some of the songs a bit more polish in the final mix, but everything else remained as it was when

Dirty Mind went on sale, four months after Prince had begun working on it, on October 8 1980. Not everybody at Warners was happy, however. "He turned [the company] into disarray," the label's vice-president, Marylou Badeaux, noted. "The promotions people would call me and say, 'I can't take this to radio! Is he crazy?'"[7]

Just in case the jacket – a stark black-and-white image of Prince, in studded trench coat, neckerchief, stockings, bikini briefs, and a 'Rude Boy' button, standing in front of the bare springs of an upturned bed in homage to James Brown's *Revolution Of The Mind* album sleeve, which saw The Godfather photographed behind prison bars – wasn't enough, the album was sent to DJs with a sticker that implored them to "please audition before airing." The doe-eyed seducer of Prince's previous albums had been replaced with a predatory look – as the singer himself put it – of "pure sexuality."

"I wasn't being deliberately provocative, I was being deliberately *me*," Prince asserted.[8] The shockwaves went off far and wide. Songs such as 'Do It All Night' and 'Dirty Mind' said it all in their titles: here was a man dispensing with the pleasantries and getting straight to business, ditching the sexual revolution of the 60s in favor of the sexual aggression of the 80s. And it got worse. 'Head' tells the story of a sordid meeting with a bride-to-be on the way to her wedding, while 'Sister' – allegedly inspired by Prince's half-sister Sharon – explores the (fictional) concept of losing your virginity in an incestuous tryst. Prince might have expected his father to have something to say about that, but John L. seemed more concerned with the language than the subject matter. "When I first played *Dirty Mind* for him," the singer told *Rolling Stone* in 1983, "he said: 'You're swearing on the record. Why do you have to do that?' And I said: 'Because I swear.'"[9]

Dirty Mind is more than just *The Joy Of Sex* set to music, however. Tracks such as 'Partyup' and 'Uptown' (about a place where "we do whatever we please") show his socially conscious side – something that would continue to surface again and again as his career progressed.

When it came to touring *Dirty Mind*, Prince was able to go back out as the headliner, rather than as somebody else's support act. The addition of Lisa Coleman, the 19-year-old daughter of Hollywood session player Gary Coleman, on keyboards had a significant impact on the group. After a three-hour audition, during which she and Prince barely spoke, it became clear that Coleman would bring much more to the group than had her predecessor. "Lisa is like my sister," Prince told *Rolling Stone* a few years later. "She'll play what the average person won't. She'll press two notes with one finger, so the chord is a lot larger, things like that. She's more abstract. She's into Joni Mitchell, too."[10]

Prince himself seemed to settle more comfortably into his own skin on the Dirty Mind tour, while the band quickly gelled into a tight musical unit. All manner of hijinks ensued on the tour, from stealing emergency megaphones on airplanes to taking it in turns – rather more dubiously – to be left slumped in wheelchairs, drooling, in airports, pretending to have been left behind.

For all the fun, the tour began on a rather inauspicious note on December 4 in Buffalo, New York, one of several smaller towns and cities that struggled to appreciate this freaky character singing freaky songs in bikini bottoms and stockings. While venues such as the 12,000-seat Cobo Arena in Detroit came close to selling out, Prince found himself playing to half-empty halls in Winston-Salem, Chattanooga, and Nashville. Sales of *Dirty Mind* itself were sluggish as 1980 drew to a close, leading his management to cut the tour short after a show at Chicago's Uptown Theater, on December 26, for fear that it would soon start losing money.

While Prince took stock in yet another new house on the outskirts of Minneapolis (which he would soon paint purple), his salvation came in the form of a *Rolling Stone* article headed by a question: 'Will The Little Girls Understand?' Prince's management team had hired publicist Harold Bloom to up their star-in-waiting's media profile. This first piece of serious rock journalism about Prince opened the floodgates for the rest of the music press, including Britain's weekly *New Musical Express*, which exalted: "Prince refuses to play it safe. If he did, he wouldn't have made this album."[11]

Dirty Mind hadn't been selling well – it was performing even more slowly than *Prince* had – but the tipping point, as Dez Dickerson put it, came with "this tidal wave of critical acclaim."[12] Perhaps most notable was Ken Tucker's four-and-a-half-star *Rolling Stone* review, which called *Dirty Mind* "the most generous album about sex ever made by a man."[13] The *Minneapolis Tribune* followed suit, heaping praise upon Prince's "unique instrumental sound, a disco-funk mode that is quite recognizable as his."[14]

The Dirty Mind tour resumed in the wake of this upsurge in critical interest, with Prince booked into smaller clubs this time around to ensure that each date was a sell-out. The press coverage did its job, and a whole new audience began to check out what all the fuss was about. Minnesota's other boy-done-good, Bob Dylan, came to the hometown opening night at Sam's Club on March 9, while Mick Jagger was part of a sell-out crowd at the New York Ritz on March 22 – the same venue that Prince had struggled even to half-fill three months earlier.

By the time the tour wound up in New Orleans on April 6, Prince had begun to make significant inroads into a new, white market. Buoyed by this success, he started working on another side project, having realized that he needed to create more of a buzz than he could simply by being 'Prince,' and needing an outlet for a fresh stream of lighter, more direct pop-funk songs that he couldn't use himself.

The way to address this, he decided, was to create a 'ghost band' that would not only give Prince another outlet for his ideas but would also make it seem like he wasn't just out there on his own. The Minneapolis Sound, as it came to be known, had its roots in the club circuit that Prince played on with Grand Central and Champagne, but this time he was (theoretically) in control of the whole scene. Each of its bands would be characterized by the same funky rhythms, pop hooks, and new wave elements, and deploy the same instantly recognizable stripped-down production, but none would be better than Prince himself.

After convincing Morris Day to donate his song 'Partyup' to *Dirty Mind*, Prince promised to repay his old friend by making him the frontman of a new band. Unsurprisingly, given that he was still playing in local bands and working as a runner for Prince, Day jumped at the chance. The rest of this new band, dubbed The Time, also came from Minneapolis. Prince single-handedly dissolved and reconstructed the Flyte Tyme group – which included bassist Terry Lewis, drummer Jellybean Johnson, and keyboardists Jimmy 'Jam' Harris and Monte Moir – with the inclusion of guitarist Jesse Johnson, who had played in other local bands, and Morris Day in his new role. (Before recruiting Day, Prince had courted another local singer and Flyte Tyme original, Alexander O'Neal, who later became hugely successful in his own right but wanted more than Prince was willing to pay him to be in The Time.) The crucial final addition to the line-up was dancer/valet Jerome Benton, who became Day's comic foil.

The Time's look was based around the retro-pimp fashions of two generations back: Stacy Adams shoes, bright suits, and long, thin ties. It was perfectly in keeping with the skinny, drainpipe suits of the emerging new wave bands of the era. Morris Day's image – that of a self-obsessed skirt-chaser, as seen in *Purple Rain* – had its origins in a pimp persona Prince used to mess around with, for which he put on an old man's 'hustler' voice. But while Day and his cohorts certainly looked the part, they weren't expecting any great success in their own right. "We knew we weren't going to make any money," Jimmy Jam recalled. "Prince was very upfront: 'There's not going to be a lot of money in this.'"[15]

Having assembled the band, Prince got to work on both his own *Controversy* and The Time's eponymous debut, while also running his new group through strict rehearsals until he was happy that they could work as a unit. As good as they got, The Time wouldn't be allowed to play a note on their eponymous debut album. Prince recorded all the music himself, crediting the production to a pseudonym, Jamie Starr, and to Morris Day (who was at least allowed to sing on the record, but had to follow Prince's guide vocals note-for-note).

While Prince was recording *The Time* across April 1981, the buzz around him had grown to the extent that he made his first trip to Europe, playing three club dates in Amsterdam, London, and Paris, from May 29 to June 4. While some musicians might have spent their first foreign trip seeing the sights, Prince used it to investigate what was going on in the clubs, seeking out new ideas to bring back home with him.

Despite the success he was now having, however, Prince was finding it difficult to keep his band together. "During the *Dirty Mind* period I would go into fits of depression and get physically ill," he told *Rolling Stone* in 1985. "I couldn't make people in the band understand how great we could be together if we all played our part."[16] More than a decade later, he identified the root of the problem: his bassist. "André's ego always got in the way of his playing," he said. "He always played on top of the beat, and I'm convinced that was just because he wanted to be heard. André and I would fight every night, because I was always trying to get him to sound like Larry Graham."[17]

André Cymone, Prince's first ever bandmate, quit the group in April 1981, although he hung around until the end of the Europen tour. It didn't come as much of a surprise. As early as 1977, Cymone had turned up at the *For You* sessions with the attitude that it would not be long before he would be doing "my thing." Now he had clearly decided that he had watched from the sidelines for long enough. Even so, Cymone continued to bear a grudge against his old friend. He later claimed that Prince had stolen many of his ideas for The Time, along with the bassline for *Controversy*'s 'Do Me, Baby.'

Ideas for Prince's new album were coming so fast that his side project were amazed he could keep going. "He'd come to our rehearsals for five or six hours, then go to rehearsals for his own band, then [work] all night in the studio," Time keyboardist Jimmy Jam recalled.[18] One happy side-effect of having a new band was that Prince could let the semi-autonomous Time take care of the R&B market while he focused his own efforts on his impending crossover into the mainstream.

When it was released on July 29 1981, *The Time*'s infectious pop-funk was a lot less challenging than *Dirty Mind*, and a lot less weighty than what Prince was cooking up for *Controversy*. Its tightly written, simple songs soon found favor with the record-buying public, many of whom quickly guessed that this Jamie Starr character – who had been previously credited as an engineer on *Dirty Mind* – was actually a pseudonym for Prince himself. Prince denied it, which of course served only to increase media interest in the record, which ended up outselling *Dirty Mind*.

After returning from Europe in June, Prince started work on his fourth album, *Controversy*, at home and in Los Angeles. While The Time's songs were funky and played to the kind of black music stereotypes Prince had seen in his youth, his own material carried on in the *Dirty Mind* vein. It wasn't a mainstream success by any stretch of the imagination, but *Dirty Mind* had attracted a new crowd, and Prince intended to build on that. *Controversy* would end up mixing funk with new wave and seductive ballads, sex with religion and politics, creating a whole that feels as confused as it is confusing. A bewildered review in Britain's *New Musical Express* wondered quite how Prince could be so "temporarily valorous" yet "ultimately conservative."[19] Is that what funk was meant to be?

When he started work on *Controversy*, having already fulfilled his initial three-album deal with Warners, Prince would have been well aware of the fact that he needed to deliver the goods this time. Having been brought in to replace André Cymone on bass, 18-year-old former International House Of Pancakes employee Mark Brown (subsequently renamed Brown Mark) asked his new boss what the plan was. "This album has to make it," Prince told him. "He definitely knew what he was doing," Brown noted, "but I don't think he had a clue if it was going to work. I think he was feeling that, if it didn't sell, he'd be dropped."[20]

In Europe, Prince discovered that new wave acts such as Gary Numan were already incorporating the cold, synthesized textures of Kraftwerk and the underground electronica scene of the 70s. On his return, Prince began to seek out ways of intertwining his synths into his sound more deeply than he had on *Dirty Mind*. He also came across the Linn LM-1 drum machine, the first device of its type capable of sampling real drum sounds, and soon realized that it would help him record entire drum parts cheaply and quickly, without having to play them in real time. His experiments with overlapping LM-1 rhythms and synthesizer parts reach their peak on *Controversy*'s 'Private Joy,' a song he wrote for his then-girlfriend Susan Moonsie. Overall, however, for all its innovative ideas, *Controversy* feels more like a halfway house between *Dirty Mind* and its fully realized follow-up, *1999*; a taster, of sorts, of a sound that Prince had not yet quite mastered.

Having made a tentative entry into the world of political debate on *Dirty Mind*'s 'Uptown,' Prince stepped wholeheartedly into that arena with *Controversy*. The jacket is almost like a color version of *Dirty Mind*'s, with Prince – wearing slightly more clothes than last time around – standing before a backdrop of newspaper headlines based on the album's sensationalist lyrics, plus one that simply reads "Joni," in honor of Joni Mitchell. (Ten years later, Alan Leeds echoed the sentiments of the design when he claimed: "Music is like a newspaper to [Prince], and his attitude is: what's the point of reading last week's paper?"[21]) On the record, 'Ronnie, Talk To Russia' and 'Annie Christian' demonstrate a desire to say something about the world at large. But the former is decidedly naïve ("Ronnie, talk to Russia before it's too late / Before they blow up the world") and the latter, ostensibly about gun control, is more of an inner-worldview than a political one, voiced by a man who "live[s] my life in taxicabs." (Even on 'Ronnie,' "the world" has become "my world" by the end.)

Perhaps the most interesting aspect of *Controversy* is the level of unrestrained self-obsession on it. 'Private Joy' might have started out as an ode to a girlfriend, but is told from the point of view of Prince himself; what she does for him, and how he likes to keep her entirely for himself, without ever mentioning what *he* brings to the relationship. Likewise, 'Do Me, Baby' plays out a seduction fantasy, almost in real time, during which Prince never once lifts a finger. Only on the final track, 'Jack U Off,' does he offer anything in the way of recompense, offering his services "in the back of a car, restaurant, or cinema." But even then he ends up deciding that "as a matter of fact, you can jack me off."

The pinnacle of Prince's self-obsession arrives on the title track, on which he attends to various concerns others might have had about him. Is he black or white, straight or gay? Does he believe in God, or himself? (In typically perverse style, the answer is: both.) He claims not to be able to understand human curiosity, but seems to have grasped the fact that it might lead to an interest in him. The inclusion of 'The Lord's Prayer' midway through the song only adds to the sense of confusion and contradiction. Here is a man trying to make sense of himself and his place in the world while also trying to make himself appealing to everybody else (and perhaps toning down the explicit image he had thus far embodied).

The confused state of the record was best summed up by *Sweet Potato* magazine, which suggested that there ought to have been "a serious side and a sex side. Which would have made everything nice and cozy if the penis weren't a political tool in Prince's worldview."[22] As far as Warners was concerned, "[*Controversy*] is a musical outrage and a sincere statement of opposing views." That might be stretching the point somewhat. What is important, however, is that each of these songs, from the rockabilly-style 'Jack U Off' to the spoken word 'Annie Christian,' served to unlock the ideas that Prince would develop and in some cases perfect on *1999*.

When it was released on October 14 1981, *Controversy* sold more strongly than *Dirty Mind* but its chart performance showed that Prince still had some way to go to achieve genuine mainstream appeal. Released as a single over a month earlier, the title track stalled at Number 70 on *Billboard*'s Pop chart, despite peaking at Number Three on the R&B listings. It might have done better had Prince deigned to give interviews to explain the ideas behind the album. Instead, hoping that the music would speak for itself, he opted not to walk the promotional treadmill at all.

Prior to setting out on tour in support of the album, Prince played a one-off showcase in Minneapolis and a support slot for The Rolling Stones in Los Angeles. For a boy with his eye on mass appeal, the Stones shows served as a sharp reminder of just how far he had to go. The average Rolling Stones fan still rode the coattails of 70s rock'n'roll, about which everything was neatly defined. Men played guitars and slept with women, who were submissive and did what they were told. Prince's songs might often have had a similar message, but his androgynous look – stockings, high heels, bikini bottoms – sent out very different signals, as did singing about jacking someone off. That was what women did to men, not the other way around. If Prince was singing about such a thing ... well then he must be gay.

Prince's first night supporting the Stones, on October 9, at the open-air Memorial Coliseum, did not go well. The first out of four acts on the bill, he was booed off after 15 minutes. "He could only stay on for two or three songs," Bill Wyman later recalled, "because the crowd threw things at him. He made great records, but he couldn't perform on stage." Prince was so shaken by the experience that he flew straight back to Minneapolis and refused to return for the second concert, which was scheduled for October 11. It took an hour-and-a-half on the phone with Dez Dickerson – following pleas from Steve Fargnoli and even Mick Jagger – before Prince would change his mind. Dickerson suggested a few changes to the set that might make the show heavier (and thus more palatable), and appealed to Prince's sense of pride, telling him: "We can't let a few dirtballs run us out of town like this ... . We got to come back, and show them what we're made of."[23]

Two days later, Rolling Stones fans turned up armed and ready for a fight, having heard about what happened on the first night. Fruit, vegetables, Jack Daniels, and even a bag of rotting chicken came flying through the air at the group. But Prince played on, completing a full set despite the hostile response, and gained a lot of ground with the LA press as a result.

Prince began a tour of his own a month later, on November 20, but even that wasn't without its own set of problems. As his longest stint so far as a headliner, however, it was a huge success in terms of his previous tours. Deciding to make his shows more theatrical, he hired set designer Roy Bennett to build a two-tier stage with hydraulics, ramps at either side, a fireman's pole, and a set of blinding lights that shone through from the Venetian blinds used as a backdrop.

Prince's stage persona had evolved at a similar rate. He now wore a shirt and trousers beneath his purple trench coat and built long segments of audience participation into the set, in which he more or less acted out the words to 'Do Me, Baby' with the women in the audience. *Dirty Mind*'s 'Head' became the centerpiece of his shows, and found him sitting on top of the speakers, virtually masturbating his guitar to the climax of a ten-minute jam.

With a setlist that largely ignored his first two albums (save for the singles 'I Wanna Be Your Lover' and 'Why You Wanna Treat Me So Bad?'), the Controversy tour presented Prince as an ambassador for sexual freedom. For some audience members, however, it was all too cerebral, particularly by comparison to the short, snappy set by The Time that preceded Prince's arrival. Little did Prince realize that, while he was concentrating on lofty conceptions, his protégés were working on becoming a tighter live unit. Like any good students, they made a point of trying to outdo their master on stage – only Prince didn't like being shown up in the same way the he had Rick James a year or so earlier.

Tensions grew as Prince refused to acknowledge the fact that, although he was the mastermind behind the music, what brought The Time to life night after night was the band itself – particularly the charisma between comedy duo Morris Day and Jerome Benton. Well aware of their own worth, The Time began to ask for more money, but Prince wouldn't give it to them. The group began to boil with resentment – particularly Jesse Johnson, whom Matt Fink later described as having "a major ego problem."[24] But when Prince started work on The Time's second album in December, during a break between legs of the tour, he still refused to give Morris Day and co any artistic control.

It wasn't only The Time that Prince was keeping at arm's length. He was also beginning to isolate himself from his own band. In January 1982 he hired Charles 'Big Chick' Huntsberry, a former professional wrestler with a grey Santa Claus beard, as his personal bodyguard. An imposing figure who stood at six feet eight inches tall, Chick immediately began to confound expectations – not least those of Dez Dickerson, whose first thought upon catching sight of Huntsberry in a Virginia hotel restaurant was: "Oh Lord, I'm gonna die in Richmond." (As it happened, Huntsberry "turned out to be one of the most interesting people I ever met," while later, having warmed to him, Dickerson found himself desperately convincing Prince not to fire his new bodyguard for being *too* imposing a presence.[25])

After a brief period during which he was avoided by almost everyone on the tour, Huntsberry – who had once had the job of carrying AC/DC's Angus Young around on his shoulders – found himself getting involved in Prince's stage show. He would pull Dez Dickerson off stage during planned altercations between the guitarist and Prince during 'Let's Work,' and on one occasion was called upon to drag The Time off one-by-one and replace them with Prince's own band. He also quickly became Prince's closest confidante, and would be seen everywhere with him, even to the extent of leading him to the stage at the 1985 BRIT Awards ceremony, where Prince won the award for Best International Artist for *Purple Rain*. (The album's liner notes credit him as 'The Protector.')

Protected and cocooned from the outside world, however, Prince seemed to grow increasingly nasty – in particular toward The Time. No longer would friends be pushing each other around in wheelchairs before an unsuspecting public. Rather, during the final show of the tour, on March 14 1982 at Cincinnati's Riverfront Coliseum, the bad blood between the headlining and supporting acts boiled over. While The Time played their final opening set, Prince and his entourage threw eggs at them. "I thought it was kind of low," Morris Day later recalled. "I know it was meant in fun, but when you're trying to do your show in front of a bunch of people, throwing eggs is not too cool."[26]

Things got even worse after The Time's set. Backstage, Jesse Johnson – the most vocal of The Time's dissenters – was kidnapped by Big Chick and handcuffed to a wall-mounted coat rack in Prince's dressing room while the star threw more food at him. Management ordered that there was to be no interruption to the headliner's set, but as soon as Prince walked off stage at the end of the show a full-scale food-fight ensued and carried on all the way back to the hotel. Refusing to concede to his underpaid side-project, Prince made Morris Day pay for the damage caused, claiming that Day had started the whole affair.

As ever, Prince seemed incapable of ending an album-tour cycle without there being some rupture within his camp. Since he didn't need The Time as musicians – only Morris Day as a singer – Prince was able to spend March 1982 working on their second album without interruption, while also working on music for a third side-project and his own follow-up to *Controversy*. One collaborator who wasn't yet indispensable, however, was Chuck Statler, a director who had been hired to shoot hours of footage of Prince on tour and at home. Entitled *The Second Coming* (after his entrance music), the project was scrapped after an argument between Prince and Statler. Despite his continued growth as a self-sufficient musician, it seemed that Prince wasn't quite ready for the realities of collaborating on film. It would be another few years before he could realize that dream.

CHAPTER 4

ALL THE CRITICS LOVE U

He embodied a change in our culture that, in retrospect, seems like it was inevitable. But at the time he was riding a wave before a lot of us recognized it coming.

ALAN LEEDS

R ather than addressing the simmering conflict with The Time, Prince loaded more work onto himself after winding down the Controversy tour in March by launching a second side project. Back in January, Prince had met Denise Matthews at the American Music Awards. A lady of Hispanic descent, she looked almost like his female counterpart, and Prince was instantly attracted to her. "Prince sent someone over to talk to me," she later recalled. "He took my number and gave it to Prince, who called me the next day. He came to pick me up that night in a white limo and we went out to dinner."[2] (In another telling of the story, Matthews recalled being invited to join him in the bathroom so that Prince could try her coat on. When he took his own leopard-skin coat off, it turned out that he had nothing on underneath it.)

Prince had already toyed with the idea of launching a female group to counterbalance The Time's masculinity. It would also give him yet another outlet for aspects of himself that wouldn't fit into his own work, and continue to build a buzz around the Minneapolis scene that he was not-so-secretly masterminding. His initial plan was to create an all-girl group called The Hookers, comprising his girlfriend Susan Moonsie; set designer Roy Bennett's wife, Brenda; and Cavallo Ruffalo & Fargnoli employee Jamie Shoop. The group's image – lacy lingerie, stockings, and heels – was supposed to turn the wholesome 60s girl-group look on its head, presenting instead a group of predatory women out stalking bars and clubs looking for sex.

After meeting Matthews, however, Prince began a stormy relationship with her, renamed her Vanity (Matthews having rejected Prince's original suggestion, which was to call her 'Vagina' – pronounced 'Vageena'). She was immediately promoted to leader of his new group – an early indication of one of the roles he would expect his girlfriends to play. Instead of finishing things with Moonsie, however, Prince cut Jamie Shoop from The Hookers and renamed the girls Vanity 6 (six being the number of breasts between them).

For Matthews, it was the dream ticket. She had left her Niagara Falls home at the age of 15 (following the death of her father and her mother's slip into alcoholism and depression) and set her sights on becoming rich and famous. Meeting Prince seven years later was exactly what she wanted. "He told me he was going to make me a star," she recalled, "so I moved out to Minneapolis to live with him."[3]

Prince recorded Vanity 6's self-titled debut album for them, while also working on The Time's *What Time Is It?* and *1999*. When it was released on August 11 1982, *Vanity 6* was a moderately successful record full of lightweight pop tunes with titles such as 'Nasty Girl,' 'Wet Dream,' and 'He's So Dull.' The general mood veered closer to new wave than funk. The album presented the group as a vampish foil to The Time's gang-of-pimps image, while once again the production was credited to Jamie Starr in an attempt to make it look like another one of this mysterious tycoon's masterpieces.

In his only interview of 1983, with the *Los Angeles Times*, Prince was keen to get certain facts straight. "One, my real name is Prince," he said. "Two, I'm not gay. Three, I'm not Jamie Starr."[4] (Only much later would he admit that he was "just getting tired of seeing my name. If you give away an idea, you still own that idea. In fact, giving it away strengthens it."[5]) Such was the confusion that, in Britain, *Melody Maker* even went so far as to call The Time and Vanity 6 plagiarists. Mining the same dancefloor-friendly funk and new wave sound as *The Time*, both *What Time Is It?* (released a fortnight after *Vanity 6*) helped Prince tighten his grip on the black market, while also allowing him to stretch out into ever-more experimental territory on his own new record.

From the end of March to mid-August, Prince shut himself away like a mad scientist to work on his fifth album. Despite the success of the Controversy tour, he once again eschewed the band because, he said: "I was working with a lot of people who weren't exactly designed for their jobs. I had to do a lot, and I had to have control because a lot of them didn't know exactly what was needed."[6] Parts of this new project were recorded in his own 24-track basement studio (which he called Uptown), with the rest completed at Sunset Sound in Los Angeles with Peggy McCreary, an engineer who had also worked on *Controversy*. Prince seemed more obsessed with this new project than he had been with any before. He often pulled 24-hour stints in the studio, with McCreary forced to stay with him around the clock. With just the two of them in the room, there were regular flare-ups – particularly if there was any sort of hold-up. Prince would pace around waiting for tapes to be rewound for playback or for technical problems to be fixed. (As much as he had embraced new studio technology, it seemed that the machines often weren't fast enough to keep up with him.)

"I remember days when Prince would come into the studio at, like, 9am, kick you out of the room for about 20 minutes, then write a song," recalled Peter Doell, who worked sporadically as an engineer on *1999*, and later with Miles Davis. "Then he'd come back ... and you'd better have the drums tuned up and ready, because he's going to play the daylights out of the drums. ... Then he'd go on and do the bass, keyboards, and by one o'clock you're mixing it, and by four o'clock you run off and have it mastered. ... He was an unbelievable cottage industry."[7]

As these long and often arduous sessions continued, Prince began to push his new ideas further and further, building on his *Controversy* experiments and taking studio trickery to the extreme, thereby keeping his peers and his listeners guessing for as long as he could. The Linn LM-1 drum machine became increasingly prominent. It had only featured on one song on *Controversy*, but can be heard all over *1999* in between layer upon layer of synthesizer. The combined effect is that of a cold, hard, mechanized take on Phil Spector's organic, eardrum-crashing Wall Of Sound. What Prince had over Spector, however, was that he could turn out hits for himself as well as for others.

By July Prince had completed a ten-track album, which he took to managers Bob Cavallo and Steve Fargnoli. As much as they liked it, however, they felt this new work needed a 'Controversy' or a 'Dirty Mind' – an opening track that could show in no uncertain terms what the rest of the record was about. "He yelled at us," Cavallo recalled, "and then he went back to Minneapolis and kept recording."[8]

Prince recorded the song in question – which would end up becoming one of his signature works – in less than a day, between late-night rehearsals with The Time. As Jimmy Jam later recalled, Prince walked in one afternoon at around 2pm and played the assembled musicians his latest creation. "We're going: 'Hey! When did you do this?' 'I did this last night after I left.' Oh, man, it's not fair!"[9]

Prince's defining statement of the era, '1999' touches on a theme that would continue to crop up in his work: partying to the end, in the face of a looming apocalypse. The previous album's 'Ronnie, Talk To Russia' voiced similar concerns, but its lyrics were too specific (and too naïve) to appeal to a wider, cross-generational audience. While '1999' has a similarly paranoid, fear-of-the-bomb theme, it isn't rooted in one spot. With one of Prince's catchiest and most danceable tunes beneath it, it remains – like Stevie Wonder's best work – as relevant today as it was when it was recorded (and at the turn of the millennium).

"Mommy, why does everybody have a bomb?" Prince asks in a sped-up voice at the end of the song. Never has certain death sounded so inviting. Mimicking the call-and-response vocals of Sly & The Family Stone's 'Dance To The Music,' Prince has keyboardist Lisa Coleman sing the opening phrase, followed by Dez Dickerson, allowing the song to build before coming in himself on the third line. The opening is inspired and disorientating in equal measure, not just because of the switch between voices but also because of the melodic changes it goes through; these came as a result of the fact that Prince, Coleman, and Dickerson recorded their vocal parts together, only for Prince to split them up later on, meaning that some 'lead' parts had been planned as harmonies.

While promoting his wildly eclectic *Emancipation* LP in 1997, Prince described *1999* as "nothing but me running the computers myself, which is why [it] isn't as varied."[10] This might well be true, but it remains one of his most successful and enduring works, not least because of the way that he was able to refine and perfect the cluttered, anything-goes approach of *Controversy*. The lyrics, meanwhile, are deeper but more accessible. 'Little Red Corvette' might sound to begin with like a simple pop song about lost love, but the line about "a pocket full of horses, Trojan" carries a safe-sex message, Trojan being a popular brand of American prophylactic. (The fact that "some of them were used" adds a rather creepy undercurrent.)

Elsewhere, 'Free' is a gospel ballad with an unusually patriotic theme, given that it was written by a man with a reputation for being pop's most morally bankrupt sexual deviant; 'Delirious' is a much stronger take on the rockabilly pastiche of 'Jack U Off'; and 'Automatic' and 'Lady Cab Driver' show off a newfound sadistic streak. ('Lady Cab Driver' features a spoken-word passage in which Prince has sex with the driver in the back of her cab, with each thrust dedicated to the likes of "the creator of man," "politicians who are bored and believe in war," or the question of "why I wasn't born like my brother: handsome and tall.") The lyrics are also much more humorous than one might have expected. Prince teaches the perennially unfunky to dance on 'D.M.S.R.' – "All the white people, clap your hands on the four" – and whisks a lover away on "Prince International" during the extended sex-as-flying metaphor of 'International Lover.'

Perhaps the most remarkable aspect of *1999* is the fact that it never feels overlong or self-indulgent, despite the fact that 'Lady Cab Driver' runs to nine-and-a-half minutes, and that half of the remaining ten tracks clock in at more than six. Taken as a whole, *1999* marks the point at which Prince had learnt to ride a groove for as long as he wanted, endlessly reworking it so as to prevent it from getting stale. For Dez Dickerson, it was "the seismic shift where all of the things that were attempted and all of the things that were pointed toward ... came together in this sort of perfect storm."[11]

Once Prince had completed work on this, his most powerful album yet, Steve Fargnoli was given the job of taking it to Warners and trying to convince the label to release *1999* as double album for the price of a standard LP. Once again the Warner executives were being asked to stick their necks out for a relatively underground artist, having already let him produce his own debut and run off into ever-stranger territory on his subsequent releases. Now the label was being asked to release an album that was in serious danger of making a loss.

Fargnoli, however, had become Prince's greatest ally when it came to dealing with the label, and was able to convince chief executive Mo Ostin that a double-album was the only way to go. (The company's European arm wasn't so easily convinced, and opted to release *1999* as a seven-track single album to begin with, omitting some of the longer songs, before issuing the full-length version in 1983.)

As it was, Ostin and his cohorts needn't have worried. A few weeks after the album's release, on October 27 1982, *Rolling Stone* praised the diversity of *1999* and its creator. "[Prince] works like a colorblind technician who's studied Devo and Afrika Bambaataa & The Soulsonic Force," the magazine declared, "keeping the songs constantly kinetic with an inventive series of shocks and surprises."[12] Even Miles Davis, in his autobiography, was moved to call *1999* "the most exciting music I was hearing in 1982" before declaring Prince himself to be "someone who was doing something different" and worth "keep[ing] an eye on."[13]

Even so, when the title track stalled at Number 44 on the *Billboard* Pop chart, it seemed like mainstream success might still prove elusive. Not everybody was impressed by Prince's "Specially priced two record set." The *New Musical Express* thought it was a prime example of the desperate moves a record company makes when "the only people who like you are the people who get their records free."[14] As with *Dirty Mind*, however, there was something of a snowball effect. Prince's live shows were fast becoming unmissable, with newspapers such as the *Philadelphia Enquirer* going out of their way to "unequivocally recommend [this] wonderful, provocative show."[15]

The 1999 tour built on the Controversy setup. This time Prince presented his full army of talent to the world in the form of a Triple Threat line-up that saw Vanity 6 open and The Time play second on the bill, while the new Roy Bennett-designed stage set included a bed that came up through the floor so that Prince could re-enact the lyrics to 'International Lover' each night. The musical arrangements were similarly ambitious. Bobby Z had his work cut out trying to figure out how to incorporate his own live drumming alongside electronic rhythms triggered by the Linn LM-1. "I felt like an auto-assembly worker looking at a robot for the first time, wondering if I still had a job," he recalled, adding that he got little guidance from his boss. "Prince said: 'Here it is, figure out what you're going to do with it.' The machine was on the record and I had to augment that and get it to work live."[16]

As with the Controversy tour, the Triple Threat dates were marred by an air of antagonism between Prince and The Time. Feeling overworked and underpaid, the group took their frustrations out on stage, doing their best to outdo Prince each night. As guitarist Jesse Johnson recalled, the band would sometimes knock on his dressing room door to tell their boss they were going to 'slaughter' him.

The Time had good reason to be frustrated. For this new tour it was requested that they perform behind a curtain as Vanity 6's backing band before playing an hour-long set of their own, with only a small pay increase to show for it. Not surprisingly, the group balked at this offer, so Prince took to bullying them after they finished playing – which naturally served to create further tension between the two parties. To make matters worse, he then decided to drop the group from the line-up when the tour reached major cities such as New York and Los Angeles.

Frustrated at the lack of creative freedom being afforded to them, Jimmy Jam and Terry Lewis had begun to produce other groups without telling their boss. Midway through the second leg of the Triple Threat tour, the pair missed a show in San Antonio after finding themselves snowed in in Atlanta, where they had been recording The SOS Band. Jerome Benton had to mime playing the bass on stage while Prince played Lewis's parts off stage; Lisa Coleman stood in for Jimmy Jam.

When the missing band-members returned, Prince fined them $3,000 each – an extortionate amount for musicians who already felt they were grossly underpaid.

When the tour finished in April, he sacked them both, wholly undermining Morris Day's authority as The Time's supposed leader. "That was fucked up," Day recalled. "For me, it was like being the president, but having to answer to the CEO. I had a fair amount of control ... but the bottom line was always his."[17] (Jam and Lewis went on to form Flyte Tyme Productions and create massive chart-busting hits in the Minneapolis Sound mould. They won a Grammy for their work on Janet Jackson's 1986 album *Control*, and subsequently worked with a wide range of R&B stars, including Gladys Knight, Luther Vandross, and Mariah Carey.)

Vanity wasn't having the best experience, either. On a professional level, she wasn't keen on Prince's instructions to "get out there, take off all your clothes, and run around naked," but at the same time she craved attention, and enjoyed putting on an aggressive front.[18] Then there was the way Prince treated his girlfriends. Still in a relationship with Susan Moonsie, too, he started an affair with another new musical interest, Jill Jones.

"He juggled the affairs on a day-to-day basis," said Alan Leeds, who would soon be called in to stop the tour from falling apart. "Some nights Vanity would disappear with Prince, then some nights Jill would appear on the Prince bus, leaving Vanity in the hotel."[19] According to Barney Hoskyns, who covered the tour for the *New Musical Express*: "Nobody seems to remark how peculiar it is that Vanity, supposedly enjoying pride of place between the little chap's sheets, actually kips on her own in a separate bus and scarcely exchanges a word with him throughout the days I'm on the tour."

Vanity's relationship with Prince had begun in a rush of passion but was slowly fizzling out. On some nights she wasn't even competing with Moonsie or Jones, but with any other girl who happened to take Prince's fancy. Overwhelmed by sudden stardom and upset by his casual approach to their relationship, she turned to drink and drugs to get through the tour.

Prince still had one confidante: the unshakable Chick Hunstberry. The closer he and Huntsberry became, however, the more the singer began to use his bodyguard as a barrier against the rest of the world – including his bandmates. Having already developed a reputation as a reclusive egomaniac, Prince now found himself having to account for his obsession with protection and privacy. A backlash was inevitable. "Nobody has to walk around their home town with a nine-foot bodyguard," the disgruntled Jesse Johnson later recalled, "but Prince has dogged so many people, ripped off so many ideas, that he knows he's gonna get his ass kicked."

Things got so bad for all concerned that, midway through the tour, Prince had to bring in Alan Leeds, who had previously served as James Brown's tour manager, to keep everything together. Leeds saved the day, despite initially finding himself having to communicate with Prince – like everyone else on the tour – through Huntsberry. In the end Leeds became as close a confidante to Prince as had

Huntsberry, but was still never quite sure when to be "Alan the big brother," "Alan the best friend," or "Alan the gofer." The key was knowing what Prince wanted, and when. "I'd better not confuse the three roles," Leeds recalled, "because if he sends me on a mission and I come into rehearsal empty-handed, and I start laughing and joking like we did in front of the TV last night, I'm not going to last very long."[20]

Within a few years it would not be uncommon for Prince to travel on a separate bus to the rest of his band, with only Huntsberry, Leeds, and various girlfriends allowed onboard. Barney Hoskyns recalled similar scenes during a post-concert dinner on the 1999 tour: "Only when everybody is settled and ready to order does Prince, engulfed in the shadow of his giant, bearded bodyguard ... enter the restaurant, gliding silently past the row of booths and making his way to the other side of the room."

Despite the internal turmoil within the Prince camp, everything seemed to be going from strength to strength on the outside. Perhaps the most crucial breakthrough came when '1999' began to appear on heavy rotation on MTV in December, just as the Triple Threat tour was taking off. The exposure was invaluable. Not only was Prince now being foisted onto television screens on a regular basis, he was also one of the first black acts to appear on the channel – several months ahead of Michael Jackson's 'Beat It' – proving to Prince that his music could break down racial barriers.

Fortunately for Prince, this newfound exposure had coincided almost exactly with his decision to take more care over his music videos, which had until now been rather mundane. The '1999' promo stuck to that same basic formula of filming a live performance of the song, but had enough fast edits – and enough shots of Lisa Coleman and Jill Jones in lingerie – to appeal to the MTV crowd.

Next came 'Little Red Corvette,' for which Prince even performed a brief but elaborate dance routine. The song itself saw him finally get to grips with a rock sound that wasn't generic, as his previous stabs at the genre had been. It even had a proper rock guitar solo, edited together from three different takes played by Dez Dickerson, one of the few musicians to get such a spotlight on a Prince album during this phase of his career. It proved to be just the hit Prince needed, reaching Number Six on *Billboard*'s Pop chart right in time for the launch of the second leg of the tour. (Interestingly, the single stalled at Number 15 on the R&B chart.)

The MTV exposure led to even greater interest in the Prince live experience, which in turn boosted his crossover appeal as a bona fide hitmaker. The *1999* LP soon broke into the US Top Ten and ended up selling three million copies within a year. By the time the year for which it was named arrived, it had gone Platinum four times over.

But while the final stages of the 1999 tour should have been one big party, things weren't quite so simple. Prince had irreparably damaged his relationship with The Time, and pushed Vanity into a world of drink, drugs, and depression, making her unreliable and irritating to be around. He was also going to have to find a replacement for Dez Dickerson, who like former bandmate Gayle Chapman had found God and had begun to feel rather conflicted about his role in Prince's band. "I knew I didn't have it in me to continue – spiritually, emotionally, creatively, mentally," Dickerson later recalled.[21] Prince let him go, but continued to support him. He had Cavallo Ruffalo & Fargnoli take over Dickerson's affairs, offered to help write and record his solo project, and later gave his band, The Modernaires, a showcase spot in *Purple Rain*.

Dickerson had long since wanted to work on his own material, so his departure from the band didn't come as a surprise. Prince had a ready-made replacement to hand in the form of 19-year-old Wendy Melvoin, a friend of Lisa Coleman who had been traveling with her in the tour bus, and who would occasionally jam with the band during soundchecks or rehearsals if Dickerson wasn't around. Melvoin was a simple, handy replacement – just the sort of musician Prince needed to capitalize on his newfound commercial appeal. And she had a twin sister, too.

CHAPTER 5

BABY I'M A STAR

Purple Rain is the pinnacle of
the whole Prince & The
Revolution experience.

LISA COLEMAN

At the start of 1983, 'Little Red Corvette' and *1999* were in the process of turning Prince into a minor crossover star in America. The 'Little Red Corvette' video – one of the first by a black artist to be shown on MTV – made him an instant small-screen icon. But few would have guessed that, in just over a year, Prince would become a big-screen legend, too, not to mention a global pop phenomenon.

By the end of 1984, Prince had become the first act since The Beatles to simultaneously top the US charts with a single ('When Doves Cry'), album, and movie (both *Purple Rain*). He had also found time to write hit albums for The Time (*Ice Cream Castle*), Apollonia 6 *(Apollonia 6)*, Sheila E. (*The Glamorous Life*), and a hit single for Sheena Easton ('Sugar Walls,' a thinly veiled exploration of her internal anatomy), while Chaka Kahn resurrected 'I Feel For You' and put it back into the charts.

While still concentrating on building a roster of controlled acts which would create a Minneapolis scene, the success of 'Little Red Corvette' also threw Prince into a high-profile global pop battle that the media would fuel for decades. A month after the release of 'Corvette' on February 9 1983, Michael Jackson released 'Beat It.' Both records immediately stormed the white mainstream market, courtesy of their respective rock guitar solos, and made unprecedented strides on MTV. Bridging the gap between black and white music in the early 80s, each could claim to being the most important figure of the decade, even if Bobby Womack would complain that both men had "groomed their music for a white audience."

Jackson's *Thriller* went onto become the biggest-selling album of all time. But while he might have surged ahead of Prince in terms of sales, it took him until 1987 to issue a follow-up, *Bad*, which received much less ecstatic reviews. During the same period of time, Prince had written and recorded ten albums for himself and others, all the while becoming more and more critically feted for his more powerful array of music. (Comparing the two men in his autobiography, Miles Davis wrote: "I like Prince a little better as an all-round musical force. Plus he plays his ass off as well as sings and writes."[2])

Prince has always been keen to play down any rivalry between the two. "I could talk to you about Michael Jackson," he told the *New Musical Express* in 1995, "but I would just be doing the job that a journalist does, so there's no point."[3] According to Robin Power, star of Prince's 1990 film *Graffiti Bridge*, Prince was offered a lucrative licensing deal with Coke shortly after Jackson signed up with Pepsi, but turned it down. "He didn't want to be compared to Jackson," Power told Prince biographer Liz Jones. "He felt he should be compared with Miles [Davis] or [John] Coltrane."[4] (This might perhaps be one of the reasons why Prince chose not to appear on 'We Are The World,' the 1984 charity single co-written by Jackson.)

Despite what Prince told the press, there clearly was some sort of rivalry between the two men. In December 1985, while working on his second film, *Under The Cherry Moon*, in San Francisco, Prince was visited by Jackson, whom he challenged to a game of table tennis. Prince's competitive streak reportedly got the better of him, leading him to hit the ball across the table at Jackson as hard as he could. While paying a return visit a month later, Prince shared a pizza with Jackson's pet monkey, Bubbles, leading to reports in the *National Enquirer* that he had used mind-control tricks to send Bubbles mad. (The two men had also been in a studio together briefly in 1978, after Prince had asked to sit in while Jackson worked on *Off The Wall*, but they never spoke.)

The *Bad* sessions threw up another interesting tale. Jackson had his producer, Quincy Jones, speak to Prince about the possibility of a duet on the album's title track. The plan was for Jackson's management to plant false news stories in the press about a bitter rivalry between the two men leading up to the release of the single – which would serve as a supposed final battle. Problems arose, however, when Prince began to look in detail at the song's lyrics – and the first line, "Your butt is mine," in particular. "Who's singing that to whom?" Prince asked, "'cause you sure aren't singing that to me." (He offered up a reworking of his 1976 song 'Wouldn't You Love To Love Me?' intead, but Jackson rejected it.)

Even as both men – and Jackson in particular – became more reclusive across the decades, the media loved to fuel a good rivalry. In 2007, Prince's 21 Nights In London residency at the O$_2$ Arena gave rise to rumors that Jackson planned to perform a 25 or 30-night run at the same venue, although Prince countered that his record-breaking run would never be broken. In 2009, Jackson announced his This Is It residency, which quickly grew from an initial ten-date run to a planned sequence of 50 shows. Tragically, however, Jackson collapsed at his rented Los Angeles home on June 25 2009 and was unable to be resuscitated, robbing the world of an original talent, whose private life – like Prince's – sometimes overshadowed his true achievements. Prince may still wear the crown for longest O$_2$ Arena residency, but Michael Jackson will always be remembered by many as The King Of Pop.

Back in 1983, however, Prince was still, as The Time's Jimmy Jam put it, "at the point where he wasn't yet a superstar, but was right at the point of doing it."[5] What Jam and everybody else wondered was: "What's your next move gonna be?" As it turned out, Prince's next move was to do what David Bowie did with *Ziggy Stardust*: write himself into fame.

Prince was (and is) an avid film fanatic, so it's no surprise that he had long courted the idea of making a motion picture of his own. The man who stamped his dominance over the recording process with the words "Produced, Arranged, Composed, And Performed By Prince" would naturally have wanted to exert a similar authority over the other main avenue of popular entertainment. He would also have noticed how Sylvester Stallone had turned himself into a superstar with *Rocky* in 1976. Six years later, when Prince first began to consider making a movie, the *Rocky* franchise was into its third installment.

According to drummer Bobby Z, Prince was "fascinated with the camera," and had already started taping rehearsals and concerts and filming short skits. He had begun to come up with the basic concept for *Purple Rain* as far back as the *Dirty Mind* period. During his Controversy tour, Prince had started to film his shows for something called *The Second Coming*, which would intersperse concert footage with dramatic elements. In the end the project was scrapped, but he returned to much the same concept for the *Sign "O" The Times* concert movie a few years later.

By the time the second leg of the Triple Threat tour in support of *1999* began in February 1983, Prince had taken to carrying around a purple notebook in which he wrote down ideas for the semi-autobiographical movie that was beginning to form in his mind: *Purple Rain*. He wasn't yet a superstar, but did have some leverage. He had told his managers at Cavallo Ruffalo & Fargnoli that if they wanted to hold onto him beyond the imminent expiration of his contract they had better get him a movie deal with Warner Bros. "I want to star in the movie," he told Bob Cavallo. "I want my name above the title and I want it to be at a major studio."

Unfortunately for Cavallo, Warner Bros Pictures wasn't particularly keen on the idea of pumping heaps of money into the pipe-dream project of a mid-level singer with only a handful of hits to his name. If he wasn't able to carry on making hit records, the company reasoned, he wouldn't be able to attract the sort of crowds a major motion picture needs to make its money back.

"There was no precedent for this," tour manager Alan Leeds recalled. "Rock'n'roll stars with a couple of hit albums did not make major movies. Let alone somebody from the black community having the gumption to do it in the mainstream."[6] Before it was to agree to such a deal, Warners needed proof that Prince was the star that the movie was supposed to turn him into.

Thankfully, Prince still had the full backing of the head of Warner Bros' music division, Mo Ostin. Although no distribution deal had been secured, Ostin put up $4 million of the label's money to get the ball rolling. Having been given at least something of a green light, Cavallo and his colleagues went out in search of a screenwriter. They soon found 46-year-old William Blinn, who had won an Emmy award for his work on the *Roots* television show and was an executive producer of *Fame*, which had just completed its second series.

By the time Blinn was introduced to Prince, the movie concept had formed into something that centered on the incestuous Minneapolis music scene and recalled

Prince's early struggle for success in bands such as Champagne. Blinn found Prince less than willing to communicate at first, making his attempts at writing a treatment (for what was then known as *Dreams*) rather difficult. "Casual conversation is not what he's good at," Blinn later said. "He's an enigma. He wants to communicate but he doesn't want you to get too close."[7] After gathering together "12 to 14 pages" of ideas Blinn flew out to Minneapolis to watch the March 15 Triple Threat show. Later that night he went to Prince's house, where it became clear to Blinn that the singer was on "an honest quest to figure himself out. He saved all the money on shrinks and put it in the movie."[8]

He very nearly didn't get the chance. After the Triple Threat tour came to an end, in May, Blinn moved out to Minneapolis to start work on the project – only for Prince to start canceling meetings or walking out of them. Blinn came close to withdrawing from the project altogether when the singer left a meeting at a cinema after 20 minutes. "You've got a rock'n'roll crazy on your hands," Blinn told Steve Fargnoli. "I know he's very gifted, but frankly, life's too short." With that Blinn got on a plane back to Los Angeles.

Whether or not Prince realized that he was to blame for Blinn's departure or simply didn't want to see his dreams crumble is unclear, but the singer quickly called his screenwriter to apologize for his behavior (which he blamed on stress). Blinn returned to Minneapolis to give the project another chance, at which point Prince played him some of the songs he had already written for the movie on his car stereo. "Behind the strange combination of shyness and creativity," Blinn realized, "he is very, very bright, quite gifted, and quite professional ... not always what you find in the rock world."[9] *Dreams* was finally becoming a reality.

While Blinn worked on the script, Prince carried on writing new songs and rehearsing them with a new line-up of his backing band, now known as The Revolution. Wendy Melvoin replaced Dez Dickerson, who had left to pursue his own music career after informing Prince that he was no longer happy with the theatrical direction in which the music seemed to be headed.

Another new addition was Alan Leeds. Having joined the Prince entourage as manager of the Triple Threat tour, Leeds was given the job of overseeing the various projects Prince was currently involved in, which now included much more than just writing and recording music. Prince & The Revolution, The Time, and Vanity 6 were all busy rehearsing in a warehouse in St Louis Park, Minneapolis. They also took acting classes three days per week for three months under the tuition of drama coach Don Amendolins.

Although each musician's screen role would essentially be an extension of his or her own personality, some seemed more cut out for acting than others. According to Amendolins, Morris Day had "natural abilities" that the others lacked; Denise Matthews (Vanity) was "lazy"; and Prince was "very, very good. He'd flip right out of his persona and be whatever character he had to be."[10] Perhaps surprisingly, he also seemed to take direction better than the rest. An even tougher job fell to choreographer John Command, who had the job of condensing years of dancing training into a few short months.

Everything seemed to be on the up. Prince had first served notice of this most famous of backing bands on the cover of *1999*, on which the words "anD thE rEVOLUtioN" are printed backward within the 'i' of his own name. He debuted the now formally named Revolution – which would later become almost as famous as Prince himself – at Minneapolis's First Avenue, the club that would become the focal point of what was now called *Purple Rain*, on August 3 1983, during a benefit concert for the Minneapolis Dance Theater Company, raising $23,000 in the process.

The show marked the live debut of guitarist Wendy Melvoin alongside longstanding Prince sidemen Bobby Z Rivkin (drums), Matt Fink and Lisa Coleman (keyboards), and relative newcomer Mark Brown (bass). Such was Prince's faith in this new group that he recorded the entire concert with a mobile truck, which yielded no-fuss backing tracks for 'I Would Die 4 U,' 'Baby I'm A Star,' and 'Purple Rain.'

While the music was going from strength to strength, and Prince was happy with his most talented band yet, problems beset the film. William Blinn's *Fame* television show was picked up for a third season, so he decided to quit work on *Purple Rain*, leaving Minneapolis for good after handing in his first script draft on May 23. It took Cavallo Ruffalo & Fargnoli until September – just two months before shooting was due to commence – before they found a new writer-director. The man in question was Albert Magnoli, who came on the recommendation of director James Foley, but whose previous experience as a director was limited to a 1979 short entitled *Jazz*.

Although Magnoli wasn't interested in rewriting Blinn's script, he had an auspicious first meeting with Prince's management team. "Cavallo asked me what kind of story it would be if I was to make a film with Prince," he recalled. "I just started telling him a story off the top of my head, and in that ten minutes I had outlined the concept of *Purple Rain*."[11] Even more promising was Prince's initial reaction to Magnoli. "We sat down, I pitched him the concept, and the first words out of his mouth were: 'You've only known me for ten minutes, yet you tell me basically my story. How is that possible?'"[12]

Magnoli's arrival might have helped, but the project still refused to run smoothly. Prince's current side-projects, The Time and Vanity 6, were supposed to be playing his rivals in *Purple Rain*, but as both groups were essentially Prince puppets, they were becoming reluctant to co-operate. In April, Prince had fired the two main musical talents in The Time, Jimmy Jam and Terry Lewis, while keyboardist Monte Moir had left of his own accord after the sacking, leaving only singer Morris Day. Replacements for Moir, Jam, and Lewis were all found in the shape of bassist Jerry Hubbard and keyboardists Mark Cardenez and Paul Peterson. But The Time didn't have much longer to run, as Morris Day made it clear that as soon as *Purple Rain* was finished, so was he. Not only had Prince undermined his power within the band, he had also begun making it more obvious to the public that the Jamie Starr/Starr Company credits were actually pseudonyms.

"When people came to realize how big a role he played in some of these projects," Alan Leeds recalled, "they started to lose a little respect."[13] By the time a third Time album – *Ice Cream Castle*, named for a Joni Mitchell lyric – was released on US Independence Day 1984, the group had ceased to exist, despite the fact that, ironically, they had been allowed to play their own instruments this time around. (Undeterred, Prince had already started to assemble a new group out of the wreckage: The Family.)

Vanity's role in the new project was also problematic. Hurt by the relationships Prince continued to have with other women, Matthews became addicted to drink and drugs ("I did [drugs] on the sly," she recalled, "but nobody tried to stop me") and embarked on affairs of her own. "She was a competitive pistol," according to Alan Leeds, and "wasn't about to let Prince's desire for control sentence her to the confines of her room."[14] For his part, Prince – whose preference tends to be for more demure ladyfriends – quickly became weary of her attitude. Nonetheless, he had her written into the *Purple Rain* script and began to work on a successor to *Vanity 6*. Then in August 1983, during pre-production of the movie, she left the project, possibly over yet another pay dispute. Depending on who you believe, she either quit or was sacked.

Still looking to cling onto her fame, Matthews retained the name Vanity and recorded two solo albums, *Wild Animal* and *Skin On Skin*, while also starring in a handful of movies. All the while her drink-and-drugs lifestyle continued to spiral out of control. When she started dating the notorious rock lunatic Nikki Sixx a few years later, his equally wild Mötley Crüe bandmate Tommy Lee was moved to remark: "There's something really crazy about Vanity."[15] Describing their first meeting in his autobiography, Sixx himself recalled: "She opened the door naked with her eyes going around in her head. Somehow I had a feeling we might just hit it off."[16]

By the time she reached her thirties, having smoked crack cocaine for years, Vanity found herself temporarily deaf and blind. She suffered kidney failure (having already lost one kidney), internal bleeding, and a stroke, and spent three days on a life-support machine. After miraculously surviving this ordeal, she renounced her Vanity days and became a born-again Christian. She now runs a ministry in Freemont, California.

Meanwhile, back in Minneapolis, Prince and director Albert Magnoli needed to find a replacement for Vanity as quickly as possible. After auditioning close to 1,000 women in Los Angeles and New York, Prince settled on 22-year-old Patricia Kotero. Despite turning up to audition in her "baggiest sweats," as she later put it, she was practically the mirror image of Vanity, proving that in Prince's world, no one was indispensable. According to Magnoli, she was also "very sweet and tremendously accessible," which to Prince no doubt meant that she was malleable enough to fit the role.[17] "Do you believe in God?" Prince reportedly asked her at the audition, and then: "Are you hungry?" Kotero answered "yes" to both. She was quickly rechristened Apollonia and given the job of leading Susan Moonsie and Brenda Bennett in the renamed Apollonia 6.

Kotero found Prince difficult to work with. "There was a side of him that was just a tyrant," she later claimed, noting that he made her keep the fact that she was married secret so that fans might believe they were romantically involved. It has also been rumored that Prince demanded she eat and drink only candy and herbal tea – just like him. "He wanted to make everyone clones of himself," she said.

As Prince soon discovered, however, Kotero might have had the look, but she wasn't the greatest of singers. With little option but to forge ahead, he soon began to take songs away from the *Apollonia* 6 album, either to record himself ('17 Days,' 'Take Me With U'), repurpose for another imminent side project by Sheila E. ('The Glamorous Life'), or hold onto until a suitable act came along ('Manic Monday,' which he donated to The Bangles after meeting Susanna Hoffs in 1985). All that remained for Kotero to sing was a sequence of lightweight pop tunes, such as 'Sex Shooter' and 'Blue Limousine.'

Purple Rain began shooting on November 1 1983, giving the cast a few weeks to complete the outdoor scenes before the bitter cold of a Minneapolis winter crept in at the end of the month. Not all of them were finished in time, however, so some members of the cast and crew were flown out to Los Angeles as indoor shooting continued in Minneapolis. Mo Ostin's $4 million was beginning to run out, leaving the whole team in desperate need of major financial backing if the project was going to be seen through to the end.

Bob Cavallo and Steve Fargnoli went back to Warner Bros Pictures, and this time were able to convince the company of *Purple Rain*'s worth – just as cast and crew were celebrating at the movie's wrap party in Minneapolis at Bloomington's Holiday Inn on December 22. Although a few scenes had to be re-shot in Los Angeles on December 27, post-production on *Purple Rain* could now begin in preparation for its theatrical release.

A perfectly orchestrated promotional campaign meant that when *Purple Rain* opened on July 27 1984 it brought in $7.3 million in just three days. It went on to make around $70 million in total – reportedly more than ten times the cost of production. According to Albert Magnoli, the movie's excellent opening weekend meant that its distribution needed to be stepped up several gears. Having initially planned to show the movie in 200 theaters, Warner Bros now decided to present it on over 900 screens across the USA. Following the word-of-mouth success of the Controversy and Triple Threat tours and the May 1984 single 'When Doves Cry,' the release of the *Purple Rain* soundtrack album raised anticipation for the new movie to fever pitch. The summer of 1984 was set to be Prince's season. Anyone who hadn't yet seen him live clamored to get a look at Prince in action; those who already had were eager to relive the excitement.

In the two decades since its release, the *Purple Rain* movie has become dated on a number of levels. That it helped define the 80s is without question, but in so perfectly capturing the zeitgeist it also came to exemplify so many of the decade's worst cliches. There's the big hair, the new romantic clothes, the obligatory topless-woman scene, in which the hapless Apollonia is asked if she wants to "purify" herself in Lake Minnetonka; there's also an awkward moment where Jerome Benton throws a stereotypically loudmouthed ex-lover of Morris Day's into a dumpster. (When challenged by MTV about the movie's alleged sexism, Prince admitted: "Sometimes, for the sake of humor, we may have gone overboard."[18]) Even the editing techniques that once helped tie the visual experience of *Purple Rain* to the fast pace of MTV aren't quite so dazzling as they once were.

As an insight into Prince's psyche, however, *Purple Rain* is indispensable. The Battle Of The Bands trials surrounding rival acts The Revolution, The Time, and Apollonia 6 are based on Prince's early days as a struggling musician in Minneapolis, during which time he played in Champagne on the same club circuit as Flyte Time. The scenes work not just as dramatic construct but also as a tribute to Prince's hometown and the people who helped him in his early days.

Most of the characters and musical acts in the film – The Revolution, The Time, Apollonia 6, and even First Avenue club owner Billy Sparks – use their real names, and are essentially extensions of themselves. Prince plays The Kid, a semi-autobiographical construction with an almost magical air. He seems to have the ability to appear and disappear at will, whether on side streets, on his purple motorcycle, or in scenes such as the one in which he seems to vanish when Apollonia turns to compliment him on a performance.

In 1996, Prince told Oprah Winfrey that the most autobiographical part of the film was "probably the scene with me looking at my mother, crying."[19] Although Albert Magnoli later suggested that the part where The Kid's father warns him never to get married was based on something Prince once told him, the singer himself was adamant, in a 1985 interview with *Rolling Stone*, that "[the] stuff about my dad was part of Al Magnoli's story. We used parts of my past and present to make the story pop more, but it was a *story*."[20]

Even so, the career of the father in *Purple Rain* – an abusive failed musician named Francis L. – seems to echo that of Prince's real father, John L. Nelson. Prince has never spoken about exactly what went on behind closed doors in his family. But given that his parents divorced when he was young, and that he then became estranged from his father for lengthy periods (and even made overt references to child abuse on record), it would seem that his was not a particularly happy childhood. That the specter of physical abuse lingers in The Kid's relationship with Apollonia – and that he even envisions his own suicide after his father attempts to take his own life – suggests that Prince was playing out something of an Oedipal nightmare on the big screen.

The *New York Post* review of *Purple Rain* noted that, in The Kid's world, "women are there to be worshipped, beaten, or humiliated."[21] Most other reviews of the movie, however, were content simply to revel in the "affirmation of [Prince's] versatility and substance"[22] (*Miami Herald*); his "taste for androgynous appeal"[23] (*Philadelphia Daily News*); or the fact that the movie "reeks of unadorned sex" (*Detroit Free Press*).[24] Perhaps the lack of armchair psychology in these reviews is a reflection of the two-dimensional nature of the movie, in which Wendy and Lisa are simply the girls of The Revolution; Morris Day – a "full-fledged young comedian" in the eyes of noted critic Pauline Kael – relaxes into a pimp persona; and Apollonia serves as the eye candy.

Albert Magnoli might have tried hard to invest some feeling and motivation into the characters, but the parts audiences tend to remember are the performances. *Purple Rain* might not have aged all too well, but the musical segments remain as incredible as they ever were, particularly those by Prince himself. He manages to wring every drop of emotion out of a character who, elsewhere in the movie, seems moody, inarticulate, and self-obsessed.

One interesting aspect of *Purple Rain* is that, although Prince's parents were both black, The Kid's mother is played by Greek actress Olga Kartalos (one of only two professional actors in the movie, the other being Clarence Williams III, who played Francis L.). This was in part another example of Prince's efforts to blur the truth of the story, but it might also say something about the light-skinned singer's attempts to appeal to a mixed mass audience. Having tasted mainstream success with 'Little Red Corvette,' Prince was keen to follow up with something simple and bombastic and cross right over – just like Bob Seger, whom Prince kept crossing paths with on his 1999 tour.

And so Prince wrote 'Purple Rain,' a guitar-led anthem that builds from a simple chordal opening to a huge crescendo with strings, almost five minutes of guitar soloing, and Prince's most impassioned vocal performance to date. The song became an instant lighters-in-the-air classic and helped the accompanying album sell 13 million copies in the USA alone.

The *Purple Rain* soundtrack album still stands as Prince's biggest-selling record. After knocking Bruce Springsteen's *Born In The USA* off the top of the *Billboard 200*, it remained at Number One for 24 weeks. It served as further evidence, as Bob Cavallo put it, of the fact that Prince was "vitally interested in music, but also in success."[25] Perhaps the most obvious example of Prince's ability to meld creativity with commerciality was the leadoff single, the ethereal pop masterpiece 'When Doves Cry.' The opening guitar riff roots the song in rock, but the overlapping vocals, complex drum-machine patterns, and complete lack of bassline came from somewhere else entirely. (It was all too much for Warners. According to vice-president Marylou Badeaux, the label's initial response was: "What kind of fucking record is this, with a bunch of strange sounds?"[26])

The rest of *Purple Rain* served as the best evidence yet of the power of Prince and his arsenal of strange sounds. The opening 'Let's Go Crazy' is perfectly pitched, beginning – as does the movie – with church organ and the words "Dearly beloved, we are gathered here today ..." before launching into an uninhibited dance track. Its promises of a mixture of sexual freedom and salvation carry the message that, if you follow Prince, you'll be free to do whatever you chose.

The album also contains one of Prince's most heartbreaking ballads, 'The Beautiful Ones.' Written for Susannah Melvoin, twin sister of guitarist Wendy – whom Prince had met in May 1983, while she was still in another relationship – it builds around gentle synths and slow drum patterns to the coy question: "If we get married, would that be cool?" Having concluded that you always lose the beautiful ones, Prince lets go for a moment of pure passion, screaming relentlessly to his unrequited love.

The pacing of the album is exemplary, with each of the ballads offset by up-tempo dance tracks. 'The Beautiful Ones' is followed by 'Computer Blue,' a track constructed out of driving drum loops and dolphin-like squalls of guitar. The emotional intensity builds on 'Darling Nikki,' with its stop-start synths and backward messages that God is coming, and 'When Doves Cry,' before peaking on the final three tracks – 'I Would Die 4 U,' 'Baby I'm A Star,' and 'Purple Rain' – all of which segue into one another, as recorded at the First Avenue benefit show.

While most of *Purple Rain* seemed to replace the crude sexuality of old with a more subtle sensuality, one song in particular landed Prince in hot water. Prince had already written songs about oral sex and incest ('Head' and 'Sister,' both included on *Dirty Mind*), and even declared his intention to "fuck the taste out of your mouth" on *1999*'s 'Let's Pretend We're Married.' But when Tipper Gore (the wife of future US Vice President Al Gore) heard 'Darling Nikki' – in which the "sex fiend" title character "masturbat[es] with a magazine" – playing in her daughter's bedroom she was suitably encouraged to form the Parents' Music Resource Center. Gore's organization led a crusade to clean up popular music, one of the results of which was the introduction of Parental Advisory stickers. It also drew up a list of the 'Filthy Fifteen' – the most offensive records of the time. 'Darling Nikki' headed the list, with the Prince-penned 'Sugar Walls' at Number Two, suggesting that the PMRC had been far too outraged to dig any deeper into Prince's back catalog.

The timing of the record releases leading up to *Purple Rain*'s premiere had been perfectly planned, and so too was the launch of the accompanying tour, which opened two months to the day after the album had reached *Billboard*'s top spot. Those who had seen the movie and bought the album (and, perhaps, some or all of The Time's *Ice Cream Castle*, *Apollonia 6*, and latest addition to the roster, Sheila E.'s *The Glamorous Life*) now had the chance to go to the concert and buy the t-shirt. As New York-based journalist Amy Liden put it, the movie had given mainstream America the chance to "see what this guy was doing on stage." Having done so, many would have been eager to check him out in the flesh.

There was no 'triple threat' this time, as Prince's own show regularly reached the two-hour mark, and The Time had disbanded as soon as *Purple Rain* wrapped. (Jesse Johnson struck out as a solo artist, as did Morris Day, who found success both with his 1985 debut, *Color Of Success*, and as an actor.)

Prince had also lost interest in Apollonia 6 by the time the tour began, so chose to take Sheila E. out as his opening act instead. *Apollonia 6* suffered as a result. Released in October 1984, the album only reached Number 62 on the *Billboard* 200, while the first single to be taken from it, 'Sex Shooter,' stalled at Number 85 on the Hot 100. With Apollonia 6 fast fading from memory, Kotero resumed her acting career (she had previously starred in a TV mini-series called *Mystic Warriors*), returning to music for just one solo album, *Apollonia*, in 1988.

Given newfound prominence within the Prince camp, Sheila E.'s debut, *The Glamorous Life*, made it to Number 28 on the *Billboard* 200, even reaching Number Seven on its R&B chart. Bassist and future Prince confidant Larry Graham aside, drummer and percussionist Sheila E. is perhaps the only musician Prince has worked with who could claim to be better attuned to their instrument than he is. As the daughter of former Santana percussionist Pete Escovedo – and Goddaughter to Tito Puente – it came as little surprise when she followed in her father's footsteps. Having already left school to tour with her dad, she found herself working with bassist Alphonso Johnson in 1976 at the age of 19. Two years later, so the story goes, she met Prince at an Al Jarreau concert. But it wasn't until 1984 that the pair really hit it off.

Prince ran into Escovedo again shortly before the release of *Purple Rain* and immediately began to think of her as a potential replacement for The Time and Apollonia 6 on his upcoming tour. But despite having played over the years with Marvin Gaye, George Duke, and Lionel Richie, Sheila E. wasn't quite ready to front a live band. She did a good enough job, but her performances lacked the pizzazz of The Time. (She did at least offer rather more depth than Vanity 6.)

Sheila E.'s records were a different story, however. Her first three albums – *The Glamorous Life* (1984), *Romance 1600* (1985), and *Sheila E.* (1987) – seem on the one hand to have been designed to keep Prince prominent in the R&B market, but were often more rhythmically complex than Prince's other output of the time, and clearly benefited from her exemplary percussion work.

It also soon became clear that Sheila E. would not be just another puppet project. Although her debut album was credited, like all the rest, to the ubiquitous Starr Company, Prince gave Escovedo the freedom to claim that her mentor was too busy with *Purple Rain* to have had much to do with it. "He'd call on the phone to see how I was doing," she told Liz Jones, "and on the last day he came to listen to it, but there was no time for him to put any parts on it."[27] (This wasn't entirely true. Prince's obvious 'guest' vocal on the title track was the first clue to the fact that, as Escovedo's father later revealed to *Rolling Stone*, Prince had actually written and performed almost every note.)

With Escovedo in tow, the Prince live show was now a much bigger production than it had been before. Set designer Roy Bennett took the fireman's pole of the Controversy and Triple Threat shows and added extra balconies, trapdoors, lighting rigs, video screens, and a bathtub that came up from beneath the stage. The tour took in 98 shows in just over six months and meant that Alan Leeds needed to take on an assistant, production coordinator Karen Krattinger (who was, ironically, the tour manager for The SOS Band, with whom Jimmy Jam and Terry Lewis had been working when they missed their slot on the Triple Threat tour).

Prince himself was also beginning to change in response to his new megastardom. "He just kind of shut himself off," recalled Roy Bennett. "He became a different person at that point. Between Prince and everyone else, a wall came up."[28] Alan Leeds's brother Eric joined the tour midway through as a saxophonist and would later claim that it was run "like it was the Marines."[29]

Perhaps Prince further retreated from the outside world because he felt threatened. By the time the *Puple Rain* album came out, The Revolution had become superstars in their own right. They were almost too much of a good thing. Prince had long sought mass appeal, but now that he had achieved it, he found himself criticized for making the white musicians – Melvoin in particular – too much of a focal point, to the detriment of the group's only black player, Mark Brown. While on tour, The Revolution were constantly reminded that that they were *his* band, not part of *the* band. (Conversely, the band-members quickly became unhappy with the size of their paychecks, which seemed to bear no relation to the huge sums Prince himself was now earning.)

Having already begun to use his newfound fame to shut himself off from those around him, Prince also took his biggest tour yet as an opportunity to start to change his image. Maybe he had been stung by Tipper Gore's attacks; maybe he just felt that, with a much bigger fanbase, he should become a more positive arbiter of social mores. Either way, the two-hour shows now incorporated a "conversation with God." But there was still a clear conflict between a Prince who "tried to be good" and an audience that "love it when I'm bad."

For the *Los Angeles Times*, Prince's newly "conservative approach sacrificed the challenge and provocation of his earlier performances." For the most part, however, the Purple Rain shows were Prince's most accomplished yet. After support from Sheila E., Prince & The Revolution presented two hours of funk-rock, choreographed dance routines, and theatrical set pieces in a show that regularly sold out 20,000-capacity arenas.

As Prince & The Revolution were fast becoming the biggest band in the world, so Minneapolis was growing into a new role as the epicenter of cool. The local press had already been writing for some time about a Minneapolis Sound, but now the rest of the world was beginning to catch on. Prince reacted to this new level of exposure in his own way. "When the film came out a lot of tourists started coming to First Avenue," he told *Rolling Stone* in 1985. "That was kind of weird, to be in the club and get a lot of 'Oh! There he is!' I'd be in there thinking: 'Wow, this sure is different than it used to be.'"[30]

The key difference was that, having achieved the fame that he craved, Prince was too big and too famous to enjoy it. In his memoir, Dez Dickerson recalls going backstage to see Prince after a show in Washington DC and inviting him on a shopping trip the following day. "At first his eyes got bright, and then sad," Dickerson recalled, "and he answered: 'I can't do stuff like that anymore.' Fame had changed things, and, sometimes, it hurts."

CHAPTER 6

U GOT 2 TRY A NEW POSITION

We didn't want him to make that *Under The Cherry Moon*: a black-and-white movie, which wasn't musical, in which he died at the end, in the South of France.

BOB CAVALLO

f Prince was using the Purple Rain tour to unveil a new and (slightly) more conservative side in order to appeal to middle America, he received a sharp reminder of his weaknesses midway through the epic five-month jaunt. On January 28 1985, Prince performed 'Purple Rain' and won in three categories at the American Music Awards – Favorite Album in both the Black and Pop fields, and Favorite Single for 'When Doves Cry.' If the assembled audience of contemporary stars and living legends didn't already think him slightly strange, more than a few eyebrows would have been raised by the fact that Prince was accompanied by his bodyguard, Chick Huntsberry, each time he went up to get an award.

Huntsberry had of course been permanently at Prince's side since joining the Triple Threat tour. His own public profile was, however, already under scrutiny following an incident the previous year on September 5, when photographers started taking pictures of Prince outside a Sheila E. concert at the Agora in Cleveland. After telling the snappers not to take photos of his charge, the fearless Huntsberry got physical, and one of the photographers ended up injured. Although it would take until October 4 1988 for the case to get to court, the reporter's claim – for which he was seeking $2.75 million in damages – would dog Prince until he took the stand himself to defend his aversion to having his picture taken.

In the event, the judge would rule a mistrial, but by then Huntsberry had long since quit as Prince's head of security as a result of another altercation: one that occurred shortly after the American Music Awards, in the early hours of January 29 1985. Directly after the awards ceremony, 45 of America's most prominent musical acts of the time were asked to take part in the recording of 'We Are The World,' a song written by Michael Jackson and Lionel Richie and scored and arranged by Quincy Jones in aid of USA For Africa, a charity set up to raise money for famine relief in Ethiopia. Prince was among the artists invited to the session, along with Bob Dylan, Bruce Springsteen, Huey Lewis, Stevie Wonder, Diana Ross, and Tina Turner – the kind of mix of rock and soul that Prince himself had helped bring together a few years earlier.

While the tape was rolling, however, Prince was having dinner at a Mexican Restaurant on Sunset Boulevard. A piece of paper with his name on it might have been taped to the floor next to Michael Jackson's, but he never turned up to sing. Prince felt he had a perfectly good explanation for this. "We had talked to the people that were doing [it]," he said a few months later, "and they said it was cool that I gave them a song for the album." This, he said, was the best thing for all concerned: "I'm strongest in a situation where I'm surrounded by people I know ... [but] I probably would have just clammed up with so many great people in the room."[2]

That might well have been true. Bob Dylan later recalled that he felt so uncomfortable that he had to be guided through the recording by Stevie Wonder. But Dylan still turned up. Prince's 'explanation' served only to fuel rumors that he was a selfish egotist. It didn't help that, after leaving the Mexican restaurant at 2am, Prince had Huntsberry forcefully eject a paparazzi photographer from his limo. All of a sudden, he had gone from being the hero of the Awards night to the villain of the piece – the man who cared nothing for charity, and would be prepared to let his bodyguards loose on anyone who dared try to get close to him. Nonetheless, Prince was incensed. "I don't have any problem with somebody I *know* trying to get in the car with me and my woman," he told *Rolling Stone* shortly after the incident. "But someone like that? Just to get a picture?"[3]

Unfortunately for Prince, Huntsberry had by this time developed a $1,000-per-week cocaine habit. Needing to fund his addiction after quitting his job in the wake of this latest fracas, the bodyguard sold his story to the *National Enquirer*, which promptly published a kiss-and-tell expose. 'The Real Prince: He's Trapped In A Bizarre Secret World Of Terror' was based largely on interviews with Huntsberry, who is quoted as describing the singer as "the weirdest guy I've ever met. He feels he's a second Mozart."[4]

Among the 'revelations' were that Prince lived in an armed fortress with life-size murals of Marilyn Monroe on the walls, which seemed to leave the singer at pains in future interviews to remind people that he lived a normal life. But despite writing a bitter song about the situation entitled 'Old Friends 4 Sale,' which remained unreleased until it was included on *The Vault: Old Friends For Sale* in 1999 – by which time some of the more personal lyrics had been cut – Prince always cared deeply for his former bodyguard. He kept Huntsberry on the payroll and even bought him a house. Just weeks after Huntsberry quit, Prince admitted to *Rolling Stone* that he had "told him that his job was still there and that I was alone ... I miss him."[5]

With his public profile tarnished, it was easy to overlook the fact that Prince had indeed agreed to donate a song of his own to the USA For Africa album. He spent February 2 recording it with Wendy Melvoin and Lisa Coleman at the New Orleans Superdome during a break in the Purple Rain tour. But although the resulting '4 The Tears In Your Eyes' was a beautiful ballad about striving to maintain hope and faith in a dire situation, it was too little too late. Whatever good Prince might have done, it was overshadowed by the no-show, and his apparently mean-spirited behavior.

Prince gave his side of the story in 'Hello,' the B-side – rather aptly – to his 'Pop Life' single, which addresses the mostly negative effects of fame. Bemoaning the press's treatment of him, he sought also to remind his critics of his past charitable work: "We're against hungry children / Our record stands tall / There's just as much hunger here at home." Or, as he told *Rolling Stone*, paraphrasing the song's lyrics: "We'll do everything we can, but y'all got to understand that a flower that has water will grow, and the man misunderstood will go."[6]

As the Purple Rain tour drew to a close on April 7 1985, everyone except Prince seemed confused as to what would happen next. Some members of The Revolution were surprised that he hadn't opted to milk the album and movie for all they were worth, but Prince had been unwilling to sign up for anything beyond a six-month tour of the USA, which meant that no one else got to experience the phenomenal live show until the VHS release of *Prince & The Revolution: Live*. As Alan Leeds recalled: "I think he really had fears of being typecast as Mr *Purple Rain*. By the time that tour was over, he was so sick of that music and that whole concept."[7]

Worse news was to follow on April 2 1985, when Prince's manager, Steve Fargnoli, announced the singer's plan to retire from live performance following the completion of the tour. "I'm going to look for the ladder," Prince had reportedly told Fargnoli by way of explanation. "Sometimes it snows in April." A decade later, Prince gave a less cryptic explanation to *Icon* magazine. "I was doing the 75th Purple Rain show, doing the same thing over and over – for the same kids who [now] go to Spice Girls shows," he said. "And I just lost it. They put the guitar on me and it hit me in the eye and cut me and blood started going down my shirt, and I said, 'I have to go on stage.'"[8]

There were suggestions from outside the Prince camp that the singer's personality had been adversely affected by the success of *Purple Rain*. The Time's former guitarist Jesse Johnson would later claim that Prince was "such an asshole" that Johnson "had to change my phone number to stop him calling me. He'd just say: 'Jesse, your album sucks,' and hang up." (A year later, having heard that Johnson's second solo album, *Shockadelica*, didn't actually contain a song by that name, Prince recorded one himself in an effort to 'prove' his idea that every great album title needed a great song to back it up. He then had his own 'Shockadelica' pressed up for club play in advance of the release of Johnson's album, which subsequently made it look like Johnson had stolen the idea from him, rather than the other way around.)

To others, however, it seemed that Prince was finally starting to get on better with people. During the Purple Rain tour he had begun to take influence from the jazz records played to him by new Revolution saxophonist Eric Leeds. The brother of tour manager Alan, Eric had been invited to jam with the band during encores midway through the Purple Rain tour – the first time that Prince had allowed brass instruments on stage with him.

Prince was also interested in the white pop and rock'n'roll acts from the 60s and 70s that Wendy Melvoin and Lisa Coleman grew up with, as well as other more recent music that the singer had missed while locked away in the studio for the past half-decade. As Alan Leeds put it, the three of them "made it their own project [to turn] Prince onto different kinds of music. He had a very genuine interest in expanding his musical curiosity."[9]

The group coalesced into a potent musical force, and, as much as he might have hated to admit it, Prince needed The Revolution – particularly Melvoin and Coleman. "The more famous he got, the more he relied on us to speak," Melvoin recalled.[10] Prince's inner circle started to resemble a kind of university clique, trading ideas and inspirations back and forth. He was, according to Melvoin, "hungry for influences to take him further, so he relied heavily on me and Lisa to guide him in the directions he couldn't think of himself."[11]

The spirit of collaboration continued in the studio. Melvoin and Coleman would hole up with Prince and help him on his way to new musical discoveries on *Around The World In A Day* and its follow-up *Parade*. "It's true that I record very fast," he told MTV in 1985. "It goes even quicker now that the girls help me."[12] Their influence fed into a newly collaborative way of working as Prince started to invite members of The Revolution – particularly Melvoin and Coleman – into the studio with him as he recorded the follow-up to *Purple Rain*.

The catalyst for this was in fact a song that that Coleman's brother David had recorded in a three-day session at Sunset Sound in June 1984, which Prince paid for as a birthday present – an act of kindness that seems to be rather at odds with Jesse Johnson's opinion of him. (In a similar moment of benevolence, Prince reportedly gave his father a co-writing credit on his forthcoming album's 'The Ladder,' just so that he could earn some money from the royalties.) David Coleman used those three days to record a demo with Wendy Melvoin's brother, Jonathan, which they promptly gave to their sisters. "There was song on it called 'Around The World In A Day,'" Lisa Coleman recalled. "Wendy and I flipped, and played it to Prince. There were a lot of different types of instruments on it, interesting sounds – Arabic music, the oud, cello, finger cymbals, darbuka."[13]

Inspired by this wide sonic palette, Prince re-recorded the song, with David Coleman's input and blessing, as the title track for his new album. He was so enthusiastic about it, in fact, that he started work on the new project straightaway, despite the fact that he was midway through recording a second solo album for Sheila E., *Romance 1600*. Whenever he had a break from touring he would stop off at any available studio to work on the record – or, failing that, use a mobile recording unit. By the early hours of Christmas Day 1984, Prince had recorded and mixed the entire album, having put down vocals for the closing track, 'Temptation,' with engineer Susan Rogers during the final session.

On February 21 1985, with the end of the Purple Rain tour still two months away, Prince played *Around The World In A Day* to executives in Warner Bros' Los Angeles office. The quick turnaround was a shock to the label, which hadn't expected a follow-up to *Purple Rain* so soon. According to a report in *Rolling Stone* magazine in April, the label received a phone call late that afternoon to say that its biggest star would be there in 45 minutes. Prince arrived in a limo, dressed in a purple kimono and holding a single rose, flanked by his father, bodyguards, management, and Wendy Melvoin. He led around 150 executives to a fourth-floor conference room, played them the album – barely speaking, except in a low whisper to Mo Ostin – and then left as suddenly as he had arrived. One employee present subsequently told *Rolling Stone*: "Everyone sort of stood up and applauded after the record was over, and then he wasn't there anymore."

The new album blindsided Warners just as it would the public when it was released on April 22, a mere two weeks after the completion of the Purple Rain tour. The label wanted *Purple Rain 2*, but what Prince gave them seemed to sound more like a late-60s psychedelic album. If that wasn't enough, *Around The World In A Day* came with an insistence that there would be no singles, no promotional videos, and not even any adverts in magazines. Prince seemed adamant that only 'real fans' find out about the album, which should be seen as the work of a creative artist and not just another commercial product.

"I had a sort of F-you attitude," Prince told The Electrifying Mojo, a Detroit-based DJ, on June 6, the day before he turned 27. "I was making something for myself and my fans, and the people who supported me through the years."[14] For some in the Prince camp, including Matt Fink, who bemoaned the timing, this seemed like a serious misstep, but the singer himself was anxious not to be pidgeonholed. "I saw kids coming to concerts who screamed just because that's where the audience screamed in the movie," he explained to *Entertainment Weekly* in 1999. "I wanted to totally change that."[15]

This might well have been the case, but most critics were left unconvinced by the album's surface-level psychedelic sheen, particularly when it came to the Eastern-sounding title track or the Beatles-esque escapism of 'Paisley Park.' These criticisms weren't entirely accurate – Prince certainly hadn't abandoned his old sound quite as dramatically as some reviewers suggested – but then nor was the singer's claim in an interview with MTV around the time of the album's release that "*Around The World In A Day* is a funky album."[16]

There are however hints of almost everything that came before it on *Around The World In A Day*. The utopian themes of 'Uptown' resurface on 'Paisley Park,' which Prince told *Rolling Stone* was his attempt "to say something about looking inside oneself to find perfection."[17] Elsewhere, there are the usual extended sexual metaphors ('Raspberry Beret' and 'Tambourine,' a barely disguised tribute to masturbation); heart-wrenching ballads ('Condition Of The Heart'); strident, rock-based patriotism ('America'); plus the usual battle between religious fulfillment (the gospel ballad 'The Ladder') and sexual obsession ('Temptation,' a close relative of 'Darling Nikki,' complete this time with a conversation with God).

All in all, it was pretty much standard Prince fare – or as close as you might get to such a thing. But coming so soon after *Purple Rain*, it was also something of an eye-opener. If the previous album's 'Darling Nikki' was, as Prince later suggested, "the coldest song ever written,"[18] then 'Paisley Park' is about as warm an invitation as you might reasonably expect to come in, sit down, and relax.

"If there was a theme to *Around The World In A Day*," Alan Leeds recalled, "[it] was that it was the anti-*Purple Rain* record."[19] This, it seems, was the only thing critics could settle on. Whether it was any good or not was a different matter. The *New York Times* was impressed, having decided that Prince was "asking, perhaps demanding, to be taken seriously."[20] For the *New Musical Express*, however, it was one creative leap too far. "Prince's position is presently unassailable," it claimed, "[but] contrary to his own high self-regard, this does not make him infallible."[21] The only thing reviewers could agree on was the album's somewhat superficial debt to psychedelia, notably The Beatles. For the *New York Times*, the album "might more accurately have been titled *Around Great 60s Rock In A Day*," while the *Detroit Free Press* noted that "The Beatles, and John Lennon in particular, bear heavily on 'Paisley Park' ('Penny Lane') and 'The Ladder' (an 'Instant Karma' for the 80s)."[22] For *Newsweek*, the album seemed like "an eerie attempt to recapture the utopian whimsy that characterized The Beatles' *Sgt Pepper*."[23]

Prince, of course, disputed this. "The influence wasn't The Beatles," he told *Rolling Stone*. "They were great for what they did, but I don't know how that would hang today."[24] He made a point, too, of defending his decision not to make *Purple Rain 2*. "You know how easy it would have been to open *Around The World In A Day* with the guitar solo that's on the end of 'Let's Go Crazy,' just put it in a different key? That would have shut everybody up who said that album wasn't half as powerful. I don't *want* to make an album like the earlier ones. Wouldn't it be cool to put your albums back-to-back and not get bored?"[25]

To his credit, much of the album's power came from subtle textures rather than rock-star posturing. But criticism seemed unavoidable this time around, even when it came to the artwork, which many took to be a rather too obvious reference to The Beatles' *Yellow Submarine*. "The cover art came about because I thought people were tired of looking at me," he explained to *Rolling Stone*. What he was going for this time, he said, was something "a little more happening than just another picture ... some way I could materialize in people's cribs when they play the record."[26] Rather tellingly, however, the gatefold jacket includes a drawing of Prince, holding his 'cloud guitar' and dressed in the cloud-covered suit he wore in the 'Raspberry Beret' promo video. The cartoon Prince looks considerably older than his real-life counterpart did at the time, as if to suggest that his recent ascent to superstardom had had quite the aging effect.

Despite the muted critical response and deliberate lack of promotion, *Around The World In A Day* still peaked at Number One on *Billboard*, ironically knocking the *We Are The World* album off the top. But while *Purple Rain* had clung onto the top spot for 24 weeks, its successor only hung on for three, by which time its creator's confidence seemed to be faltering. Relaxing his earlier standpoint, he rush-released 'Raspberry Beret' as a single, shot a promo video for it, and gave his first interview for two years to *Rolling Stone*. "I think the smartest thing I ever did was record *Around The World In A Day* right after I finished *Purple Rain*," he said, clearly on the defensive. "I didn't wait to see what would happen with *Purple Rain*."[27]

For the most part, however, Prince seemed too busy to let the response to *Around The World In A Day* bother him, noting that it had been bought by "the same three million" people who bought *1999*. "It's important to me that those people believe in what we're trying to say," he said, "as opposed to just digging it because it's a hit."[28] He would go on to boast that "George Clinton told me how much he liked *Around The World In A Day*. You know how much his words meant than those from some mamma-jamma wearing glasses and an alligator shirt behind a typewriter?"[29]

Even before the album was released, Prince was well on the way to making the follow-up, *Parade*. He might not have ended 1985 as the most bankable pop-star of the year, but was still the most creative, and still had enough credit in the bank that his carte blanche would not yet be revoked. If nothing else, *Around The World In A Day* put Prince on the path toward what he considered to be the ultimate artistic expression. Although some of his critics didn't like what he was doing, he retained a level of respect as he forged on, bucking ever more against the conventional wisdom about what a commercially successful musician should do.

With *Purple Rain*, Prince had shown himself to be just as capable of making hit movies as hit records. For his follow-up movie, however, he was keen to produce a more serious, artistic affair – something that proved him to be more than just a flash-in-the-pan pop star who had made a lucky break onto the big screen. "I'm hoping that everyone understands where I was trying to go with it," he told Detroit DJ The Electrifying Mojo in 1985. "There's a message behind it all and I hope people think about it when they leave. That's the main thing."[30]

Given the huge success of *Purple Rain*, Warner Bros seemed happy to stump up $10 million to produce the follow-up. Prince and Steve Fargnoli hired screenwriter Becky Johnson to come up with a draft script, which was based on an idea the singer had had about playing a bar-room pianist-cum-gigolo who falls in love with an heiress in the Côte d'Azur (a concept he planted the seeds for on *Around The World In A Day*'s 'Condition Of The Heart').

Setting it in the South of France was important to Prince, who had developed a taste for travel after years of never leaving North America. In June 1985 he and

Steve Fargnoli went looking for shooting locations, following much the same MO as had The Beatles for *Help!*: find a place you've not visited before and make a movie there.

Having settled on Nice – hardly the cheapest place to make a movie – Prince and Fargnoli returned to Minneapolis to work out the details of the shoot. By then Prince had decided that he wanted to shoot the movie in black-and-white – a risky business, given that most popular movies of the time tended to be bright and brash. (Black-and-white movies wouldn't hold much mainstream appeal to modern audiences until Steven Spielberg made *Schindler's List* in 1993.)

Prince should have been making a bright, poppy movie held together by a string of live musical performances. Instead, *Under The Cherry Moon* was inspired by black-and-white comedies from the 20s, 30s, and 40s, and included just two musical sequences – one of them over the end credits. Prince was keen to show his serious side, but since much of the praise for *Purple Rain* had been for the musical segments, this didn't seem like the greatest of ideas. Both label and management started to object. "We had a whole different plan, a whole different screenplay," manager Bob Cavallo later recalled. "We had secret writers writing on it and all that, but he wouldn't [do it]."[31]

Warners did at least manage to convince Prince to shoot in color first, and convert to black-and-white later – presumably in the hope that he would change his mind in due course and stick with color. In an effort, once again, to give *Under The Cherry Moon* some artistic weight, Prince asked the French photographer Jean Baptise Mondino to direct it, but Mondino was too busy. (He would later photograph Prince for *Lovesexy*, and direct his 'I Wish U Heaven' promo.) Instead, Prince brought in a German cinematographer, Michael Ballhaus, as lighting and photography director, and gave the job of directing to Mary Lambert. Like *Purple Rain* director Albert Magnoli, Lambert had no major experience of moviemaking, but had recently shot stylish promo videos for Madonna's 'Like A Virgin' and 'Material Girl,' which suggested that she might be able to make a movie for the MTV generation.

Casting wasn't particularly straightforward, either. Since this was no rock'n'roll movie, Prince was keen to avoid using The Revolution, but wanted his girlfriend of the time, Susannah Melvoin, to play Mary Sharon, the heiress with whom Prince's Christopher Tracy falls in love. Susannah had herself been just as influential on Prince's post-*Purple Rain* activities as her twin sister. When Prince hired Wendy Melvoin to replace Dez Dickerson in 1983, he had no idea it would lead to one of the most intense relationships of his life, but that's exactly what happened. Shortly after hiring Wendy in May 1983, he met her twin. The pair were instantly attracted to each other, and it wasn't long before Susannah had split up with her boyfriend of the time and moved from California to Minneapolis to be near Prince. She quickly took pride of place among Prince's girlfriends, further driving the despairing Vanity away and pushing Jill Jones into the background.

Coming from the same stock as her sister Wendy, it's no surprise that Susannah had an affinity for music. She quickly began to introduce Prince to new influences in literature, art, and music, too, and would soon be working in the studio with him as one of two singers in The Family, a post-Time band some felt Prince had formed just so that he could keep her nearby. (There were also suggestions that Prince had proposed to her shortly before they flew out to Paris together in August 1985 to begin pre-production.)

But Melvoin was far too inexperienced – particularly given that the cast already included another novice actress, Emmanuelle Sallet – and when it became clear that she couldn't act, Prince sent her home, replacing her with Kristin Scott Thomas, who had initially only read for a much smaller role. Jerome Benton, Morris Day's old sidekick in The Time, who enjoyed a relatively small part in *Purple Rain*, was promoted to the role of Prince's comedy foil, Tricky, in an attempt to re-create *Purple Rain*'s much praised comedy-duo element. (Since The Time's dissolution, he was the only member who had hung around the Prince camp, joining an augmented line-up of The Revolution as a dancer.)

After a quick rewrite of the script, shooting began on September 16 in Victorine Studios, Nice, and on the French Riviera itself. "The preparation and filming of *Under The Cherry Moon* was an exciting time in the Prince camp," Alan Leeds recalled. "That we spent three months in the South of France didn't hurt."[32]

That might well have been true, but the project quickly ran into trouble. Having moved out to France with Susannah Melvoin in August – before promptly sending her home again – Prince soon decided that a movie set was no place for monogamy, and allegedly started an affair with Kristin Scott Thomas (he would later write 'Better With Time,' as featured on 2009's *MPLSound*, with her in mind). Director Mary Lambert was hot on Susannah's heels, having already been demoted to an 'advisory' role just four days into shooting. Having previously spoken positively of working with someone who "knows what he wants," Lambert issued a statement to confirm that she was leaving "under totally amicable circumstances," noting that "Prince has such a strong vision of what this movie should be ... that it makes no sense for me to stand between him and the film anymore." Lambert was followed by the actor Terence Stamp, who had been due to play Scott Thomas's father, but left because of "timetable clashes." He was replaced by Steven Berkoff.

Prince soon found himself stuck directing the movie and working with a European crew who spoke limited English. He shot the movie quickly, often happy to go with the first take. The whole thing was done by November 21, two months after the shoot began. A day later, Prince shot the promo video for 'Girls & Boys' with The Revolution, and then returned to Minneapolis. A few extra scenes were shot in April 1986, by which time Prince had almost completed editing the rest. As far as he was concerned, he had taken to moviemaking as easily as he had to recordmaking. "There's no difference [between the two]," he told The Electrifying Mojo. "People have tried to tell me [that] a movie is a little bit more complex, but to me it's just a larger version of an album."[33]

Under The Cherry Moon received its world premiere on July 1 1986 in the less-than-glamorous location of Sheridan, Wyoming, as a result of an MTV competition in which the 10,000th caller to a special hotline had the event staged in his or her hometown. The winner was a 22-year-old hotel chambermaid, Lisa Barber, who also won the right to be escorted to the screening (at the Centennial Theater) by the leading man, who sat with her throughout. After the movie, Prince & The Revolution performed at the local Holiday Inn – the only local venue big enough to stage a concert.

The fact that a publicity stunt such as this was employed spoke volumes about how the movie was expected to perform. Had this been another *Purple Rain*, it would almost certainly have opened in Los Angeles to hordes of screaming fans. Instead, it was shown in a town best known, according to one local resident, for its fishing lures. "We don't care about no boy who wears tight pants and struts around like a woman," the man told *People Weekly*.

The media's response to *Under The Cherry Moon* was similarly harsh. "Don't even turn up on the same continent where this is playing," *USA Today* warned, while Glenn Lovell of the *San Jose Mercury News* described Prince's performance as the most "outrageous, unmitigated display of narcissism" since Barbra Streisand in *A Star Is Born*.[34] The movie's storyline – gigolo falls in love, gives up his lifestyle for the woman he loves, but ends up being assassinated by her father – just wasn't very appealing. It didn't help that Prince gave himself one of the most self-indulgent death scenes ever – perhaps fittingly, given that the *New York Times* would call his character "a self-caressing twerp of dubious provenance."

Prince fans still had plenty to latch onto, however, as they watched him act coy, funny, and cute for the camera. "That film went through many drafts," he said in an AOL web chat in 1997. He admitted that "much was lost in the shuffle," but felt that there are still "some very funny scenes."[35] But while some moments – such as when Prince's Christopher Tracy mocks Scott Thomas's Mary Sharon for being unable to pronounce the word 'wreckastow' (a slangy pronunciation of 'record store') – are still fondly remembered by fans, there's little else to savor. Warners had reportedly wanted a greater sense of conflict in the script, but Prince himself mistakenly felt that the 'atmosphere and music' would be enough to keep audiences entertained. The *Philadelphia Daily News* summed the movie up perfectly: "*Purple*

Rain is a psychological/autobiographical glorified rock video starring Prince & The Revolution, while this new one ... is a movie starring Prince."[36] *Under The Cherry Moon* ended up winning eight Golden Raspberry Awards, losing out only in the category of Worst Actress, which was won by Madonna for her role in *Shanghai Surprise*. (Back on the defensive, Prince claimed to have no regrets in a 1990 interview with *Rolling Stone*, in which he said: "I learned that I can't direct what I didn't write."[37])

Thankfully, the first major artistic misstep of Prince's career could be overlooked to some extent in favor of its soundtrack album. *Parade* is another relatively collaborative album in the *Around The World In A Day* mold. This time, however, Prince shifted the focus from 60s rock'n'roll to jazz, as introduced to him by saxophonist Eric Leeds. *Parade* is also notable for being the album on which Prince returned to playing live drums in favor of the programmed patterns of the Linn LM-1, and finally assented to using real horns in place of synthesized ones. It is also the first Prince album to feature string arrangements by Clare Fischer, who would go on to add color and character to some of his greatest works.

Fischer had previously worked with Rufus, the group that launched Chaka Khan. He was subsequently brought in by David Rivkin to add strings to Prince's latest side project, The Family. After hearing his contribution to tracks such as 'Christopher Tracy's Parade,' the superstitious Prince decided they were so perfect that he never wanted to meet Fischer face-to-face for fear of breaking the magic on future recordings. (They have still never met.)

The collaboration with Fischer established the method by which Prince now preferred to work: "sending tapes back and forth, and just being interested enough hearing what he would do left to his own devices," as Alan Leeds put it.[38] Between April and December 1985, Prince worked on most of the basic tracks for *Parade* on his own, but would send them to Lisa Coleman and Wendy Melvoin for augmentation. He found this to be the most comfortable method of collaborating, and would stick to it throughout his career – even when working with Miles Davis.

Prince took over the three studios at Sunset Sound while working on the album. He used one for *Parade*, another for The Family, and a third for an album by Mazarati, which was being produced by David Rivkin and Revolution bassist Mark Brown. Legend has it that he had cut the first four songs for *Parade* on the spot, in sequence: that he sat down behind the drums, asked Susan Rogers to roll the tape, and played through all of the drum tracks, using only his handwritten lyrics as guidance, then added the bass, keyboards, guitars, and vocals to each of the songs, one after another.

All that was left was for Susannah Melvoin to provide vocal overdubs, Clare

Fischer to add his string arrangements, and Wendy Melvoin to sing the lead vocal for 'I Wonder U.' "He would get an idea and just couldn't rest to the degree of burning out engineers," Alan Leeds recalled. "He was an engineer's nightmare, because he had no patience with the technology – just waiting for them to rewind tape was tedious for him, to the point where he would yell, 'Can't you make that move a little faster?'"[39]

The only truly collaborative track on *Parade* is 'Mountains,' which was recorded with the newly expanded line-up of The Revolution. (Drummer Bobby Z had been usurped by Sheila E. when it came to adding cowbells to 'Life Can Be So Nice.') This put The Revolution in the odd position of being asked to contribute to a project that they were generally being kept at arms' length from.

Released on March 31 1986, *Parade* met with a critical fervor that *Under The Cherry Moon* had failed to attract and was hailed as a total artistic comeback by those critics who had disliked *Around The World In A Day*. "Stunning in its scope" was how the *Sunday Times* chose to describe it, while the *Detroit Free Press* called it "a confirmation of Prince's place as a superior melodist, arranger, and player, as well as a celebration of his creativity."[40]

The album is so concise and tightly written that it seems a lot shorter than its 40-minute run time. With its off-kilter rhythms, weird ebbs and flows, and instrumental subtleties, it doesn't sound like anything else in the Prince canon. From a musical perspective it's one of Prince's densest records, but the production is closer to the stripped-down sound of *1999*.

Jazz is the main influence on piano-led tracks such as 'Under The Cherry Moon' and the instrumental 'Venus De Milo,' but even the 'rock' tracks – including 'Anotherloverholenyohead' – don't sound like anything Prince had recorded before. The funky 'Girls & Boys,' the celebratory 'Mountains,' and the piano-ballad 'Sometimes It Snows In April' – one of Prince's most affecting songs – are all augmented with such unusual instrumentation and unexpected twists that they still manage to surprise even after they seem to have settled into a recognizable structure.

The highlight for most listeners was 'Kiss,' a song Prince almost didn't record. His cavalier attitude to giving away new songs (see 'Manic Monday,' reclaimed from Apollonia 6 during the *Purple Rain/Apollonia* 6 sessions, but unreleased until Prince gave it to The Bangles) made him believe that he could write hit tracks for just about anybody, even if he hadn't masterminded the band's image and sound.

Next door to where Prince was recording *Parade*, Revolution bassist Mark Brown and Bobby Rivkin were working on a self-titled album by a group known as Mazarati. Brown had started playing with the group on the Minneapolis club scene during a break from touring with The Revolution. Not wanting to end up the same way as Jimmy Jam and Terry Lewis, he wore a mask on stage and called himself The Shadow. After a while, however, Brown knew that he would have to come clean to

Prince or face serious consequences. But when he did, Prince surprised him by deciding to take Mazarati under his wing.

Prince was too busy to produce the group himself, but donated one song to the project, '100 MPH.' Then, as the sessions continued, he offered them another unused track: a bluesy acoustic number called 'Kiss.' Rivkin and Brown sat up all night wondering what to do with the song before opting to give it a strident funk backing. When Prince returned to Sunset Sound the following day, he quickly changed his mind about the song's worth. "It's too good for you guys," he told them. "I'm taking it back." He had originally suggested that he would reward Rivkin for his efforts by giving him a co-production credit, but eventually listed him only as the song's arranger, even though the main elements of the song originated from Rivkin and Brown's version. ("Terence Trent D'Arby asked me where 'Kiss' came from," Prince later boasted. "I have no idea. Nothing in it makes sense. Nothing! The hi-hat doesn't make sense."[41])

Before long, Prince had completed the minimal final version of 'Kiss,' stripping away a lot of the detail Rivkin and Brown had added, and chose it to be the first single from *Parade*. Warner Bros felt that it sounded like a demo, but Prince was determined to release it without any changes, and he was right to. A taut, sparse blend of funk and R&B, sung in a falsetto Curtis Mayfield would have envied, 'Kiss' would become Prince's first transatlantic Number One hit since 'Let's Go Crazy.' (The other song he had written for Mazarati fared rather less well. '100 MPH' stalled at Number 19 on the R&B chart, and didn't even register on the Hot 100.)

"I remember the first time that I heard the song 'Kiss,'" Dez Dickerson later recalled, "really feeling that he had managed to recapture some of that raw R&B emotion from some of his earlier music."[42] The promo video is equally stripped-down. It features just Prince, Wendy Melvoin, and an unidentified female dancer, proving just how valuable Melvoin was to Prince at the time.

Part of *Parade*'s overall genius is the way that it runs through all sorts of tried-and-tested Prince tricks while still sounding like nothing that came before it; part of its charm is the way that it sounds like Prince is stretching himself beyond his comfort zone to incorporate influences he hasn't fully mastered. It marks one of the few occasions where he has sounded out on a limb. Ironically, it would be kept off the top of the US charts by Janet Jackson's *Control*: an album produced by sacked former Time members Jimmy Jam and Terry Lewis.

CHAPTER 7

GOT ANY DREAMS YOU AIN'T USIN'?

He was constantly pissed off at us. It was a very strange time. We were fighting. There was fire coming out.

WENDY MELVOIN

In March 1986, the casual observer might have expected Prince's focus to be on *Under The Cherry Moon*, which was still in need of a few extra scenes, and *Parade*, which was due to go on sale in a couple of weeks' time. Continually discarding old ideas in favor of new ones, however, Prince had already started work on yet another new project, under the glow of a stained-glass window in his new home studio in Chanhassen, Minnesota, which would serve as his main base of operations while waiting for his new Paisley Park studio to be built. That project was *Dream Factory*, the culmination of his recent embrace of the spirit of collaboration.

Having traded tapes regularly with Wendy Melvoin, Lisa Coleman, and Clare Fischer while making *Parade*, Prince took things a step further at the tail end of 1985, forming The Flesh with Sheila E. on drums, Levi Seacer Jr on bass, and Eric Leeds on saxophone. The group made a series of impromptu, jazz-based recordings at Sunset Sound studios around the turn of the year. Prince had them pressed up as *The Flesh* but never released it, although 'Junk Music' found its way into *Under The Cherry Moon* and 'U Got 2 Shake Something' turned up as 'Shake!' by The Time on *Graffiti Bridge*.

The Flesh might never have materialized, but it was clear that Prince had grown more interested in the idea of recording with a group in the studio. So it was that he invited The Revolution to work on what is now one of his most famous unreleased albums, *Dream Factory*. Although Prince recorded most of 'The Ballad Of Dorothy Parker' and 'Starfish & Coffee' on his own, remaining songs prominently feature The Revolution – notably 'Visions,' a solo instrumental piano piece by Lisa Coleman, who also sings the lead vocal on 'A Place In Heaven.'

The sessions seemed to gratify the band, particularly Melvoin and Coleman, with whom Prince worked most closely. Having expanded the live line-up of The Revolution to a point where some felt the chemistry had been ruined, Prince seemed to be using these sessions to assuage tensions within the group.

Further complicating things between Prince, Wendy, and Lisa was his relationship with Wendy's twin, Susannah. That Prince adored her was in no doubt: she sang on *Parade* and designed the jacket artwork for the *Dream Factory* project. Despite trying to behave like a committed monogamist, however, Prince continued to flaunt his affairs. This made life difficult not just for Susannah but also for her sister and Lisa Coleman. Whenever Prince upset her, she would confide in Wendy, who in turn would talk to Coleman – which had made it almost impossible for them all to work together. "It was hard," Coleman told Prince biographer Liz Jones. "We couldn't take sides. Prince was trying to draw the lines all the time."[2] Such was Prince's hold over his girlfriends that Susannah stuck it out until December 1986, and even then moved only to a nearby apartment.

Prince, it seems, just didn't know how lucky he was at the time. Susannah inspired some of his greatest ballads, including 'The Beautiful Ones' and 'Nothing Compares 2 U,' and had a profound impact on *Parade*'s follow-up, *Sign "O" The Times*. His obsession with her is writ large on a song once slated for *Dream Factory*, 'Big Tall Wall,' on which he declares his intention to build said wall around his lover "so U can't get out," and is confirmed by the dark themes of much of the material he wrote during and immediately after the break-up of their relationship.

Prince was so obsessed with Susannah that he made her a co-vocalist of The Family, created out of the remaining members of The Time, and released their self-titled debut album before even beginning filming on *Under The Cherry Moon*. Time keyboardist Paul Peterson was given the task of performing frontman duties, while Jerome Benton carried on as dancer/comic foil, with Jellybean Johnson on drums. They were joined by Miko Weaver, who also played guitar with Sheila E., but here seemed to be more of a nominal presence than a fully-fledged group member.

Prince had begun work on *The Family* during the summer of 1984 in much the same way as he had The Time's albums: writing all of the songs, playing all of the instruments (except for saxophone and strings), and laying down guide vocals for Peterson – now known as St Paul – to follow. Unlike Morris Day, however, Peterson was clearly a sideman, not a frontman, and struggled to keep up with the recordings.

Leaving aside the quality of the material, *The Family* just didn't have the drive of The Time – nor did it have Prince's total commitment. It was released on his Paisley Park label in August 1985 while the singer himself was in France working on pre-production for *Under The Cherry Moon*. He had little interest in promoting the album, so simply left it to Warner Bros. Peterson ended up leaving the group after just one concert at First Avenue, citing a lack of creative input, while the remaining members of The Family then found their way into the ever-evolving line-up of The Revolution.

Ultimately it seems that forming The Family was just Prince's way of keeping Susannah Melvoin by his side for as long as possible. The album artwork makes plain his infatuation with her. She dominates the main jacket artwork (by *Vogue* photographer Horst P. Horst), and features in several interior snaps taken by Prince himself.

Just as importantly, however, The Family gave him an outlet for his first tentative experiments with both live saxophone (played by Eric Leeds) and string arrangements by Clare Fischer. Both of these elements were more fully developed on *Parade*, but for now just meant that *The Family* was jazzier and less accessible than anything The Time had done.

The Family also released a single, 'The Screams Of Passion,' but the group's most lasting legacy came with their recording of the original version of 'Nothing Compares 2 U,' as famously covered by Irish singer Sinead O'Connor. Prince had nothing to do with O'Connor's rendition, however, and in fact – if she is to be believed – later had a fiery meeting with her. "Prince started to give out to me for swearing in interviews," O'Connor told the UK's *Mirror* newspaper in 2007. "When I told him to go fuck himself he got very upset and became quite threatening. ... A few blows were exchanged. All I could do was spit. I spat on him quite a bit."[3]

Prince never responded to these claims, but some commentators have made clear their cynicism, noting that O'Connor's remarks were timed to coincide with Prince's 21 Nights In London residency. Others meanwhile have expressed doubts that the diminutive Prince could ever hold his own in a fight with the taller and rather more imposing O'Connor.

That Prince never fully let go of the girl the song was written for became clear in a 1997 web-chat with AOL, however. Despite usually being so deft at avoiding anything approaching a personal revelation, he gave a simple, honest response to the question of who had inspired 'Forever In My Life' (despite being married to Mayte Garcia at the time): "Susannah. She knows."[4] It seems fitting, then, that the song most directly inspired by her has never been heard by anyone other than Prince and his engineer, Susan Rogers.

Shortly after Susannah finally left him for good, Prince recorded a song called 'Wally,' in which he reportedly confided his deepest thoughts about her to his bodyguard and dancer, Wally Safford. Prince erased the song once, before recording it again for posterity but never releasing it.

Given that Warners had put up $10 million to make *Under The Cherry Moon* but only recouped $3 million, it was decided that the best way to turn both projects into full-blown commercial successes would be for Prince to go out on tour. Prince, however, was busy prioritizing work on *Dream Factory* and looking to his own empire. After hitting his commercial peak with *Purple Rain* – and establishing himself as a successful hitmaker with The Time and Vanity 6 – Prince was able to convince Warners chief executive Mo Ostin to put up $2 million so that the singer could start his own Paisley Park Records label. "Paisley Park is an alternative," he told *Rolling Stone* in 1985. "I'm not saying it's greater or better. It's just something else. It's multicolored and it's very fun."[5] In reality, however, it was little more than a name.

Although Warners made a significant investment to get it off the ground, Paisley Park was essentially a vanity label, created to keep the singer under the impression that he had more control than he really did, much like the Stones' Rolling Stones Records. The Paisley Park logo would subsequently be seen alongside the Warners logo on Prince's own records, those of his side projects, and any other acts Prince chose to work with (or that his management signed to keep the label afloat as a commercial entity).

As it turned out, the multi-colored novelty would soon wear off. Paisley Park was an alternative, but not in the way Prince had anticipated. Instead, it became a shining example of how not to run a record label. While Warners continued to reap success with each new Prince record, the singer didn't seem to be pulling his weight when it came to the other Paisley releases. By the end of the 80s he seemed to be coming to the end of his run of great records, leaving him with little to spread around elsewhere.

He also adopted a rather passive approach to the business of running a label. Instead of signing new artists to try to build a formidable roster, he only seemed to be interested in working with members of his existing tight-knit group – Sheila E., The Family, Jill Jones, and his 1987 Madhouse project. According to Alan Leeds, who would serve as president of Paisley Park Records until 1992: "Prince wasn't taking the responsibility to produce competitive records and turn the label around."[6] In the rare instances that he did branch out, Prince ended up working with the likes of George Clinton, who was well past his best by the time of 1989's *The Cinderella Theory*. His attempts to refashion Mavis Staples as a modern R&B star in the early 90s were similarly unwise.

Therein lay the problem: Prince knew how to make records, but he was not a 'producer.' Rather than let an artist's personality shine through, he forced his own ideas onto them, resulting in a series of records that each sounded too similar to the last. As Alan Leeds recalled, Prince rarely had much enthusiasm for the outside groups Cavallo Ruffalo & Fargnoli brought in, and "failed to disguise his lack of interest."[7]

Paisley Park quickly became home to half-baked ideas that came and went in a flash. Prince's interest could seemingly only be roused by album projects that involved girlfriends: Jill Jones, Taja Sevelle, Ingrid Chavez, and The Family. Asked in 1990 why nothing from a reported session with Bonnie Raitt ever saw release, Prince told *Rolling Stone*: "I was just working on a lot of things at the same time, and I didn't give myself enough time to work with her … I used to do that a lot – start five different projects and only get a couple done."[8]

Such was the situation with *Dream Factory* when Warners requested that Prince tour. As ever, however, he was still of a mind to do things the hard way. His US 'tour' consisted of ten Hit & Run dates, starting at First Avenue on March 3 1986, for which the city and venue of each performance would only be announced a few hours before showtime. This created enough fervor that each night would sell out, but still came as a disappointment to Warners, who had high hopes for a blockbuster tour. Prince did play a further 15 shows in Europe and four more in Japan, but that was as far as the promotional jaunt for *Parade* went.

The Hit & Run dates introduced a new, iconic part of Prince folklore: the after-show gig, which would see the band take to the stage of a smaller venue in the early hours of the morning and play a much looser, jam-based set. "The after-shows were a natural outgrowth of an artist who was intrigued [by] the idea of performing often and in a variety of venues," Alan Leeds explained. "Prince enjoyed the intimacy and immediacy that small clubs provided."[9]

The tour itself was bittersweet. Tensions between Prince and The Revolution had grown, largely because the show was now essentially a funk revue. The props of previous tours were replaced by Matt 'Atlanta Bliss' Blistan on trumpet, bodyguards-turned-dancers Wally Salford and Greg Brooks, Sheila E. – who was increasingly replacing Bobby Z in the studio – on percussion, Miko Weaver on rhythm guitar, and various members of the now-defunct Family, including ex-Time dancer Jerome Benton and Susannah Melvoin on backing vocals. "I was behind the piano, next to Bobby Z," Mark Brown recalled, "and behind three guys that used to be bodyguards. I started feeling a little underappreciated."[10] Eric Leeds seemed to sum the situation up best when he dubbed the band the "counter-Revolution."

Few among the original line-up were happy about this turn of events, but for Prince, it all made perfect sense. Having been criticized for courting the white market, he wanted to return to his roots with a larger-scale soul/funk revue in the same vein as George Clinton's P-Funk groups. He was also keen, as always, to make his shows more theatrical. This was simply the live equivalent of his sometime habit of sacrificing subtlety on his later records in favor of building up layer upon layer of overdubs.

Prince had made some concessions to The Revolution in the recording studio, such as giving Melvoin a lead vocal on *Parade*'s 'I Wonder U' and working with them on *Dream Factory*, but the tensions continued to rise. "Prince is an entertainer," Wendy Melvoin later recalled. "He wanted more entertainment, and Lisa and I wanted less."[11] In July 1986 Melvoin, Coleman, and Mark Brown all threatened to quit before the European *Parade* tour kicked off, but all three were convinced to ride it out.

Keen to avoid conflict, Prince worked on in the studio alone. By the end of June he had assembled enough material to expand *Dream Factory* to a 19-track double album featuring lengthy solo tracks such as 'Crystal Ball' and 'Movie Star.' At one point he even reportedly considered turning the project into a Broadway musical about the trappings of fame.

On July 18, Prince had a final master of *Dream Factory* pressed. The artwork, which was designed by Susannah Melvoin and included a space for each member of The Revolution to draw something to represent him or herself, seemed to suggest that this was very much a group record, but many of the truly collaborative songs – including 'Sexual Suicide,' 'Big Tall Wall,' and 'Teacher, Teacher' – had been removed and replaced by solo recordings (some of which would later resurface on *Sign "O" The Times*).

The Revolution felt foxed again. Midway through the Parade tour it became clear that these would be their last shows together. But by then Prince was already thinking about shelving *Dream Factory* and moving on to something new.

Although the album that rose from its ashes, *Sign "O" The Times*, is widely considered to be among Prince's finest works, *Dream Factory* could have been even better. It would certainly have been his most eclectic record. The tentative sessions during 1984–85 from which Prince picked up rock, pop, and jazz influences from his bandmates here reached their natural conclusion, with the band hitting new creative peaks all the time. Perhaps their greatest moment together came with the recording of 'Power Fantastic' at Prince's home studio. As Alan Leeds writes in the liner notes to *The Hits/The B-Sides*: "Lisa Coleman found herself playing the grand piano in the upstairs living room while the rest of the band huddled in the basement studio. Connected only by mics and earphones, The Revolution still managed to pull off the exquisite song in a single take – even the jazzy intro that Prince suggested just as tape was ready to roll."[12]

There weren't too many other moments like this on the final version of *Dream Factory*, but Prince was still wise enough to hold onto the group recordings of things he couldn't do alone. Lisa Coleman's solo-piano piece, 'Visions,' is about as low key an opener as one might find on a Prince record, but contrasts well with what follows: the squelchy funk of the title track, on which Prince – in the sped-up voice of his new alter-ego, 'Camille' – renames Hollywood "Holly Rock" and describes fame as a dream factory, designed to keep you unaware of reality. Elsewhere, 'Strange Relationship' has an Eastern psychedelic feel that's missing on the *Sign "O" The Times* version, and 'All My Dreams' takes the carnivalesque sound of *Parade*'s opening tracks to its logical conclusion.

Despite being a sprawling double album, *Dream Factory* is brighter and more cohesive than its eventual follow-up, *Sign "O" The Times*. The material set for inclusion on it spanned the length and breadth of Prince's abilities, from 'Movie Star,' a hilarious spoken-word piece about a Morris Day-like character trying to woo clubbers with his looks, to 'Crystal Ball,' a nine-minute run through jazz, funk, and reggae that sounds more like a mini-album than a single song. Written in the wake of Prince's sudden return from France following America's air raid on Libya in April 1986, 'Crystal Ball' reprises the '1999' theme of partying in the face of death – or, in this case, staying close with an expert lover who draws "pictures of sex" on the walls.

Much of the solo *Dream Factory* material later appeared in altered form on either *Sign "O" The Times* or the three-disc out-takes collection *Crystal Ball*. But the fact that nobody got to hear it as it was originally intended – alongside the last gasps of The Revolution – is a travesty. *Dream Factory* proved exactly how important the group was to Prince's artistic growth, and could well have had an even greater impact than *Sign "O" The Times*. Not one to look backward, however,

Prince let the *Dream* fade away, and instead turned his attention to a new, semi-collaborative project, Madhouse, and the eventual follow-up to *Parade*.

Having shelved their collaborative masterpiece, Prince now needed to sack the band. On the final night of the *Parade* tour – September 9 1986 at Yokohama Stadium, Japan – he smashed all of his guitars and walked off stage after a final encore of 'Sometimes It Snows In April.'

Prince had never done anything like it before. Perhaps unsurprisingly, it marked the end of his association with The Revolution. In early October, he invited Melvoin and Coleman to dinner at his rented Beverly Hills home and fired them both. He then called Bobby Z to tell the drummer that he was going to be replaced by Sheila E., with whom Prince had been working in the studio for several years already. Matt Fink opted to stay on, but Mark Brown quit, partly out of loyalty to the others but also because he was unhappy at Prince's decision to return to making funk-based music.

As far as Prince was concerned, they all "needed to play a wide range of music with different types of people" so that they could "come back eight times as strong."[13] Others around him were less than convinced. Having hit what looked like a creative peak with The Revolution during the aborted *Dream Factory* sessions, he now seemed to want to go back to where he had been several years ago: recording everything on his own.

Melvoin and Coleman were left further embittered by what they saw as a lack of credit on 1987's *Sign "O" The Times*, which features re-recorded versions of tracks from the *Dream Factory* sessions (even Susannah received a credit on the album). The pair did nonetheless go on to establish themselves as session players, and as a duo in their own right (as Wendy & Lisa). They have also composed a number of movie soundtracks together, including *Dangerous Minds* and *Toys*, and in 2008 self-released their first new album in ten years, *White Flags Of Winter Chimneys*.

Prince made intermittent contact with the duo during the 90s, but neither of the collaborative projects that he suggested came to fruition. Having initially invited them both to play on a song entitled 'In This Bed Eye Scream' (released on the 1996 triple-album *Emancipation*), he eventually decided it would be better just to dedicate it to them. He then toyed with the idea of making a new Revolution album based at least in part around older recordings, to be called *Roundhouse Garden*, but that never made it beyond the planning stage either. Asked why not, Prince told fans at a Q&A session to "ask Wendy and Lisa," fuelling rumors that, having by this time become a Jehovah's Witness, he would not work with them unless they publicly renounced their homosexuality.

It took until the early 21st century for the trio to patch things up. Prince and Wendy Melvoin played together as a duo on the *Tavis Smiley Show* in February 2004 in support of *Musicology*. Then, on February 15 2006, both Melvoin and Coleman joined Prince for his show-stopping appearance at the BRIT Awards. The duo also appear on two tracks on his 2007 *Planet Earth* LP, 'The One U Wanna C' and 'Lion Of Judah.'

At the end of 1986, however, Prince was closing the curtain on the most collaborative phase of his career, aborting the *Dream Factory* project and dismantling one of his most celebrated backing bands. He would subsequently put together a new backing band from the musicians he had left, but things would not continue as they were. With the *Parade* era over, Prince decided that he wanted to reclaim everything for himself again.

CHAPTER 8

TALKIN' STUFF IN A VIOLENT ROOM

It was really a song a day coming out of the studio … Concepts for albums were coming to him almost as quickly as the songs were.

ALAN LEEDS

Musically alone for the first time since 1978, and with *Dream Factory* on the shelf, Prince went back down to his basement studio to start up a new project with only engineer Susan Rogers for company. The recordings Prince made would prove to be a lot darker than the *Dream Factory* songs, suggesting that he had been deeply affected by the loss of The Revolution and arguments with Susannah Melvoin – and also perhaps the fact that sales of his albums continued to slip, despite the ever-increasing critical fervor with which they were greeted.

Prince's response to all of this, of course, was to retreat into the studio and let his anger manifest itself on tape. Within ten days he had completed work on an album called *Camille*, which had its roots in 'Erotic City,' the B-side to his 1984 single 'Let's Go Crazy.' Prince had figured out a way of recording high-pitched vocal tracks by slowing the tape down, singing in real time, and speeding it back up. The result made it sound like he had recently ingested a large quantity of helium.

Prince used the effect again on 'Dream Factory' to ask the question: "Got any dreams you ain't usin'?" The voice fascinated him to the extent that he decided to give it the name Camille. Although he has never quite admitted it, it seems likely that Prince took it from the nickname of the 19th-century French hermaphrodite Herculine Barbin. (When an interviewer for Yahoo! put it to him that his brother believed this to be the case in 1997, Prince replied: "Your brother is very wise."[2]) Prince's plans for Camille even extended at one point to a movie, for which he planned to play both himself and his high-pitched alter ego.

While messing around with Camille in the studio in late October, Prince recorded a new song that set James Brown-style horn and guitar riffs against murky, hollow-sounding drums. 'Housequake' would become an important signifier of his continuing musical evolution. "It came at a time when there were other changes in his life," Susan Rogers recalled. "'Housequake' represented a new [style of] dance music for him."[3] Prince himself has never doubted its importance – or its genius. Reflecting on the breakthrough song to *Rolling Stone*, he said: "You'll be sitting there at the Grammys and U2 will beat you. And you say to yourself, 'Wait a minute, I can play that kind of music, too … but *you* will not do 'Housequake.'"[4]

With 'Housequake' in the bag, Prince quickly cut a whole album's worth of Camille material. By November 5, a self-titled album (to be credited to Camille, not Prince) was ready for mastering. A 'Housequake'/'Shockadelica' test pressing went out to clubs soon after that – partly so that Prince could get 'Shockadelica' out there before Jesse Johnson's album of the same name was released – but the album ended up being shelved almost as quickly as it had been recorded, despite already having a catalog number and artwork (a stick drawing of a man with crosses for eyes). Prince's work on the project wasn't entirely in vain, however. 'Rebirth Of The Flesh' aside, all of the *Camille* songs resurfaced in some form or other, either on *Sign "O" The Times*, as B-sides, or on the soundtrack to *Bright Lights, Big City*.

82

Prince's reasons for scrapping *Camille* aren't clear, but it's likely that he had concerns about the commercial viability of the project. With sales of his recent albums dropping incrementally, he knew that he needed to come up with a sure-fire hit this time around – particularly with The Revolution gone, and all eyes on him alone. He needed to show that he had grown as a musician, and that he hadn't relied on The Revolution to get where he was. Picking up the pieces of *Dream Factory* and *Camille*, Prince decided that his next release would be his defining statement: a three-LP set called *Crystal Ball*, with the song of the same name as its centerpiece.

Continuing at the same frantic pace that had yielded *Camille*, Prince had completed the 22-track triple album by November 30 and promptly sent Steve Fargnoli to play it to Warners. "He knew that just having the balls to do three records would create a big bang," Alan Leeds noted.[5] It did, of course, but the 'bang' was more destructive than creative. Having made concession after concession for Prince up until now, the label balked at the idea of putting out a triple album.

Prince's attitude, as Alan Leeds recalled, was: "Don't mess with me, this is it!" But this time Warners flatly refused. Prince might have been the label's most creative artist, but that wasn't enough to justify the expense of putting out a three-record set. It would be too costly to produce, and too expensive for the casual fan to want to buy. Already concerned by the rate at which Prince put out new albums – which confused casual buyers and made it virtually impossible to maximize their commercial potential – Warners refused to agree to release an album that seemed to be aimed only at critics and die-hard fans. Chief executive Mo Ostin insisted that Prince's next album be no longer than a double, forcing Prince to cut down his carefully constructed masterpiece.

This was the first real feud between label and star, but is indicative of problems that would emerge down the line. As far as Prince was concerned, Warners had no business telling him what to do with his art. Despite losing interest in what *Crystal Ball* ended up being almost as soon as it was completed, he retained a bitterness about the overall situation for much longer. "I delivered three CDs for *Sign 'O' The Times*," he said in 1996. "Because people at Warners were tired, they came up with reasons why I should be tired too. I don't know if it's their place to talk me in or out of things."[6]

As 1986 came to a close, Prince had lost his biggest battle to date with Warners, watched Susannah Melvoin walk out of his door for the last time, and been forced to trim his masterpiece by a third. Stripping away the lengthy 'Crystal Ball,' along with several *Camille* songs and others dating back to *Dream Factory*, Prince pushed 'Sign "O" The Times' up to the front and made it this new, slimmer album's title track. (The songs featuring sped-up vocals are still credited to Camille.)

The only new addition was the second disc's hard-rock opener, 'U Got The Look,' which Prince recorded in December, and which went on to become one of his most successful singles. But had it not been for Sheena Easton, who happened to visit Prince while he was working on it, the song might never have been completed. Prince had been struggling to get the song right until Easton turned up and added her vocals. (Her presence on the record – and in the accompanying promo video, which was shot during a day off in Paris in June 1987 – led to speculation that she had become yet another one of Prince's girlfriends. Easton would later laugh this off, noting: "According to the press, he bought me an apartment, which then became a mansion. ... And how our affair ended telepathically, so I think that speaks for itself."[7])

Sign "O" The Times was finished by the middle of January 1987, and released on March 30 to some of the strongest reviews Prince has ever received. Unaware that the material had once extended across an even wider musical terrain, critics fell over themselves to praise the album's diversity, scope, and musicianship. "Prince's virtuoso eclecticism has seldom been so abundantly displayed," *Rolling Stone* exclaimed.[8] For the *New York Times*, Prince wasn't just "rearranging ordinary songs; he's started to warp the songs themselves."[9]

The *New Musical Express* was slightly more cautious. Noting that some of the tracks on side one sounded like demos, the paper nonetheless concluded that, while this might signal the end for any other artist, for Prince it could "only enhance" a career that has "so far been brilliantly stage-managed."[10] There were still a few criticisms from elsewhere: some reviewers simply found the whole thing too eclectic for its own good, suggesting perhaps that trimming down *Crystal Ball* hadn't been quite so bad an idea after all. Not one to easily forget criticism, Prince countered these complaints three years later, in an interview with *Rolling Stone*. "What people were saying about *Sign "O" The Times* was: 'There are some great songs on it, and some experiments on it,'" he said. "I hate the word 'experiment.' It sounds like something you didn't finish."[11]

The *Sign "O" The Times* jacket shows a more mature-looking Prince on the set of a local production of *Guys & Dolls*. He has his musical equipment set up in front of fading city lights screaming about Drugs, Arcades, and Girls Girls Girls, suggesting that he had decided to put music before the rock'n'roll lifestyle. In contrast with the backdrop, Prince himself is out of focus, staring out into space, perhaps leaving his sex-obsessed past behind him. One rather pointed addition, however, is the glowing, purple crystal ball sitting on top of the drum riser – a clear sign that he had not yet forgiven or forgotten Warners' decision to veto the original triple-album concept.

Such personal messages would of course have been lost on the casual buyer, who would have had no choice but to marvel at this two-disc magnum opus. As he had with *1999*, Prince chose to open the record with a note of social commentary, but 'Sign "O" The Times' is no call to hedonistic arms. Over a sparse drum pattern,

Prince makes reference to AIDS, gang violence, and drug addiction. "Some say a man ain't happy," he concludes, "unless a man truly dies."

'Sign "O" The Times' was the most mature statement Prince had yet made, but it also served to wrong-foot his audience. It's not until 'The Cross' – two thirds of the way through the second disc – that he returns to the world outside of his usual themes of sex, love, and partying. The way he treats these themes, however, marks *Sign "O" The Times* out as a much more mature work than anything that came before it. Alongside typical tales of lust – 'Hot Thing,' 'It,' 'U Got The Look' – Prince deals with the breakup of his relationship with Susannah Melvoin in a much more honest, conflicted manner than might have been expected. Having closed disc one with 'Forever In My Life''s declaration that "I wanna keep U 4 the rest of my life," he then goes on, in 'If I Was Your Girlfriend,' to express his jealousy at the close bond between the Melvoin sisters, asking: "Would U run 2 me if somebody hurt U / Even if that somebody was me?" Then, on the aptly named 'Strange Relationship,' he admits he "can't stand 2 see U happy," but also "hate[s] 2 see U sad."

Sign "O" The Times does more than just play out the demise of a relationship: it gave Prince the chance to show the world exactly what he was capable of musically. At its best, the album can be seen as the culmination of everything Prince had done – and been exposed to – previously, without ever betraying his musical roots. As *Q* magazine put it, the album's funk edge "slices straight through the white gut of pop."

'Housequake' and 'It's Gonna Be A Beautiful Night' (the latter recorded live in Paris with The Revolution in 1986) are the album's funkiest moments, while the likes of 'Play In The Sunshine' and 'I Could Never Take The Place Of Your Man' offer up perfect pop-rock for the mainstream. For all its brilliance, *Parade* betrayed Prince's struggle to harness new sounds and styles that he wasn't yet familiar with, but on *Sign "O" The Times* he seems to have mastered them effortlessly, shifting with ease from rock to psychedelia, funk to jazz, all the while maintaining his role as the world's leading loverman. (The closing 'Adore' is one of his greatest ballads and a vocal tour de force with overlapping harmonies that are among Prince's most complex.)

Sign "O" The Times is a perfect blend of Prince's own formative influences and the new musical worlds he had been introduced to by The Revolution. In many ways it is his equivalent of Sly & The Family Stone's *There's A Riot Goin' On*: a masterpiece built on a foundation of subdued, murky funk, and the culmination of a creative surge that would never again be repeated.

Part of the album's unusual feel stems from Prince's acceptance of happy accidents. A snowstorm caused a power shortage during the recording of 'The Ballad Of Dorothy Parker' (a song he claimed to have written in a dream, but which seems to reflect his arguments with Susannah Melvoin). When the electricity came back, Prince carried on recording, but the sound desk wasn't yet up to full power.

"Half the new console wasn't working," Susan Rogers recalled, "[and] there was no high end at all."[12] But rather than try to rework or remix the song, Prince stuck with the supposed imperfections of the recording, willing perhaps to accept it as a sign of good fortune from a higher power.

The same was true of the recording of 'If I Was Your Girlfriend.' The distortion on Prince's voice wasn't planned, but came from a mistake Rogers made while setting up the equipment – the kind of thing Prince would never have stood for in the past. Having "inadvertently switched something the wrong way," Rogers was relieved to find that Prince "never said a word. He had this attitude [of] 'Well, maybe that was meant to be.'"[13]

Despite the acclaim with which it had been received by the critics, *Sign "O" The Times* peaked at Number Six on the *Billboard* chart, two spots lower than where *Parade* had ended up. The title track reached Number Three on the Hot 100, but any momentum was broken by Prince's surprising choice to follow it with 'If I Was Your Girlfriend,' which staggered in at Number 67. Undoubtedly a brave choice as far as single releases went, its gender-twisting lyrics and unflinching honesty were too much for the charts. According to Alan Leeds, it "stopped radio in its tracks. Homophobes misinterpreted the lyrics, and its charming eccentricity didn't fit a format." Everybody else had expected 'Housequake' to be the next single, but for Prince, Leeds recalled, that would have been "*too* obvious."[14]

The album's initial commercial impact was slowed further by Prince's decision to begin the accompanying tour in Europe rather than America – and to take his jazz-funk side project Madhouse with him as the support act. His latest external group endeavor, Madhouse marked a change in the way Prince approached his side projects, which he had previously used as a means of maintaining his standing in the R&B world while his own work veered off in ever more experimental directions. This time his intention was to explore new ideas that didn't fit on his solo records.

By the mid 80s, Prince was becoming increasingly interested in jazz, as evidenced by his shortlived experiments with The Flesh. Having scrapped plans for a fully collaborative jazz record, however, he spent four days at the end of September 1986 recording a jazz-funk album by the name of *8*, with contributions from Eric Leeds (saxophone and flute) and Matt Fink (a few synthesizer solos).

The album had been released on January 21 1987 and credited to Madhouse, with no other names anywhere on the jacket. While in the past Prince had left clues to his involvement in records by The Time, Vanity 6, and others, he was keen this time to distance himself from the project completely, either out of a genuine wish to let the music speak for itself, or because he feared a backlash from 'serious' jazz critics.

He was right to be wary: *8* demonstrates only a superficial understanding of how jazz works, and is far too regimented – because Prince played most of the instruments himself – to sound truly improvised. By comparison to Miles Davis's fusion work on late-60s and early-70s albums such as *Bitches Brew* and *On The Corner*, *8* is incredibly tame. Nonetheless, it didn't take fans long to recognize the Prince sound and buy enough copies to push *8* – a completely instrumental oddity – to Number 25 on *Billboard*'s R&B chart, and Number 107 on the Pop chart. One of its eight numbered tracks, 'Six,' reached Number Five on the R&B singles chart.

On his European Sign "O" The Times tour, Prince was keen to mask Madhouse's identities as much as possible, to the extent that they performed in sunglasses and hooded black robes. (Prince would even step out to play drums with them from time to time.) Why he chose to launch the tour in Europe is unclear, but it could well have been that, like other groundbreaking American artists, including jazz legends such as Miles Davis and Charlie Parker, he found his European fans to be more open to new ideas. (It might also have had something to do with his irritation at the way his record sales in America continued to decline.)

The Sign "O" The Times tour began in Sweden on May 8 1987. Rehearsals had begun four months earlier with an almost entirely new band. While Matt Fink remained from The Revolution, and Eric Leeds and Atlanta Bliss stayed on to play live horns, the nucleus of the group came from Sheila E.'s band: Sheila herself on drums, Levi Seacer Jr on bass, Miko Weaver on guitar, and Boni Boyer on keyboards and backing vocals. Jerome Benton, Wally Safford, and Greg Brooks reprised their dancing roles, but were often sidelined to make way for Prince's new foil, Cat Glover. A longtime fan, Glover choreographed the shows and brought a charged sexuality to the performances, which saw Prince slide through her legs, tear off her skirt, and emerge with it in his mouth during 'Hot Thing.'

The European tour took in 34 concerts during May and June (surprisingly missing out Britain), and focused largely on the *Sign "O" The Times* material. "The music was first rate, the band was on fire, and the show was wonderfully imaginative, without the over-the-top largesse of the [next year's] Lovesexy tour," Alan Leeds recalled.[15] Impressed by his new group's proficiency, Prince designed the set to showcase their talents on songs such as Charlie Parker's 'Now's The Time' and his own 'It's Gonna Be A Beautiful Night.' The show as a whole was his most exciting yet, performed on a stage designed to mirror the album artwork.

The *Sign "O" The Times* songs seemed to change every night as the band grew in confidence. But any progress that was being made came to an abrupt halt in June, when Prince opted not to tour the USA. Despite the recent success of 'U Got The Look'/'Housequake,' which hit Number Two on the Hot 100, he had no desire to perform an album he had little interest in for an audience he was unhappy with. Instead, he opted to film the final four European dates, deciding that any market he hadn't yet visited could make do with seeing the Sign "O" The Times tour on the silver screen.

When Prince returned home to Minneapolis, the construction of his soon-to-be legendary Paisley Park studios had been completed. Aside perhaps from the symbol to which he changed his name in the mid 90s, the 65,000-square foot complex in the Chanhassen district of Minnesota, on the outskirts of Minneapolis, would be the one physical thing most commonly associated with the musician.

Prince had long dreamed of owning his own studio complex, having found himself much more comfortable recording at home than anywhere else. Flush from the success of *Purple Rain*, he was able to make this a reality in May 1985, buying a 200-acre plot of land just ten minutes away from his home in Edina. Keen never to have to risk losing the property, Prince paid in cash. ("He had no mortgages on anything,"[16] his manager of the time, Bob Cavallo, recalled.)

Asked why he wanted to withdraw into his own castle, Prince told *Details* that he had "heard 'Prince is crazy' so much that it had an effect on me. So one day, I said, 'Let me just check out.'"[17] Paisley Park gave him the "solitude" and the "controlled environment" that he craved. But he was keen, too, to point out that this large, concrete block wasn't just a retreat from the world. "I don't live in a prison," he told *Rolling Stone*, in response to Chick Huntsberry's earlier 'revelations' in the *National Enquirer*. "I am not afraid of anything. I haven't built walls around myself."[18]

Prince officially opened the doors to Paisley Park on September 11 1987, and has used it to record all of his albums from *Lovesexy* onward. The complex boasts four studios (two of them with 48-track consoles), an editing suite, a games room, a 12,000-foot soundstage, a nightclub, dressing rooms, a hair salon, production offices, conference room, and an art department – all of which need to be manned. Every single room is wired for sound so that Prince can record whatever he likes, wherever he likes – and perhaps so that he can hear what's going on when he's not in the room. He held his Celebration weeks on site during the early 21st century, and has shot all of his promo videos – as well as *Graffiti Bridge* and *The Undertaker* – on its soundstage. He has also staged benefit gigs, playbacks, and even fan question-and-answer sessions in the building. "Man, Prince has got a hell of a complex out there," Miles Davis exclaimed in his autobiography. "[There's] record and movie equipment, plus he had an apartment for me to stay in. The whole thing seems like it's about half a block."[19]

Paisley Park's vast scale meant that, having ploughed $10 million into building it, Prince soon found he had stretched his finances to the limit. The obvious solution might have been to rent the facilities out to others, but for a long time he refused to let any outside groups in. "It became evident to all of us that he had enough projects in mind that he could fill up every studio and soundstage in the building with," Alan

Leeds recalled.[20] This might have been a good thing from a creative perspective, but also meant that it soon became "an enormous [financial] drain" – as did the fact that Prince had the studios manned 24 hours per day, just in case he decided to drop in on a whim.

Even after he did start letting in other acts, Prince just didn't have the skills required to run a business. When his financial situation threatened to spiral out of control in 1994, he gave his stepbrother and head of security, Duane Nelson, the job of arbitrarily firing staff. Since then Paisley Park has been run on more of a skeleton crew, and is no longer open to the public. Even so, in 2004 Prince told *Ebony* magazine of his plan to "have interns in here working and learning every aspect of the music business."[21]

Perhaps most famously, Paisley Park is home to The Vault, a storeroom for countless songs, albums, and even full-scale promotional videos that Prince has made but never released. Given his work rate, it's possible that there might be thousands of different projects stored inside – a prospect so tantalizing that it ensures some fans' continued interest in the star, if only for what might one day see the light of day.

So protective is Prince of Paisley Park that when the Spanish newspaper *El País* asked what he would do if the complex was destroyed by a fire, he angrily replied: "This will never happen. If you leave a piece of bread on a table, someday it will become moss, and this will become medicine. In the same way, Paisley Park will never be destroyed, it will just become something else."[22]

The first project Prince undertook at Paisley Park was the completion of his *Sign "O" The Times* tour film. His failure to maintain the momentum of the tour itself was, in a lot of people's eyes, one of the biggest mistakes he ever made. To make matters worse, he found that most of the concert footage he had was too grainy to be useable. He did what he could by shooting new performance scenes and short dramatic segments at Paisley Park, but this in turn served only to interfere with the energy of the live show.

The *Sign "O" The Times* movie concept was similar to what Prince had envisioned for *The Second Coming*. It ended up receiving rave reviews from critics who were no doubt pleased not to have to sit through another *Under The Cherry Moon*. *Rolling Stone* called it "a first-rate concert film" that captures Prince and his band "at the top of their form,"[23] while the *Philadelphia Daily News* saw it as a reaffirmation of Prince's status as "the most provocative, all-things-to-all-people sex symbol to hit the pop arena since Elvis Presley."[24]

Once again, however, critical acclaim was no guarantee of commercial success. *Sign "O" The Times* struggled to compete with a rush of seasonal hits aimed squarely at the Christmas market. "A number of us told him that the release date was a mistake," Warners' Marylou Badeaux recalled, "but in his mind we were just trying to undermine him."[25] Its impact was dented further by the fact that concert movies tend as a rule not to hang around for too long anyway. Unsurprisingly, then, it failed to make the kind of money that Prince would have earned from touring the USA. Many of the people who would surely have gone to see him play just weren't interested in seeking out a limited-run concert movie. (Because of the company's unwillingness to back another potential turkey, *Sign "O" The Times* was independently distributed, and opened in only 30 US cities.)

Also failing to attract attention as 1987 drew to a close was the second Madhouse album. When it came to recording *16*, Prince brought in drummer John Lewis as well as Eric Leeds, Levi Seacer Jr, and Matt Fink from his live band. Released on November 18 1987, *16* had a harder-edged group dynamic than its predecessor, but failed to make as much impact. The single 'Ten' stalled at Number 66 on the R&B chart, while the album itself didn't chart at all.

Since then Madhouse has been stuck in a kind of limbo, with Prince recording several prospective *24*s over the years. A ten-day session with Eric Leeds in December 1988 yielded eight more tracks, each with subtitles, such as '17 (Penetration)' and '18 (R U Legal Yet?),' but none have been released. ('21' to '24' were grouped under the name 'The Dopamine Rush Suite.')

He made another attempt in July 1993, bringing in Eric Leeds and various members of the New Power Generation – Michael Bland on drums, Levi Seacer Jr on guitar, and Sonny Thompson on bass. The only numerically titled track, '17,' ended up on the compilation album *1-800-NEW-FUNK*, but Warners had no interest in putting out the likes of 'Asswoop' and '(Got 2) Give It Up.' A few years later, Prince reportedly reworked some of his *Kamasutra* album (included alongside 1997's *Crystal Ball*) as a third Madhouse record. But although a couple of tracks surfaced in 1998 and 2001, no full-length third album has never appeared.

The two surviving albums, *8* and *16*, are not masterpieces in any sense, but are interesting because of their dissimilarity to anything else in Prince's 80s output. But if this is the best jazz-fusion that Prince could offer, it's clear that he had only just begun to scratch the surface of what Eric and Alan Leeds had been introducing him to. It's unsurprising, however, that Prince wanted to make music in this vein, as he had been idolizing Davis's work since the mid 80s. By this time, Davis had changed the face of jazz at least five times in as many decades. He had also become known for his no-nonsense attitude to other people. This might have been seen by most as a sign of arrogance, but was actually symbolic of the survival instincts of a man who had been through everything from heroin addiction to racist beatings at the hands of the New York City police force.

"Young black guys were attracted to Miles because of his politics – he was an icon," Alan Leeds later noted. "I think as Prince learnt more about [him], he started to see some of himself in Miles."[26] This certainly seems plausible. It's not hard to imagine Prince being in awe of one of the few musicians who had been even more prolific than he had himself.

Prince himself has not spoken often about Davis, but his recollections of a visit by the self-styled Prince Of Darkness to his home are telling. "As he was passing by my piano," Prince told *Musician* in 1997, "he stopped and put his hands down on the keys and played these eight chords, one after the other. It was so beautiful. ... I couldn't decide whether it was him or an angel putting his hands on the keys."[27]

Davis had a similarly high opinion of Prince. "[He can be] the new Duke Ellington of our time if he just keeps at it," he wrote. "I learn things from Prince. [His] music is pointing toward the future." Davis did however find some elements of Prince's career amusing. "If I said 'Fuck you' to somebody they would be ready to call the police," he noted. "But if Prince says it in that girl-like voice that he uses, then everyone says it's cute."[28]

Despite the obvious respect the two men had for each other, their attempts at collaboration were not particularly successful. They first met at an airport in early December 1985, shortly after Davis moved from Columbia to Warners. Davis later claimed that Warners had first proposed the idea of a collaboration; it's certainly not hard to imagine that the label would have been keen to have two of its highest-profile stars work together.

After that initial meeting, Prince proposed a more relaxed get-together, suggesting that Davis spend some time with him and Sheila E. By December 26, a new project seemed to be taking shape. Prince sent Davis a track called 'Can I Play With U?' and suggested that he record whatever he wanted over the top and include it on his forthcoming album, *Tutu*. But when Prince received a tape of the finished song in March he didn't seem to like what Davis (as well as his keyboardist and bassist) had done to it. "When we sent him the tape and he heard what was on there he didn't think his tune [worked with the rest of *Tutu*]," Davis recalled. "Prince has high musical standards, like me."[29] The song was pulled from the album, but with the hope that something could be done with it at a later date.

Davis continued to hold out for a proper in-studio collaboration, but Prince shied away from the idea. He preferred instead to send tapes back and forth to see if the recordings could fit together, giving himself time and space to work at his own pace. Working with Davis in real time posed all sorts of problems. "If Miles is a control freak," Alan Leeds said, "multiply that by five when you come to Prince." Davis had surrounded himself with younger musicians throughout his career, but Prince didn't want to put himself in the position of having to tell his idol what to do. "The idea of being in a studio with Miles and trying to direct him was foreign to him," Leeds added, "and he just couldn't even conceive of that scenario."[30]

Davis wasn't prone to giving up easily, however, and would leave messages at Paisley Park telling "that little purple motherfucker" to contact him.[31] But while they met several times following the failure of 'Can I Play With U?,' it was never in a recording studio. Davis had dinner at Prince's home in 1987, and sat in and watched Prince rehearse at Paisley Park later the same year, but he didn't have his trumpet with him.

Davis did bring his trumpet along to Prince's New Years Eve benefit show on December 31 1987. Looking to raise money for the Minnesota Coalition For The Homeless, Prince charged $200 per ticket for a performance at Paisley Park, while simultaneously using the event to say goodbye to *Sign "O" The Times*. At the end of an 80-minute set, Davis took to the stage for a rendition of Madhouse's 'Six.' Prince, however, seemed so shy that he barely looked at his idol, let alone tried to interact with him, save for a bit of scatting in response to Davis's trumpet playing.

The Prince-Davis partnership largely fizzled out after that, but the two men continued to show their respect for each other. Davis took to playing *Dream Factory*'s 'Movie Star' during his 1991 concerts, and worked on a few tracks from the aborted third Madhouse album for himself. But when Davis played at Prince's Glam Slam club (a later entrepreneurial venture), Prince declined several requests to jam with him on stage.

The opportunity for these two musical giants to work together in the studio disappeared when Miles Davis died on September 28 1991. Two days later, Prince recorded his 'Letter 4 Miles' at Paisley Park. Like many of the songs closest to his heart, it has never been released to the public – nor has the "indescribable music" Prince once told *Guitar World* he had made with Davis before he died.[32] (It seems doubtful that such recordings actually exist, however, given that there is no documentary evidence to support this.)

Despite seeing the New Year in by jamming with his idol, Prince seemed to be heading into 1988 lonelier than ever. Warners might have wanted more time to work with *Sign "O" The Times* and maximize its commercial potential, but as far as Prince was concerned it was done with. He had a great new band, but would never allow himself to become as close to them as he had to The Revolution, having decided that he had already learnt everything he needed to know. In a few short years he had pushed away almost everybody close to him, from Dez Dickerson and Chick Huntsberry to Lisa Coleman, Wendy Melvoin, and, most devastatingly, Susannah Melvoin. He continued to date Sheila E., but his closest confidante was probably Alan Leeds.

Prince had begun 1987 alone, but had at least felt that he was on an artistic high. Now, a year later, reality seemed to be seeping through. He was still alone, and now had to follow what most people felt to be his crowning artistic achievement – with or without Camille.

CHAPTER 9

I'VE SEEN THE FUTURE

When I talk about God, I don't
mean some dude in a cape and
beard coming down to Earth.
To me, he's in everything, if
you look at it that way.

PRINCE

With the Sign "O" The Times tour behind him, Prince decided it was time to face up to what some felt to be a marked 'whitening' of his sound in recent years. During October and November 1987 he spent time in the studio revisiting a selection of funk songs recorded the previous year (to which he added one new composition, 'When 2 R In Love') to create one of the most contentious albums of his career: *The Black Album*.

Some have since suggested that *The Black Album* was never intended for general release. According to Susan Rogers: "The tracks were odds and ends, things we would do on a day off ... sometimes he wanted to break away and do something [different] just to get it out of his system."[2] That this was the case is given further credence by the fact that Prince sat on the recordings for so long, since he tended to release new material as soon as he completed it.

'Le Grind,' 'Bob George,' and '2 Nigs United 4 West Compton' had all appeared on an acetate pressed up for Sheila E.'s birthday on December 11 1986, but none were deemed suitable for *Sign "O" The Times*. Having been stung, once again, by suggestions that he had left his roots behind, Prince perhaps felt the need to prove to his critics that he still had it in him to be out-and-out funky. At any rate, an album began to take shape after he called in Eric Leeds and trumpeter Matt Blistan to play on the songs, and dancer Cat Glover to sing on them. ("We were just kidding around," she recalled. "[Prince] didn't want everyone listening to [it]."[3]) The album was scheduled for release on December 8 1987 – less than a month after the opening of the *Sign "O" The Times* concert movie.

The trouble was that, after ten years in the business, Prince wasn't having as many bright ideas as he used to. And, without a Revolution to bounce them off, they weren't as varied, either. His prolific workrate seemed to be getting the better of him. "For every great song [he wrote]," Marylou Badeaux recalled, "there were ten kind-of-okay songs."[4]

Originally set to be called *The Funk Bible*, *The Black Album* certainly constituted a return to Prince's roots. It's a dark, uninviting record that harks back, with its lyrics about masturbation and uncharacteristically aggressive attitude to sex, to the controversial themes of *Dirty Mind*. But it served also to highlight Prince's struggle to fit into the musical climate of the late 80s – particularly when it came to hip-hop, which by then was well on its way to becoming one of popular music's most commercially successful strands.

As far as Prince was concerned, hip-hop was distinctly unmusical. His feelings are summed up by 'Dead On It,' on which he laments switching on the radio to hear a "silly rapper talking silly shit." The largely instrumental '2 Nigs 4 West Compton,' meanwhile, was intended as a musical swipe at the likes of NWA, whose *Straight Outta Compton* was just around the corner, and whose glorification of gang violence and misogyny Prince detested. (Changing his tune somewhat, Prince

94

would later take the misguided decision to add rapper Tony M. to his backing group, and would tell Spike Lee in 1997 that he "did" gangsta rap years ago, citing his "half-sung" vocals on tracks such the 1982 B-side 'Irresistible Bitch.')

All in all, *The Black Album* seemed symbolic of Prince's concerns about his place in the contemporary music scene. (On one track, 'Bob George,' he slows his voice down to an approximation of an overbearing pimp and calls himself "that skinny motherfucker with the high voice.") It's a fun, funky record, but hardly groundbreaking. Prince might have felt that he had more musical talent than any of the hip-hop acts out there, but his sales were slipping. His frustration was later borne out in an interview with *Rolling Stone*, where he admitted to being "very angry a lot of the time back then, and that was reflected in [*The Black Album*]."[5] Going back to the sexually explicit material of the past might not have been the best way to boost his profile – particularly when the album in question contained just seven funk tracks and a ballad ('When 2 R In Love'), stitched together without the care and consideration of past glories such as *Dirty Mind* and *1999*.

When Prince presented the new album to Warners, the label was once again concerned about the lack of downtime between his previous album and this prospective follow-up. It was also alarmed by Prince's design concept for the record: no credits, no image, just a plain black jacket with a catalog number (in peach) on the spine. With sales falling, the label felt, Prince needed to make his latest releases easier to find, not harder.

This coupled with its less impressive musical content meant that *The Black Album* was something of a thorn in the company's side. Even so, Warners still agreed to release it. This time it was Prince who got cold feet, calling Mo Ostin and begging him not to put the record out. Several differing reasons have since been given for this volte-face. Some have suggested that, just before the album's release, Prince took ecstasy for the first time and had a 'bad trip' that resulted in him thinking *The Black Album* was the work of the devil. But these charges are at odds with the fact that hardly anyone has ever even claimed to see Prince drink alcohol, let alone take drugs. (When pressed on the subject by the *New Musical Express* in 1995, Prince would admit only that he is "interested in all experiences."[6])

Prince himself has claimed that he saw the word 'God' floating above him in a field and was convinced from then on that *The Black Album* was an 'evil' recording. Others have put this down more tangibly to the influence of the spiritual poet Ingrid Chavez, with whom Prince had recently begun to work. The furthest Prince has gone toward explaining his decision came in the Lovesexy tour program, in which he describes how his alter-ego, Camille, had "set out to silence his critics" and found a new color: "black: the strongest hue of them all" – perhaps suggesting that he truly felt that *The Black Album* might revive his commercial fortunes. Camille, however, subsequently realized he had allowed "the dark side of him to create something evil."

Leaving aside any religious or drug-related epiphanies, it seems most likely that, having, in his own words, "[cut] off people in my life and disappear[ed] without a glance back," Prince then decided that he ought to be making something more spiritually uplifting instead of returning to morally bankrupt funk.[7] *The Black Album* was recalled from warehouses a week before its release. While this did at least leave Warners with a longer gap between Prince albums, the company still had to shoulder the cost of pressing (and then destroying) the first run of around 500,000 copies.

What happened next, of course, was that *The Black Album* became the biggest-selling bootleg since the first, Bob Dylan's *Great White Wonder*. The album became so notorious, in fact, that it was even reviewed in some of the more trendy music magazines. Alan Leeds remains of the opinion that *The Black Album* would have represented "a turning point, for better or worse, at a time when he needed one" – and would have had a much bigger impact than *Parade*, *Sign "O" The Times*, or its replacement.[8]

Having fought off his dark urges, Prince immediately set about recording another new album. *Lovesexy* would become his defining spiritual statement, leaving no doubt as to where his heart and soul really lay – while also making amends for its 'evil' predecessor. Prince recorded the whole thing in seven weeks, taping the songs in more or less the order in which they appear on the album, and performing everything himself except for a spoken-word introduction by Ingrid Chavez (billed as Spirit Child), a rap by Cat Glover, and some of the more complex drum tracks performed by Sheila E. So strong was his belief in this new work that he had begun rehearsing his band for a Lovesexy tour before Warners had heard a note.

When it came to presenting the album to the label in March, Prince once again arrived with a series of awkward demands. This time around, instead of wanting to have a plain black jacket, he enlisted Jean Baptiste Mondino (his original choice of director for *Under The Cherry Moon*) to photograph him sitting naked on a large flower. There he sat, staring out as though in a trance, his genitalia covered only by a raised thigh. Warners was concerned that some stores would refuse to stock the album, which did prove to be the case, even though the imagery is rather more passive than the covers of *Dirty Mind* and in many ways even *Purple Rain*. For Prince, however, there was nothing to be concerned about. "All that album cover was, was a picture," he told *Rolling Stone* in 1990. "If you looked at that picture and some ill came out of your mouth, then that's what you are – it's looking right back at you in the mirror."[9]

Further headaches ensued when Prince announced that the nine-track CD should be presented as a single 45-minute piece, without track breaks. To him, of course, this was just another way of ensuring that the listener appreciated his art as a single entity, not as a collection of songs. To Warners, however, it was another way of alienating the casual fan. (Prince got his way, although later pressings of the album are split into individual tracks.)

Prince had also decided that, as with *Around The World In A Day*, the album should be taken on its own artistic merits, and thus released without the accompaniment of promo videos or anything else that might diminish the air of mystery around it. It was fast becoming clear that, while still a bona fide musical genius, Prince had begun to lose his business savvy. Thankfully, he eventually relented and made a promo video for 'Alphabet St' – but only at the 11th hour, resulting in Alan Leeds having to scrabble around to find a director at short notice on a Sunday morning. The result was a quickly dated, blue-screened affair that sees Prince dancing and driving his "white rad ride" through a dense fog of letters which, at one point, spell out the phrase "Don't buy *The Black Album*, I'm sorry."

As far as Prince was concerned, *Lovesexy* was his most intensely personal album yet. Most critics agreed, but were unsure exactly what conclusions to draw from the battle between sex and religion expressed in the songs. Even those closest to Prince weren't entirely sure what to make of it, although Alan Leeds was privy to indirect allusions. "I don't think Prince ever directly explained *Lovesexy*," he recalled. "But casual conversations with some of us revealed a lot."[10] Without the luxury of chatting to its creator before its May 10 1988 release date, *St Paul Pioneer Press* described the album as "a hasty note from a troubled soul,"[11] while *Rolling Stone* saw fit to exclaim that "the hardest questions may not lend themselves to easy answers, but make for much better music."[12] Others were more cagey, with the *Detroit Free Press* suggesting that it "may take some time for listeners to get a handle on."[13]

Most of the strengths and weaknesses of *Lovesexy* stem from the fact that it came from such an honest splurge of this-is-what-I-am-thinking recording. As Alan Leeds later noted, Prince responded to "an unpleasant reality" in the same way he always did: by "construct[ing] a reality of his own."[14] In this case, having reached a low ebb and apparently unnerved himself with the darkness of *The Black Album*, he had found religion. Luckily for Prince, this particular religion was one that allowed him to reconcile his sexual and spiritual feelings with ease; one that allowed him to sing about "drippin' all over the floor" ('Lovesexy') and bodies jerking "like a horny pony" ('Alphabet St'), while also exclaiming: "Love is God, God is love" ('Anna Stesia').

Elsewhere on the album, the likes of 'Dance On' and 'Positivity' mark a return to socio-political concerns, notably gang warfare, while 'Anna Stesia' can be read as a direct acknowledgment of Prince's loneliness and need for salvation. The opening 'Eye No,' meanwhile, welcomes listeners to "the New Power Generation," which marks Prince's first use of the term.

Musically, however, there was nothing particularly new about *Lovesexy*. The beats might have been harder and more complex than before – evidence of the fact Prince had become a semi-regular fixture on the Paris and London club scenes – but by now it was hardly surprising to hear a blend of different musical styles on a Prince record. The main talking point concerned whether or not Prince had forgotten how to write tight, structured, melodic songs, or whether he had deliberately wanted to try to create one long movement. His insistence on a 'one track' CD suggests the latter, as does his later declaration that the album was intended to be "a mind trip, like a psychedelic movie."[15] There are some neat production tricks throughout, too, not least the way Prince and either Glover or Sheila E.'s vocals mutate into each other on the title track. (Somewhat ironically, given Prince's recent attitudes toward hip-hop, 'Alphabet St' features a rap by Glover.)

Prince himself was clearly happy with how *Lovesexy* turned out, but it sold only 750,000 copies, making it his least successful album since his debut, *For You*. It remains a firm fan favorite, although there is still some debate as to whether it marks a final creative peak or the start of a slow, steady decline into mediocrity. Its failure to sell irked Prince, who clearly felt that his most honest work to date should have been received with unparalleled enthusiasm.

It's unlikely that releasing *The Black Album* would have made a difference to Prince's overall career path. It might, however, have helped reassert his dwindling credentials in the R&B world, and held a slightly broader appeal, despite showing no real progression or departure from what came before. Both albums were simply consolidations of old tricks – it just depended which tricks listeners preferred.

Even after *Lovesexy* struggled in at Number 11, Prince refused to believe that his most personal concept to date could fail, and had begun to plan the most extravagant tour of his career. Until now, he had worked with neat, economical stage sets. The Controversy and Triple Threat tours made much of a simple set of ramps, lights, and a fireman's pole, while the Sign "O" The Times stage set was essentially a large-scale reproduction of the album art.

The Lovesexy set took in swings, a miniature basketball court, and a set of hydraulics that would lift its star up toward the roof during the 'spiritual rebirth' part of 'Anna Stesia.' It cost $2 million even before the costumes were made and a 90-person team was brought in to run the show. Then there was the wireless technology required for the band to be able to get around the massive stage, set in the round, not to mention the three-quarter-scale '67 Thunderbird Prince had had built – at a cost of $250,000 – to take him to and from the stage. One final extravagance was nixed during planning. "There was also supposed to be a fountain that poured hundreds and hundreds of gallons of water down into the center of the stage," set designer Roy Bennett recalled. "That would have been a very short show."[16]

As well as generating the vast expense of building, storing, and transporting the set, Prince put his band on the payroll for six months of rehearsals before the tour had even started. He then took the crucial decision to switch the tour around right before it was due to kick off, scrapping the US leg in favor of taking the show to Europe, where *Lovesexy* was performing much more strongly. As with the Sign "O" The Times tour, however, it would surely have been more prudent to try to boost the album's performance at home first, rather than allow it to sink even further down the charts. Switching territories at the last minute incurred all manner of costs, suggesting once again that Prince had lost his business sense.

From a musical perspective, however, the Lovesexy tour was as astounding as it was ambitious. Played in the round, it was set up to tell the good-versus-evil story of Prince's spiritual awakening. After running through a greatest hits set of earlier, sex-obsessed songs – 'Erotic City,' 'Jack U Off,' 'Dirty Mind,' and so on – Prince (as Bob George) would be shot down by a fleet of policemen. Then, after an extended reading of 'Anna Stesia,' during which he would literally be taken higher and higher into the arena, bathed in golden light, the show turned into a celebration of *Lovesexy*, with a smattering of old favorites such as 'When Doves Cry' and 'Purple Rain.' (When the accompanying tour movies, *Livesexy 1* and *Livesexy 2*, were released on VHS, the sets were reversed, giving the *Lovesexy* songs prominence.)

By the time the Lovesexy tour made it to the USA in September, Prince fans seemed to be losing interest in *Lovesexy* and the man himself – somewhat surprisingly, given that he had not been out on a full-scale tour of the country since 1985. It all ended up being reminiscent of the Dirty Mind tour, with sell-out crowds in Prince strongholds such as New York and Detroit, followed by a struggle to half-fill arenas elsewhere.

The US leg of the tour ended in November 1988. More than ever before, Prince was in need of a hit. As he sat at home in the months before an eight-date Japanese tour scheduled for February 1989, he found his focus returning to an idea he had drafted more than a year earlier. After years of trying to escape it, he was beginning to come around to the idea of making a *Purple Rain Mk II*.

As with *Purple Rain*, however, the project that would become its big-screen follow-up, *Graffiti Bridge*, was beset with pre-production problems from inside the Prince camp. Following disagreements about how to proceed with this new film, Prince sacked his long-standing management team of Cavallo, Ruffalo & Fargnoli. Fortunately, he had recently been back in touch with *Purple Rain* director Albert Magnoli, who had shot some of the Lovesexy shows for a planned documentary. Magnoli's movie-industry contacts would, Prince knew, certainly prove useful when it came to trying to get *Graffiti Bridge* made. (Unlike Cavallo, Magnoli seemed unconditionally supportive of the project – to begin with, at least.) But while his loyalty was so far uncontested, Magnoli had yet to prove himself able to turn around Prince's deteriorating financial situation and do battle with Warners.

Nonetheless, Prince brought him in to handle his affairs. Magnoli knew he had a difficult job on his hands. Prince was desperate to re-establish himself as a creative force within the movie industry and repeat the commercial success that had eluded him since *Purple Rain*. Doing so would halt an alarming financial freefall, exacerbated recently by the losses made on the Lovesexy tour and the hefty severance packages paid to Cavallo, Ruffalo & Fargnoli. Fortunately for all concerned, Magnoli's first move was a masterstroke (or at least a slice of extremely good luck); before *Graffiti Bridge* could get off the ground, he found a sure-fire commercial hit for his charge. Happily for Prince, it was attached to another movie project. Tellingly, it wasn't one of his own.

In October 1988, Warner Bros Pictures had started shooting the first serious big-screen adaptation of *Batman* with goth-lite director Tim Burton at the helm. While putting together rough edits of some early footage, Burton had used '1999' and 'Baby I'm A Star' to backdrop specific scenes. Prince's songs worked so well that Burton got in touch with Magnoli to see if the singer would be interested in contributing to the soundtrack.

"When I heard about the movie I felt in my heart that Prince was perfect for it," Magnoli later claimed.[17] Burton wasn't looking for a full Prince-penned soundtrack, however: his original scheme was for Michael Jackson to soundtrack the 'light' side of the movie, with Prince providing the 'dark' songs, but that didn't last for long. As the film progressed, producer Jon Peters quickly realised "it was obvious … that we needed a unified approach to the score."[18]

Prince wasn't sure about the idea at first, but flew out to London in January 1989 to meet Burton on the Gotham City set at Pinewood Studios. Suitably impressed by a 20-minute showreel, Prince decided to put his own movie plans on hold and work on the *Batman* soundtrack instead. The fact that one of the first songs he learnt to play on his father's piano was the original 60s *Batman* theme would have helped – as indeed would the reported commissioning fee of $1 million and the worldwide exposure a blockbuster film would afford. As *Rolling Stone* noted: "Doubtless the one-man band from Minneapolis knew from the get-go that *Batman* … was going to be the biggest tie-in this side of shoeleaces."[19]

Aside from the financial gains he made, Prince came away from Pinewood Studios having met female lead Kim Basinger, who was playing the part of Vicki Vale. Prince fell so hard for Basinger at first sight that some suggested her involvement in the movie was what made him want to record the soundtrack – particularly 'Scandalous,' which is essentially a Basinger tribute. (It's also not hard to imagine Prince relishing her seductive admission to The Joker: "I just *love* purple.")

With Basinger to impress, Prince tried to cancel the Japanese leg of the Lovesexy tour in order to get straight on with the *Batman* recordings, but was convinced otherwise. On his return, he spent six weeks in February and March working on songs for the soundtrack. Despite having originally been asked only to 'contribute,' he presented Burton and Warners with a full eleven-track album. Deciding that the *Batman* brand had enough commercial clout to warrant both a Prince soundtrack and an instrumental score by Danny Elfman, the company gave him the green light. Burton, however, rejected two of the songs Prince had recorded, '200 Balloons' and 'Rave Unto The Joy Fantastic.' (Prince subsequently released '200 Balloons' as the B-side of 'Batdance,' but ended up hanging on to 'Rave' until 1999's *Rave Un2 The Joy Fantastic* LP.)

The final nine-track *Batman* album went on sale on June 20 1989, three days before the movie opened in the USA. Those who bought it after having seen the movie might have been slightly confused by its contents, however: only 'Partyman' and 'Trust' appear prominently in the movie, while 'Scandalous' (co-written by Prince's father, John L. Nelson) plays over the second half of the end credits. Nothing more than snippets of the other tracks were used, suggesting that Prince's over-enthusiasm might have gotten the better of him.

Batman is hardly a great piece of work. While some reviews praised its commercial appeal (notably the *Detroit Free Press*, which screamed: "Holy hit singles, Batman! Prince has done it again!"), others were quick to note a distinct lack of major artistic progression.[20] The stripped-down funk sound is closer to *The Black Album* than *Lovesexy*, but despite Prince's efforts to interject the psychological quirks of Batman/Bruce Wayne and The Joker into most of the songs, there are no great stretches of the imagination.

Rolling Stone was correct to assume that some of the songs had simply been "sitting around Paisley Park" and not written specifically for the movie, since 'The Future,' 'Electric Chair,' and 'Vicki Waiting' all came from 1988 recording sessions.[21] The song that Prince seemed to put the most effort into is 'Batdance,' a dance-orientated collision of samples of movie dialogue and other songs from the soundtrack put together so meticulously – in the manner, somewhat ironically, of hip-hop acts such as Public Enemy – as to suggest that Prince had spent more time on it than anything else on the record.

Nonetheless, the success of the movie helped push the genuinely catchy singles, 'Partyman' and 'Batdance,' up the charts (the latter beat the *Ghostbusters II* soundtrack single 'On Our Own' by Bobby Brown to Number One) and resulted in the album selling more than four million copies, making it Prince's most commercially successful offering since *Purple Rain*. It also added him to a very select group of artists to have released two *Billboard* Number One soundtrack albums. The only downside, it seemed, was that Prince had had to agree to sign the publishing rights to the songs used in the movie over to Warner Bros, which means that only the single B-sides '200 Balloons,' 'Feel U Up,' and 'I Love U In Me' appear on the comprehensive compilation *The Hits/The B-Sides*.

For Prince himself, the sales success of *Batman* was a mixed blessing. On the one hand, it must have irked him to some extent that something so commercially minded, throwaway, and unrepresentative of his true artistic vision had become such a big hit when albums much closer to his heart (particularly *Lovesexy*) were widely ignored. What Prince couldn't argue with, however, was the fact that *Batman* had re-established him as a commercial force in both the music and movie worlds after years of diminishing financial returns, giving him much greater clout when it came to convincing Warners to back his *Graffiti Bridge* project.

After winding up the Sign "O" The Times tour in June 1987, Prince took to working on a treatment for *Graffiti Bridge* – named for a real Minneapolis landmark – in September the same year, prior to working on *The Black Album*. Back then the plan was for Madonna to play Ruthie Washington opposite Prince's Camille Blue. But when Madonna came to Paisley Park to look at the script, she told Prince that it was terrible and that she wanted nothing to do with the project. (The pair did nonetheless collaborate on 'Love Song,' as featured on her 1989 LP *Like A Prayer*.)

Similarly, Bob Cavallo assumed that the 20-page treatment Prince gave him in advance of a meeting with Warners in December was a draft, and suggested hiring a professional writer to turn it into a screenplay. Prince of course felt that the 'draft' was all he needed, but for Cavallo it looked like a disaster waiting to happen. "He didn't really want to work with us anymore," Cavallo later claimed, "but if I could have gotten that film made, I think he would have."[22] As things stood, however, Cavallo didn't feel particularly inclined toward raising funds for a project that already seemed doomed to failure.

Prince's response to this, on December 31 1988, was to fire his entire management team, along with his lawyer and financial advisor. This would prove to be a big mistake. Cavallo Ruffalo & Fargnoli – and Steve Fargnoli in particular – had played a crucial role in keeping Prince's career on track over the years. They had done all the fighting with Warners on his behalf, and had managed to get him almost everything he wanted. Without them, Prince would find himself in a much weaker position at the negotiating table. Sacking his lawyers and financial advisors at the same time only exacerbated the problem, and left him in the position of having to install a new team at a time when his financial situation was less than buoyant.

Fortunately, Albert Magnoli's arrival turned around Prince's fortunes when he secured his client the *Batman* soundtrack. Magnoli's success reversed a run of seemingly poor decisions that Prince himself had made – withdrawing *The Black Album*, replacing it with the poor-selling *Lovesexy*, and then going off on a loss-making tour – that had left Warners feeling decidedly unsure about the idea of investing in another risky, big-budget project. But once Prince had proven he was still capable of multi-million sales, the company became more open to the *Graffiti Bridge* project – particularly now that it was being billed as a follow-up of sorts to *Purple Rain*.

Prince came away from *Batman* with a newfound commercial clout and Kim Basinger – whom he now planned to cast as *Graffiti Bridge*'s female lead – on his arm. (Basinger had also worked with Prince on a third draft of *Graffiti Bridge*, with Prince offering to record an album for her in return.) But while Albert Magnoli was already talking about setting up a movie production company in partnership with Prince to "do projects that are diversified and take the entire gamut of entertainment," the singer was in fact still struggling to raise enough money for the first one.[23] As 1989 drew to a close, Magnoli started to feel the same way as Bob Cavallo had a year earlier.

"My idea for the film was for a higher-budget, more elaborate concept," he recalled. "But Prince wanted a lower-budget approach and to get the film out within a year. So I just said: 'Why don't you do that, 'cause I'm shooting for the moon here.'"[24] And so it was that Prince found himself looking for his third management team in the space of a year.

This time he hired Arnold Stiefel and Randy Phillips, who had promised to secure the financial backing needed to make *Graffiti Bridge*. In what can be seen as an important shift in priorities, Prince now seemed to be hiring people who would tell him what he wanted to hear, not what he needed to hear. "He was beginning," Warners' Marylou Badeaux recalled, "to not listen to anyone who was not a 'yes' man."[25] As Alan Leeds later noted, the obstinance that followed 1989's "house-cleaning" led Prince to go "through three different management structures, sometimes including legal and financial teams, in less than five years."[26]

In fairness to Stiefel & Phillips, they did make good their promise to secure $7 million of Warner Bros Pictures' money – exactly the same amount that Mo Ostin had put up in order to get *Purple Rain* off the ground. Warners had been sold on the fact that the movie was set to reprise the feud between Morris Day and The Kid, and agreed to finance it on the condition that the original line-up of The Time would appear.

This didn't seem like it would be a problem. Prince had already started working with Morris Day and Jerome Benton on a new album called *Corporate World*, so could easily use those recordings as a springboard to The Time's *Pandemonium*. He was also able to convince Jimmy Jam, Terry Lewis, and Jesse Johnson to return on the basis that *Graffiti Bridge* would tell The Time's side of the story.

Unsurprisingly, however, the plot emphasis began to shift almost as soon as the movie entered production. Six years after *Purple Rain*, The Time still found themselves forced to stand in their creator's shadow. *Purple Rain* "had told Prince's story," Jimmy Jam later recalled, but *Graffiti Bridge* was just "a Prince movie with a cameo by The Time."[27]

With yet another disappointment in the can for Morris Day and co, *Graffiti Bridge* would end up as virtually their last stand. The group has been sporadically active in the years since, however. A new line-up, billed as Morris Day & The Time, began touring during the mid 90s, and made an appearance in Kevin Smith's 2001 movie *Jay And Silent Bob Strike Back*. The group also formed part of Prince's 1999 New Years Eve show (actually recorded on December 17) and supported him on a handful of Musicology tour dates in 2004. The original line-up then reconvened in 2008 for a duet with Rihanna at the Grammy Awards, followed by a run of shows in Las Vegas – not unlike the 3121 residency Prince staged there in 2006. In June 2010, during a four-date Stingy tour, Morris Day revealed that The Time had a new album of "cool, sexy music with attitude" almost ready for release – possibly in time to coincide with the 30th anniversary of their debut in 2011.[28]

As seems to be the case whenever Prince tries to make a movie, one step forward (reuiniting The Time, in this case) was followed by another step back. Over the years, Prince has tended to avoid having relationships with other public figures – except, of course, those involved in his various side-projects. What this tells us about him is open to interpretation, but it's interesting to note what happened when Prince tried to pull another star with a profile as high as his own into his orbit.

Kim Basinger had previously played the female lead in *9½ Weeks*, a steamy look at the dark side of relationships that was, perhaps unsurprisingly, one of Prince's favorite movies of recent times. When it came time for her to join Prince in the studio to add her vocals to 'Scandalous,' the pair reportedly staged their own homage to *9½ Weeks*' sex-and-food shenanigans, leaving the Paisley Park engineers to clean honey off the mixing desk the following morning. (Basinger's contributions to the main edit of the song are limited to a few groans of pleasure, but the 'Sex Suite' mix includes a series of suggestive exchanges between the pair.)

The relationship was strange and shadowy from the start. It was once rumored that Prince offered up as much as £5 million to speed up Basinger's immediate divorce from her make-up artist husband, Ron Britton, while others have suggested that Prince had an almost hypnotic hold over her. She even sacked her manager and installed Albert Magnoli in his place.

Almost as suddenly as the relationship had started, however, it was over. Basinger left Paisley Park in January 1990, throwing another spanner into the

Graffiti Bridge works. It's not entirely clear what happened between them, since almost every word spoken about the relationship is based on rumor and allegation. Perhaps the weirdest claim is that Basinger's family had become so concerned about her infatuation with Prince that they essentially had to kidnap her from Paisley Park. Whether this is true or not, Basinger did leave in such a hurry that she left her car in Prince's driveway. (He eventually had it towed.)

Neither party has said a lot about the affair following its demise. In 1990, Prince told *Rolling Stone*: "I really don't know her that well."[29] But he seems to have harbored feelings for her since, and even allegedly offered to help with the $8-million lawsuit she faced after pulling out of the movie *Boxing Helena* in 1993. (That same year, he also released 'Peach,' another track based around her distinctive moans and groans.)

Just as had been the case when Vanity quit on the eve of shooting *Purple Rain*, Prince was left looking for a last-minute replacement female lead. Since his other on-off girlfriend of the past few years, Anna Garcia, had already packed her bags and flown back to Britain, Prince approached Ingrid Chavez, whom he had met around the time of *The Black Album*. (Chavez has been credited with kick-starting Prince's spiritual rebirth – she appears as 'Spirit Child' on *Lovesexy* – so seemed like an obvious candidate for *Graffiti Bridge*, which has a strong spiritual grounding.)

Having already completed work on the accompanying soundtrack album, Prince and his cast of bandmates and friends – including Mavis Staples and George Clinton, both of whom were signed to Paisley Park Records at the time – shot the movie in six weeks during February and March 1990. Most of the scenes were shot on the Paisley Park soundstage on sets that Prince admitted were cheap, before musing, in a *Rolling Stone* interview: "Man, what I'd do with a $25 million budget. I'll need a big success to get that, but I'll get it. I *will* get it."[30]

Elsewhere in the interview, which runs the gamut between cheeriness and defensive uncertainty, Prince refuted the idea that he had taken a gamble in making *Graffiti Bridge*. "What gamble?" he asks. "I made a $7 million movie with somebody else's money, and I'm sitting here finishing it."[31]

Graffiti Bridge might not have seemed like a gamble to Prince, but it certainly was for Warners, whose money the singer was cheerfully spending. When test audiences reacted poorly to the movie in April, the company demanded that Steve Rivkin – brother of Prince alumni David and Bobby – be brought in to oversee further edits and try to salvage the project. Prince postponed a planned European tour by six weeks in order to work on a new edit, but still hadn't completed it by the time he stepped onto the stage at the Stadion Feijenoord in Rotterdam, Holland, on June 2.

For the three-month Nude tour of Europe and Japan, Prince assembled a line-up of old hands – Matt Fink, Miko Weaver, and Levi Seacer Jr – and new members, among them keyboardist Rosie Gaines, drummer Michael Bland, and three hip-hop dancers, Tony Mosley, Damon Dickerson, and Kirk Johnson, whom he christened The Game Boyz. Sheila E. may have left the fold, but she continued to maintain her own musical career, and later co-founded the Elevate Hope Foundation with George Clinton's former Bride Of Funkenstein Lynn Mabry. On December 13 2003, the foundation put on the Family Jamm in aid of victims of child abuse. Escovedo was joined by numerous Prince alumni, including Carmen Electra, Jill Jones, Eric Leeds, Apollonia, and Matt Fink. In 2007 she formed the group C.O.E.D. (Chronicles Of Every Diva) with former Prince bassist Rhonda Smith and released the single, 'Water Of Life.' Three years later, she began selling her *From E 2 U* EP, which contains the Prince-penned 'Leader Of The Band,' online and at concerts.

The Nude tour marked another change of approach for Prince. Whereas in recent years he had played on extravagant stage sets and focused on new material, he now seemed content to run through the hits against a less showy backdrop of ramps and poles – the sort of stripped-down stage set he had utilized on earlier tours. There was some suggestion that the move was financially motivated – a claim given further credence by the fact that the singer had recently started construction of a Minneapolis nightclub, Grand Slam, which put a further strain on his resources. But as far as Prince was concerned, "kids save a lot of money for a long time to buy tickets, and I like to give them what they want."[32] To that end, having seemingly conceded defeat in his war on hip-hop, he even let Tony Mosley rap during *Batman*'s 'The Future.'

The Nude tour might have been slicker and less experimental than previous Prince shows, but it was still a resounding success. The promise of back-to-back hits provoked a huge response from concertgoers, notably in London, where Prince played a record-breaking 16-night run at Wembley Arena. (Dire Straits had held the previous record of nine nights.)

Even so, Prince was still left to sort out the mess of *Graffiti Bridge*, which he was now attempting to edit on VHS machines in hotel rooms. He then had to shoot additional scenes in Hollywood in September after completing the Japanese leg of the tour. The movie had been due for release during the summer, but was delayed until November 2, whereupon it received even more scathing reviews than had *Under The Cherry Moon*, and took only $4.2 million at the box office.

"I didn't want to make *Die Hard 4*," Prince told *Rolling Stone* in an attempt to defend *Graffiti Bridge*. "But I'm also not looking to be Francis Ford Coppola. I see this more like those 50s rock'n'roll movies."[33] For *Entertainment Weekly*, however, Prince's latest cinematic outing could "barely muster the energy to get from one shot to the next."[34] The *St Paul Pioneer Press* did its best to take a positive perspective, noting that there are "so many good musical numbers ... that the plot barely has time to exist."[35] The *Washington Post*, by contrast, simply begged Warners to "stop him before he films again!" before charging that "*Graffiti Bridge* should be bronzed immediately and delivered to Hollywood's Hall Of Shamelessness, where it might draw bigger crowds than it's likely to at movie theaters."[36]

Graffiti Bridge is essentially a visual version of *Lovesexy*: a confusing splurge of Prince's innermost thoughts, continuing to explore that album's preoccupations with spiritual rebirth. In his defence, Prince claimed that it was "one of the purest, most spiritual, uplifting things I've ever done. Maybe it will take people 30 years to get it. They trashed *The Wizard Of Oz* at first, too."[37]

His close-cropped beard says it all: this will be my defining, most mature artistic statement. But while *Purple Rain* had an element of psychodrama, *Graffiti Bridge* merely proves that Prince believed that the movie (like its predecessor, *Under The Cherry Moon*) could succeed on the strength of its music and the barest of good-versus-evil plotlines. He would later claim that the aim of the movie was to be "non-violent, positive, and [have] no blatant sex scenes," having apparently forgotten that the scene that test audiences had most objected to was the one of him masturbating to the song 'Tick, Tick, Bang.'[38]

It's difficult to think of *Graffiti Bridge* as anything other than an abject failure, from the weak plot to the terrible acting and unconvincing rivalry between Morris Day and The Kid (who do battle over the ownership of a fictional nightclub). Unsurprisingly, it marked the last time Prince ever received financial backing for a big-screen feature.

Fortunately, however – and just as had been the case with *Under The Cherry Moon* – the accompanying soundtrack album was much stronger, and gave critics something to rally around. *Rolling Stone* gave it a four-and-a-half-star review that praised the work of an artist "reasserting his originality ... with the ease of a conqueror."[39] *Time* called the album a "groovable feast,"[40] while *Q* felt it "practically impossible to choose anything that doesn't deserve to be there. How long is it since that can honestly be said about a Prince album?"[41]

For the *New York Times*, *Graffiti Bridge* was the work of a "far less conventional" Prince now able to "take chances that didn't exist for him with *Purple Rain*."[42] The singer himself seemed to be in total agreement. "'Thieves In The Temple' and 'Tick, Tick, Bang' don't sound like *nothing* I've ever done before," he told *Rolling Stone*.[43] The level of praise heaped upon the record seemed to be based mostly on the fact that *Graffiti Bridge* is much more song-based than *Lovesexy*, and also a lot more varied. It also makes good use of songs by other artists featured in the movie, including Mavis Staples, George Clinton, the child R&B star Tevin Campbell, and The Time.

The fact that many of the songs had been around for quite some time probably helped, too. 'Tick, Tick, Bang,' the most explicit track on the album, dates back as far as 1981, while the masterful 'Joy In Repetition' was originally slated to appear on *Crystal Ball*. The funk-gospel 'Elephants & Flowers' had been reworked from a 1988 recording session, while the fan-favorite ballad 'The Question Of U' was written in 1985.

Of the three songs recorded with *Graffiti Bridge* in mind, only lead-off single 'Thieves In The Temple' hits the heights of the older material, while the 'joy of repetition' seems a little more dubious on the opening 'Can't Stop The Feeling I Got,' which does nothing that earlier rockabilly-style tunes such as 'Jack U Off' and 'Delirious' hadn't done better before. (*Village Voice* was in on the emperor's new clothes aspect when it noted: "It's amusing to hear Prince singing and Morris Day playing drums on a song called 'New Power Generation.' New? These brothers are both over 30."[44])

All in all, *Graffiti Bridge* seemed like the perfect album for those fans who had been turned off by the high concepts but wanted something a bit meatier than *Batman*. It proved that, even if the best tracks came from The Vault, Prince could still put together an album of proper songs. But for all its strengths, and all the praise heaped upon it, the album sold less than a million copies, putting it on a par with *Lovesexy* in terms of commercial success (or failure).

CHAPTER 10

WE R THE NEW POWER GENERATION, WE WANT 2 CHANGÉ THE WORLD

Prince's music in the 90s suffered because, for the first time, he allowed outside trends to influence his work.

ALAN LEEDS

A s *Graffiti Bridge* found itself exiled into the hall of shame, it was thankfully not indicative of Prince's next move in 1990. His live shows more clearly signposted where Prince was heading. The Nude tour got the singer to focus on his past hits (and thus start thinking about writing some new ones), while its incorporation of hip-hop elements suggested that Prince was ready to reconnect with the black audience many felt he had left behind in the 80s.

In a previously unpublished interview with noted soul and jazz critic Charles Waring, backing singer and keyboardist Rosie Gaines recalled: "The whole concept was to strip the show down and show actual talent. You just play, go out there and enjoy it. And I have to say that was the finest tour we did. That was the most fun. The more elaborate the thing got [with the later Diamonds And Pearls tour], the less fun it was."[2]

After the tour wound up on September 10 at Japan's Yokohama Stadium, Prince returned home and immediately began working on his next record. It would be his first with a band's input since *Dream Factory*, and would bring him back to his black roots like nothing since the shelved *Black Album*.

In the past few years, Prince's singles had seemed to perform better on *Billboard*'s R&B chart than the Hot 100, and it now seemed that he was returning to the idea of recording songs for songs' sake, and not to serve grand, overlying concepts. Rolling the project out wasn't without the now usual difficulties, however. In December 1990, shortly after completing work on his follow-up to *Graffiti Bridge*, Prince decided once again to shake up his managerial infrastructure. One might have expected him to re-hire Arnold Stiefel and Randy Phillips, who had done a reasonable job for the duration of their initial 12-month contract, but Prince saw things differently.

As far as he was concerned, they had done what he wanted of them – securing financial backing for *Graffiti Bridge* – and could now be shown the door. When it came to replacing Stiefel and Phillips, Prince opted not to seek out professional businesspeople but to promote from within his already close-knit circle. And so it was that Gilbert Davison stepped up from head of security (a role he had inherited in 1985 from Chick Huntsberry) to manager and president of Paisley Park Enterprises, while press officer Jill Willis, formerly of the New York PR company Rogers & Cowan, was installed as the company's vice-president.

Prince's touring band was given a similar overhaul. When Matt Fink told the singer that he wasn't available for two appearances at the Rock In Rio festival in January 1991, he found himself replaced by Tommy Elm, whom Prince rechristened Tommy Barbarella after the cult movie starring Jane Fonda. (The move was similar to the sacking of Jimmy Jam and Terry Lewis from The Time in 1983, in that Fink had been busy producing another band.) Meanwhile, Levi Seacer Jr switched from bass to guitar, following the departure of Miko Weaver at the end of the Nude tour, and Sonny Thompson came in on bass. "We were his first black band," Rosie Gaines recalled of the group that would soon become known as The New Power Generation, "and our thing was to help him get his audience back."[3]

More than that, however, was that – as with his 'love symbol' – the very phrase 'New Power Generation' has come to represent much more to Prince than just a name. To the man himself, it has always been more of a concept than a tangible entity. On 'Eye No,' recorded in 1987 and included on 1988's *Lovesexy*, he welcomes listeners to his new power generation, explaining that his "voice is so clear" because "there's no smack in my brain."

Right from the outset, the NPG concept seemed to symbolize self-improvement and the quest for a better, healthier lifestyle. That it first emerged on Prince's most spiritual album to date was no accident. He took the concept even further a year later, on *Graffiti Bridge*, when he named the album's second track 'The New Power Generation' and declared: "We want 2 change the world." Even before he started referring to his band by the same name, Prince seemed to have decided that the NPG should lead the way when it came to advocating a better life.

It's somewhat ironic, then, that the band that eventually took the name, and was deemed important enough to be credited alongside him on albums such as *Diamonds And Pearls*, seemed initially to be nothing more or less than a tight, proficient group of session musicians. As far as Prince was concerned, this was just what he needed. He could, he told *Rolling Stone*, "keep switching gears on them and something else funky will happen."[4] But while The New Power Generation certainly had the hard R&B chops required to keep up with current trends in the black music market, they would never be anywhere near as innovative and influential a band as The Revolution.

Prince had planned to spend the early months of 1991 trying to drum up interest in his forthcoming *Diamonds And Pearls* LP, but instead found himself distracted by other matters. On February 1, he was sued by his former managers, Cavallo, Ruffalo & Fargnoli, who claimed $600,000 in severance pay and damages for breach of contract, fraud, and denial of contract in bad faith. Prince was also charged with ignoring his managers' advice since 1985 and continuing to flood the market with competing product (a claim that would perhaps have hurt the singer more than the others). He retaliated by suing his former lawyers, arguing that they had negotiated an unfavorable settlement with Cavallo, Ruffalo & Fargnoli.

The whole mess was eventually settled out of court, but meant that Prince couldn't really concentrate on the business of convincing Warners to release his new album until March. The company had been keen instead to release a greatest hits set in an effort to break a run of increasingly low-selling records. What the label executives hadn't anticipated, however, was that, on *Diamonds And Pearls*, Prince had stopped chasing his artistic muse and decided, for the first time ever, to concentrate specifically on writing hits.

In fact, Prince was so determined to make a success of *Diamonds And Pearls* that he went out on the promotional circuit well before the album's release, performing at industry showcases, making one-off television appearances, and playing 'Gett Off' in his 'assless' pants at the MTV Video Music Awards. He even hired a pair of high-profile dancers, Lori Elle and Robia La Morte, to play the roles of 'Diamond' and 'Pearl.' These were the very sorts of promotional activities that he would have balked at a few years earlier, but now they were helping to push his media profile up to its highest point since *Purple Rain*.

Another change could be seen in relation to the singer's attitude toward promo videos. In the past he had sometimes refused to make them at all, insisting that his art be judged on its own merits, but this time he went into overdrive, issuing a video EP with promos not just for the album's first single, 'Gett Off,' but also for its B-sides. According to the director, Rob Borm, Prince worked like a man possessed on the main 'Gett Off' promo, even going so far as to make executive decisions on the edit from the back of his limo. "He would call me up," Borm recalled, "and say, 'Rob, you know that third shot in [the] sequence? Trim two frames off the tails.'"[5] The high-concept piece, which Prince wanted to look like the 1979 movie *Caligula*, ended up costing five times more than its original $200,000 budget.

The well-oiled promotional machine had certainly done its job by the time *Diamonds And Pearls* went on sale in October 1991. Prince might almost have driven himself and his band – who had had to get used to nine-hour rehearsals and three hours' sleep – into the ground, but it all paid off in the end. The album ended up selling more than six million copies worldwide and found its way into the upper reaches of both the British and American album charts. It's not hard to see why. *Diamonds And Pearls* has a neat, polished, early-90s sound and contains little that might challenge the casual listener. "You know when you buy someone's record and there's always an element missing?" Prince asked *Details* magazine. "The voice is wrong or the drums are lame or something? On mine there's nothing missing."[6]

In reality, however, that was part of the problem. Denser even than *Lovesexy*, the album almost sinks under the weight of its over-production. Tracks such as 'Thunder' and 'Cream' – two of six singles to be drawn from the album – are undeniably catchy, but are so slick that they could easily pass as standard pop-radio fodder. So too could the fan-favorite title track, which shows Prince at his most bombastic. The falsetto-sung 'Insatiable' is more subtle, but is essentially a re-write of 1989's 'Scandalous.' And while Prince's heart is in the right place on 'Money Don't Matter 2 Night' and 'Live 4 Love' (which focuses on the Gulf War), neither song quite manages to drive its message home.

Prince recorded much of *Diamonds And Pearls* live in the studio with The New Power Generation – something of a bone of contention among the band-members, who later felt that he had failed to credit them properly for their input. As talented a bunch as these musicians were, however, they lacked The Revolution's capacity for risk and experimentation, resulting in a series of arrangements largely devoid of the quirks and twists that made otherwise simple songs such as 'Mountains' work so well. (Interestingly, while *Sign "O" The Times* had been recorded on a six-track machine, *Diamonds And Pearls* makes use of as many as 48 tracks.)

The album is hampered further by a smooth R&B sheen designed to win back the favor of the black audience many critics felt Prince had left behind. Even those involved with the record weren't entirely convinced by this particular change. "I was dismayed that Prince wanted to emulate the sound of current black music," engineer Michael Koppelman recalled. "It was frustrating to see what I consider to be a very talented musician fucking around with a lot of trendy crap."[7]

The most glaring change to the Prince sound is the singer's wholesale embrace of hip-hop – something he had spoken out against several years earlier. During the previous year's Nude tour, Prince had brought in three male backing dancers, The Game Boyz, and quickly discovered that one of them, Tony Mosley, could rap. After giving him a few solo spots on the tour, Prince invited the rechristened Tony M. to rap on a number of tracks on *Diamonds And Pearls*, even basing an entire song, 'Jughead,' around his less than engrossing delivery about managers being "parasites" and "money minders."

'Jughead' certainly had an impact, but not in the sense that Prince might have anticipated. After hearing it, Steve Fargnoli served him with a $5-million lawsuit, claiming defamation and breach of contract. (Prince and Cavallo Ruffalo & Fargnoli were forbidden from talking publicly about each other as part of their previous settlement.)

Prince's attempts to ingratiate himself with the hip-hop world didn't end there. "Black awareness is really taking an upturn today," Tony M. noted, "and he really wants to be a part of that."[8] In case anyone had missed the point, Prince took to singing into a gun-shaped microphone on stage, but it didn't seem to have the desired effect. As Alan Leeds later recalled: "The 'keep it real' hip-hop community wasn't buying Tony M. or a gun-shaped microphone from a guy Prince's age [33] who had grown up in a relatively middle-class Midwestern environment."[9]

Prince, of course, tried to distance himself from the obvious message he was sending. Reminding people that he was brought up in a black and white, rich and poor world, he "always said that one day I would play all kinds of music and not be judged for the color of my skin but the quality of my work."[10] But even his most supportive critics failed to rally round him when the album was released on October 1. The general feeling was that Prince needed a rest; or, as *Entertainment Weekly* put it, that "too many years churning out records by himself in his Paisley Park complex have taken their toll."[11] As far as the *New Musical Express* was concerned, it all served as proof that Prince was no longer a "vital force acting on pop music's zeitgeist."[12]

Prince's use of a gun-shaped microphone was all part of a concerted effort to reassert his 'masculine' qualities. He seemed determined to keep that going offstage, too. "When he was with the boys I was just another woman to him," keyboardist Rosie Gaines recalled. "He was kind of a male chauvinist at that point."[13] Gaines found herself stuck for long stretches on a tour bus with the rest of the male membership of the group, by whom she was often bullied. Unsurprisingly, she left at the end of the tour and was replaced, for the next album, by Morris Hayes. "Toward the end of the Diamonds And Pearls tour," Gaines told Charles Waring 13 years later, "I'd really had enough of the whole thing. ... It really was him changing and not ... We had a love-hate relationship. I felt at that time that he was not really taking good care of us and looking out after [us] like the way he should be. And we didn't get paid the way we should have."[14]

Somebody who did quickly became a permanent fixture in the Prince camp was Mayte Jannell Garcia. Born in 1973, she had grown up in Germany and the USA, moving around a lot as a result of her father's job in the military. At the age of eight she became the youngest professional bellydancer to appear on television when she performed on *That's Incredible!* On July 25 1990, her mother took her to see Prince's Nude show in Barcelona, Spain. Although Mayte wasn't much of a Prince fan before the show, her mother sensed that there might be opportunity for her to dance professionally for the singer, and so encouraged her to send him a videotape of her dancing.

The tape Mayte sent to Prince, via Kirk Johnson of The Game Boyz, is said to have contained footage of her dancing to 'Thieves In The Temple.' (The song was chosen by her mother, who had enthused about its Middle Eastern overtones.) Mayte was quickly invited to bring another tape to Prince, which she did two weeks later after a show in Germany. When she met him, Mayte's first thought was: "Wow, he's really small!"[15] Prince would later claim to have fallen in love the moment he saw her.

This isn't so surprising, given that Mayte shared many of the best elements of his past girlfriends. She had the exotic looks of Vanity (her parents are both of Puerto Rican ancestry) and the enrapturing charm of Susannah Melvoin and Kim Basinger. When Mayte left the backstage area, having performed her party trick of flipping coins on her belly, Rosie Gaines reportedly told Prince that he had just met the girl he would marry.

Mayte was still only 16 at this point, so she and Prince began a long-distance courtship designed to bring her closer into the Prince fold in time for her 18th

114

birthday. "Prince was very protective of me," she later recalled, "and my father was happy to place me in his care. ... It was all quite innocent, but quite intense."[16] With her father's blessing, she and Prince wrote to each other regularly, while Prince sent her tapes of new songs, which she filmed herself dancing to. By the time of the Diamonds And Pearls tour, Mayte was living in Minneapolis and working as part of the backing group as a supplementary dancer to Diamond and Pearl.

Like the album itself, the Diamonds And Pearls tour was Prince's most conventional to date. The stage set, which included various statues and a 'love symbol'-shaped spaceship, was certainly extravagant, but the musical arrangements left little room for improvisation and felt more like a revue, while the newly hired brass section – which brought total membership of The New Power Generation up to 17 – played much more of a straightforward R&B role than the jazzy duo of Eric Leeds and Matt Blistan had in years past. In an attempt to keep his band well-drilled, Prince introduced a 'Whoever's The Funkiest' competition each night. "We had this bonus thing," Gaines later recalled. "Whoever's the funkiest that night, they get to have a bonus. So everybody's always on, 'cause everybody's trying to get that bonus. So that [made] everything interesting."[17]

The tour was a resounding success, but the cost of the show, huge entourage, and regular bonuses for band-members who played at after-shows cut right into any potential profits. "The amount of money spent on the road was just ridiculous," Prince's UK publicist of the time, Chris Poole, later recalled. "His accountants told me later that it didn't make any money. That he spent it all, basically."[18]

This didn't appear to matter to Prince, who still seemed not to have grasped how precarious his financial situation had become. Perhaps he simply felt that, having re-established himself as a commercial success, he didn't need to worry anymore. He had almost completed his next album even before the Diamonds And Pearls tour finished, and was so confident in the material that he took to playing tracks from it over the public address system before taking the stage during his eight-night run at London's Earl's Court Arena. His intention was to release these new songs on an album with an unpronounceable title as quickly as possible.

In August 1992, two months before the album's release, Prince sat down to renegotiate his contract with Warners. The label must have been happy to learn that Prince was already recording promo videos for his intended singles, while the success of *Diamonds And Pearls*, his best-selling record in years, put Prince in a much better bargaining position. From a Warners perspective, this new deal was geared toward encouraging Prince to carry on making hit records. It reportedly gave him a 20 per cent royalty rate and a huge advance of $10 million per album – on the condition that the previous album managed to sell more than five million copies. Prince's view on this was that his new '$100 million' deal put him on an even higher pay-scale than Madonna and Michael Jackson, who had both recently negotiated $60 million contracts with Warners and Epic respectively. More conservative estimates suggested that Prince stood to make around $30 million. As far as the public was concerned, however, the new deal made him pop's most bankable act.

For Warners, the litmus test would be Prince's 14th studio album, which he had once again recorded with (and co-credited to) The New Power Generation, and which he gave an unpronounceable symbol for a title. The label had high hopes that, despite its unpronounceable title, the new album, later dubbed *Love Symbol*, would repeat the success of *Diamonds And Pearls* when it was released on October 13 1992, almost exactly one year after its predecessor. In the event, however, it barely managed to sell a million copies. So much for the $10-million advance on the next one.

Part of the problem lay in the choice of singles used to promote the album. The first was 'Sexy MF,' which was unplayable on radio because of its coarse lyrics and had limped in at Number 66 on *Billboard*; the second was 'My Name Is Prince,' a hip-hop track unlikely to attract any new listeners, which stalled at Number 36. (*Rolling Stone* did, however, paraphrase the song's hook with its declaration that "His name is Prince and he is funky – funkier, in fact, than he's been in ages."[19])

Both songs were designed to let Prince burrow further into the hip-hop market. He had recently opened his Glam Slam club in Minneapolis, and wrote 'Sexy MF' after hanging out there. "The sexier the dancers," he later told Spike Lee, "the bigger the revenues."[20] While noting that AMG's 'Bitch Better Have My Money' was the biggest club song at the time, however, he seemed less aware that he had still failed to convince as a hip-hop artist himself.

Warners had wanted to release the majestic, Eastern-tinged '7' instead, and would be vindicated when it eventually reached a fitting Number Seven on the Hot 100 when issued as the album's third single. NB then, however, *Love Symbol*'s fate had been sealed. The critics found the album as confusing as any Prince release to date. Some reviewers even confused themselves, with *Spin* arguing on the one hand that the record broke no new ground, but on the other that it served as further evidence of Prince's "silly and crafty genius."[21] The *Minneapolis Star-Tribune* was firmer in its findings, declaring the album to be "a royal disappointment."[22]

The confusion was Prince's own fault. In the press release that accompanied the album, he described it as a "rock soap opera" designed to play out across the record's 75-minute runtime. The plan – at least to begin with – was for it to tell the story of how he met and wooed the Crown Princess Of Cairo, played by his new love interest, Mayte Garcia, while being hounded in a series of spoken-word segues by a news reporter (played by Kirstie Alley). Then, right at the last minute, he decided to add a new song, 'Eye Wanna Melt With U,' and had to cut some of the segues to make room for it. This left just his battles with Alley – which seem only to confirm the singer's obsession with avoiding interviews and frustrating journalists – and made it virtually impossible to understand what was going on in narrative tracks such as '3 Chains O' Gold.' (The *3 Chains O' Gold* VHS, which strung together several promo videos, helped clarify matters a little – until you get to the '7' clip, which serves only to muddy the waters further as Prince suddenly finds himself having to kill off seven of his past selves.)

Love Symbol is much more impressive without the 'rock soap opera' tag. In terms of scope, it's not quite up there with *Sign "O" The Times*, but certainly trumps *Graffiti Bridge*. One major improvement on *Diamonds And Pearls* is the performance of The New Power Generation, who appear on around half of the songs. After tightening up on the road and growing more accustomed to working in the studio, the musicians sound willing and able to go wherever their leader wants to take them. (On *Diamonds And Pearls*, by contrast, Prince seemed at times to be pandering to his cohorts' limitations.)

The album isn't without its flaws – the reggae-lite touches on 'Blue Light,' Tony M.'s raps on both 'My Name Is Prince' and 'Sexy MF' (a catchy riff in search of a song), the throwaway ballad 'Sweet Baby' – but they are more than outweighed by its strengths. The straightforward R&B tracks on *Diamonds And Pearls* seemed to get lost under the weight of over-production, but here Prince manages to pull his songs back from the brink of bloated excess. The Eastern-tinged '7' remains one of his finest moments on record, its interlocking vocal parts as accomplished as anything else he has recorded. 'Eye Wanna Melt With U' might not push many boundaries, but its hard club beats sit perfectly between the softer 'Blue Light' and 'Sweet Baby.' All in all, the competing elements of rock, hip-hop, funk, reggae, jazz, and dance music might sometimes be baffling, but they're always intriguing. When he does fail, you can at least tell that Prince is doing his best to reassert himself as pop's greatest risk-taker.

In March 1993, Prince began Act I, his first full American tour for five years. He might have ditched Diamond and Pearl, but the show was very much the 'rock soap opera' that *Love Symbol* had set out to be. The first half of the set saw him act out the album's attempted storyline in a manner that made a lot more sense on stage than on record. Having plucked his Arabian princess, Mayte, out of the audience, he would find himself on the run from assassins desperate to reclaim the Three Chains Of Turin from her. After an interval, the second half of the set comprised a more straightforward run through the hits.

A lot had changed by the time Prince commenced Act II in Europe at the end of July. Not only had he disposed of The Game Boyz, he had also changed his name to the unpronounceable symbol that gave his most recent album its title. Taking to the stage each night with gold chains hanging down over his face, he would begin by explaining his dissatisfaction with Warners – who had started to object more strongly to the rate at which he wanted to release his music – to the audience. Then, having scrapped the high-concept theatrics of Act I, he would play a straightforward, career-spanning greatest hits set. This would, he claimed, be the last opportunity to hear these songs live, since they now belonged to Warners and 'Prince' – somebody that O{+> was no longer willing to be.

For a while it seemed that, despite the name change, Prince would carry on working exactly as he had done before. He had already recorded his next project – *I'll Do Anything*, a movie soundtrack that would ultimately be scrapped when the director opted to cut the movie's musical element – and would continue to put out low-selling albums by other artists on Paisley Park Records while gearing up for the release of his next solo album. Without any side projects to touch The Time in terms of appeal (and quality cast-off Prince material scarce), however, Paisley Park Records' releases were becoming a laughing stock. Prince had recently thrown few musical bones to the likes of T.C. Ellis, whose 1991 album *True Confessions* includes three Prince co-writes, but for the most part he had lost his enthusiasm for running a label and let the projects govern themselves.

Back in 1989, Paisley Park had taken on two veteran artists who then made cameo appearances in *Graffiti Bridge*: George Clinton and Mavis Staples. Clinton, who had been as big an influence on Prince as Jimi Hendrix, Joni Mitchell, James Brown, or Sly Stone, offered up a half-baked, dated album called *The Cinderella Theory* that hardly anyone bought. Prince became more involved in the making of Staples's *Time Waits For No One*, but his modern production techniques served only to make her sound like a fish out of water. (He tried again in 1993 with Clinton's *Hey Man ... Smell My Finger* and Staples's *The Voice*, but neither reached a wide audience.)

In these two cases, Prince was at least trying to give something back to the musicians who had influenced him so much during his formative years. "I thought it was good that a little genius like Prince and a young person would be listening to Mavis and would want to write songs for me and record me," Staples told jazz and soul critic Charles Waring in 2005. "I was flattered that Prince called me."[23] Indeed, Prince was so in awe of Mavis Staples that even when it came to recording her second Paisley Park album, 1993's *The Voice*, he still couldn't talk to her. "I had to start writing him letters to communicate with him. And if Prince has kept all my letters, he has a big book on me. ... He really wrote my life on that album. And it was such a shame [that] the album couldn't get played because I got caught up in Prince's and Warner Bros' fight."[24]

When it came to newer artists in greater need of a leg-up, however, he hardly seemed to care. Ingrid Chavez had been something of a spiritual guide for Prince while he made *Lovesexy*, but he kept putting off work on her debut album. Sessions began in 1987, but the album wasn't released until September 1991, and even then it relied as much on the work of guitarist Levi Seacer Jr and engineer Michael Koppleman as it did on Prince himself.

Prince's long-term sax player Eric Leeds was another member of his inner circle to receive the gift of a Paisley Park album release. Unfortunately for Leeds, however, the album was based around scrapped sessions for a third Madhouse record. By 1991, hardly anyone was interested in Prince-related jazz excursions – least of all Prince himself, who was busy chasing current trends in R&B and hip-hop. The album was simply stamped with the Paisley Park logo and sent off into the wilderness.

The artist most damaged by Prince's lack of interest was Rosie Gaines. "Rosie is like a tornado," he had gushed in an interview with *Details* after the Nude tour. "There's never enough hours in the day for her voice. There's never enough tape for her voice."[25] As usual, he had promised to make her a solo album, with the working title *Concrete Jungle*. Shortly after the sessions began in the summer of 1990, however, he met 18-year-old Tara Leigh Patrick in a Los Angeles nightclub. True to form, he lost interest in Gaines's record almost immediately and started work on a rap album with Patrick instead.

Patrick became Carmen Electra, and was given a support slot on the Diamonds And Pearls tour. Her set revolved around her struggle to rap terrible, half-baked material such as 'Go Go Dancer' and 'Step To The Mic' in front of an audience that wasn't even particularly keen on Prince's own hip-hop excursions, let alone those of a low-level Vanity. Prince did his best to blame the hostile critical response on anything but Electra – her backing band, which he sacked and replaced with his own; the venues – before finally dropping her from the bill in June.

Warners was similarly unconvinced by the music on *Carmen Electra*, which ended up being delayed until February 1993. Even then it sank without a trace, but not before the entire project – which included several promo videos shot in Egypt – had cost a couple of million dollars. Later the same year, Prince had Electra play both Penelope and Calypso in his *Glam Slam Ulysses* stage production, a loose adaptation of Homer's *Odyssey* for which he wrote all the music. (The show closed down after two weeks and a critical mauling, and plans to give the production a full US tour were quietly dropped.)

Throughout the Carmen Electra debacle, the Rosie Gaines recordings – perhaps the most commercially and artistically viable of all of Prince's early-90s side projects – were left stagnating in The Vault. Anyone who had witnessed her performances on the Nude and Diamonds And Pearls tours could see how talented she was. Prince failed to take full advantage of that talent, but he didn't want anybody else to, either. When Gaines quit Prince's group following the Diamonds And Pearls tour, he refused to let her out of her contract with him. It's possible that he genuinely wanted to return to the recordings, which Gaines continued to work on without him; and it's quite feasible too that he was scared that, if he allowed her to take them to Motown (as she wanted to), they would become a hit without him.

Either way, *Concrete Jungle* sat on the shelf until it was formally scrapped in 1994, at which point Gaines was finally allowed to sign to Motown. Her debut album was eventually released in June 1995 as *Closer Than Close*, featuring two songs co-written by Prince, 'I Want U (Purple Version)' and 'My Tender Heart.' But although the title track was a modest chart success, the album as a whole suffered from years of being sat on and soon disappeared from the charts.

Despite everything she had been through over the years, Gaines has remained thankful for Prince giving her a start in the music business. "He did expose me to the rest of the world, [took] me out to do a lot of things I didn't get a chance to do, so I still look at him as probably the most exciting and greatest experience I had," she said in 2004. "It was miserable and it was wonderful at the same time."[26] She even returned to Prince's side to add vocals to *Emancipation*'s 'Jam Of The Year' and *1999: The New Master*. She has since claimed that she was never paid for either appearance, while also stating that there could be as many as five Rosie Gaines albums locked in The Vault.

Meanwhile, with Prince losing interest in his own roster, his bosses at Warner Bros HQ were beginning to show signs of a serious case of fatigue when it came to the most famous artist on theirs.

CHAPTER 11

EYE HATE U

According to some people I'm bankrupt and crazy. I woke up one day and the radio said I was dead. People say: "He changed his name, he doesn't even know who he is." … I know exactly who I am.

PRINCE

W arner Bros had been keen to take a break from saturating the market with new Prince material ever since the singer came along with *Diamonds And Pearls* – his 13th album in as many years – in March 1991. A greatest hits set, the label reasoned, would give consumers a break from the endless stream of new Prince product that seemed increasingly to be competing with itself, while also consolidating and celebrating a remarkable body of work accrued at such a frantic pace since the late 70s. "Our dispute was not the content but the quantity," Warners' senior vice-president Bob Merlis recalled. "He had artistic control. We didn't want to stifle his creative spirit."[2]

As far as Prince was concerned, putting out greatest hits albums was something you did once you had passed your prime. Fortunately, *Diamonds And Pearls* proved to be his most commercially minded work in years. There were no convoluted concepts, the overall sound was aimed squarely at the contemporary R&B market, and it ended up selling better than any Prince record since *Purple Rain*.

The idea of a greatest hits set didn't go away completely, however. It did not help that Prince was once again rapidly launching himself into new projects with little commercial viability. Rather, he seemed more determined than ever to make self-indulgent music that – even moreso than *Love Symbol* – was wholly uninteresting to anyone but its creator. A few weeks after announcing his intention to concentrate solely on "alternative media projects, including live theatre, interactive media, nightclubs and motion pictures," Prince holed himself up on the Paisley Park soundstage for most of June and July 1993 to film *The Undertaker*. The original plan was to make a feature-length movie starring Nona Gaye and the television actress Vanessa Marcil, but that ended up being scrapped in favor of a wholly musical project.

Most of what became *The Undertaker* was drawn from a 30-minute live set recorded by Prince and NPG bassist Sonny T and drummer Michael Bland in mid June. Some of the footage featuring Vanessa Marcil was later inserted in between the seven songs, reducing the 'feature-length movie' concept to a slick, three-man jam interspersed with barely related dramatic moments – a half-baked mess attractive only to die-hard Prince fans hungry for long, blues-based jams. (None of the scenes shot with Nona Gaye were used.)

The movie begins in black-and-white with Marcil's character entering Paisley Park needing to use the phone. She is told where to find one, but ordered not to go past "the sign," because there's a rehearsal going on. After the man she calls, Victor, refuses to believe that she's "changed," the girl becomes distraught and takes an overdose of pills before wandering into the rehearsal room. From here the viewer is treated to stripped-down versions of 'The Ride,' 'Poorgoo,' 'Honky Tonk Women,' 'Bambi' (from *Prince*), a snippet of 'Zannalee,' 'The Undertaker,' and 'Dolphin,' a studio version of which would subsequently appear on *The Gold Experience*.

As the band plays, Marcil's character dances, becomes ill, and then seems to die while Prince is singing the title track (another warning about the dangers of gang warfare and drug addiction). During 'Dolphin,' however, the girl comes to, throws her pills away, and leaves Paisley Park. A line from the title song – "Don't let the Devil make U dance with the undertaker" – flashes up on the screen as the credits roll, but the film's overall message is lost in a mess of muddled editing and overuse of primitive visual effects such as negative coloring and image warping.

All in all, it's hard to ascertain the point of the project beyond Prince's need to keep recording music. *The Undertaker* was given a limited VHS release through the NPG music store at the end of the year and then distributed more widely by Warner Music Vision in March 1995, but seems mostly to have been an exercise in wasting money at a time when Prince really should have been more frugal. (He also reportedly pressed up CDs of the soundstage recording and planned to give them away free with *Musician* magazine in early 1994, but was blocked from doing so by Warners.)

Two years later, Prince had slightly more success with the March 1995 release of *The Sacrifice Of Victor*, a 45-minute edit of a live performance shot at Bagley's Warehouse in London during the early hours of September 8 1993. He had ended his Act II tour a few hours earlier at Wembley Arena and hired the Warehouse for an all-night end-of-tour party. Taking the stage at 3am, he performed a full set with The New Power Generation that included a number of tracks from *The Undertaker* and previews of material from two newly recorded albums, *Come* and *The Gold Experience*. Mavis Staples popped up at one point to sing 'The Undertaker' and 'House In Order' (from her Paisley Park Records LP *The Voice*), while The Steeles and the NPG (fronted by Tony M.) also played brief sets.

The Sacrifice Of Victor is certainly more enjoyable than *The Undertaker*, but is still not one for the casual fan, with 'Peach' the only well-known song on the setlist. It is probably most interesting as an indicator of Prince's mindset during the latter part of 1993. The opening footage is taken from the September 7 Wembley Arena show, and shows him taking to the stage in a black-and-white suit that could easily be mistaken for a skeleton costume and announcing: "London, my name is not Prince, and my name damn sure ain't Victor" (in response, it seems, to suggestions that *Love Symbol*'s 'The Sacrifice Of Victor,' which references child abuse, is autobiographical). After this announcement he is wrapped up in a black shroud and carried off stage as if in a funeral procession, ending the Act II tour with a reminder of one of his latest concerns: doing everything he could to make it clear that 'Prince' is dead.

The concert had taken place only two months after Prince presented yet another new record to Warners, having already followed *Diamonds And Pearls* with the *Love Symbol* album the previous October. *Goldnigga* was billed as the full-length debut by his backing band, The New Power Generation, but Warners flatly refused to release it and instead decided to finally unveil the greatest hits collection it had been sitting on for the past two years. *The Hits/The B-Sides* gave Warners a chance to recoup some of the money it had lost when *Love Symbol* failed to generate even a fifth of the revenue of *Diamonds And Pearls*. The first two *Hits* discs (also made available as separate albums to begin with) are largely focused, as one would expect, on Prince's single releases, and provide a remarkable non-chronological document of one of the greatest artistic trajectories of any musician in the history of pop. For anybody wondering where Prince might be going in the 90s, it served as a reminder that he had done more than enough in the 80s. The likes of 'When Does Cry' sounded no less innovative in 1993 than they had when originally released nine years before.

The *B-Sides* disc, available only as part of the three-disc set, would have been revelatory to listeners who had not bought the original singles. It contains some of Prince's greatest material, from the electro-funk 'Erotic City' and the pop-rock 'She's Always In My Hair,' to the live favorite 'How Come U Don't Call Me Anymore' and two genuinely moving ballads, 'Another Lovely Christmas' and 'I Love U In Me' (another track in the gender-shifting mould of 'If I Was Your Girlfriend').

The package also includes a handful of rarities aimed squarely at the Prince completist: 'Power Fantastic,' from the *Dream Factory* sessions; an alternate version of '4 The Tears In Your Eyes' originally broadcast during Live Aid; two recent recordings, 'Peach' (a rock track built around a Kim Basinger sample) and 'Pope' (another less-than-essential excursion into hip-hop); 'Pink Cashmere,' a ballad written for ex-girlfriend Anna Garcia; and a flawless live duet of 'Nothing Compares 2 U,' sung with Rosie Gaines on the Diamonds And Pearls tour. The only thing missing, because of contractual complications, was anything from *Batman*, but nobody seemed to mind.

By the time *The Hits/The B-Sides* was released, Prince had publicly declared that he would now only offer Warners archival material from The Vault and not new songs, but *Rolling Stone* didn't seem too concerned. "If 'She's Always In My Hair' and 'Another Lonely Christmas' are any indication of the reported 500 songs Prince has in his vaults," the magazine supposed, "his label might just get its money's worth." The review concluded by stating that *The Hits* stood among the "essential documents of the past decade."[3]

Rolling Stone's opinions were amplified elsewhere. According to *Q* magazine, "Most truly essential compilations contain a few stars from pop's astrological map; these three [discs] contain a whole galaxy."[4] *Entertainment Weekly* described *The Hits* as a "vital affirmation that, at one time, Prince's very strangeness and eccentricities had a point; he was never weird simply for weirdness' sake."[5]

Running to 56 tracks and more than three hours of music, with illuminating liner notes by Alan Leeds, *The Hits/The B-Sides* remains the best one-stop for Prince's Warners years, covering as it does pretty much everything except *The Gold*

Experience. Subsequent Warners compilations pale in comparison. *The Very Best Of Prince* (2001) and *Ultimate Prince* (2006, with a second disc of relatively obscure 12-inch mixes) are just slimmed-down versions of what came before.

It's interesting to note that Warners released all three compilations – at least in part – with the intention of knocking the wind out of the sales of whatever else Prince was doing at the time. *The Hits/The B-Sides* came out right when Prince had begun to publicly criticize the label in the media, somewhat undermining his attempts at waging war with the company. In July 2001, *The Very Best Of* was released a few months before the singer's return to using the name 'Prince' with the rather more challenging *The Rainbow Children*, while *Ultimate Prince* was initially intended to coincide with his much trumpeted major-label return, *3121*, before Prince and then-label Universal managed to convince his old sparring partners to delay its release until August 2006. Even a decade after Prince and Warners officially ended their relationship, it appears that at least one party couldn't help but return to the battlefield from time to time.

Given the embarrassment that both parties suffered during the very public battle between them, it's perhaps no surprise that Warners have since sought to undermine their former charge. It's also worth remembering that tensions between the two had existed for over a decade: Prince had, of course, been giving his employers cause for concern ever since the release of his third album. The company was shocked by the lyrical content and overall image presented on *Dirty Mind*, but had been convinced by Cavallo Ruffalo & Fargnoli to release it as it was.

The album wasn't a huge commercial success, but it paved the way for Prince to become one of the most progressive and innovative musicians of his age. Further risk-taking strategies followed, such as selling the double-disc *1999* at the price of a single album, and releasing the bass-less 'When Doves Cry' as a single. These gambles paid off. But as the hits began to dry up, and Prince's ideas grew increasingly introspective, Warners began to lose confidence in his decisions. *Batman* and *Diamonds And Pearls* aside, each of his releases since the mid 80s seemed to sell less well than the last.

Prince insisted on putting out an album a year, tossing each record aside almost as soon as it came out to make way for the next one. His work rate meant that his albums were directly competing with each other for space on record-store shelves, which made it almost impossible for Warners to make its money's worth out of each one. The singer also seemed increasingly unwilling to compromise on any decisions relating to his recorded output. Generally speaking, an artist would bring his or her new record to the label and, as Warner Bros vice-president Jeff Gold later recalled, "decide mutually" about what tracks stood out as singles, how best to promote the record, and so on. Prince, however, "would show up … and kind of railroad you. All you could do was present your best case, appeal to the management."[6]

The final straw – for Prince at least – came when Warners refused to release the decidedly uncommercial New Power Generation record *Goldnigga*. Around the same time that he was working on the *Love Symbol* album, Prince had started this new project with his band, putting particular emphasis on rapper Tony M., one of the Game Boyz. M. might not have featured as prominently on *Love Symbol* as he did on *Diamonds And Pearls*, but Prince was still keen to prove that he could corner the hip-hop market as easily as he had the worlds of rock, pop, and funk.

Prince seemed to have more faith in *Goldnigga* than in any of his other early-90s projects, but the album has more significance as an artifact than as a piece of music. When he presented it to Warners, the label decided that now might be a good time to take a break from new Prince product. The singer's recent collaborations with Tony M. on his own material ('Sexy MF,' 'My Name Is Prince') had not exactly set the charts alight, so basing an entire album around the rapper hardly made good business sense.

The most important aspect of *Goldnigga* is that it was the first self-released Prince album. He had copies of it pressed up and ready to sell at NPG stores and concerts, and thus took in all of the profits himself. This seemed to fit well with the album's main lyrical themes: a 'goldnigga' is defined on the record as a black man who earns money through "knowledge and creative efforts," and who, working without a label, "can feel good because there's no blood on his hands."

Prince had already made clear his feeling that record labels and managements did nothing but steal profits from their artists' work on 'Jughead' (another showcase for Tony M., as featured on *Diamonds And Pearls*). He used *Goldnigga* to drive the point home, even going so far as to include a skit in which the title character squares up to record label executives. It was almost as if Prince knew what Warners' reaction to the record would be, and was using Tony M. to air his views about the company, without having to say them himself.

Goldnigga was credited to The New Power Generation, but nobody was fooled as to whose work it really was. Despite not taking any direct action, Warners was less than happy that one of its artists had made an album outside of the terms of his recording contract. Prince himself features prominently on several of the album's funky jams, while several more are focused on his usual preoccupations (sex and race). But while *Goldnigga* might sound like a Prince record, Warners was certainly right to pass on it. Only the truly devoted would have been able to stomach 47 minutes of Tony M. rapping over the most turgid, jam-based funk Prince had yet recorded. The whole thing was aimed squarely and transparently at black audiences, with song titles such as 'Black MF In The House,' and artwork full of fast cars, scantily clad women, and gaudy jewelry.

Goldnigga was only given a limited release, and as such has become rather collectable among Prince completists. The first CD pressing – featuring an extra song, 'Guess Who's Knockin',' that had to be removed from later editions because it lifted the chorus from Paul McCartney's 'Let 'Em In' – is particularly sought-after. But in the grand scheme of things, the album is mediocre at best, and important only in that it helped accelerate the break-up of Prince's relationship with Warners.

Refusing *Goldnigga* wasn't the first time the label had turned down one of Prince's albums: in 1987, the singer had agreed to cut down the three-disc *Crystal Ball* to a more manageable, two-record *Sign "O" The Times*. Six years on from the *Crystal Ball* disappointment, however, Prince began telling audiences on the Act II tour exactly what he thought of Warners and its attempts to hold him back and stifle his creativity. The singer's views quickly spilled over into the press, kickstarting a battle that would ultimately become a source of embarrassment for all concerned.

Further stoking the fire beneath Prince and Warners was the singer's lacklustre approach to the label he'd so enthusiastically launched in the mid 80s. "I ended up spending several very frustrating years trying to get Warners and the industry to take Paisley Park Records seriously when [it] simply didn't want to be taken seriously,"[7] Alan Leeds recalled. Among Prince's demands during his 1992 contract renegotiation were that the label continue to fund Paisley Park Records as a joint venture – despite the fact that it had quite obviously become a monumental waste of money.

Desperate to keep Prince happy, Warners agreed, and even gave him his own office suite and 12 members of staff in the West LA commercial district of Century City. But there was no improvement in the quality of Paisley Park's output. Eyebrows were raised in 1993 when Rosie Gaines' album was postponed so that Prince could focus on his latest discovery, Carmen Electra: the album with genuine promise disappeared to make way for an awful rap record by an identikit Prince-girl that sank without a trace.

This might well have been the final straw. In February 1994, just as Prince was beginning to wage war against Warners, the company pulled the plug on Paisley Park Records, refusing to throw more money away on vanity projects that brought nothing in return. "All the other artists that were on that label, that was over once Warner Brothers and he got in that battle," Rosie Gaines later lamented.[8] Mavis Staples maintains that her second album with Prince, *The Voice*, could have been a platinum-selling hit if it weren't for the conflict between Prince and Warners. "They would use me to get at Prince," she said. "I mean, you're arguing with Prince and why stop my record because of that? But they stopped it because it was on his label and they didn't want his label to be successful. ... I got caught in the middle, and that was another one gone down the drain for Mavis."[9] Prince took the label's master-tapes with him, but has never reissued any Paisley Park albums. In a further demonstration of his lack of interest in the label, it later transpired that he never set foot in his Century City office suite during the two years he owned it.

Prince of course blamed Warners for the failure of Paisley Park Records. "I was under the assumption that it was a joint effort," he told the *LA Times* in 1996. "All we do as artists is make the music. I didn't think I'd have to be marketing the records, or taking them to the radio station. If Michael Jordan had to rely on someone to help him dunk, then there would be trouble."[10] According to Alan Leeds, however, Warners took the view that "a succession of 'girlfriend' records and Prince's generosity toward legacy artists past their prime weren't representative of a real label."[11]

Prince's response to this setback was to launch NPG Records on his own and to set about haranguing Warners into letting him release a single on it. On the face of it, NPG Records became much more successful than its predecessor. Prince might not have attempted to assemble a roster as big as Paisley Park's, but he did release one-off albums by artists such as Chaka Khan and Larry Graham as well as the occasional NPG record. He has since claimed that, in some cases, he made up to 90 per cent profit from NPG releases over the years because there are fewer overheads and no parent label to pay. Despite selling to a more limited fanbase, he can boast of having made more money from NPG than he ever did with Paisley Park.

With his Paisley Park label no more and Warners increasing despairing over Prince's public attacks, a further threat to his reputation – at least in the eyes of the wider public – came on June 7 1993, his 35th birthday. As a celebration, Prince announced that he had legally changed his name to an unpronounceable symbol and that he would no longer be providing Warners with new songs, but instead planned to fulfill his contract by giving the company previously unreleased material from his vast archive, The Vault. Even the singer's UK publicist, Chris Poole, was stunned by this latest development. "My immediate reaction," he later recalled, "was pretty much the same as everybody else's: 'he's finally gone mad.'"[12]

"Everybody at Paisley Park was on a short leash and couldn't say 'Prince' after this press release had gone out," Jeff Gold recalled. "We'd have fun with it, because you'd call Paisley Park to talk to somebody in his management [and] try to get them to say 'Prince,' which they would never do."[13] Warners continued its gentle mockery of the name change with an advertisement in *Billboard* for the singer's forthcoming retrospective set *The Hits/The B-Sides*. "We here at Warner Bros treat our artists with a lot of heart," the ad – made up from a mixture of words and symbols – began, before requesting: "Don't call him Prince, call him O{+>, OK?"

A week later, Prince retaliated with a similar advertisement, which read, "We here at NPG treat our artists with respect. It makes us sad when they are sad. If they have new music they want to give to their fans, that's cool." What should have been a private battle was fast becoming very, very public.

Prince's decision to change his name is sometimes said to stem from a spiritual awakening the singer claimed to have had in Puerto Rico in December 1992. But while there might be some truth in this, it seems also to have been borne out of naïvety. Despite what his press release said, the change was simply not legal: it's impossible to change your name to a soundless glyph, even if you hope "one day [to] hear a sound that will give me a feeling of what my name will sound like."[14] (In the meantime, Prince seemed quite happy for people to call him "Sir.") It seems quite likely, however, that the singer believed that changing his name would release him from his contractual obligations, since Warners had signed 'Prince,' not 'O{+>.' His plan now was to release as much new music as he wanted under his new name while killing off the old one with music from The Vault. "I was a little ashamed of what Prince had become," he told Spike Lee in 1997. "I really felt like a product."[15]

Having already used a number of pseudonyms in the past, Prince appeared to have no qualms about taking things a step further, and seemed adamant that this O{+> character represented an entirely new persona. "Prince never used to do interviews," he told *Time Out* in 1995. "You'd have to ask Prince why … but you're not talking to Prince now. You're talking to me."[16]

The press response to all of this was a mixture of skepticism and ridicule. Some thought it was a mere publicity stunt; others thought the singer had finally lost his mind. Warners had sent out floppy disks with the glyph on, requesting that it be used instead of the word 'Prince,' but the most common response was to call him The Artist Formerly Known As Prince or TAFKAP.

Prince's PR team shortened the new name, somewhat pretentiously, to The Artist. Still, media commentators began to come up with their own nicknames. New York shock jock Howard Stern began to refer to the singer as The Artist People Formerly Cared About, while *Minneapolis Star-Tribune* columnist and Prince-watcher Cheryl Johnson took to calling him Symbolina. Prince later wrote the bitter 'Billy Jack Bitch' in response to some of Johnson's comments, but took most of the criticisms in his stride. "I hear they're calling Diana 'The Artist Formerly Known As Princess' now," he joked on *The Oprah Winfrey Show*, before revealing, "Recent analysis has proved that there's probably two people inside of me." (The "other person," he added, appeared to be "someone I created when I was five years old."[17])

All jokes and media battles aside, Prince was lucky not to be sued by Warners, given that he was doing his best to destroy one of the company's most bankable brands *and* refusing to hand over any new material. "We have a new album finished," he told *Vibe* magazine brazenly in 1994 (referring to *The Gold Experience*), "but Warner Bros doesn't know it. From now on Warner Bros only gets old songs out of The Vault."[18]

The label's position was made all the more difficult by the fact that Prince's management team was shifting at such an alarming rate that nobody ever really knew who to talk to. Similar changes were taking place at Warners, too. The two most artistically sympathetic chairmen at the company, Mo Ostin and Lenny Waronker, both left in 1994 after several years of restructuring following its takeover by Time Inc in 1990, and the subsequent adoption of a more corporate mindset as Time Warner.

These changes left little room for long-term artistic development of the kind that Ostin and Waronker had championed. When Danny Goldberg replaced former Warner Music Group Chairman Robert Morgado, he took on the job of trying to repair the company's relationship with Prince. As far as the singer was concerned, there were two major sticking points: The New Power Generation's *Goldnigga* follow-up, *Exodus*, and the matter of the next official 'Prince' product.

Having had to sit through 1993 without a major release, Prince made clear his intention to make up for lost time when he presented Warners with two new albums during the first half of 1994. First came *Come*, which consisted mostly of old material recorded before his name change, and then *The Gold Experience*, made up largely of new songs.

Prince's plan was for *Come* to be credited to 'Prince,' with *The Gold Experience* to be credited to O{+>, and for both to be released on his 36th birthday (one year to the day since his name change). His exact reasoning is unclear, but it seems that he wanted to pit his two 'brands' against each other and see which one the public responded to best.

This kind of deliberate sabotage went against all good business sense, and Warners refused point blank. One new Prince album would be more than enough – particularly at a time when record-store shelves were already swamped with his recent output. The label found little to get excited about when Prince first delivered *Come* in March and requested he rework it – and add the newly-recorded 'O{+>' song, 'The Most Beautiful Girl In The World,' to the tracklisting.

'The Most Beautiful Girl In The World' had long been a thorn in Warners' side. *Goldnigga* had taught him that he didn't need a label in order to release his music, while Warners' refusal to handle the New Power Generation-credited album furthered Prince's resolve to release his music on his own terms – as much of it, and as often, as he liked. In February 1994, he'd kicked up enough of a fuss for his employers to let him release 'The Most Beautiful Girl' through the newly formed NPG Records. Warners reluctantly agreed to this scheme with the proviso that Prince put up all of the money to promote and release the single himself. He duly spent $2 million manufacturing and marketing the single, enlisting the help of Bellmark, an independent label run by Al Bell, a former vice-president of Stax, to distribute it.

Prince saw this as his one chance to prove he should be left alone to do things his way, and devised an ingenious promotional scheme guaranteed to draw

130

attention for what was perhaps his most important release since *Purple Rain*. In December 1993 he booked advertising space in European and American magazines as an "eligible bachelor seek[ing] the most beautiful girl in the world to spend the holidays with," requesting that photo and video responses be sent to Paisley Park. Seven of the 50,000 applicants were chosen to appear in the promotional video for the single, while photographs of a further 30 of them were used in the artwork.

The campaign was an unqualified success. Released, fittingly, on Valentine's Day 1994, 'The Most Beautiful Girl In The World' sold 700,000 copies, rising to Number Three on the *Billboard* Hot 100 (and Number Two on the R&B chart). It also became Prince's first ever Number One hit in Britain. But there was a lot more to the single than just clever marketing. A love song to Mayte, it was nothing short of a masterpiece from an artist whose best days had seemed to many to be far behind him. Prince's vocal delivery is one of his most convincingly impassioned, while the multiple layers of vocal harmonies and instrumental overdubs prove that he was capable of piling up the production without sapping a song of its energy and emotional power. The song's euphoric peak and climax are almost as grand as 'Purple Rain.'

'The Most Beautiful Girl In The World' was a much-needed artistic and commercial success, suggesting that O{+> could be just as vital as the singer's former incarnation. (The joy was retrospectively tainted when, in January 2009, it was revealed that Italian songwriters Bruno Bergonzi and Michele Vicino had, as soon as 'TMBGITW' was released, sued Prince for plagiarism, claiming that he'd "borrowed heavily" from their 1983 song 'Takin' Me To Paradise.' After having their claim rejected in 2003, the songwriters appealed, and are still awaiting the necessary 'third degree' ruling in the Italian courts.) For Warners, however, the whole affair was particularly galling, the label having only agreed to the release in an attempt to get Prince off its back, not expecting the song to become his most successful single since 1989's 'Batdance.'

For Prince, all of this was proof that Warners didn't know what it was doing, and by extension that he should be allowed to release what he wanted, when he wanted. The single's success made him even more determined to break free from the label and encouraged him to drum up further support by publicly declaring that the album from which the song was taken, *The Gold Experience*, would never see the light of day because Warners refused to release it.

He was, however, able to convince the label to let him put out a second record through NPG a few months later: a full-length compilation album named for the free-phone telephone number he had set up to take orders for Prince and O{+>-related merchandise. Distributed once again by Bellmark, *1-800-NEWFUNK* was unable to repeat the success of 'The Most Beautiful Girl.' It barely sold at all, in fact, and only reached Number 45 on the *Billboard* R&B chart. The only song on the album credited to O{+> is 'Love Sign,' a duet with Nona Gaye, the daughter of Motown legend Marvin Gaye. Prince wanted to release it as a single but Warners refused to grant him permission, perhaps fearing a reprise of 'The Most Beautiful Girl In The World''s storming success. Undeterred, Prince pressed up promo copies for R&B radio stations, performed the song live on several television shows, shot a video for it, and placed adverts in *Billboard* magazine. But the single never materialized.

The rest of *1-800-NEWFUNK* mixes previously released material, such as George Clinton's 'Hollywood,' with new work, including '17' by Madhouse, 'Minneapolis' by the NPG offshoot MPLS, and Mayte's remarkably successful version of 'If Eye Love U 2Night,' a Prince-penned song previously recorded by Mica Paris. Despite its poor commercial performance, the 11-track album remains a worthy addition to the Prince canon, its mixture of upbeat funk and ballads yielding a number of fine examples of Prince's 90s update of the Minneapolis Sound. It might not have sold very well, but to Prince it served as further proof that he could carry on alone, without Warners' backing.

In the meantime, the castoffs Prince was throwing Warners' way did nothing to soothe the tensions between them. He returned in May with a new, much darker-sounding pressing of *Come* which, pointedly, still didn't feature his recent smash-hit and now omitted upbeat tracks such as 'Endorphinmachine' and 'Interactive,' which he had since decided were O{+> songs, not Prince songs. At the same time he also delivered *The Gold Experience*, which did include 'The Most Beautiful Girl' (and 'Endorphinmachine'), but was credited to O{+>.

Of the two, Warners eventually opted to release *Come*, largely because it was the one credited to the still-bankable Prince moniker. But this ultimately meant that on August 16 the label put out a dated album by a man who had no interest in promoting it, and whose audience had probably already grown tired of the soap opera surrounding his name-change and public battles with his label. *Come*'s jacket shows Prince staring out gravely in front of a cathedral, with his birth and 'death' dates, 1958–93, emblazoned across the front. (As if to hammer home the point, there are photographs inside of a live-and-well Prince dated 1958 and a 'dead' Prince dated 1993.)

Sick of the name-calling and name-changing, *Rolling Stone* headed its review 'Oh, whoever,' before imploring its readers to "appreciate these moves as part of what has become the most spectacular slow-motion career derailment in the history of popular music."[19] The *Detroit Free Press* voiced its disappointment by calling *Come* a "toss-off that doesn't merit the excitement usually accorded Prince albums."[20]

The album does have its moments. The *St Paul Pioneer Press* drew attention to the inclusion of a few songs that sound like "an old friend exposing something of himself, risking something real."[21] Perhaps the strongest of these is 'Papa,' a brutal, spoken-word retread of the child-abuse story hinted at on *Love Symbol*'s 'Sacrifice Of Victor.' Over a sparse musical backdrop, Prince declares: "Don't abuse children, or else they turn out like me." The song eventually rises to a more upbeat, cathartic conclusion, with Prince singing of how "there's always a rainbow at the end of every rain." 'Solo,' meanwhile, is a largely a cappella meditation on loneliness on which Prince's voice seems to echo out from the biggest, emptiest mansion in Minneapolis.

It's moments like these that mark *Come* out as one the singer's most interesting (and downright weird) albums, particularly when compared to the Prince-by-numbers themes that dominate the rest of the songs. The opening title track is an 11-minute paean to oral sex, 'Race' yet another so-so socially conscious collision of hip-hop and funk, 'Space' a largely unsuccessful attempt at trip-hop, and 'Loose!' and 'Pheromone' aimless retreads of early-90s dance music (the latter a blatant re-write of *Love Symbol*'s 'Continental').

While *Come* sold only 345,000 copies on its release in the USA, some fans now think of it as something of a 90s classic. But while it might sound good by comparison to the likes of later travesties *Chaos And Disorder* and *Newpower Soul*, it certainly doesn't come close to his best work of the 80s.

Comparing old and new Prince became a legitimate exercise in November when Prince opted finally – and somewhat puzzlingly – to allow Warners to release *The Black Album*. Although it didn't get him any closer to fulfilling his contractual obligations to the label, Prince did reportedly pick up a fee of $1 million for *The Black Album* as part of a three-album deal (from which he later withdrew) that also included *The Gold Experience* and an unnamed movie soundtrack.

Warners might have been glad to finally release *The Black Album*, but it didn't fare well with fans or critics. Seven years late, it was now, as the *Detroit Free Press* put it, "little more than an interesting period piece."[22] *Time* magazine seemed to hit the mark when noting that, while listeners in 1987 "probably wouldn't have known what to make of [the album's] bitter outlook, today it [sounds] almost conventional."[23]

Most of the fans who might have bought *The Black Album* had it been released in 1987 had moved on by 1994, or would have been content with their bootlegs of the original. The hardcore supporters that remained weren't enough to send the record hurtling to the top of the charts. Prince, meanwhile, seemed ever more desperate to reverse his fortunes. "If I knew the things I know now before," he was soon saying, "I wouldn't be in the music industry."

CHAPTER 12

THE EXODUS HAS BEGUN

I'm not scared of poverty. I grew up being poor … and these times are positive because they force you to decide if you're interested in living on this planet or not.

PRINCE

f Prince's situation with Warner Bros was turning into a major public embarrassment, behind Paisley Park's doors he had yet another crisis on his hands. After *Purple Rain* made him an overnight millionaire, he was suddenly thrust into a world where money was no longer a concern. According to Bob Cavallo, his manager throughout the 80s, Prince had even paid for Paisley Park in cash; by the time he was 27, had $27 million in the bank.

One might justifiably assume that this would have made him financially secure for life. It certainly made him brash enough to claim, in a radio interview: "I wouldn't mind if I just went broke, you know."[2] He subsequently reminded *Rolling Stone*: "I never was rich, so I have very little regard for money now. I only have respect for it inasmuch as it can feed somebody."[3] But just a few years later, Prince was facing severe financial difficulties following the loss-making Lovesexy tour and a string of albums that, while critically successful, had failed to reap the financial returns their reviews warranted.

In attempting to scrap the Japanese leg of the Lovesexy tour in favor of getting on with the *Batman* project, Prince was also beginning to demonstrate a tendency toward making less-than-sound business decisions. Had manager Steve Fargnoli not been able to convince him otherwise, Prince could have been sued for as much as $20 million for pulling out of the concerts.

Prince still seemed unwilling to listen to sound financial advice, choosing instead to do what he wanted, when he wanted. "We had a big graph," Bob Cavallo later recalled. "I put it on an easel showing the decline in revenue and increase in spending. He just walked [up] and turned it over."[4]

Fortunately, *Batman* was Prince's biggest commercial success since *Purple Rain*, and was followed in 1991 by another hit, *Diamonds And Pearls*, that helped put him back in the black following the failure of the previous year's *Graffiti Bridge* movie. Within a few years, however, Prince's finances would begin to fall apart again. By January 1995 the situation had become so bad that the *St Paul Pioneer Press* was reporting, "Paisley Park Enterprises, the company that oversees most of Prince's business interests, is not paying its bills on time or at all."[5]

Prince's extravagant spending appeared to have finally caught up with him. Since opening Paisley Park he had kept the studios fully manned 24 hours a day on the off chance that he might want to record. In Los Angeles, meanwhile, he spent around $500,000 per year on having a studio manned and ready at the Record Plant just in case he decided to drop in on a whim.

Studio costs were just the start of it. Paisley Park's in-house catering team and ten-strong tailoring department, employed to make bespoke clothes for Prince, his band, and his girlfriends, were all employed full-time, as were his band and road crew – even if they weren't recording or touring. By the mid 90s, Prince was also filming expensive promotional videos on the Paisley Park soundstage for songs that would never get released, even though the space was supposed to be hired out for movie productions such as *Grumpy Old Men*. (In the end, Warners executives had to get involved in order to clear the soundstage long enough for the movie to be shot.)

Prince might have claimed to have signed a $100 million contract with Warners in 1992, but the reality was that his albums were not selling enough for him to be earning anywhere near that. Even so, he had no problem wasting $2 million on his Glam Slam Minneapolis nightclub, or another $2 million on recording and promoting the hopeless Carmen Electra album. He made numerous other decisions without giving any consideration to cost or practicality, such as opening further Glam Slam clubs in Miami and Los Angeles, setting up a series of NPG music stores, building extravagant stage and movie sets, and even buying multiple copies of the same bespoke canes from a local company during a brief period in which the cane became his fashion accessory of choice.

Prince's decisions weren't just costly to the singer himself. Having previously worked on the 'Gett Off' promo video (which went five times over its $200,000 budget in less than a week), director Rob Borm found himself working on '7.' "Before we even shot film," he later recalled, "we had probably spent $90,000."[6] Then, with a set almost complete at Paisley Park, Prince decided he had had a better idea and moved the entire project to Los Angeles.

This was all very well except that, by 1993, Borm was due $450,000 for his work. When he tried to get it, Paisley Park could only afford to pay him 70 cents on each dollar owed. By the time he did get paid Borm had already fallen into debt himself, and ended up giving all $315,000 to his creditors before declaring bankruptcy.

Borm might even have been one of the lucky ones. Plenty of others found themselves up against a brick wall when it came to collecting debts owed by Paisley Park. Cane-makers Suzy and Gary Zahradka were forced to threaten legal action before receiving a belated check in return for their $4,500 invoices, while Record Plant studios ended up withholding a master tape Prince had accidentally left on the premises in order to ensure that a $150,000 bill got paid. Others simply met with a wall of confusion when they tried to get in touch with Paisley Park.

Part of the problem stemmed from Prince's revolving-door employment policy, and his decision to put people with little or no experience in charge of various key divisions of Paisley Park Enterprises. When the management team of Arnold Stiefel and Randy Phillips reached the end of their initial 12-month contract with Prince in late 1990, the singer opted not to renew it and instead named former bodyguard Gilbert Davison as the company's new president, promoting his PR Jill Willis to the position of vice-president.

In October 1994, with Paisley Park's finances spiraling out of control, Davison resigned. Prince brought in his half-brother and former head of security Duane Nelson as Davison's replacement, flanked by Julie Knapp-Winge and Therese Stoulil. Nelson was then left in charge of what have since been called arbitrary firings at the company. Rather than cutting back on his spending, Prince was keen to cut back on his staff. All wardrobe director Heidi Presnail was told was that she was "being fired on a cutback, and they were eliminating my position."[7]

Within two years Nelson, Stoulil, and Knapp-Winge were also gone, which meant that there had been more changes in the company during the past five years than there had been throughout the 80s. Even Levi Seacer Jr, the bassist who took over as head of Paisley Park Records after Alan Leeds resigned in 1992, had upped and left in November 1994 – along with his girlfriend, publicist Karen Lee – while Prince was safely out of the country at the European MTV Awards.

By 1996 what remained was a corporation without a head, and with nobody for Prince himself to answer to. Less and less information has come out of Paisley Park in the years since, making it difficult to determine the continuing state of Prince's financial situation. It does appear to have improved since he left Warners and struck out on his own, however: releasing albums himself to a dedicated fanbase has allowed him to sell fewer copies but make more from each one. Prince took a much larger cut of the profits from 1996's *Emancipation*, his first self-released album with large-scale distribution in the stores, than he would have done under his contract with Warners. When it came to the follow-up, the multi-disc *Crystal Ball* set, he even waited until he had received enough pre-orders to make the project commercially viable before pressing it up, thus ensuring that he would break even at the very least. In the years since, Prince has cut several deals with major labels, but only when it has suited him, signing one-off distribution deals with Arista for *Rave Un2 The Joy Fantastic*, Columbia for both *Musicology* and *Planet Earth*, and Universal for *3121*. Even then he has continued to pay for all of the production costs, leaving the promotional work to the label.

As the record industry changes and big-name stars look to sign so-called '360 degree' deals with live promoters – taking the focus away from album releases, which in turn become a mere adjunct to the tour – Prince appears once again to have been ahead of the game. He has certainly made a lot of money in recent years from lengthy live residencies such as the 3121 Jazz Cuisine at the Rio All-Suite Hotel in Las Vegas during 2006–07 and the 21 Nights In London run at the O$_2$ Arena in 2007, having perhaps realized that staying in one place for an extended period removes the expensive transport costs usually associated with touring. He has also taken to playing one-off events, including private parties, for vast sums. In December 2007, he reportedly earned $2 million for a set at the 40th birthday of Turnberry real-estate heir Jeffrey Soffer, while he is rumored to have made more than double that for an appearance at the 2008 Coachella festival.

Some might call him a sell-out, but Prince seems to need to do these things in order to maintain his spending, both on himself and his music. The success of the 21 Nights In London shows allowed him to give away copies of his then current album, *Planet Earth*, to all attendees (having already negotiated an innovative distribution deal with the *Mail On Sunday* newspaper), and to shoot an entire *21 Nights In London* photo book released in September 2008.

Similarly, the movie director Kevin Smith, who was involved in yet another unreleased Prince project in 2001, recalls speaking to a senior Paisley Park employee who told him: "I've produced 50 music videos. You've never seen them, 'cause they're for songs you've never heard. He puts them in The Vault. Fifty fully produced music videos with costumes and sets. Everything. That's just the way Prince is."[8]

Fortunately for Prince, he remains an incredible live performer, no matter how many times he plays the hits "for the last time." If he were relying on sales of new albums alone at this stage in his career he might well have ended up in the same sort of financial mess that rumor suggests Michael Jackson was in before his death. Instead, he remains in the position he spent the mid 90s fighting to be in: one that allows him to do what he wants, when he wants.

As 1994 rumbled to a close, however, Prince looked to be fighting a losing battle. A verbal agreement was reportedly made in September to release *The Gold Experience* before the year's end, but nothing had come of it. Prince's despair over the fate of his latest work was writ large when he told the British tabloids. "A lot of the guys [at Warners] who caused me problems have gone now, but I'm still waiting to see if things change," he said. "I still believe that *The Gold Experience* will never be released. They wouldn't even let me release a ballet I had written."[9] It was later alleged that Prince had withdrawn the album because Warners had told him that it would not count toward the four albums he still owed the company. His newest work, about which he felt most enthusiastic, remained in limbo; the older material that did make it out onto the shelves had failed to set the world alight. All he wanted to do now was make more records, but even that would prove difficult.

Having already turned down The New Power Generation's *Goldnigga* a year earlier, Warners passed on its follow-up, *Exodus*. Prince had started work on the album in May, shortly after being sent back to the studio to make *Come* more commercially appealing. Fully ignoring his contractual obligations to the label, he wrote and recorded all of the material on the album and released it on his own NPG Records on March 27 1995. (He also appears prominently throughout as both musician and singer, but used the pseudonym Tora Tora in the linernotes and covered his head with a scarf when making promotional appearances with the band in order to mask his identity.)

If *Goldnigga* was Prince voicing his dissatisfaction with Warners, *Exodus* is a long, meandering expression of his complete and utter disdain. For once it's the full-band performances that stand out; the solo pieces, by contrast, are conspicuously colder and less engaging. The album's most forward-thinking concept comes during the spoken word intro, in which it is announced that NPG Records is looking for new talent – with the proviso that any prospective musicians be "free" because, "when it comes to downloading your work into your fans' computers, you can't have any contractual obligations."

What follows is, for the most part, a densely produced mess. While it might have been paper-thin, *Goldnigga* did at least have a plotline. *Exodus* is just a series of jam-based funk ramblings and dull ballads held together by a series of loose, uninteresting segues, most of them featuring bassist Sonny T., who takes the place of Tony M. in pushing the stereotypically black angle.

Everything that happens within these 12 dramatic segments – including various seductions and childhood reminiscences, and the drinking of some spiked soup – turns out to have been a dream, although few listeners are likely to have cared either way by the time they got to the last of the album's 21 tracks.

Exodus does contain a couple of moments worth hearing. 'Get Wild' is a dense, funky number that stands as a triumph of Prince's busy, mid-90s production style, while his attempt at an Italian accent during the 'mashed potatoes' segue provides a genuinely (if unintentionally) funny moment. The rest is eminently forgettable. The album is dedicated to 'His Royal Badness,' in memory of 'Prince,' but it probably would have been more appropriate to dedicate it to his dearly departed sense of quality control.

Prince had also seemed to lose his sense of respectibility, and was now talking to Warners directly rather than leaving the job of negotiating with the company to the likes of Cavallo Ruffalo & Fargnoli. This led only to further frustrations between the two parties. Prince would go in shouting and arguing in the label executives' faces, demanding not just that he be allowed to release what he wanted, when he wanted, but that he be given full ownership of his entire back catalog. As Warners' Jeff Gold later noted, it's not unheard of for established artists to request such a deal, "but there's always some compensation for it. They'll take a lesser royalty, or they'll re-sign for less money than they ordinarily would." Prince, however, "wanted to have his cake and eat it, too."[10]

Things took a sharp turn for the worse when Prince started coming to meetings – and making public appearances – with 'SLAVE' written on his face in eyeliner. This served only to detract from whatever considered, salient points he might have been making about artists' rights and the inherent unfairness of recording contracts. More than anything, he was setting himself up for ridicule by the media, particularly when he decided to compare his adoption of O{+> to the decisions of Cassius Clay to become Muhammad Ali and Malcolm Little Malcolm X (thereby erasing the slave names given to their respective families). Why should I call myself Prince Nelson, he asked himself, if I don't know who 'Nell' was?

For many in the media (and elsewhere), this was a step too far. For a man who had boasted about signing a $100 million contract a few years earlier to compare his plight to that of African-Americans being forced to work as slaves was nothing less than an outrage. Prince might have been making a point during the early 90s of trying to identify more closely with his black roots, but this was something else. Watching from the sidelines, the departed Alan Leeds would conclude that Prince "has good points in his arguments and tons of sympathy from other artists, young and not so young, but … it seemed like he spent more energy in promoting his views and marketing concepts than creating the music itself."[11]

Prince tried at first to justify his stance. "People say I'm a crazy fool for writing 'SLAVE' on my face," he told *Rolling Stone* in 1996, "but if I can't do what I want to do, what am I? When you stop a man from dreaming, he becomes a slave. … If you don't own your [master tapes], your master owns you."[12] But it wasn't long before he realized that he was losing support in his crusade against Warner Bros, and started to backtrack. Within a few months he would be claiming only to have written on his face to remind the label "that I know what time it is,"[13] and that he "never meant to be compared to any slave in the past, or any slave in the future."[14] He went even further in a subsequent interview with the *St Paul Pioneer Press*, in which he explained that he did it "because I had become a slave to myself … I felt like I was in a box spiritually, not creatively."[15]

Also still in a box, however, was *The Gold Experience*. As 1995 began, Prince had taken to telling anyone willing to listen that his employers were holding back his "best album yet." He'd spent much of 1994 ignoring *Come*, which he completely refused to promote. When he did make a public appearance – either at Paisley Park or at his Glam Slam clubs – he would use it to showcase the unreleased *Gold Experience* material, or would give copies of its songs to DJs to play over the PA system. The battle showed no sign of slowing down. On February 20, Prince was named Best International Male at the BRIT Awards. "Prince? Best?" he began, in a speech that left many thinking he had totally lost the plot. "*Gold Experience* better. In concert, perfectly free. On record, slave. Get Wild. Come! Peace, thank you."

Things became a little clearer a month later when he launched the Ultimate Live Experience tour, on which he intended to play mostly new material, going back no further than *Batman*-era B-side 'I Love U In Me' and '7.' The 20-date tour stopped at various European cities during March 1995, but it was not the success Prince had envisioned. "This tour is crucial for him," UK promoter Chris Poole pointed out at the time. "He has a small cash-flow problem. He's not broke, but he's been spending his money on his music."[16]

Unfortunately for Prince, while he had previously been able to play a record-breaking 18-night stint at London's Wembley Arena, he was now struggling to sell tickets for four shows at the same venue. It got worse elsewhere: the Sheffield Arena was reportedly less than half full on the two evenings he played there. With touring being the main way for a musician to make money, this was not a good sign. (In a desperate attempt to raise more funds, fliers were handed out at each concert advertising that night's official after-show event in the hope that fans would be willing to pay for another live experience immediately after the first.)

Prince made no secret of the fact that he was planning to play a lot of new, previously unheard material from *The Gold Experience*. He even implored fans to bring their tape recorders – somewhat ironically, given his subsequent aggressive stance toward those who trade in live recordings – telling them that this would be their only chance to hear the music. Such a scenario was no doubt off-putting to those casual fans who had come to see Prince on his record-breaking Nude tour in 1990, and continued to queue up to hear him run through the hits in the years since.

The poor turnout affected the show itself, with Prince finding himself having to cut back the production costs for fear of ending up seriously out of pocket. When the Ultimate Live Experience opened at Wembley Arena, he emerged from the Endorphinmachine – an extravagant structure flanked by representations of male and female genitalia, which took its name from one of the *Gold Experience* songs – and traveled to the front of the stage on a conveyor belt. Because of the expense of transporting the hugely cumbersome set, however, he ended up leaving most of it, save the womb-like center, in London.

Even then the show was beset by technical problems that made the tour his most shambolic in a long time. After hiring and firing several sound engineers along the way, Prince had taken, by the end of the 20-date tour, to mixing the sound himself from within the Endorphinmachine's womb. If this was the only chance his fans would get to hear the *Gold Experience* songs, he wasn't exactly presenting them in their best light.

The tour continued sporadically back in America, with several shows at Paisley Park after it was opened up to the public on August 1. Then, after much wrangling with Warners, *The Gold Experience* was finally released on September 26 1995. Despite the fact that much of it was already two years old, the album was well worth the wait, and sounded fresher than anything Prince had recorded in years. Finally, for the first time since *Sign "O" The Times*, he seemed able to put together an album full of commercial hooks and a sense of adventure that wasn't bogged down by weighty concepts.

Aside from references to Prince being "muerto" and further suggestions of a growing interest in internet technology and interactive media, *The Gold Experience* is, more than anything else, a collection of mostly great songs. It covers little new thematic ground, but that barely matters when the songs are as good as 'P Control,' 'Endorphinmachine,' and of course 'The Most Beautiful Girl In The World.' Even when he tries out Shuggie Otis-like sunshine funk on 'Shy,' or lets fly with his anger toward *Minneapolis Star-Tribune* columnist Cheryl Johnson on 'Billy Jack Bitch,' the effect is much more powerful – and in the latter case, funnier – than *Come*'s lumpen funk or *Exodus*'s dreary diatribes against Warner Bros. All in all, Prince seemed to have rediscovered his muse, notably on 'Dolphin,' one of his most lyrical and inventive power ballads, and the anthemic closer 'Gold,' a kind of 'Purple Rain' for the 90s.

Commercially, however, *The Gold Experience* was a disappointment. After two decades in the music business, Prince seemed to have reached a point whereby hardcore fans would continue to buy whatever he released, but younger listeners were more interested in a new generation of stars. The album only just managed to sell 500,000 copies in America – partly, perhaps, because Prince had done most of his promotional work in support of it long before it was actually available to buy, and partly because everything he did seemed to be overshadowed by his battle with Warners – but did at least allow O{+> to beat Prince in the charts. (*The Gold Experience* reached Number Six, compared to *Come*'s Number 15.)

To those critics who had rolled their eyes at the Prince/O{+> shenanigans, *The Gold Experience* was evidence that all was not lost. According to the *St Paul Pioneer Press*, it "fully redeems O{+> as the ruler of his wildly imaginative, funky, sexy kingdom,"[17] while *Vibe* called it a "Prince experience par excellence" and "his best effort since the 90s almost happened without him."[18]

At least Prince still had enough of a fanbase to prove his worth to the critics, if not to his label. He also seemed to have done enough to retain the support of the black market he had gone to such lengths to chase during the early 90s. "Black people still call me Prince," he told Spike Lee in 1997. "Sometimes I ask them [why], and they say, 'Because you are a prince to us.'"[19] In other quarters, however, he seemed to be living on borrowed time. The name change, the public outbursts, and the 'SLAVE' incidents were simply too much for Warners.

Twenty years earlier, a young Warners employee, Russ Thyret, had sat on the floor talking about music with Prince and his manager of the time, Owen Husney, eager to convince the other two men that his was the right label for this bright young star in the making. By 1996, that same man had become the chairman of the Warners music division, but even he had had enough, and decided that the best thing for all concerned would be to officially end the two parties' 18-year union – a relationship that had generated an estimated $300 million.

"We've come to a point where we feel that if he's happier somewhere else, we don't have any beef with him," Warners vice-president Bob Merlis told the *Los Angeles Times*.[20] Noting that the company had been puzzled by – rather than angry about – the singer's behavior, Merlis confirmed the reasons behind the split: "He wanted to release more albums than his contract called for; he wanted a different contract, which ran contrary to good business practices. Eventually, we agreed that his vision and ours didn't coincide."[21]

On April 26 1996, Prince successfully amended his 1992 Warners contract with the help of a new lawyer, L. Londell McMillan (a replacement for Gary Stiffleman, who had helped broker the original '$100 million' contract). After *The Gold Experience* was finally released on a joint NPG Records/Warners imprint, Prince had still been required to deliver three more albums, but this was cut down to two sets of unreleased material – *Chaos And Disorder* and *The Vault ... Old Friends 4 Sale* – in return for a reduced royalty rate and an agreement not to publicly slander his former employers.

"I have decided to part company with Warners," Prince told *The Times* on July 6, "but surprisingly we're now on the most amicable terms we've been on for a long time."[22] His final appearance with 'SLAVE' written on his face came two days later, during a performance of 'Dinner With Delores' on *The David Letterman Show*. "I was bitter before," he explained a week later, "but now I've washed my face. I can just move on. I'm free."[23] (He did however continue to use the name O{+> until his publishing contract with Warner Chappell Music expired at the end of 1999.)

Shortly after helping Prince terminate his contract with Warners, L. Londell McMillan asked *Forbes* magazine: "Is this artist the kind of mercurial crazy some people say, or is he the wise one who understands where he fits at the start of a new century?"[24] Once the dust settled, it became clearer what Prince had actually been fighting for. He had never had a problem with anyone in particular at the label, he said, just the system they were governed by. "They don't even realize what they're saying," he explained in an interview with *USA Today*. "It's all habit now."[25] What Prince wanted was a new system in which artists owned their work, and were free to distribute it themselves. "In Mozart's time, word of mouth built an audience. People found him and heard him play. Then someone came along and said: 'We can sell this experience.' Right there, you got trouble."[26]

"I want to find out who the first person was who saw fit to sell music," he told the *St Paul Pioneer Press* in 1996.[27] Continuing on the same theme a year later, he told the Spanish newspaper *El País* that it would be "fantastic" if one day artists could achieve independence from their record labels. "But that is a very delicate question," he said, "because many artists are too weak and frightened to just go outside."[28]

A decade on, Prince has emerged as the pioneering champion of business practices such as these. "It was through Prince that I think I gained my own sense of what people say," Terence Trent d'Arby has said. "Forget what the record company says you must do to be successful. Do what the voice in your head tells you to do." In 2007, shortly before Radiohead released *In Rainbows* online without any input from a major label (allowing fans to pay whatever they saw fit for the record), Prince shook the industry again by becoming the first artist to give away his brand new album for free with a UK newspaper. Despite the embarrassment and humiliation he faced from the press at the time, his mid-90s battle with Warners can now be seen to have provoked a major rethink of the entire music industry.

"I gave [Warners] my music for years and they gave me a lot of golden albums," Prince concluded in 1997. "Look at what I do with them: I just hang them on a wall. They don't make me happy."[29] He didn't regret having a relationship with the company, and was smart enough to realize that he wouldn't have got where he was – particularly when it came to building Paisley Park – without any outside assistance; it was simply that, as he put it: "Contracts don't interest me any more."[30]

Neither again did bands, it seemed. While it's true that *The Gold Experience* is Prince's best album of the 90s by some distance, it's also something of a backhanded compliment to focus on it purely in those terms. The album proved, after a string of disappointments, that Prince still had some spark left. The question was: how much? After touring Japan in January 1996 with what was essentially a continuation of the Ultimate Live Experience, Prince sacked The New Power Generation, many of whom had been playing with him since 1991. Having officially announced his intention to terminate his contract with Warners in December 1995 it seemed that, just as had been the case when he let go of The Revolution almost a decade earlier, Prince now wanted to take back his music for himself in 1996. Seven months after striking the deal to free himself from Warners, Prince was ready to show the world what he could do with his freedom.

ABOVE: In 1980, Prince won a support slot for Rick James, but it wasn't long before he started to steal the headliner's thunder. **RIGHT**: The Triple Threat tour of 1982–83 was Prince's most extravagant yet.

ABOVE: According to keyboardist Lisa Coleman, the *Purple Rain* period marked "the pinnacle of the whole Prince & The Revolution experience." **RIGHT**: The *Parade*-era Hit N Run shows were Prince's last with The Revolution.

During the 1988 Lovesexy shows, Prince would
symbolically kill off an old persona each night before
performing his most religious material to date.

In 1991, *Diamonds And Pearls* revived the fortunes of Prince and his new band, The New Power Generation. "We were his first black band," singer Rosie Gaines (pictured, with Prince) recalled. "Our thing was to help him get his audience back."

OPPOSITE: Between the Act I and Act II tours of 1993, Prince changed his name to an unpronounceable symbol and announced his retirement from music.
ABOVE: With dancers Diamond and Pearl.
LEFT: On the Ultimate Live Experience Tour, during which he took to the stage with 'SLAVE' written on his face.

MAIN PICTURE: Prince with his first wife, Mayte, whom he married in 1996.
INSET: With Mayte at the opening of the NPG music store in Camden, London, April 1994.

ABOVE: In 1996, Prince released *Emancipation* on his own label to wide acclaim. **RIGHT**: By the start of the 21st century, Prince had converted to the Jehovah's Witness faith and turned his back on his more salacious past work.

At the time of his performance at the 2006 BRIT Awards,
Prince was riding high on the success of *3121*, his first
album ever to debut at Number One on *Billboard*.

EMANCIPATION

My music wants to do what it wants to do, and I just want to get out of its way. I want the biggest shelf in the record store, the most titles. I know they're not all going to sell, but I know somebody's going to buy at least one of each.

PRINCE

nyone still interested in Prince in 1996 would be forgiven for thinking that his first release of the year was simply another consolidation of former glories in the wake of *The Gold Experience*'s disappointing sales. *Girl 6* is another compilation album, but there is very little overlap with *The Hits/The B-Sides*, released three years earlier. Only 'Erotic City,' 'How Come U Don't Call Me Anymore,' and 'Pink Cashmere' appear on both. The rest of *Girl 6* is made up of recordings by Vanity 6, The New Power Generation, and The Family, alongside 'Girls & Boys,' three tracks from *Sign "O" The Times*, and three previously unreleased Prince recordings.

The album was compiled as a soundtrack to Spike Lee's movie of the same name, which tells the story of a phone-sex operator – all of which seemed surprising, given how protective Prince tends to be of his music. Similarly surprising was how pleased the singer was with how the project turned out. "The scene where you used 'How Come U Don't Call Me Anymore,' he told the director in 1997, "is my favorite scene. In fact it forced me to put that song back into our set. ... I used to think I couldn't do it better than I did with my band, The Revolution, but your film gave me a newfound respect for the music."[2]

While the old songs on *Girl 6* are pretty flawless, the three previously unreleased recordings don't exactly set the world alight. 'She Spoke 2 Me' and 'Don't Talk 2 Strangers' were recorded in the early 90s. The former passes by in a light, jazzy way, while the latter is a more moving piano ballad, sung in falsetto and originally intended for a mother to sing to her daughter in the movie *I'll Do Anything*. The third new song, 'Girl 6,' is credited to The New Power Generation, presumably because of its hip-hop influence, but Prince himself features prominently. It samples various old songs of his as well as snatches of dialogue from the movie, but contains no real hooks.

Those who did bother to review *Girl 6* were fairly positive about its mix of old and new. But despite being plastered with the words 'SONGS BY PRINCE,' the album still only reached Number 45 on *Billboard* and ultimately sold less than 100,000 copies.

Back at Paisley Park, Prince was giving more serious thought to what he considered his next proper album release, and how best to market his work without the backing of a major record label. Having left Warner Bros, the artist now known as O{+> was free to record and release as much music as he wanted. Setting up his own New Power Generation label to do just that, he became the first musician to seriously harness the power of the internet. In his efforts to remold the music business, however, he still struggled to make the kind of music that would send him back to the top of the charts.

Having broken his bond with his record label, Prince conversely strengthened his commitments at home. Mayte Garcia had become more and more of a rock for

Prince to cling to as his personal troubles grew during the early 90s. In 1995, he gave an interview to the UK TV show *The Sunday Show*, whispering his answers to Mayte, who in turn relayed them to the host. He began telling the press that she made it easier for him to talk to God, among other things, and wrote a series of ballads for her, the most notable being 'The Most Beautiful Girl In The World.' "Mayte grounds me," he told *Harper's Bazaar* in 1997. "She doesn't try to change me, but she makes me aware of certain things."[3] Prince even wrote a solo album, 1994's *Child Of The Sun*, for her, but as with Susannah Melvoin's record with The Family, it seemed to have been designed mostly as a means of keeping her close by in the studio.

Prince and Mayte were married on Valentine's Day 1996 in a small ceremony at Minneapolis's Park Avenue Methodist Church. Only Mayte's parents and sister attended from her side, while Prince invited his mother, stepfather, and Bernadette Anderson, but not his father. By then the couple were virtually inseparable, with Mayte pointing to a O{+> symbol hanging around her neck rather than speaking her husband's name to the priest. It wasn't long before they were expecting a baby.

Prince has always been reticent about discussing personal matters, but seemed to change his tune when it came to Mayte. He took great pleasure in pointing out the similarities between the two of them, such as that Mayte's mother's name was Nell, and that his surname was Nelson – or Nell's son. This, he decided, was proof that they were "made to be together," and that "all the ingredients were there to unite us."[4] He would even claim, in an interview with Oprah Winfrey, that it "felt like she was either my sister or we were the same person or something in another life. There's a closeness [that] you know is right and you don't argue with."[5]

Mayte's influence clearly changed Prince for the better. With his wife by his side, he began to see the world in a different light. "When I opened Paisley Park, I was so excited to have my own studio that I just started recording and didn't come out for 20 years," he told MSN Music Central in 1996. "After I got married I finally looked at the place."[6] (Mayte, he later told *Guitar World* magazine, had put him on "studio rehab."[7]) He seemed to surprise even himself with the revelation: "I haven't had a nightmare since I decided to get married. That's extraordinary!"[8]

Prince and Mayte's relationship might have looked like textbook married bliss to the outside world, but it wasn't quite as traditional as it seemed – perhaps unsurprisingly, given the age difference, and how easily the elder Prince would have been able to influence the younger Mayte. "I wasn't allowed to call him, ever," she later revealed. "Even when we were married; I had to wait for him to call me. I've no idea why, he never actually said."[9]

Outside pressure began to mount during the spring of 1996. Prince and his new wife were expecting their first child in the fall, and impending fatherhood threatened to change his life irreversibly. His terrible financial situation added to the strain, with the threat of bankruptcy looming large, and his battle with Warners due to reach its conclusion.

These stresses and strains came to a head on April 21. Prince had been suffering heart palpitations for the past few months, and had been taking painkillers in an effort to combat them. He had also recently become a strict vegetarian, and was perhaps lacking in nutrients when, that evening, he polished off a bottle of wine and suffered bouts of nausea before being rushed to Minneapolis's Fairview Southside Hospital. He had become notorious over the years both for not sleeping much and for drinking even less. Now it seemed his body had almost collapsed under the strain of a sudden combination of painkillers, alcohol, and a radical change in diet.

Three days after the scare, Prince finally came to an agreement to terminate his contract with Warners. He spent much of the next few months out of the public eye, his focus presumably on looking after himself and spending time with Mayte. (He also started rehearsals with a new line-up of The New Power Generation, retaining only Morris Hayes on keyboards, and hiring bassist Rhonda Smith, guitarists Kat Dyson and Mike Scott, and drummer Kirk Johnson.)

Following the April agreement, July saw Warners release the first of its two final Prince albums, *Chaos And Disorder*. According to Prince, the album was recorded in little over a week, with input from The New Power Generation and Rosie Gaines, and certainly sounds like it. "Someone told me Van Halen did their first record in a week," Prince seemed pleased to report. "That's what we were going for [with *Chaos And Disorder*]: spontaneity, seeing how fast and hard we could thrash it out."[10] The liner notes seem at pains to point out that the material was originally intended "4 private use only," and that it serves as "the last original material recorded by O{+> 4 Warner Bros." The cover artwork – which includes a footprint over a smashed record – carries much the same message: this relationship is over.

Chaos And Disorder's 11 tracks tend toward the most boring, straightforward rock Prince had yet recorded, his conflict with Warners seemingly having consumed him to the point where even his biggest fans might struggle. While he might have taken a certain perverse satisfaction from the fact that it sold less than 500,000 copies worldwide (thus generating very little in the way of profit for Warners), he was also putting the loyalty of his fanbase at risk by releasing something so lackluster. The lyrics to the closing track, 'Had U,' say it all. Having opened his debut album, *For You*, by stating that "all of this and more is for you," he now sang of how he had "hurt U," "disappoint[ed] U," and "fuck[ed] U."

As far as Prince was concerned, everything else paled in comparison to the battle he had won. But this in turn made it impossible to find any real excitement anywhere on *Chaos And Disorder*. 'Dig U Better Dead' might offer a fairly interesting take on the singer's label troubles (including such notes-to-self as "One minute you're hot / Tell the truth and you're not" and a paraphrasing of record label advice not to "dress 2 freaky and make their daughters stare") but it's spoilt by the music. Confirming the absence of fresh ideas was 'I Will,' its squealing, echo-laden finale sounding just like the end of *Sign "O" The Times*' 'I Could Never Take The Place Of Your Man.'

The only single to be drawn from the album was 'Dinner With Delores,' a dull, Prince-by-numbers tale of an encounter with a sexually forthright woman. Although he made a less-than-engaging promo video for the song and performed it, under duress, on *The Late Show With David Letterman*, the single was not released commercially in America, and stalled at Number 36 in the UK.

Incredibly, *Chaos And Disorder* was hailed by some reviewers as "a welcome return to basics" (*Billboard*)[11] and even "Prince's best effort since *Purple Rain*" (*Chicago Sun-Times*).[12] The *New Musical Express*, on the other hand, seemed to offer a more accurate appraisal, noting the thick layer of irony in 'I Rock Therefore I Am''s claim that "I sing the song / The best I can" before concluding that the album is "the sound of a man with too much time and too many names pouring his talent straight down the plughole."[13] It's hard to argue with that.

Prince's attention was, of course, focused on his forthcoming *Emancipation* album, his first 'proper' release since negotiating the split with Warners, and the one with which he aimed to show the world that he could do it all on his own. "All the stakes are higher," he told the *New York Times*, "but I'm in a situation where I can do anything I want."[14] And that's exactly what he did. With a nod perhaps to Warners' refusal to release the similarly sprawling *Crystal Ball* ten years earlier, he unveiled a three-disc set of 36 songs that ran to 180 minutes. With his triple-album dreams finally realised, Prince would mark the record's landmark importance as "the first time that I've recorded an album, a complete album, in a state of complete freedom."[15]

Prince also made clear his dedication to Mayte on 1996's *Emancipation*, a triple-album love-song to his wife and their unborn child. (Her pregnant stomach is pictured in the liner notes.) Shortly after the album's release, he claimed: "You can now hear that my soul has been in love with Mayte for thousands of years."[16]

Just as he was about to plow his efforts into promoting the album, however, another tragedy struck. In mid September, Mayte was rushed to hospital with sharp abdominal pains. She was seven months pregnant at the time, and feared that she was about to give birth prematurely. Although this wasn't the case, it was subsequently revealed by doctors that the couple's baby was likely to be born with physical abnormalities. The child was born on October 16 with Pfeiffer syndrome, a rare genetic defect that causes an unborn baby's cranial bones to fuse together prematurely, resulting in severe physical deformities. After a week of unsuccessful operations, Prince and Mayte took the heartbreaking decision to take their son off life support and let him pass away as peacefully as possible.

Although the fate of the child identified only as 'Boy Gregory' on his death certificate would soon become public, Prince began making cryptic comments about the baby's health in the media. "It's all good, never mind what you hear," he told Oprah Winfrey a few weeks after the baby had died.[17] A year later, he told Spike Lee: "I'm a firm believer in reincarnation for people who either have more work to do or have so much debt to pay back that they have to be here ... my work was finding Mayte and having a child, which we will continue on until there are several here."[18] Prince's denials drew a number of criticisms, but according to Mayte: "We believed he was going to come back, that souls come back. We didn't want to acknowledge he was gone. It was our way of grieving."[19]

It's impossible to know exactly what effect the tragedy had on Prince, but he seems to have responded to it by doing what he always does: throwing himself into his work. He had signed a pressing and distribution deal with EMI-Capitol for *Emancipation* a week before the baby's birth; now, three days after his death, he was playing a warm-up show with the NPG at Paisley Park. He then went on a quick promotional trip to Japan before he and Mayte filmed a perplexing promo video for the album's first single, a cover of The Stylistics' 'Betcha By Golly Wow!,' in which the couple act out a happy childbirth.

The video's theme was puzzling, but then it did come at a time during which Prince felt he had been through something of a spiritual rebirth. He certainly felt like a different person now that the Warners cloud no longer hung over his head. A year later he made a telling remark while describing a newly written song, 'Comeback,' to Spike Lee. "If you ever lose someone dear to you," he told Lee, "never say the words, 'They're gone,' and they'll come back."[20] Perhaps it was all as simple as that: avoid the pain, don't wallow in it.

Avoiding the pain was made more difficult, however, by the fact that his new album so enthusiastically proclaimed his love for Mayte and impending fatherhood. (The beat of one song, 'Sex In The Summer,' came from a recording of an Ultrasound scan of his unborn child's heartbeat.) With Prince at his most open and talkative in years, interviewers were inevitably going to take this opportunity to dig into his private life. This put him in the position whereby he had to talk about where the music came from, but didn't want to tell anybody about what he had just been through.

The result was a muddying of the waters. Prince would describe *Emancipation* as coming from a period of reflection on his life. "Having a child helps you do that," he told *Rolling Stone*, seemingly suggesting that his son was still alive. Then, in an interview with *USA Today*, he appeared to deny outright the suggestion that his son had died. "My skin is so thick now," he said. "I care much more about my child than what anyone says or writes."

With *Emancipation* set for release on November 19, Prince showed no sign of stepping off the promotional machine. As well as having the weight of his own private tragedy to deal with, he had also forced himself into a position where he had to prove, beyond any doubt, that releasing an album on his own was the right move, and that he was blazing a trail for future artists. "This is my debut," he told *USA Today*. "My name represents this body of work, not what came before."[21]

Such declarations were tempered by a hint of fear. "I ain't scared of nobody," he told *Rolling Stone*, although he seemed to be trying to convince himself as much as anyone else. "Tell me how many singles you hear," he continued. "I wanna read that."[22] Speaking to the *New York Times* around the same time, he seemed keen to preempt any suggestion that the album might be too sprawling. "I play a lot of styles," he explained. "This is not arrogance; this is the truth. ... Sometimes I just stand in awe of what I do myself. I feel like a regular person, but I listen to this and wonder, where did it come from?"[23] After a year of recording, Prince had amazed himself, telling the media that *Emancipation* was the best album of his career.

Fortunately, the majority of reviewers seemed to agree with him. The press response to *Emancipation* set out the stall for the way most of Prince's subsequent high-profile albums of solid yet safe music would be received. *USA Today* gave the album four out of four and called it "outstanding"; the *Detroit Free Press* declared it to be his best effort since *Sign "O" The Times*.[24] "By reviving a flair for songwriting long gone in modern R&B," the *New York Daily News* concluded, "while rendering his vocals more sober and his lyrics more thoughtful, one of pop's most maddening figures rewards our patience at last."[25]

At the heart of most of the reviews, it seemed, was a sense of relief that Prince had returned to making music to a formula that was relatively easy to understand, rather than putting together concept albums about things that were only fully defined in the singer's mind. By comparison to his previous album, *Chaos And Disorder*, it's hard not to see *Emancipation* as a bit of a masterpiece. It's also not inconceivable that the press genuinely wanted to see Prince do well now that he'd ended his long, drawn-out battle with Warners and stepped out on his own.

For Prince, *Emancipation* was "probably the most joyous [album] I've made. It's by far the most romantic because I've never been this much in love."[26] Ultimately, it can be viewed in much the same way as most of Prince's more popular, post-*Lovesexy* output. The songs are well written and the production is immaculate, but the overall package was never likely to set the world alight. In the context of mid-90s R&B it was certainly a success, but then R&B at the time was in a decidedly unhealthy state. That Prince wanted to make the album palatable to the mainstream listener is made clear by his inclusion, for the first time, of covers of other artists' songs alongside his own, including a version of Joan Osborne's 'One Of Us.'

The album is full of wonderfully inventive touches, particularly the way that Prince harmonizes with himself throughout. Thematically, it's also much clearer than a lot of his other work of the time. It's hard to listen to the run of songs at the end of the second disc – 'The Holy River,' 'Let's Have A Baby,' 'Savior,' 'The Plan,' and 'Friend, Lover, Sister, Mother/Wife' – without being overwhelmed both by Prince's apparent joy while recording them and a knowledge of what soon followed. Elsewhere, there are enough unusual moments to keep the listener engaged right through to the end, from 'Emale''s tale of sexual blackmail by email to 'In This Bed Eye Scream,' which is something of an apology to Wendy Melvoin and Lisa Coleman. (Prince contacted the pair at one point to ask them to work on the song with him, but ended up finishing it off on his own and dedicating it to them instead.)

Overall, *Emancipation* might be a little too polished, but it's certainly got more grit than the likes of *Diamonds And Pearls*. It didn't sell quite as well as Prince had hoped, but the pressing and distribution deal he had struck with EMI-Capitol made it a resounding success in business terms. The deal provided the model on which Prince would base all of his future arrangements, whenever he felt like working temporarily with a label that had more clout than his own NPG Records. He retains the copyright and master tapes, and receives a much larger royalty rate than he would under a normal contract. In return, Prince assumes all recording and promotional costs, while the label pays for manufacturing and distribution, charging a fee for each copy sold. Or as Prince later put it, labels are like "a florist – they just deliver the flowers."[27]

Under the terms of his old Warners deal, *Emancipation* would have needed to reach sales of 500,000 just for Prince to break even. Now however it was being reported that, having sold 450,000 copies, he was already $5 million in profit. If these figures are even close to the truth, the move away from Warners had proved to be very successful indeed, even if it was hampered somewhat by the shutting down of EMI-Capitol in April 1997.

After pushing *Emancipation* so strongly in the press, Prince's next job was to take it out on the road. On January 7 1997 he embarked on the 21-date Love 4 One Another Charities tour – his first full-scale US tour in four years, for which he gave some of the profits to good causes. Perhaps surprisingly, his set was made up largely of old 'Prince' songs, with only a handful of *Emancipation* tracks thrown in, suggesting that the singer had already put the album – and its difficult themes – behind him.

The tour was originally intended to be a small-scale warm-up for a full-scale trek around the world but that idea was scrapped following EMI-Capitol's demise. Instead Prince simply took a month off before starting again with a longer run of shows dubbed Jam Of The Year. The 65 US dates amounted to his longest American tour since the Purple Rain shows a decade earlier.

Just as *Emancipation* had inaugurated a new way of releasing and distributing albums, the Jam Of The Year shows provided a template for future tours. The

Prince team would book 15,000-seater venues just a few weeks in advance and then handle ticket sales and promotion itself. Once again, cutting out the middleman – and performing on a much less extravagant stage set – yielded greater financial benefits. It has since been estimated that Prince earned $30 million from the Jam Of The Year tour alone, and had completely turned his financial situation around by the time it came to a close in January 1998.

During the tour, however, the ghost of 'Boy Gregory' would not go away. Perhaps the most telling of Prince's promotional appearances – in a year which had arguably seen him at his most confessional before the press – was on *Muppets Tonight*. Season two of the spin-off from the long-running *Muppet Show* opened with a bang on September 13 1997 when it featured Prince (still calling himself O{+>) as a guest star. The culmination of a series of Prince-as-everyman television appearances, which had begun a year earlier with an incredibly open interview on *Oprah*, it was taped during a break from the Jam Of The Year tour, with the singer still ostensibly promoting *Emancipation* almost a year after its release.

He also seemed keen still to score points against Warners, a year after his departure from the label. At one point a ventriloquist's doll asks the singer if he would consider working with dummies, to which Prince replies: "I already have, but in my business they're called executives."[28]

For the most part he was there to have fun, however, and appeared to be a lot more relaxed with The Muppets than he tended to be when fulfilling press and media obligations with human beings. Cue gentle mockery of his new name (a security guard tells Prince he is "the bear currently known as unamused"); a group of Muppets dressed as Prince from different eras, singing 'Delirious'; the singer himself dressed as a country bumpkin, with an alligator disguised as a pet dog; and a re-recorded version of 'Starfish & Coffee' filmed as a black-and-white school days flashback, featuring a Muppets' take on the young Prince.

The show closed with 'She Gave Her Angels,' one of the many Prince songs of the time written for and inspired by Mayte. All in all, *Muppets Tonight* is one of the most bizarre television appearances Prince has ever made. It's also one of the few times in his career that he has seemed to let his guard down and make light of his own public persona.

But while Prince was on TV declaring his love for Mayte, she was barricaded in at Paisley Park. To make matters worse for Prince, who had thrown himself into his work when many would have argued that he should have stayed home with his wife, two former Paisley Park employees decided to make Prince and Mayte's personal heartbreak public by selling their story to the press. In doing so, they turned an unavoidable tragedy into a homicide case.

Erlene and Arlene Mojica were twins from Puerto Rico who had been employed as Mayte's nanny and bodyguard respectively. They were fired in December 1996, reportedly because of suggestions that they were planning to speak to the press about life behind the closed doors of the Prince estate. (Prince later claimed that they had signed confidentiality agreements, but the Mojicas have said that their signatures were forged.)

Shortly thereafter, and apparently in retaliation to their having been sacked, the sisters contacted a local Minneapolis journalist, Tom Gasparoli, and gave their side of the story. Among their claims was the groundless insinuation that Prince had not given the baby enough of a chance to live before taking him off life support. Having heard the sisters' testimony, Gasparoli told them to go public with their claims. "I don't know if it's a crime," he told the Minneapolis radio station KSTP, "but it sure didn't sound right to me."[29]

On March 9 1997, Britain's *News Of The World* ran a story entitled 'Bizarre Truth Behind Death Of Star's Baby.' The article was based on a number of the Mojicas' claims, including one that Prince refused to allow Mayte to eat any meat during her pregnancy (and that the sisters had to sneak her out to a nearby TGI Friday's so that she could); that he wouldn't let her have an Ultrasound scan during her first trimester; and that he prevented doctors from giving her magnesium in order to avoid a miscarriage when she first started having contractions.

Thanks to Gasparoli, who shared the Mojicas' claims with any media outlet that would listen, the noise became so loud that local homicide detectives in Minneapolis were forced to become involved. Thankfully, it didn't take long for them to decide that what had occured was the result of "a natural death. We don't plan to investigate. There's no case here."[30] The verdict was made official in June, and the Mojicas were taken to court. They haven't spoken publicly about the affair since, but their 'revelations' clearly put further strain on Prince and Mayte's relationship.

"Some couples are brought together after the loss of a child," Mayte later noted. "Others are driven apart. In our case the latter happened."[31] Their split was complicated and drawn out, but appears not to have been bitter. With Prince on tour for so much of 1996–97, it's entirely possible that he and Mayte simply grew apart at a time when they should have been working on making their relationship stronger.

The situation was further complicated by reports that Mayte had become involved with the Spanish dancer Joaquín Cortés, shortly after Prince bought her a mansion in Marbella. (The lyrics to *Rave Un2 The Joy Fantastic*'s 'I Love U But I Don't Trust U Anymore' appear to support these theories.) Meanwhile, Prince himself is alleged to have started dating his second wife, Manuela Testolini, as early as 1998.

A further strain was placed on the marriage when Prince became a Jehovah's Witness. He had been introduced to the faith, while at a rather low ebb, by Larry Graham, the former Sly & The Family Stone bassist, at the after-show party following the Nashville date of the Jam Of The Year tour during the early hours of

August 22 1997. Prince's new religious beliefs seemed to replace Mayte as the guiding force in his life. He told *Paper* magazine that marriage contracts originated from Pontius Pilate's consensus to crucify Jesus, before explaining to the *New York Times* that he and Mayte had renounced their marriage vows after "read[ing] them over" and deciding that "there were a lot of things in there we didn't like."[32]

A little while later he told the *Minneapolis Star-Tribune* that he and Mayte had "decided to do this whole thing together" for the benefit of their "spiritual wellbeing."[33] He subsequently sent the newspaper a follow-up letter spelling out his distaste for "CONtracts" and reasserting various views that he felt had not been given adequate space in the original article. "These days Mayte and O{+> refer to each other as 'mate' or 'counterpart,' not husband and wife," he wrote, before explaining that the couple planned to renew their marriage with new vows that better suited them.[34] (This never happened.)

Several years after splitting up with Prince, Mayte made a number of illuminating comments about him in an interview with the online magazine *Fiya*. "Now I know other men," she said, "I can see how in tune [Prince] is with women. It's the way he notices every detail about you ... and when he looks at you he makes you feel like you're the center of the universe. That's very beguiling."[35] Lamenting the fact that their marriage was allowed simply to fade away, she conceded: "I hate the fact I'm divorced. I'm now very wary of ever getting married again, because I believe marriage should be for life." Noting that Prince himself had since remarried, she added: "He's getting a divorce now."[36]

As his private life crumbled, Prince – who had been so close to bankruptcy just a few years before – did at least have a financial turnaround to celebrate. As 1998 dawned, however, he found himself struggling once again to produce a worthy follow-up to his recent critical and financial success. He might have taken control of his business situation, but he was also on the verge of slipping slowly but surely from musical prominence.

CHAPTER 14

U EVER HAD A CRYSTAL BALL?

This is a poet, a Renaissance man, an iconoclast. This is someone who is bringing the state of music further along. I don't want to get involved in whether this is hype or not – this man is at the top of his form.

CLIVE DAVIS

With Prince having boasted of his newfound freedom to release as much new music as he wanted, it was perhaps slightly curious that he didn't release any new material at all in 1997. Without Warner Bros to push him, it seems that Prince himself had finally realised that, in order to maximise profits from a new record, he needed to give it time to sell – and to tour properly in order to promote it. Although sales of *Emancipation* were lower than expected, Prince had few overheads to settle, while his 1996–97 Jam Of The Year kept the money rolling in.

It almost seemed as though, in the wake of his son's tragic death, and with the financial successes of his latest album and tour, Prince had all but forgotten about actually recording new music. His recent albums might not have pushed the musical envelope in the same way as had his 80s output, but he was still plugging away at reinventing the music business itself. Following the fallout of his battle with Warners, it took quite a few years for the dust to settle and everyone else to catch up, but Prince was one of the very few people on the planet then trying to harness the potential of the internet. "Once the internet is a reality the music business is finished," he told the *New Musical Express* in 1995. "There won't be any need for record companies. If I can send you my music direct, what's the point of having a music business?"[2]

All of this might have been news to the world at large, but not to Prince. "As early as 1989 he was envisioning a cyber world," Alan Leeds told housequake.com in 2007. "I know because he told me so, teasing me – and everyone else on his payroll – for not completely co-signing his vision."[3]

It wasn't until 1997 that Prince found himself in a position where he could advertise his next release, *Crystal Ball*, over the internet, checking online orders to gauge how many fans were interested in the record before he started manufacturing it. As he explained to *Guitar World* a year later, he was just "testing the water to see if people would buy music over the internet … since the album was a success, it leads me to believe that the whole interactive thing offers great possibilities."[4]

Prince's testing of the waters was also a landmark event for the music business as a whole. *Crystal Ball* was the first full album to be released online by any artist on the planet – and he did it all without anyone else's help. By then he had already opened and closed at least one website, thedawn.com, and would continue to set up others throughout the late 90s, including love4oneanother.com, which offered individual tracks for download on occasion; the mail-order site 1800newfunk.com; and npgonlineltd.com (which later became the celebrated npgmusicclub.com).

In May 1997, Prince started taking pre-orders for the multi-disc set via love4oneanother.com, and his 1-800-NEW-FUNK hotline. *Crystal Ball* was set to include three discs of archival material and a fourth disc of new songs, *The Truth*.

Prince was footing the bill for the production of the set himself, so decided not to start manufacturing it until he received a certain number of pre-orders (somewhere between 50,000 and 100,000). Whatever the figure, it didn't take long to reach it. With the promise of unreleased material cherry-picked from The Vault, demand among hardcore fans was high.

Crystal Ball was originally due to be sent out in June, but that proved to be a somewhat optimistic goal. Lacking the kind of manufacturing and distribution setup available to proper record labels, Prince's organization was overwhelmed from the start and couldn't keep up with demand. The first copies of the set were not sent out until January 29 1998, and even then there were problems with the mail-order system, resulting in some fans receiving more than one copy while others didn't get theirs for months. As if to add insult to injury, *Crystal Ball* was then made available through conventional channels in March – and with a full-color booklet that wasn't included with pre-ordered copies. (Prince encouraged his fans to download the artwork from his website instead, as he would later do with *Planet Earth* in 2007.)

The disastrous distribution served only to fuel fans' loss of faith in Prince as the 90s progressed, but that wasn't the only disappointment. *Crystal Ball* was supposed to come in a spherical clear-plastic case, but when it finally saw the light of day it arrived in a flat, circular dish. The musical content, meanwhile, seemed hardly to represent the promised explosion of choice recordings from The Vault. Most of the unreleased songs from *Dream Factory* are present, but had been overdubbed since the original 1986 sessions. The oldest track on the collection, 1983's 'Cloreen Baconskin,' might have offered the tantalizing prospect of a vintage collaboration with Morris Day, but is actually just an aimless 15-minute jam. And for every enjoyable mid-90s rarity, such as 'She Gave Her Angels' or the *Gold Experience* out-take 'Interactive,' there are dire remixes of *Come* and *Love Symbol* material. "As usual the music is funky and fun," the *Minneapolis Star-Tribune* concluded, "but most of it is for fanatics only."[5]

The best part of the set was *The Truth*, an album of new material, most of it solo, acoustic, and embellished with only the lightest of overdubs. The performances are more intimate than anything Prince had recorded in years, while the songs pick up where *Emancipation* left off, continuing to trace the singer's life as a mature artist. The blues-based 'Don't Play Me' alone makes the whole set worth owning for the way it demonstrates Prince's ability to assert himself without resorting to the bluster of *Chaos And Disorder*.

The *New Musical Express* described *The Truth* as a "minor revelation [that] sounds like nothing Prince, Squiggle, or The Artist has ever recorded."[6] It's a shame then that pre-ordered copies of *Crystal Ball* followed it with a fifth disc tacked on in an attempt to appease those fans who felt they had wasted time and money on it. Prince wrote *Kamasutra* for his wedding to Mayte, and credits it here to The NPG Orchestra. The overall effect, however, is something that would better suit a new-age mail-order TV channel than a marriage ceremony, and suggests that Prince had little idea about the workings of classical music.

Despite *Crystal Ball*'s failings in terms of both content and delivery, Prince had established a business plan that would see him reap more success – in financial terms at least – than he ever did with Warners. But then, having established his O{+> brand as an unbridled commercial success, he decided to credit his second new album of 1998 to The New Power Generation. His reasons for returning to the name, for the first time since 1995's *Exodus*, are unclear, since he no longer had to hide behind it to avoid the wrath of Warners. It's worth noting, however, that at the time of *Newpower Soul*'s release, the concept of the NPG had expanded to include a record label (replacing Paisley Park Records) and an Orchestra. It would later also incorporate npgmusicclub.com, Prince's successful online website, fan club, and download store. Perhaps he wanted simply to remind people of the brand.

As a band, The New Power Generation has mirrored George Clinton's P-Funk crew in its revolving-door membership policy. There have been more than 35 official members over the years (not including dancers and guest players), among them Rosie Gaines, Maceo Parker, and esteemed musicians such as Rhonda Smith, John Blackwell, and Renato Neto. Prince has continued to credit the group on his albums, right up *3121* (2006) and *Planet Earth* (2007). Whatever the line-up, his goal seems to be to surround himself with the best musicians he can find at any given time. "I love this band," he told *Vibe* magazine in 1994.[7] (A few years later, he told AOL that the *Newpower Soul*-era musicians "stomp much booty."[8])

Letting the group change and evolve over time – almost of its own accord – seems always to have been particularly important to him. "I have been blessed with having these people come to me," he told Spike Lee in 1997.[9] Seven years later, he seemed keen to explain that using new musicians is "one of the ways we keep it fresh. ... I like to find new young kids that have something that they can bring to the sound."[10]

Unfortunately, however, the band brought nothing fresh to *Newpower Soul*. Perhaps Prince credited the record to the NPG simply because he had finally come around to the idea that flooding the market with too many Prince/O{+> albums might be unwise; or perhaps he realized that it wasn't very good, and didn't want to highlight it as a bona fide solo record. If the latter is true, it doesn't really fit with the fact that *Newpower Soul* is the NPG album on which Prince features most prominently (he even put himself on the cover). If he thought he was revealing a great secret in doing so, however (having previously made an attempt to cover up his input), he was mistaken.

Released on June 30, *Newpower Soul* performed more strongly than *Chaos*

And Disorder, suggesting that Prince fans were more willing to indulge his funk missteps than his rock follies, despite the fact that it's one of the worst and least interesting albums of his career. Prince spends most of the record plundering George Clinton – until he gets to 'Push It Up,' which cannibalizes his own 'Jam Of The Year.' The UK single 'Come On' is the best of a bad bunch of aimless funk songs; only 'Mad Sex' and the hidden track 'Wasted Kisses' – a particularly dark tale sung from the perspective of a man who has just killed his lover – offer anything different. The rest of the album is made up of the sort of lukewarm funk everybody knew Prince to be capable of making, but hardly anybody wanted to hear.

Prince put a fair amount of effort into promoting *Newpower Soul* live and on television, but most of the interviews he gave were focused not on the music but on his assertion that he had made the right decision to go out on his own. "I think I'm better suited to market my own music," he told Tavis Smiley on *BET Tonight*. "I am in a position now with New Power Generation Records that I can take the music and repackage it. ... I was never allowed this before. You're talking about a lucrative sum of money, and I've made a lot of money since I left Time-Warner."[11]

More interesting than *Newpower Soul* itself was the series of short tours Prince undertook in support of the album in the USA and Europe, giving fans another chance to see stripped-down performances of the hits, this time without second guitarist Kat Dyson but with the addition of backing singer Marva King. In a decade full of low points, however, *Newpower Soul* stands as Prince's lowest.

Helping to keep his 1998 live shows interesting were regular guest appearances by Larry Graham and Chaka Khan, funk veterans who both had NPG Records albums of their own to promote. With the financial success of his own releases, it seemed that Prince had once again decided that he could run a successful roster of artists after all.

As a member of Sly & The Family Stone during the late 60s and early 70s, Larry Graham pioneered the 'slap bass' technique and is widely considered to be one of the best bassists of the rock era. He met Prince in August 1997, at an after-show party at the Music City Mix Factory in Nashville, Tennessee, and the two men quickly became inseparable. It wasn't long before Graham had become Prince's foremost spiritual guide – or before Prince had offered to produce an album for his new mentor in much the same way as he had in the past for romantic muses such as Susannah Melvoin and Mayte.

Prince started work on the album shortly thereafter, at the same time as recording his own *Newpower Soul*. *GCS2000* would be Graham's first album since 1985 – and the first to be released under the name Graham Central Station since 1979 – and was scheduled for release in early 1999. By then Prince had also recorded and released *Come 2 My House* by Chaka Khan, famed for her role in the late 70s disco band Rufus and her 1984 cover of Prince's 'I Feel For You.'

The making of these two albums echoed the time at the start of the decade when Prince had attempted to resuscitate the careers of Mavis Staples and George Clinton. Instead of letting Graham and Khan shape their own musical identities, he tried to remold them in his image, giving *GSC2000* and *Come 2 My House* the same sound as his own *Newpower Soul*. He was also throwing his weight behind two artists well past their prime – just as had been the case with Staples and Clinton. While there might have been some interest in seeing Graham or Khan live, younger audiences were unlikely to want to listen to new records given an artificial contemporary sheen by either artist.

Prince took Graham and Khan out with him for the press tour in support of *Newpower Soul* but did little to promote either act's new album beyond having them sit beside him while he praised their work. He seemed more interested in pushing the NPG label and its ethos. "I have no contract with Larry," he told *Good Morning America*. "We have a joke, you know, he says to me: 'Contract? Let's see, what would we put on it?' The prefix of contract is 'con.' I'm not trying to con him. I trust him and he trusts me."[12]

The situation was much the same, it seemed, with Khan. "Chaka is another artist who was temporarily choked by restrictions, contracts, and bad business deals," Prince told *Guitar World* around the same time. "She's free now. ... One of the pleasures of my life is being able to work with some of my musical heroes, and in doing so pay back some dues and have a great time."[13]

It wasn't long before Prince realized that he didn't have the resources to run a label in the way he had previously, when Warners was bankrolling his Paisley Park imprint. Tellingly, his comments in the media began to take the form of pleas to bigger fish in the music industry to pick up Khan and Graham's albums for distribution. In doing so he seemed to distance himself from the responsibility of having let them down with NPG Records' failings. "I don't want to see [Khan] get lost," he told Tavis Smiley on *BET Tonight*. "I challenge the radio stations, I challenge the record stores, to take care of her."[14] After praising Best Buy, Blockbuster, and HMV for being "really cool with us" for stocking the record, he noted how so many contemporary artists – "the Lauryn Hills and the Erykah Badus" – have "much love for her." Larry Graham, he continued, "is Michael Jordan on the bass. Open and shut book. Now how do you not stock that if you love music?"[15]

What the poor uptake of *Come 2 My House* and *GSC2000* proved, however, was that record retailers also loved money, and tended to avoid stocking records that were unlikely to generate a profit. At a time when Prince's own albums weren't selling too well, his side projects were even less successful. It's no coincidence, then, that Khan and Graham's comeback LPs were the last non-Prince albums to be released on NPG Records until 2009's *Elixer* by Bria Valente – suggesting that

Prince has since realized that to become a major player he needs major-label backing, but that he had frittered away just such an opportunity in the early 90s with a series of half-baked projects that were never going to sell.

The major label that still owned all of Prince's old music was, however, gearing itself up for another success at the expense of its former charge's creative losses. With the new millennium fast approaching, it came as no surprise that '1999' began to play on the minds of Prince, his fans, and even casual listeners who had heard the singer's breakthrough hit at some point since its release in 1983. Warner Bros would have been only too aware of the commercial potential of so timely a song, but when the label decided to reissue it as a single in December 1998, Prince was enraged.

As far as Prince was concerned, the dissolution of his contract with Warners meant that only he should be able to make money off new releases bearing his name. But since Warners owned the '1999' master tapes, the label could release the song whenever it wanted (and indeed would do so again the following December). In retaliation, Prince decided to re-record and overdub the original '1999' for a new release on his own NPG label, the *1999: The New Master* EP.

"Once Warner Bros refused to sell me my masters, I was faced with a problem," he told *USA Today* shortly after the EP's release. "But 'pro' is the prefix of 'problem,' so I decided to do something about it."[16] What he seemed to have decided to do, however, was damage the legacy of the original, replacing a lean blast of future-funk with an overproduced mess that made misguided concessions to dance and hip-hop. Ironically, the new additions – DJ scratches, sampled Rosie Gaines vocals, a rap by Doug E Fresh, and a Latin breakdown that probably would have worked much better live than on record – made the 'new master' sound more dated than the original.

The remaining six tracks on the EP comprise a series of tired variations on the same theme, including an 'Inevitable Mix' that replaces Lisa Coleman and Dez Dickerson's original vocals with the less fitting voices of Larry Graham and Rosie Gaines. The EP's most interesting moment is a poem read by actress Rosario Dawson over the instrumental intro of 'Little Red Corvette,' an anti-Christmas rant drawing on the Jehovah scriptures that says much about Prince's mindset at the time.

Perhaps the most notable aspect of the release was the fact that singer broke his 'Prince' boycott and credited it, somewhat cynically, to Prince & The Revolution. But not even that was enough to encourage his fans to buy it when it was released on February 2 1999. *The New Master* EP only reached Number 150 on the *Billboard* pop albums chart, and Number 58 on the R&B albums chart. By contrast, Warners' reissues of the original single in 1998 and 1999 made it to Number 40 and Number 56 on the Hot 100 respectively.

For a while Prince threatened to tackle the rest of his back catalog in the same way, telling *Paper* magazine that, since Warners wouldn't give him back the original masters, he planned "to re-record them. All of them." This, he claimed, would result in "two catalogs with pretty much the same music – except mine will be better – and you can either give your money to WB, the big company, or to NPG. You choose."[17] On the evidence of *1999: The New Master*, it's just as well he didn't bother. There would have been plenty of disappointment on both sides.

Warners' success with its reissue of '1999' would have further reminded Prince of the limitations he faced when it came to getting his new releases on the shelves. With *Newpower Soul* failing to set the charts alight, and the same fate befalling NPG Records releases by Chaka Khan and Larry Graham, he must have started to wonder whether he would ever have any major commercial clout again. After Warners' first reissue of the single, the year that titles this major breakthrough hit was fast approaching, and the song itself looked likely to overshadow almost everything he had done during the 90s.

Asked by *BET Tonight* host Tavis Smiley about the ominous approach of the year 1999, Prince said: "If the sky has blood in it, blue and red make purple."[18] He gave a slightly less cryptic response during a similar discussion with *Details*. "I have nothing against the music industry," he said, "I just wanted to be free of it to explore all options for releasing my music. And I'll tell you this – I'll work with the music industry again, probably to release my next album."[19]

Aside from his torrid 'new master' of '1999,' Prince's only other act of note had been to lash out with lawsuits against fan magazines and websites that he claimed were cashing in on his copyrights. Just as the man himself was beginning to cultivate his presence on the internet, some of his more forward-thinking fans started setting up their own Prince websites. In February 1999, however, Prince started filing lawsuits against fan-run magazines and sites, claiming they were making money from bootlegging his music, creating unfair competition with his own activities, and, most ridiculously, breaching copyright laws by using the symbol he had changed his name to.

Most of the sites buckled under the pressure, but a few managed to stick around. The most notable of these was the print fanzine *Uptown*, which defended its right to continue in court with the help of lawyer and future Prince biographer Alex Hahn. The two parties eventually agreed an out of court settlement that allowed *Uptown* to stay in business provided it refrained from discussing bootlegged albums (individual songs were fine), stopped using the 'love symbol' glyph, and added a disclaimer stating that it was not an official Prince product.

Even so, most onlookers were bemused. The most forward-thinking man in music was now suing his own fans. "From a public relations standpoint," Alan Leeds told prince.org, "the situation was badly bungled."[20] Further criticism came in from David Bowie, who had launched his own BowieNet portal a few years earlier and was making similar strides in harnessing the power of the internet. "To understand your presence on the net you have to be a part of it and work within it," he told *Shift* magazine. "I thought it looked so reactionary, for instance, of someone like Prince to clamp down on everything in terms of the lawsuits. You can't stop the sea from coming forward."[21]

As would prove to be the case in the future, when Prince waged wars with fan websites, the lawsuits were an attempt to silence unofficial sources of Prince information at a time when he had some big news of his own to announce. In April 1999 he began making tentative contact with various major labels with the help of L. Londell McMillan, the lawyer who had negotiated the deal to extract the singer from his Warner Bros contract. Most of the meetings went badly. Prince found himself making the same complaints as before: that the labels wanted him to record identikit 'Prince' music, and stood to make much more out of it than he would himself. He seemed to have stepped right back into his mid-90s mindset in an interview with *Paper*, in which he compared the modern music industry to the movie *The Matrix*. "All the levels keep dissolving until you can't see what's behind anything," he said. "I'm not against the record industry. Their system is perfect. It benefits the people who it was designed to benefit: the owners."[22]

Fortunately for Prince, one of the men he met with was Clive Davis at Arista. Davis was and is a legend in the music business, having signed Janis Joplin, Billy Joel, and Bruce Springsteen while at Columbia during 1967–72, before founding his own label, Arista, and putting together one of the most varied rosters in the business. By 1999 the label had been purchased by the Bertelsmann Music Group; Davis himself was gearing up for the release of Carlos Santana's *Supernatural*, a star-studded collaborative album that would eventually sell more than 25 million copies worldwide. Davis was the man with the midas touch, and was ready to put his powers to work on lifting another fallen star out of the doldrums and back onto primetime radio.

A deal was struck in May, shortly after Davis listened to what Prince had recorded so far. In return for agreeing to work with a major label for the first time in three years, Prince was given an $11 million advance and a one-album deal that allowed him to keep his master tapes. All he had to do now was complete the album, which Arista would then use its own resources to promote and distribute, leaving Prince free to go his own way if he wasn't happy with the results. "People are looking for drama," he told the *Minneapolis Star-Tribune*. "[The deal is] for one album. There could be a second. The contract is [only] this thick," he added, holding his thumb and forefinger slightly apart in front of the reporter.[23]

Prince went to tell USA Today that the new deal was "like going back to school and knowing that you don't have to stay."[24] There was nonetheless some surprise in the media that the man who had declared himself a slave to the industry three years earlier could even consider returning to a major label. Prince justified his decision by praising Davis, making it clear that he felt a bond with the man, not the company. "People say to me: 'Congratulations on your new deal,'" he shrugged, "but they ought to find the president of the record company and congratulate him!"[25]

Explaining how comfortable he felt with Arista and Davis, Prince seemed to have forgotten the personal support he'd received in the early days. "When I was at Warner Bros I always heard from a third party," he told the *Minneapolis Star-Tribune*. "Record companies want to own [our] creations, but no one owns the creations but the creator. ... Clive agrees you should own your masters. He also told me, 'I have free will, too.'"[26]

For his part, Davis went around telling journalists what a genius Prince was, making it clear that this was a comeback of the highest order. (The singer himself challenged journalists who used the 'c' word, asking: "Comeback from what?") In an attempt to spoil the fun, however, Warners decided to release the last Prince album it was owed as part of the deal to terminate the singer's contract. The label had been sitting on *The Vault ... Old Friends 4 Sale* since putting out *Chaos And Disorder* in 1996, but finally chose to release it in August 1999, three months after Prince signed his new deal with Arista. That Warners credited *The Vault* to Prince – rather than O{+> – only heightened the snub.

Like *Chaos And Disorder*, *The Vault* came with a number of reminders that it was not necessarily something that Prince wanted released, from the "originally intended 4 private use only" disclaimer to the lack of detailed information in the liner notes (particularly by comparison to NPG Records' *Crystal Ball*). The prospect of more unreleased material from The Vault was enough to send the album to Number 85 in the USA and Number 47 in the UK, but most of those fans who bought it were left disappointed. As far as the *New Musical Express* was concerned, *The Vault* had been "cobbled together to cash in on a dwindling hardcore rump of completist fans."[27]

Perhaps the biggest fault to be found with *The Vault* is the fact that it contains material that had previously been available on bootlegs and that might now be of superior sound quality but was far less impressive from a musical standpoint. 'Old Friends 4 Sale,' for example, was written in the immediate aftermath of Chick Huntsberry's story about the singer appearing in the *National Enquirer*, and could potentially have resulted in one of Prince's most brutally honest recordings. The *Vault* version was recorded in the early 90s, however, and any meaning to be found in the lyrics is crushed under the weight of schmaltzy over-production.

The Vault might be marginally more enjoyable than *Chaos And Disorder*, but many of the songs included on it are either unfinished or simply aimless. Three tracks come from the aborted soundtrack to *I'll Do Anything*, of which 'There Is

Lonely' is an interesting ballad without a conclusion and 'My Little Pill' an odd spoken-word piece that doesn't make much sense outside of its original context. Much of the rest of the material is jazz-orientated, but it's often so vague and bland that it passes by unnoticed. The album's musical value is summed up by 'Extraordinary,' which is anything but. It sounds instead as if Prince entered the title into a songwriting machine, pressed the 'falsetto ballad' button, and put the results onto disc without even listening to them.

One or two tracks do make for pleasant listening, among them 'Old Friends 4 Sale' and '5 Women+.' But if *The Vault* was designed to offer tantalizing evidence of the vast collection of unreleased excellence that Prince has everyone believe exists, it failed miserably. Many fans would have been thinking the same as the *Guardian* newspaper, which asked: "What became of the talent formerly known as Prince?"[28]

Undeterred by Warners' release of *The Vault*, Prince pushed his new album, *Rave Un2 The Joy Fantastic*, harder than any since *Emancipation*, with an aggressive promotional campaign starting in September. With *Rave* featuring guest appearances by the legendary saxophonist and former James Brown sideman Maceo Parker, Public Enemy's Chuck D, Ani DiFranco, and Gwen Stefani, comparisons to Santana's *Supernatural* were obvious, with all eyes on Davis's power to mastermind another smash-hit.

Prince, of course, tried to play down the comparison. "I knew nothing about [Davis]," he told the *New York Times*, somewhat dubiously, "but he knows me. We agreed that this album is full of hits. It was just a question of whether or not we could agree on how it should be put out."[29] As with *Emancipation*, Prince seemed rather too eager to prove his continuing relevance. "Tell me that's not a hit,"[30] he almost begged Anthony DeCurtis of the *New York Times* after playing him the album's first single, 'The Greatest Romance Ever Sold.'

Interest in the album grew when it was announced that, for the first time ever, a guest producer would be brought in on *Rave*, only for the excitement to die down when the man in question was revealed to be 'Prince' (the album itself is credited to O{+>). Despite 'O{+>"s assertion that 'Prince' had always been his best editor, many observers began to suspect that they would be getting another lackluster album in the *Newpower Soul* vein.

The identity of the 'guest' producer wasn't the only link back to Prince's heyday. The title came from a track he had shelved in 1988 because it "sounded so much like 'Kiss' that I wanted to put it in The Vault and let it marinade for a while."[31] He also returned to using the Linn LM-1 drum machine for the first time in years. But none of this would be enough to make *Rave* a hit. Prince had been on the promotional trail for almost a month when 'The Greatest Romance Ever Sold' was released on October 5, but the single still failed to make a major impression. Part of the problem was that, after the success of 'The Most Beautiful Girl In The

World,' he believed ballads were his best route into the charts. While Santana's Latin rock had lain dormant for long enough that it felt almost like a 'new' sound, 'The Greatest Romance' was just another Prince ballad.

When *Rave* itself was released on November 9, the most reviewers could agree on was that it was the sound of Prince at his most unashamedly commercial, which is true: it's undoubtedly his most chart-orientated album since *Diamonds And Pearls*. But while *Diamonds* did its best to capture the zeitgeist of early-90s R&B, *Rave* seemed to lag far behind the sound of contemporary producers such as The Neptunes and Timbaland, who had created a jittery hip-hop-funk hybrid for the new millennium. As far as the *New Musical Express* was concerned, *Rave* suggested that Prince had been "killed at the turn of the decade, and his record company have kept the incident a secret, releasing off-cuts from his previous sessions as new albums."[32] *Entertainment Weekly* was kinder, noting that "when he's on, almost anything – even that nasty messiah complex – seems 4giveable," but still describing his cover of Sheryl Crow's 'Every Day Is A Winding Road' as a "borderline travesty."[33]

Rave has its moments – notably 'I Love U But I Don't Trust U Anymore' – but for the most part it sounds like a tired, cynical attempt to get back into the charts, with the likes of 'Baby Knows' coming off like a tenth-generation retread of 'U Got The Look.' Of the guest collaborators, meanwhile, only Gwen Stefani was truly contemporary enough to attract a younger audience.

Taken as a whole, the album suffers from the same complaint as Prince's debut, *For You*: in trying to prove his ability to make hit records, he made everything sound much too clinical. There's none of the fun, spontaneity, or trust in happy accidents that so benefited the likes of *Sign "O" The Times*. "Once again I don't follow trends, they just follow me," he sings on the hip-hop-edged 'Undisputed,' but the album's musical content does nothing to back up the claim.

"I've gotten some criticism for the rap I've chosen to put in my past work," Prince told *Interview* magazine in 1997. But there again, it came during my friction years ... not a lot of that stuff is incorporated into my sets now."[34] 'Undisputed' only adds to the sense that *Rave* is an album of panic recordings, put together in the hope that something would stick.

Ironically, with Prince keen for once to focus his efforts on pushing a major release in the USA, Arista's German-based parent company forced him to start in Europe, making television appearances and giving a handful of live performances in major cities such as Madrid, London, Paris, and Cologne. Given that the album only reached Number 145 in the UK, for example, it seemed like a wasted effort – particularly when it had hit Number 18 on *Billboard*. Some might have been happy enough with that – it was, after all, Prince's best US chart placing since the release of *Emancipation* – but the man himself felt that Arista had botched the promotional campaign, and that Clive Davis had failed to deliver on his promise of hits.

Prince made a final stab at promoting the album in December, appearing on TV and even filming a pay-per-view New Year's Eve celebration, *Rave Un2 The Year 2000*, at Paisley Park. But as the millennium drew closer, he felt once again that he had been let down by a major label, and started posting messages on his website suggesting that Arista lacked commitment (while also calling time on his own promotional efforts).

Prince demanded that the label release a second single from the album, but Davis refused to spend more money on an artist who had lost all interest in working the record himself. A stalemate ensued, resulting in Davis pulling the plug on *Rave* and leaving it to slide back down the charts.

Mirroring the release of *1999: The New Master* a year earlier, Prince then chose to release a remixed version of the album, entitled *Rave In2 The Joy Fantastic*, to members of his NPG Music Club in April 2000. He left some tracks alone, remixed others, and replaced 'Every Day Is A Winding Road' with 'Beautiful Strange,' a murky soundscape reminiscent of some of the weirder moments on *Come*.

All in all, the new *Rave* was another case of preaching to the converted, and as such was unlikely to find its way onto casual fans' stereos, even if it is marginally more interesting than its predecessor. As the new millennium dawned, Prince seemed like nothing more than an independent artist with a firm yet modestly sized fanbase.

CHAPTER 15

THIS IS THE WORK WE MUST DO 4 REVOLUTION 2 COME 2 PASS

I want to put up the words "Jesus Christ is the son of God" on the screen and let them deal with it. … I want to talk about religion and lead that into race and lead it into the music biz and radio, and basically at the end of the week I want to change the world.

PRINCE (AS QUOTED BY KEVIN SMITH)

A fter failing to re-establish himself as a major artist with *Rave Un2 The Joy Fantastic*, Prince spent most of 2000 out of view, seemingly stung by the disappointment. His only public appearances before November were at Paisley Park, taking the form of a series of early-hours parties and the first annual Prince: A Celebration fan event, which ran from June 7-13.

Then, on November 7, he embarked on the first leg of his Hit N Run tour of the USA, giving fans yet another chance to see him perform the hits with another revamped NPG. The line-up this time included a second keyboard player, Kip Blackshire, brought in to bolster Morris Hayes's sound; Jerome Najee Rasheed on saxophone; Geneva, Prince's first official dancer since Mayte; and John Blackwell, perhaps the most powerful Prince drummer since Michael Bland. A second leg followed in April 2001, prior to a six-date mini-tour in June, again dubbed A Celebration.

To the wider world, Prince appeared to have lost his way, with nothing left to offer but the same old greatest-hits sets. Anyone paying closer attention, however, would have noticed the release of a new single, 'The Work Pt. 1,' via Napster, the controversial, pioneering file-sharing program, in April 2001 – one month after the site was legally ordered to prevent the sharing of copyrighted music. But while the method of distribution was certainly innovative, the song itself was little more than a James Brown-style pastiche reminiscent of *Rave Un2 The Joy Fantastic*'s 'Prettyman.'

Two months later, Prince opened Paisley Park for a second weeklong fan event, which this time took its name from the title of his forthcoming new album, *The Rainbow Children*. Prince had been quietly working on the record since the fall of 2000, and gave it its first airing at listening sessions during the event. Fan opinion was polarized, just as the critical response would be when the album went on sale in November (having been available to NPG Music Club subscribers as a download since mid October).

One of the most striking aspects of *The Rainbow Children* is the fact that, after letting his publishing deal with Warner/Chappell expire, Prince had decided to return to using his name – for the first time since *Come*. Anyone expecting this to herald a return to pop-orientated material would have been disappointed, however, as *The Rainbow Children* instead marked the return of Prince the artist, rather than Prince the hit-maker. But while the move away from turgid funk delighted some fans, others just couldn't get past the subject matter.

Having been introduced to the Jehovah's Witness faith by Larry Graham in 1997, Prince used *The Rainbow Children* to make public his feelings about the religion. In the past, on albums such as *Lovesexy*, he had attempted to reconcile his sexual desires with his religious beliefs; on *The Rainbow Children*, his focus is entirely spiritual. A fully fledged concept album, it tells the story of how The

Rainbow Children and their leader, The Wise One, have been penned in by a Digital Garden built by a group of evildoers known as The Banished Ones, and now have to go knocking door-to-door to find people willing to do The Work and help deconstruct the Garden.

So far, so thinly veiled, but some fans were at least glad that Prince seemed to be returning to more mature themes than the sex'n'dancing of old. Those who found it hard to stomach, however, seemed to have forgotten that he had often sought to intertwine the sexual with the sacramental.

Prince's early grounding in religion came from the Bible classes he attended as a child at Minneapolis's Seventh Day Adventist church. Like most adolescents, he then grew interested in sex, leading to all manner of rumors about what he got up to in the basement of bandmate André Anderson's house. Much of his subsequent recording career can be seen as an attempt to reconcile his spirituality with his sexuality.

In the early days, on songs such as 'Let's Pretend We're Married,' Prince appeared to have no qualms about setting statements such as "I'm in love with God, he's the only way" against his desire to "fuck the taste out of your mouth." By the mid 80s, however, he seemed to have realized that, in his new role as a musical superstar, he ought to be a little more measured in his opinions, and took to addressing (on stage) his divided loyalties to a God who wants him to be a good, and an audience who "love it when I'm bad."

"I believe in God," he told MTV in 1985. "There is only one God. And I believe in an afterworld."[2] Acknowledging the fact that he has been accused of "a lot of things contrary to this," he added: "I'm sincere in my beliefs. I pray every night and I don't ask for much. I just say 'thank you' all the time."[3]

By 1988, Prince's beliefs had strengthened to the point where he seemed to be erasing parts of his past self entirely. The overall message of *Lovesexy* was muddled, but at its heart was a wish to fuse his sexual desires with a deeper faith in God. It might have been lost on many, but as far as Prince was concerned he was gradually getting closer to God – hence his symbolic killing-off of one of his old personae on stage each night on the accompanying tour.

Prince's spiritual struggles continued right through the 90s. "The only time you can get tranquil is when you are at one," he told the *New Musical Express* in 1995. "The only time that happens is when you are with God. He tells me to carry on doing what I'm doing, which is my music."[4] With the music in question still gravitating toward the carnal, it's no wonder he was conflicted.

When Prince changed his name to O{+> in 1993, he claimed he had been told to do so by his 'spirit.' In subsequent interviews it did genuinely seem as though a huge burden had been lifted, and that he had become a better man in the process. But as the 90s progressed he seemed continually to be struck by one tragedy after another. At his lowest ebb following the death of his infant son in October 1996, he once again went looking for spiritual guidance. His search would lead him to reconnect with God in a deeper way than ever before.

Toward the end of 1997's Jam Of The Year tour – arranged in support of *Emancipation*, an album written the previous year in celebration of marriage and impending fatherhood – Prince met Larry Graham, who had become a Jehovah's Witness in 1975 after the hectic fallout from Sly & The Family Stone. Graham quickly began to open up to Prince about the faith, which takes a literal approach to *The New World Transcription Of The Holy Scriptures*, a revised edition of The Bible published in 1950.

Prince took to the religion almost immediately. Before long Graham had replaced Prince's then-wife Mayte as the singer's spiritual and emotional confidante and had moved his family to Chanhassen, Minnesota. "Larry's a special individual," Prince told *Guitar World* in 1998. "Not only has he shown me so much spiritually about The Truth, he's given me a lot of bass licks I can steal."[5]

Prince went on to explain how his newfound faith had changed his perspective. "['The One'] went from a love song to a song about respect for the Creator," he said, adding that the meaning of the lyrics changed significantly for him after he read the *New World* Bible. "It has to be the *New World* translation because that's the original one," he added. "Later translations have been tampered with in order to protect the guilty."[6]

Prince's religious conversion provoked a mixed response from fans when the singer started changing the lyrics to some songs and refusing to play others on account of their lyrical content. *Controversy*'s 'Sexuality' became 'Spirituality,' with a new cry of "Spirituality is all we ever need"; 'The Cross' became 'The Christ,' reflecting the Jehovah's Witnesses' rejection of Christian symbolism.

Many were upset by this. The man who once made it his business to break down as many barriers as possible was now advocating a conservative worldview and following a straight doctrine that ordered the world in a precise hierarchy: God, Man, Woman, Child, Animal. The more Prince became engrossed in his new faith, it seemed, the more withdrawn he became from real life, and even less accessible. "I don't believe in idol worship," he told *Entertainment Weekly* in 2004. "When I get asked for my autograph, I say no and tell them why, because I'm giving them something to think about."[7]

Prince had spent much of his life changing on an almost yearly basis, but seemed to establish a more settled routine after converting to the Jehovah's Witness faith. In 2006, he was praising The Bible in *Giant* magazine as "the guidebook to help men and women with their sins," noting that, if he needed advice about anything, there was nobody better to consult than Solomon: "the guy who had a thousand women!"[8]

After polarizing opinion in 2001 with the overt religious content of *The Rainbow Children*, Prince reportedly began a more direct method of recruitment two years later – at least according to Cheryl Johnson, the *Minneapolis Star-Tribune* columnist with whom he had become embroiled in a public feud during the 90s. In 2003, Johnson reported that Prince and Graham had turned up in a "big black truck," knocked on a door, and started preaching the good word to a woman by the name (in the article at least) of Rochelle. Not only was this a Jewish household, but the two men had picked the evening of Yom Kippur to try to convert a Jewish woman to the Jehovah's Witness faith.

Prince has appeared to mellow somewhat in the years since. Although he remains a devout believer, his *Musicology* and *3121* LPs include enough innuendos and gentle sexual references as to suggest that he was once again seeking to reconcile his carnal urges with his spiritual ones. Mavis Staples made a telling remark about the singer in a 2007 issue of *Humo* magazine. "I really wonder if his faith still means that much to him," she said. "Recently, in Vegas, he seemed very much like the old Prince."[9]

The latest twist came in 2008, when rumors began to spread that Prince had become disillusioned with the Jehovah's Witnesses and started looking into Scientology. Some gossipers claimed that he had attended a Scientology seminar in Minneapolis on February 14 2008. These rumous came to nothing, but the singer's *21 Nights In London* residency allegedly outraged some Jehovah's Witnesses, who felt that his song choices were too racy, and his dances far too seductive. (While he did play instrumental snippets of a few old songs, such as 'Erotic City' and 'Nasty Girl,' he stopped short of singing anything that might be deemed 'outrageous.')

With Prince's early 21st century embrace of a newfound faith came a re-embracing of marriage. But where he had seemed to live out most of his relationship with Mayte Garcia – from the highest peaks to the most tragic lows – in the public eye, his union with second wife Manuela Testolini proved to be much more low key.

Testolini is 18 years younger than Prince, and was a fan of the singer long before she met him. She is known to have posted occasionally on the online fan-forum at alt.music.prince, which somehow seemed to lead to her being hired to work for his charitable organization, Love4OneAnother. Strange as it may sound, such unorthodox assimilation is typical of a man whose world is so insular. Instead of taking the time to seek out a woman in a more conventional manner, Prince gave Testolini a role in his company, making it easier for him to stay close to her, and for her to see what his life was like.

Rumor has it that Prince started dating Testolini, who became his personal assistant in 1999, while he was still married to Mayte. The fact that she was chosen to appear in his 1998 promo video for 'The One' suggests a certain closeness. Her ascension within the Prince organization coincided with the singer's continued immersion in the Jehovah's Witness faith. It has been suggested that Testolini's religious beliefs were so close to Prince's own that she became almost as important to him, from a spiritual perspective, as Larry Graham.

Testolini became a more visible presence in Prince's life after he finalized his divorce from Mayte in May 2000. The new couple were seen together at basketball games, and at the annual Paisley Park celebrations, and were married on New Year's Eve 2001 in a Jehovah's Witness ceremony in Hawaii. Testolini remained by Prince's side throughout his conversion and during the promotion of *The Rainbow Children*, and is said to have had a strong positive influence on him, aiding his emergence from a period of artistic and commercial decline.

With Testolini by his side, Prince started opening Paisley Park up to fans again, and even took to attending Q&A sessions during the annual celebrations, but the end of the relationship proved to be as inconspicuous as the start. While it is known that Testolini filed for divorce on May 24 2006, her reasons have never been made public, but it's entirely possible that married life with Prince was not quite as idyllic as a fan might have imagined.

Since then, Prince has not entirely renounced religion, but his monogamous worldview seemed to slip when he was briefly linked to the t-shirt designer Chelsea Rodgers in 2007, as well as to his hired dancers, The Twinz. At the age of 52, he seems to have hit a dead-end when it comes to find a lasting relationship. "[W]ith years of celibacy," he told *USA Today*'s Ednea Gunderson, "it all goes into the music. This time, it has to be the right person."[10] In an interview with the *LA Times*' Ann Powers, he acknowledged that, having studied Solomon and David, he had come to realize that sex was always beautiful in Biblical times, and that he wanted to "try to find a woman who can experience that with you."[11] He was seen at various public events around the time of his 21 Nights In London residency, but never with a woman on his arm other than The Twinz. (His latest protégé, Bria Valente, is perhaps the closest Prince has come to having a 'partner' in recent years.)

Perhaps his current stalemate with women is more to do with beliefs linked to *The Rainbow Children*. What's troubling is not only his apparent subscription to a theocratic order that puts women below men, but also that the Jehovah's Witness faith seemed to have instilled in him some distinctly questionable views on race. "Holocaust aside, many lived and died," he sings on *The Rainbow Children*'s 'Muse 2 The Pharaoh,' before seemingly suggesting that it is better to be "B dead" than to be sold into slavery. He makes a similarly unwise claim on 'Family Name,' reminding listeners that, when all is said and done, the Jews were at least allowed to retain their original surnames, unlike those slaves whose names were taken by their white masters.

Coming from a man who once reveled in breaking down racial and sexual barriers, all of this was nothing short of a travesty – not least because there is much to enjoy elsewhere on the album. Many found *The Rainbow Children* to be Prince's most daring and experimental release since the 80s – at least once they got past the distracting, slowed-down voice he used to narrate it (a deliberate contrast, perhaps, to his high-pitched evil twin, Camille). The album's organic, live-sounding production is certainly preferable to the over-egged R&B sound of much of his 90s output. Not all of its jazz-funk excursions are successful, but there is more flair to the arrangements than anything since *Lovesexy*.

The likes of 'Last December' and the title track make good stabs at stretching out and taking the listener on their own microcosmic journeys, and sound positively revelatory by comparison to Prince's other recent output. Some tracks do fall into Madhouse-lite territory, however, while the standout dance-track, '1+1+1=3,' bears more than a passing resemblance to the 1984 B-side 'Erotic City.' This time, instead of promising a night of unbridled passion, Prince explains to his future wife that him, plus her, plus God, equals three, and that there "ain't no room 4 disagree."

The critical response to the album was about as polarized as could be expected. On the one hand, *USA Today* called it "one of Prince's most challenging and fascinating works to date, whatever your take on the enigmatic valentines to God."[12] The *Boston Globe* seemed in broad agreement, noting that, while it was not a "classic," *The Rainbow Children* "may be the most consistently satisfying Prince album since 1987's *Sign 'O' The Times*."[13] *Rolling Stone* however took a rather different tone, bemoaning "a long trudge across the desert ... with freak-in-the-pulpit leading the way, waving his synthesizer of holy justice."[14]

For all its flaws, *The Rainbow Children* was at least a valiant attempt at creating something interesting. That Prince himself thought highly of the album is clear from the effort he put into promoting it, touring it determinedly like nothing since *Love Symbol* or even *Diamonds And Pearls*. Named after a stripped-down album sent out to members of the NPG Music Club in May 2002, the One Nite Alone ... tour took in 64 dates in the USA, Canada, Europe, and Japan, plus a one-off show recorded for a DVD released the following year.

Whereas recent tours in support of albums such as *Emancipation* and *Newpower Soul* had often seen Prince play to the strengths of his back catalog, One Nite Alone ... put the focus on his band, marginally revamped since the Hit N Run shows. The rhythm section of Rhonda Smith and John Blackwell remained, while keyboard virtuoso Renato Neto replaced both Kip Blackshire and Morris Hayes.

Prince also hired a full brass section for the first time in a while, with Maceo Parker taking most of the saxophone duties alongside Candy Dulfer, who joined mid-way through the American leg, and a new trombonist, Greg Boyer, coming on board from the start. When the hits eventually arrived they were given radical new arrangements designed to show off the band's versatility. Prince threw a few more obscure songs into the set, such as *The Vault*'s 'Extraordinary,' *Parade*'s 'Venus De Milo,' and the instrumental 'Xenophobia.' He also played a fair number of songs from *The Rainbow Children*, using the likes of 'Family Name' to proselytize the audience.

During the shows he would challenge fans in the front rows about whether it was better to give or to receive. If they opted to 'give,' he would ask them to swap seats with someone at the back of the hall. "For those of you expecting to get your 'Purple Rain' on, you're in the wrong house," he told the assembled throng. "We're not interested in what you know, but what you are willing to learn."

These heavy-handed, didactic moments aside, the One Nite Alone ... tour was one of Prince's most artistically successful live engagements in recent memory. He ended the tour in November as content as he had been in some time. *The Rainbow Children* might have been the first major Prince album since his debut to fail to reach the *Billboard* Top 100, but he seemed happy to enter 2003 as a niche musician more interested in creating pure art than chasing chart placings. Through the NPG Music Club, he could now show his most devoted fans that he didn't have to try to make hits anymore, but instead serve up new music that charted his artistic maturation.

The album after which the tour was named, *One Nite Alone ...* itself, proved to be a case in point. For those who reveled in *The Truth*, the acoustic guitar-based album included with pre-ordered copies of *Crystal Ball*, *One Nite Alone ...* was its solo-piano counterpart. Prince isn't strictly alone on the album, as drummer John Blackwell features on a handful of tracks, while others are overdubbed by synthesized sound-effects, but it is certainly one of the most intimate-sounding albums he has ever made.

Released to NPG Music Club members in May 2002, *One Nite Alone ...* was recorded at the tail end of the *Rainbow Children* sessions. The result is a 35-minute oddity that feels intimate but never quite lets you decide whether or not you're listening to the 'real' Prince. Although it's a joy to hear him singing and playing so openly, and without layers of overproduction, the overall effect is somewhat contradictory. One minute he's extolling the virtues of a loving relationship on a cover of Joni Mitchell's 'A Case Of U,' the next he's raging bitterly against a former lover on 'Have A Heart' and 'Pearls B4 The Swine.'

One song that breaks the happy-sad tension is 'Avalanche,' a return to the dubious themes of *The Rainbow Children*'s 'Family Name.' After branding Abraham Lincoln a racist who was "never in favor of setting R people free," he makes the groundless claim that the legendary A&R man John Hammond ripped off all of the acts he signed to Columbia Records.

One Nite Alone ... was still a welcome treasure for the many devoted fans who relished the prospect of hearing Prince at his most fragile-sounding. However, the live album that shares its name – Prince's first official live release – is not quite what one might have expected. Given that Prince had played numerous legendary shows over the years (and recorded most if not all of them), it would have made sense for him to do something in the same vein as Bob Dylan's *Bootleg Series*. Instead, he decided to release a three-disc document of his recent One Nite Alone … world tour.

That's not to say that releasing *One Nite Alone … Live!* was a mistake. The first two discs feature a smattering of old hits and rarities mixed with *Rainbow Children* songs, recorded across eight nights, and do an excellent job of capturing one of the best Prince tours in years.

The third disc, taken from a pair of after-show performances, is less successful. Its mix of funk jams, extended rearrangements of old songs, and obscure covers might have sounded electrifying from within the confines of a small venue, but the magic doesn't quite translate onto CD.

One Nite Alone … Live! remains the only standalone live release in the Prince catalog. It will probably never take the place of the bootlegs cherished by hardcore fans, but it's a fine place to start. Furthermore, after years of honing his pioneering internet distribution methods, it seemed that Prince was finally gearing up to providing his fans with the quality brand new material he'd been promising them for years. Now, at last, he was finally perfecting the cyberworld he had first envsioned all those years ago.

While groups such as Metallica were working themselves into a frenzy over Napster, the illegal file-sharing program, Prince took a more measured view. "File-sharing seems 2 occur when people want more QUALITY over quantity," he wrote in an email interview with *Wired* magazine in 2004. "One good tune on a 20-song CD is a rip. The corporations that created this situation will get the fate they deserve 4 better or 4 worse. … An MP3 is merely a tool. There is nothing 2 fear."[15]

As Alan Leeds later put it, the internet was "the ideal invention … for a somewhat reclusive artist who enjoys contact with fans under the guise of anonymity."[16] Prince's greatest breakthrough yet had been the launch of the NPG Music Club (NPGMC) on Valentine's Day 2001. For a one-off subscription fee of $25, members of the club were offered exclusive merchandise, priority concert tickets, and previously unreleased music from The Vault, delivered in the form of digital downloads and members-only CDs. (The membership fee was originally set at $100 before being lowered when Prince's release schedule slowed.)

In an interview with Yahoo! Internet Live, Prince described the NPGMC as "the experience for those who know better," claiming it as an antidote to the "packaged pop stars" then dominating mainstream radio. "Sometimes I want to ask those people: 'Do you even know a D Minor chord?'"[17]

Whether "those who knew better" were attracted to the club is unclear, but it was certainly a success, with fans eager for more exclusive albums such as *One Nite Alone ...*, those long-promised live recordings, and the tantalizing prospect of whatever lay in The Vault. Prince's artistic and commercial success had fallen into a sharp decline during the 90s, which had, as one reviewer put it, "almost happened without him."[18] But the rate at which he changed his mind and scrapped one project in favor of another remained the same. Given the quality of the material that *did* make it out into the world, it's unlikely that any of these unreleased works would have bothered the charts. But the lack of information about projects such as *The Dawn* (1997), *Madrid 2 Chicago* (2001), *High* (2001), and *Last December* (2002) has served only to increase speculation about them.

Little is known about any of these albums except for their titles and the fact that they were all 'announced' at some point or other. (One or two tracks earmarked for each may perhaps have ended up being released officially elsewhere.) There were also plans for several boxed sets: a seven-disc set of Prince samples for DJs with a suggested retail price of $700; a second volume of *Crystal Ball*, with the tracklisting set to be chosen by the fans; and another seven-disc set, *The Chocolate Invasion*, comprising all of the material that had been made available through the NPG Music Club until 2003. There were even rumors of a *3121* movie to accompany the 2006 album of the same name.

The most tantalizing of all the unreleased albums of the period was *Roundhouse Garden*, which Prince announced in 1998 as being a Revolution reunion based on recordings from the mid 80s. Whether it would have entailed a full-scale reunion is unclear, but Prince did meet with his former bandmates at some point to discuss working together again. Problems arose when he allegedly demanded that Wendy Melvoin and Lisa Coleman renounce their homosexuality before he would agree to working with them again, leading Bobby Z to withdraw from the project. (Prince later blamed Melvoin and Coleman for the fact that the album never saw the light of day, suggesting that people ought to ask *them* why it was never released.)

If *Roundhouse Garden* was the dream collaboration that never was, the weirdest of all the unreleased projects Prince began around the turn of the millennium was a planned *Rainbow Children* movie, to be directed by Kevin Smith. While shooting his fifth movie, *Jay & Silent Bob Strike Back*, Smith got in touch with Prince to ask whether he could use 'The Most Beautiful Girl In The World' on the soundtrack. Prince declined, but offered The Time's 'Jungle Love' instead, while also proposing an idea of his own.

It transpired that Prince was an avid fan of Smith's fourth movie, *Dogma*, a satire of Catholicism that led to him receiving death threats. As the director later recalled in *An Evening With Kevin Smith*, Prince seemed to have got the wrong end of the stick. "Sitting there, listening to him talk about it," Smith later recalled, "it's starting not to sound like the movie I made."[19]

Prince nonetheless felt that Smith was the man to direct his next movie project, and invited him to Paisley Park to film his second annual fan event in June 2001. Part of the director's job was to film a series of Q&A sessions, as well as fan responses to playbacks of *The Rainbow Children*. According to Smith, Prince wanted to make something that was "kind of like a concert film," but which included "bold things" like putting the words "Jesus Christ is the son of God" on a screen and letting the crowd "deal with it."

Despite finding it impossible to connect with the project, Smith spent a week at Paisley Park and shot hours of footage. He picked up a lot of curious information about the laws of 'Prince World' along the way. (According to a producer by the name of Stephanie, the singer would often make outlandish requests, such as once asking for a camel to be brought to him at 3am.)

Perhaps unsurprisingly, the *Rainbow Children* movie never materialized. Smith was later asked to return to Paisley Park to edit the footage, which had already been through the hands of a number of other film technicians, after Prince decided to try to turn it into a recruitment video for Jehovah's Witnesses. Smith felt that he had already made his "recruitment film for Catholicism," so passed on the project. "If you're ever approached by a bunch of Jehovah's Witnesses and they say we'd like you to watch this video," he joked at the taping of *An Evening With Kevin Smith 2: Evening Harder*, "that's my latest film."[20]

With or without his recruitment film, having made what he clearly felt was a major artistic breakthrough on *The Rainbow Children* and the One Nite Alone ... tour, Prince threw himself into recording a series of experimental instrumental albums, echoing his decision to follow *Parade* with the first Madhouse record. But while the Madhouse recordings had a sense of fun about them, the three low-key albums Prince released in 2003 smacked of pretension. (Two of them were even subtitled *New Directions In Music From Prince*.)

The first of the three albums was made available to NPG Music Club members for download on New Year's Day 2003. It was called *Xpectation*, but any high hopes were quickly dashed upon listening to it. With songs called things like 'Xosphere' and 'Xemplify,' and each one given a patronizing subtitle ('Xotica''s being 'Curiously unusual or excitingly strange'), a more appropriate title might have been *Xcrement*.

Recorded with current band-members John Blackwell (drums), Rhonda Smith (bass), and Candy Dulfer (sax), alongside pop-classical violinist Vanessa Mae, the album's ten songs are mostly in the pseudo-jazz vein of Madhouse. The title track in particular could have been lifted straight from *8*. There are a few interesting avant-garde touches, but for the most part Prince's jazz explorations show no real progression from his first attempts 16 years earlier. The overall sound is slick and sophisticated, thanks to the quality of the band as a whole (and Mae in particular, who contributes some of the album's standout moments), but most of the songs still pass by unnoticed. Perhaps the greatest disappointment is that the ten-minute long 'Xenophobia,' played live during the One Nite Alone ... tour, was left off the final tracklisting.

Two days after releasing *Xpectation*, Prince made another album available for download. Like its predecessor, *C-Note* is a largely instrumental affair with thematically linked song titles: this time around each song is named for the city it was recorded in during soundchecks, with the first letter of each spelling out the title. 'Copenhagen,' 'Nagoya,' and 'Osaka' are all instrumental, while the only word sung on 'Tokyo' is the name of the city. The album closes with a ballad, 'Empty Room,' that was once earmarked for *The Gold Experience*. The rest of the material is very much in the *Xpectation* mold, but the fact that it was recorded live with a seven-piece band gives it a more varied, organic sound.

Both *Xpectation* and *C-Note* can be viewed as test runs for *N.E.W.S.*, the only one of Prince's three LPs from 2003 to be given a conventional release. Perhaps he needn't have bothered: this latest set of *New Directions In Music* would prove to be his lowest-selling album ever. The cruel irony is that *N.E.W.S.* is probably the most interesting set of instrumentals he has ever recorded. There is still a general air of pretension – the four tracks are titled 'North,' 'East,' 'South,' and 'West,' and each run to exactly 14 minutes – but the overall effect is much more dynamic and eclectic than previous instrumental efforts, with a sound that blends the most experimental side of Madhouse with the organic feel of *The Rainbow Children*.

N.E.W.S. was recorded in a single day, with Eric Leeds returning on sax alongside keyboardist Renato Neto, drummer John Blackwell, and bassist Rhonda Smith. The album's key strengths stem from the fact that Prince seemed finally to have realized that he didn't have to try to cram his understanding of jazz into five-minute pieces. The four lengthy tracks have a definite ebb and flow to them, taking in everything from Eastern intonations to harsh, abrasive guitar. All in all, *N.E.W.S.* remains Prince's finest jazz-infused album.

Prince didn't tour in support of any of these albums, but instead decided to revisit some of his more crowd-pleasing material on what was dubbed the World Tour 2003/2004 but which actually only entailed one date in Hong Kong, five in Australia, and two in Hawaii during October and December 2003.

Nonetheless, these eight concerts – Prince's first live shows in almost a year – were important in that they gave him a chance to reconnect with his back catalog for the first time since the Hit N Run shows of 2000–01. Cynics might argue that he needed little encouragement to revisit the hits 'for the last time' yet again, but the singer had genuinely seemed to distance himself from his best-known work on his

2002 tour. Now, away from the media glare he would have faced had he chosen to play in Europe or America, he took the opportunity to have fun with his past work, reinventing old songs with new arrangements, while also introducing some of the songs from his forthcoming *Musicology* LP.

Coming at the end of a year in which the only new Prince releases had been instrumental albums aimed purely at the hardcore, the mini-tour seemed to give him the opportunity to reassess his status as a pop star. *Musicology* would see him make another grasp for the mainstream, for the first time since 1999, while the 2003 live shows seemed to have a similarly invigorating effect.

During a break from the tour in November, Prince set about planning a full-scale tour of the USA. It would end up running to 95 dates, and would be his longest trek across the country since the Purple Rain tour. Although the current year had been the quietest of his career to date, he was poised to launch his biggest comeback yet in 2004.

CHAPTER 16

DON'T U MISS THE FEELING MUSIC GAVE YA BACK IN THE DAY?

Prince saw it as a creative marketing tool, to share his music with the widest audience possible ... What better place to sell music than the live venue? We have a captive audience.

L. LONDELL MCMILLAN

Despite ending 2003 with the completion of a successful mini-tour of Hong Kong, Australia, and Hawaii, Prince threatened to alienate even his most loyal fans after an incident at Minneapolis International Airport in December. According to a report by *Minneapolis Star-Tribune* columnist Cheryl Johnson, the trouble started when a fan tried to take a picture of the singer shortly after he landed; Prince's bodyguard then swiped the fan's camera and made off with it in a luggage cart.

A follow-up report on January 15 2004 quoted a number of fans' disgust at their idol's actions. The *Tribune* continued to follow the story until April 7, when the fan involved in the incident, one Anthony Fitzgerald, sued Prince and his bodyguard for "assault and battery, loss of the camera, and intentional infliction of emotional distress." (Reports suggested that it had taken until then for the lawsuit to be put into motion because Prince's people had initially refused to accept it.)

Fortunately for Prince, only his most devoted followers were watching, and most of them quickly forgave him once his busiest and most successful year in recent memory began to take shape. At the end of January, he started playing one-off shows in anticipation of the release of a new album, beginning a promotional blitz that reached its pinnacle on February 8 during a duet with Beyoncé at the Grammy Awards. The pair performed a medley of hits from *Purple Rain* (including 'Baby I'm A Star' and 'Let's Go Crazy') alongside her 'Crazy In Love.'

For those outside the Prince hardcore, the Grammy performance was a timely reminder of the heights the singer could reach. Dressed in purple and gold, he seemed to have leaped out of the doldrums and onto the front pages almost overnight – just in time to mark *Purple Rain*'s 20th anniversary year.

Not everyone was impressed. Alan Leeds told the *St Paul Pioneer Press* that he found the level of performance "Vegas-y," while Prince himself noted: "I get asked every year to play at the Grammys. This year I did it because I have an album out that I want to promote and a concert tour that I want to promote."[2] But it did enough to draw a large chunk of the world's media to the February 24 press conference at which Prince officially unveiled the forthcoming *Musicology* album and tour.

The tour itself promised to be another 'all the hits for the last time' affair, but few of the assembled journalists seemed to mind. It seemed to most of them that Prince had disappeared completely during the time he had spent making records steeped in his Jehovah's Witness faith and releasing instrumental albums over the internet. After giving the wider world a breather, the returning Prince would be gratefully received – as would the news that he would be giving priority seating on the tour to NPG Music Club members – but the singer once again found himself having to challenge the idea that he was making a comeback. "I never went anywhere!" he told *Gallery Of Sound*. "I've been touring for a while. I took a break to make the *Musicology* project. It hasn't really stopped."[3]

As well as recording, Prince had also been busy working on expanding his internet empire. On March 24 2004, he launched the Musicology download store. To Prince this was just one more way of getting his music direct to fans as quickly as possible. "We didn't create r club to make other labels nervous," he explained in an email to *Business 2 Magazine*. "We make a lot of music and needed a worldwide distribution service that works as fast as we do. ... U can get music from r club in the time it takes 2 open an emale. 4 once, eye have a distribution service that actually works FASTER than eye do."[4]

With the launch of the NPG Music Club's download store, Prince made the album of the same name available to download for $9.99 – one month before it was due to go on sale in stores. Alongside *Musicology*, were two compilations of 'Trax' previously made available online or on the singles given away during the 2001 Hit N Run tour: *The Chocolate Invasion*, which took its name from a scrapped seven-disc boxed set originally set for release in 2003, and *The Slaughterhouse*, both also on sale for $9.99. Most of the music on both albums seems to have been compiled from material recorded during the late 90s and early 21st century; and it seems possible to construct the unreleased *High*, which was once set to come out in 2001, from the two.

The fact that Prince opted not to release *High* suggests that he made a conscious decision not to try to release a commercial hit record in the immediate aftermath of the chart failure *Rave Un2 The Joy Fantastic*. In some ways that's a shame, as the best of the material – 'When Eye Lay My Hands On U'; 'The Dance,' which was later re-recorded for *3121* – might well have given Prince the radio hit he longed for at the turn of the millennium.

The strongest track is *The Chocolate Invasion*'s 'Judas Smile,' a stop-start slow-burner with a jittery beat that's not a million miles away from Timbaland's groundbreaking late-90s productions. It's one of the most commercial yet inventive Prince songs of the period, and proves that, while he might no longer lead the charge, he could at least keep up with it. By contrast, some of the lesser material evokes *Newpower Soul*'s dull funk, notably 'S&M Groove' from *The Slaughterhouse*, so it's entirely possible that Prince scrapped *High* for fear of sending another potential failure out into the world. Still, releasing two more albums of mostly strong material on the same day that he made *Musicology* available for download served as a reminder that he was still making music as prolifically as ever, but just didn't always want you to hear it.

What Prince wanted everyone to hear, however, was that, five years after the disappointment of *Rave Un2 The Joy Fantastic*, he was ready to have another go at working with a major label. At the time of the press conference, he had not yet decided which one; given the choice, he said, he would have asked "all of them to release it at once," but he was willing to settle for working with the company "most hyped about pushing the product."

Perhaps the most interesting aspect of all of this was that, as well as making *Musicology* available as a download first, Prince was also giving away free copies to concertgoers – a concept he'd envisioned as far back as 1996, when he told *Forbes*: "Maybe we could put a [CD] sampler on every seat. Or give them the whole [album] and build it into the ticket price."[5] Now, eight years later, the idea was becoming a reality. "The CD is more or less a companion to the concert," he explained.[6] Somewhat amazingly, he was able to convince Columbia Records to agree to promote and distribute the album through conventional channels even while he continued to pursue his own non-traditional methods.

"Sony [Columbia's parent company] has graciously agreed 2 augment the *Musicology* project with worldwide promotion and distribution," he wrote in an email to *Wired* magazine. "They r cool because they do not restrict NPG's ability 2 sell the product as well. It's a win-win situation."[7]

The scheme might have looked like a catastrophe in the making, but it worked. On April 20, three weeks after Prince had started giving copies away on the accompanying tour, *Musicology* appeared on record-store shelves as a combined Columbia/NPG release. According to Sony president Don Ienner, the label started making money "with the first copy shipped."[8]

By then Prince had filled up further column inches after being inducted into the Rock And Roll Hall Of Fame and leading an all-star rendition of 'While My Guitar Gently Weeps' alongside Tom Petty and Jeff Lynne in tribute to the recently departed George Harrison. (Prince played the famous Eric Clapton guitar solo.) He had become a hot property once again. "There are many kings," Alicia Keys gushed in her introductory speech at the induction ceremony, "but there is only one Prince."

The singer himself then took to the stage to note: "When I first started out in this music industry, I was most concerned with freedom: freedom to produce, freedom to play all the instruments on my records, freedom to say anything I wanted to. After much negotiation, Warner Bros granted me my freedom, and I thank them for that." The event put Prince firmly back on the map. "After a decade spent tending only to his faithful," *Time* magazine wrote, "Prince has had a revelation: He's supposed to be a rock'n'roll star."[9]

The American Musicology tour opened to ecstatic praise, with the initial run of 26 dates gradually expanding to include 96 shows in 69 cities – his longest run since the days of *Purple Rain*. Performing in the round, as he had done on the Lovesexy tour, Prince took to an X-shaped stage in the center of the arena and played a hits-based show with a smattering of *Musicology* songs. The highlight for many was the acoustic section, during which he treated rapt audiences to solo versions of 'Raspberry Beret,' 'Little Red Corvette,' and other early classics.

Prince tried to push *Musicology* as the tour's equal, telling interviewers that "school is back in session." Most of the reviews were suitably positive, with *Billboard* noting that the album "focuses on a fun and playful Prince, whose turns of phrase and instrumental dexterity call to mind why we embraced him in the first place,"[10] and *Rolling Stone* finding it "as appealing, focused, and straight-up satisfying an album as Prince has made since who can remember when."[11] The *New York Times* was one of the few publications to suggest that the album fell short of its early promise, describing it as "a casual exhibition of Princeliness" that could have done with some of the "fighting spirit" of *The Rainbow Children*.[12]

The general consensus was that *Musicology* was a good, solid record, but the *New Musical Express* got closest to the truth with its conclusion that the album offered "a kind of flawed redemption, neither inspired enough to be a true classic nor insipid enough to make it unworthy of your attention."[13] Free from the turgid overproduction that marred much of *Rave Un2 The Joy Fantastic*, Prince seemed finally to have worked out how to make a contemporary-sounding record without losing his own style. Some of the songs might be lacking a little in terms of structure, but they work in the context of a concise, easily digestible album. Whereas some of his recent albums had been spoilt by bitterness, excess, or a determination to drive a funk riff home to the point of banality, *Musicology* is the sound of Prince having fun. He even finds time to poke fun at Michael Jackson with the lines: "My voice is getting higher / And eye ain't never had my nose done."

The rest of the album's musical and lyrical content is pretty tame by comparison. The most controversial aspect of *Musicology* turned out to be the promo video for its third single, 'Cinnamon Girl.' A response to the newly suspicious mindset brought about by the terrorist attacks of September 11 2001, it cast a 14-year-old actress from New Zealand, Keisha Castle-Hughes, as an Arab-American schoolgirl who fantasizes about blowing herself up in an airport after being subjected to racial harassment. Prince seemed to be making the point that arbitrary suspicion can lead good people down dark paths, but the video was deemed too sensitive and banned by a number of television networks in Britain and America.

Despite Prince's desire for *Musicology* to become a byword for "letting the music come first," the music on the album seemed to be completely overshadowed by his business practices.[14] Even the Musicology tour, which ended in September, was reduced to a series of statistics by the end of the year, when *Pollstar* magazine put it at the top of its list of the year's biggest concert draws. Prince, the magazine claimed, had earned more than $87 million from the 96 performances – $7 million more than Céline Dion had picked up that year during her residency in Las Vegas. (Reports elsewhere suggested that one-and-a-half million people attended the Musicology tour.)

Perhaps the most amazing aspect of *Musicology* was the fact that it led to another music industry shakeup, albeit unintentionally. After a period of much confusion, Neilsen SoundScan, the organization responsible for counting record sales and compiling charts, decided that it would include copies of *Musicology* given away at concerts from the date of the album's official release (April 20) onward. Industry executives lined up to express their outrage, noting that, while *Musicology* was being presented as a 'free' CD, the cost of purchasing it had been incorporated into the price of the concert ticket.

"Nobody can say no to that new CD if they want to see the show," one anonymous executive complained in the *Los Angeles Times*.[15] Another panicked over a hypothetical situation whereby "a dinosaur act that no longer sells records but does great live business can do a stadium tour over the summer and dominate the *Billboard* 200."[16] The executive in question was "violently against this. ... The charts are supposed to represent what consumers are spending money on. With the Prince album there is no choice."[17]

Neilsen SoundScan CEO Rob Sisco sought to justify the decision, telling *Billboard*: "The manufacturer was paid by the promoter, who is reselling the merchandise to the customer. Given that there is a sale, with the album ending up in the hands of the consumer ... we feel we should count the sales."[18] As far as Prince was concerned, exploiting the loophole was a masterstroke. Doing the calculations for *Newsweek*, he boasted: "If I sell 400,000 tickets to my shows, that would make me Number One on the charts before I even release a CD into record stores. You feel me? Then Norah Jones is gonna have something to worry about."[19]

Ultimately, *Musicology* achieved double-platinum status in the USA and reached Number Three on the *Billboard* chart. (It also peaked at Number Three in the UK without any sort of promotional gimmick.) *Billboard*'s chart editor Geoff Mayfield estimated that 25 per cent of the album's recorded sales came from ticket sales, leading most commentators to agree that *Musicology* would have achieved much the same success even if Prince had not given it away. But that didn't stop *Billboard* from altering its policy so that all future ticket-and-album bundles had to give concertgoers the chance to opt out of buying the album alongside the ticket.

After completing the tour and maximizing its commercial potential, Prince was content to lay low for the rest of 2004 and enjoy the accolades that came flooding in. *Purple Rain* was given a deluxe 20th anniversary reissue on DVD in August to further rave reviews, while the end of the year brought with it a glut of awards from magazines: Funkmaster Of The Year from *GQ*, Best Use Of Technology from *Billboard*, and Artist Of The Year from his local newspaper, the *Minneapolis Star-Tribune*.

In a year where it had finally been deemed safe to like Prince again, none of this was surprising. More refreshing was the personality shift that seemed to occur within the star, as reflected in *Musicology*'s more mature material (notably 'If Eye Was The Man In Ur Life' and 'Reflections'). "What we're trying to do is put the family first," Prince told interviewers who commented on the fact that he had left his 'rude' material behind. "When you come to a certain age, you have certain responsibilities to deal with."[20]

Inevitably, given the recent anniversary of his greatest critical and commercial success, Prince found himself looking back over his career to date. "When I was making sexy tunes," he told *Newsweek*, "that wasn't all I was doing. Back then, the sexiest thing on TV was *Dynasty*, and if you watch it now it's like *The Brady Bunch*."[21] Laughing off the furor over his use of the word 'masturbate' in 'Darling Nikki,' he nonetheless encouraged contemporary acts not to try to emulate the controversies of his earlier career. "There's no more envelope to push," he said. "I pushed it off the table. It's on the floor."[22]

After all the excitement of the previous year, 2005 looked like being Prince's quietest since he signed to Warner Bros in 1977. He spent most of it jamming and performing private concerts at his rented Los Angeles home. Aside from releasing 'S.S.T.'/'Brand New Orleans' in response to the Hurricane Katrina tragedy, and giving all proceeds to associated charities, he had not issued any new music or given notice of any forthcoming albums or tours.

To even the keenest of observers, it looked like 2005 would end with Prince still trying to figure out how to follow the astounding success of *Musicology*. Then, on December 9, *Billboard* claimed that the star had signed a deal with Universal for the release of a new album, *3121*. Four days later, on December 13 – picked deliberately to mirror the album's title – the singer held a press conference to make the news official. "I don't consider Universal a slave ship," he told reporters, in response to the usual questions about why he had decided to work with a major label again. "I did my own agreement without the help of a lawyer and sat down and got exactly what I wanted to accomplish … I got a chance to structure an agreement the way I saw fit instead of the other way around."

He also took the opportunity to give those present the first taste of *3121* in the form of its lead single, 'Te Amo Corazón.' There was nothing particularly remarkable about the song, a gentle ballad with a slight Latin feel, but according to Prince it was not representative of the album as a whole. The wider world would have to wait a while to hear the rest, however, as he would spend the first quarter of 2006 acting as a sideman for his latest protégé, Támar.

Prince might have rediscovered his own muse during the early 21st century, but he didn't seem to have very much to offer anyone else. The last time he looked beyond his own work was when he attempted to bring Chaka Khan and Larry Graham back into the spotlight in 1998. Eight years would pass before he chose to take another artist under his wing. But although the album he produced for Támar was probably his mostly satisfying R&B disc in a decade, it ended up going almost the same way as Rosie Gaines's long-delayed Paisley Park album, and hardly anyone ever got to hear it.

Prince brought Támar Davis with him when he signed to Universal in December 2005, and originally planned to release her *Milk & Honey* LP on March 21 2006, the same day as his *3121*. But after being postponed for "various reasons," according to an official statement made by Támar a month later, it never saw the light of day, except for a hastily withdrawn Japanese release. (Leaked copies subsequently sold for up to $800 on eBay.)

Prince must have believed in her at one point. Asked by *Billboard* about what he had been listening to recently during the *3121* promotional run, Prince named Támar, describing her as "a brilliant writer and a kind soul," and noting that her album would now be coming out in May.[23] "Prince has a willingness to promote *3121* because of Támar," explained Universal marketing executive Ted Cockle, adding that she is "basically his musical muse at the moment. She is with him at all times."[24]

Prince's warmth of feeling for his new charge was such that he gave her top billing on the short promotional tour in support of both of their forthcoming albums during January and February, and on the duet 'Beautiful, Loved And Blessed,' which features on both *3121* and *Milk & Honey*, and on the B-side to Prince's 'Black Sweat.' "Who the bleep is Támar," the *Minneapolis Star-Tribune* asked, "and why is she getting top billing over Prince for Saturday's quickie concert at the Orpheum?"[25] Given that she seemed to have appeared out of nowhere, the newspaper was justified in questioning the decision. But as the tour wound on, with dates and venues announced only a few days before each performance, Prince and his band continued to back Támar for what were mostly hour-long nightclub shows during the early hours of the morning.

Most of the reviews still focused on Prince, whom the *Washington Post* described as a "superb wingman," but he seemed content to play guitar and keyboards while Támar belted out a selection of her own songs and well-known soul covers.[26] That's not to suggest that the headline act was poorly received. "If audience reaction counts for something," the *Chicago Sun Times* concluded, "then Támar impressed."[27] But what looked like the start of a promising career ended up coming to nothing. No sooner had Támar appeared than she disappeared, and despite all the effort Prince put into promoting it, *Milk & Honey* never actually made it into record stores. After being postponed from March to April to May to August, the album was finally, quietly shelved. No official reason was ever given, but it was once suggested that the media's 'lying' over the release date had something to do with it.

Milk & Honey's disappearance has left fans wondering about what might have been for both Prince and Támar. Had it been released, it could well have been a breakthrough release for the younger singer, and one that served as further evidence of the creative resurgence of her mentor. The album's 12 tracks are a masterclass in contemporary R&B, with a fresher, more modern sound than anything else Prince has attempted to do with the genre in recent times. Several of the funkier cuts, such as the title track, 'Closer To My Heart,' and 'Holla And Shout,' would almost certainly have made themselves at home on commercial radio.

Of all the missteps and disappointments of Prince's later career, *Milk & Honey*'s failure to launch is one of the great lost opportunities. The *Minneapolis Star-Tribune* saw the initial emergence of Támar as proof that Prince knew when to share the spotlight, but subsequent events seemed to suggest the opposite. It's unlikely that Prince would end up riding anyone else's coattails, but when it came down to it, it seemed he didn't want to risk Támar getting in the way of his continued commercial resurgence.

There was no way that Prince could top the *Musicology* marketing campaign, however, and no point in giving away 'free' albums with concert tickets now that *Billboard* had changed its chart-eligibility rules. Instead, he made a series of high-profile television appearances, the most notable of which was a show-stopping performance at the BRIT Awards in February, for which he was reunited with Wendy Melvoin, Lisa Coleman, and Sheila E. for the first time since the mid 80s.

To entice fans to buy the album itself, he launched a *Willy Wonka*-style search for the handful of 'Purple Tickets' that had been slipped into random copies of *3121*. The lucky few who found a ticket were invited to attend An Evening With Prince on May 6 2006. A different set of chart regulations meant that Britain was exempt from the promotion, but a small band of fans from the USA, Mexico, and The Netherlands were flown to Los Angeles, given $250 of spending money, and treated to an intimate performance in Prince's rented '3121' house.

By then, however, the house itself had become something of a thorn in Prince's side. According to the *Minneapolis Star-Tribune*'s favorite Prince-watcher, Cheryl Johnson, the singer had moved to Los Angeles in 2005 after demolishing his purple home in Chanhassen, Minnesota. His first LA residence actually had the street address 3121, but in September of the same year he moved to a rented property at 1235 Sierra Alta Way, for which he paid $70,000 per month, and which he subsequently renamed '3121.'

The setup seemed perfect until it was reported in March 2006 that Prince was being sued by his landlord, the C Booz Multifamily I LLC, for redecorating the property without consent. His dream home had become a legal nightmare. Papers filed with Los Angeles Superior Court on January 13 2006 reveal that the landlord took exception to the fact that Prince had painted purple stripes and the 'O{+>' and '3121' logos on the exterior; removed carpets and baseboards and cut a large hole in a bedroom wall; installed "plumbing and piping in a downstairs bedroom for water transfer for beauty salon chairs"; and used "unlicensed carpenters and contractors."

News of the lawsuit was still trickling out when Prince performed at Sunset Boulevard's Tower Records at the stroke of midnight on March 21 to launch the album. The title was officially explained as a reference to the singer's current home, but there were a number of suggested Biblical links, not least Psalm 31:21: "Blessed be the LORD, for he hath showed me his marvelous kindness in a strong city." (The fact that *3121* was subtitled *The Music* also led to speculation that there had once been a movie project attached to it.)

With no 'comeback' story this time around, *3121* was given a slightly more muted welcome than its predecessor. Most of the reviews were positive: *Billboard* praised "one of those rare artists who can remain relevant without compromising his eccentric style;"[28] The *Times* enjoyed the sound of "an artist learning to make peace with his past without turning into his own tribute act."[29] *Entertainment Weekly* was a little more measured, noting that some of the tracks are not quite worthy of "Prince's prodigious gifts," suggesting that he "hasn't figured out how to reach back into his 80s bag of tricks and create something that feels contemporary" in the way that "disciples" such as OutKast and The Neptunes have.[30]

Nonetheless, *Billboard*'s prediction that the record "could well return him to the top of the charts" rang true.[31] Amazingly, *3121* was the first Prince album to debut at Number One in the USA, and his first chart-topper at all since 1989's *Batman*. Interestingly, while *Musicology* had sold 191,000 copies in its first week but only reached Number Three, *3121* sold slightly less – 183,000 – but still claimed the top spot.

Like its predecessor, *3121* is competent without showing off many new tricks, aside perhaps from the modern electro-funk of second single 'Black Sweat.' There's nothing wrong with the guitar rock of 'Fury,' the jazz-infused 'Satisfied,' or the upbeat, funky 'Get On The Boat,' but there's nothing particularly challenging about them either. It might be slightly more eclectic than *Musicology*, but *3121* is largely self-referential, right down to the way 'The Dance' references the screaming conclusion to 'The Beautiful Ones,' or even the fact that it was another album with a four-digit title. This, the *Minneapolis Star-Tribune* noted, only leaves you wanting more: "There's definitely a throwback vibe to … a mostly one-man-band effort that favors the musical minimalism and reliance on synthesizers of early-80s Prince."[32] ("I think in a lot of ways I still sound like I did before," Prince said, acknowledging this, "so with this new album, it helps make the connection."[33])

The accolades kept pouring in when Prince made a surprise appearance on the season finale of *American Idol* and contributed the Golden Globe-winning 'Song Of The Heart' to the *Happy Feet* soundtrack. Most importantly, his pioneering efforts with the internet were given the recognition they deserved on June 12 2006 at the tenth annual Webby Awards, where the singer was given a Lifetime Achievement Award. "Prince is a visionary who recognized early on that the web would completely change how we experience music," Webby founder Tiffay Shlain said in her official statement. "For more than a decade he has tapped the power of the web to forge a deeper connection with his fans and push the boundaries of technology and art."

Within just a few weeks, however, the NPG Music Club had been shut down. On July 4 a statement was sent out to members claiming that, in the wake of the Webby victory, "there is a feeling that the NPGMC [has] gone as far as it can go. In a world without limitations and infinite possibilities, has the time come 2 once again make a leap of faith and begin anew?" Prince seemed to be taking it upon himself to answer these questions, and put the club on hiatus until further notice.

Fans were dismayed. Not only had they lost their direct route to Prince, but also the music they had downloaded from the site, thanks to the encoding software used on it. Prince might have claimed to be taking time off to come up with ways to push the internet further, but it seemed that his boundary-breaking run had come to an end. (It was later revealed that a trademark infringement lawsuit had been filed by the Nature Publishing Group against Prince's use of 'NPG' on the day that the website was shut down.)

On December 19, Prince launched another internet venture, the 'online magazine' 3121.com. It didn't have the benefits of the NPGMC, but it was a start. Prince began offering news reports, photos, and a weekly Jam Of The Week in streaming audio through it the following year. This latest site didn't hang around for long, however, as another round of lawsuits led to Prince removing himself from the internet entirely.

In the meantime, Prince was happy to have returned to the top of the charts with an album he acknowledged was "a trip back," and set about putting the next stage of *3121* into promotion. "I know that a lot of people thought that *Musicology* and the tour didn't bring them anything new," he admitted. "And to be honest it didn't, but it was my way of saying: I'm still Prince. I'm the same who made those songs. But now it's time to move on – and still respect my flavor in music."[34]

Having made a guest appearance with Morris Day & The Time at the Rio Hotel's Club Rio in Las Vegas on May 12, Prince had set about planning his own Vegas engagement. By October, he had moved into the Rio's top suite. The news that he would be staging an indefinite run of Friday and Saturday shows at the newly renamed Club 3121 caused consternation. The man who once broke down so many barriers now seemed to be settling into one of rock'n'roll's biggest cliches, the fat Elvis decline, in an attempt to emulate the success Céline Dion had achieved in recent years with her own Vegas residency.

"It's pretty much the Prince world brought to Vegas!" one of the singer's backing dancers, Maya McClean, said in his defense. "The fans can come and really experience what it's like to be in Prince's home."[35] To that end, Prince even brought his own personal chef, Lena Morgan, to run the adjoining 3121 Jazz Cuisine restaurant, where he performed early-hours after-show jams for VIP ticket holders. (The $312 ticket also included dinner and a complimentary bottle of champagne.)

In fact, the Club 3121 shows were something of a break from the tacky Vegas tradition. Instead of presenting a glitzy, Barbra Streisand-style revue, he was playing modest, stripped-down sets in a relatively intimate 900-seater club. The shows included a mix of classics ('Kiss'; a truncated 'Let's Go Crazy'), *3121* material, loose funk jams, and jazz and soul standards. He even let his band stretch out on an instrumental version of 'Down By The Riverside,' just as he had done with his 1987 group during renditions of Charlie Parker's 'Now's The Time.' The shows proved so successful that they ran until April 28 2007, with 'normal' tickets costing $125 each. Local reports suggested that Prince was spending his days off pursuing his love of photography, and was planning to put a *3121* magazine into print to show off the results of his new hobby.

For the man who had previously undertaken massive international engagements, perfected the Hit N Run style mini-tour, and hosted numerous concerts in his Paisley Park home, the 3121 residency gave Prince another option when it came to live performance. He still seemed to have an almost pathological compulsion to play music, but had long since grown tired of extended jaunts, as evidenced by two decades of about-turns, curtailments, and complete refusals to tour certain albums.

Playing in Vegas proved to Prince that he could make just as much money by staying in one place as he could by taking an entire stage show and entourage across the country. Although he played a few more Club 3121-style shows in the middle of 2007, including four dates at the Roosevelt Hotel in Los Angeles in June, he had for all intents and purposes finished promoting *3121* after his final night at the Rio on April 28. Despite launching a 3121 perfume in July with three performances in Minneapolis, he had already moved onto his next scheme, appearing in London in May to announce the Earth Tour.

CHAPTER 17

U NEED 2 BE A SUPERSTAR OR GROW UP — BUT NOT BOTH

I'm single, celibate, and sexy. I feel free.

PRINCE

P rince focused largely on the UK – and more specifically London – for the launch of his *Planet Earth* album. But having perfected the art of using one high-profile television appearance to herald a new release, he knew he needed to leave his home country with something to remember him by. Having unleashed show-stopping performances at two of the world's most high-profile music awards shows – the Grammys in 2004 and the BRITs in 2006 – it made sense that he would now fill the halftime spot at the biggest US sporting event of the year.

Much had been made of recent Super Bowl halftime performances by The Rolling Stones, whose set was something of an anti-climax, and Janet Jackson, whose 'wardrobe malfunction' in 2004 led to widespread condemnation and an investigation by the FCC. (Even Prince felt compelled to chime in on the controversy, telling *Entertainment Weekly* things had gone "too far" before asking: "What's the point?"[2])

Three years after the Jackson incident, and after more than six months of negotiations, Prince was given the chance to show how these things should be done. On February 4 2007 he took his 'love symbol'-shaped stage to the Dolphin Arena in Miami, Florida, to play a 12-minute set of *Purple Rain*-era tracks alongside covers of 'Proud Mary,' 'All Along The Watchtower,' and, surprisingly, Foo Fighters' 'Best Of You,' complete with a full marching band. A few tetchy criticisms aside (some observers felt that Prince had deliberately thrown a phallic pose with his guitar while his silhouette was projected onto a large sheet), the show was a resounding success. Despite having to perform in torrential rain after a storm threatened to ruin the whole event, Prince was deemed to have delivered the most successful halftime show in years.

According to former manager Alan Leeds, Prince's appearance at Super Bowl XLI was "a landmark appearance that will be remembered for years to come." Perhaps the most notable aspect of it, Leeds noted, was that Prince "hasn't had a genuine hit record in many years [but] is still viewed in the fickle world of pop music as a major force."[3] With more than 140 million Americans watching – and plenty more viewers tuning in around the world – this was probably the biggest promotional opportunity of his career. Not only did it mean that all eyes were on him in advance of a new album release, it also raised the bar for future halftime shows. (The comparatively lackluster Tom Petty had no chance of competing in 2008.)

But Leeds was right – by the time Prince touched base in London in May to announce his Earth Tour, the world was waiting to see what new business model Prince would unveil this time. To begin with, *Planet Earth*'s release would follow the standard trajectory of recent years. After signing a pressing and distribution deal with a major label (Columbia again), he made a one-off appearance in the market he intended to focus on (a 1am performance at London's Koko club, his first UK concert in five years, on May 10) in anticipation of a 21-date residency at the O$_2$ Arena.

Prince also intended once again to include a copy of his new album in the ticket price. So far so normal. Then, a few weeks before *Planet Earth*'s planned UK release date, July 16, he announced plans to give the album away free a day earlier, with the July 15 edition of the *Mail On Sunday* newspaper.

Free CD and DVD cover-mounts were not a new phenomenon; they had been used as an incentive for customers to buy magazines and newspapers for years. (The *Mail On Sunday* had already caused a minor stir in April when giving away a copy of Mike Oldfield's *Tubular Bells*, with the artist himself complaining that it devalued his already well-worn music.) The difference with *Planet Earth* was that it marked the first time any artist had given a brand new recording away, and it seemed to carry with it a damaging message: screw the expensive middleman, have the album for free instead. Not surprisingly, the industry was outraged, with SonyBMG reportedly tearing up its UK contract with Prince. "It was ridiculous to have a UK deal," a spokesman told Yahoo! News, "when two million copies are going out free with papers."[4] (Prince would later claim that he wasn't trying to upstage the record company: he just wanted to get new music out. "I asked Sony: 'Were you planning to sell three million copies in London?'" he told *USA Today*'s Edna Gunderson. "I sold three million copies overnight. That's a good, clear business deal."[5])

Record retailers – already losing revenue to online sales and digital downloads – were similarly incensed. "Retailers figure that he owes them because they supported him in his early days," a *Billboard* columnist remarked, "but Prince probably figures he's paid them by providing multiplatinum sales throughout his career."[6] As far as Entertainment Retailer's Association chairman Paul Quirk was concerned, however, the man once known as The Artist Formerly Known As Prince was in danger of becoming known as "The Artist Formerly Known As Available In Record Stores."

The battle didn't stop there. It also stirred up trouble between the UK's two major music retailers when HMV decided to stock copies of the *Mail On Sunday* for the first time ever, despite having already publicly criticized Prince's marketing coup. "We're stunned that HMV has decided to take what appears to be a complete U-turn," Simon Douglas of the Virgin Megastores chain told the *Telegraph*. "Only a week ago they were so vocal about the damage it will cause."[7] As far as HMV was concerned, stocking the newspaper was simply a way of making the most of a bad situation.

Prince knew that signing the deal with the *Mail On Sunday* would destroy his contract with Columbia, but he probably didn't care. Rumor has it that he was paid somewhere between £200,000 and £500,000 for the giveaway, which is much more than he was likely to have made from a record-label advance. (It was also reported that, although the *Mail On Sunday* sold more copies than it had since the death of Princess Diana, the newspaper ended up losing money on the deal because of the cost of promoting the scheme.)

Cynics have since suggested that Prince might well have needed to give *Planet Earth* away anyway. It was well received by fans – some of whom felt it to the best album he had made since his commercial resurgence – but the media response was decidedly lukewarm. "By no means terrible" was about the best thing the *Guardian* could find to say about it.[8] *Rolling Stone* called it "one of those albums he makes when he's trying a little harder than usual."[9]

Planet Earth's opening title-track plays the same wrong-footing game as 'Sign "O" The Times' did 20 years earlier. It begins with the sense that Prince is about to make an important statement about global warming, but the overall message is as naïve as ever, and soon gives way to yet another round of commercially-minded funk'n'ballads. 'Chelsea Rodgers' is a tired disco-lite affair; 'Somewhere Here On Earth' another uneventful, jazzy croon; lead single 'Guitar' a rock riff in search of a song that recalls U2's 'I Will Follow.'

In any case, Prince had bigger plans than just putting out a new album. He knew that he had a captive audience of 504,000 during the course of his 21 Nights at the O_2 Arena, for which he was charging £31.21 for standard tickets – as well as offering VIP passes for the hardcore followers, and playing after-hours shows at the smaller $IndigO_2$ venue for a further fee. Casual fans who enjoyed a hits-based live set might also decide to seek out his past work in record stores. Instead of touring to promote an album release, he was using the album release – and the attendant controversy – to promote his live show.

Given the amount of money he stood to make from tickets, merchandise, and back catalog sales, this was something of a masterstroke, and a sign of things to come. Within months, a number of other high-profile acts, including Madonna and Jay-Z, had followed Prince in stepping away from the traditional music industry contract toward '360 degree' deals with concert promoters. (As it turned out, Prince felt that 360 deals were no better than standard contracts. "Anybody that signs one of those," he told Tavis Smiley, "[is] absolutely crazy."[10])

As with the Jam Of The Year shows, Prince quickly dropped material from his new album in favor of old hits on what started out as the Earth Tour but ended up becoming known as 21 Nights In London. In doing so he seemed almost to be admitting that his new music had no hope of matching his best work from the past. Nobody seemed to mind. Performing in the round on a symbol-shaped stage, he treated his audiences to a wide range of full-band classics, adding a solo-piano section midway through the residency for intimate versions of songs such as 'Sometimes It Snows In April.' He would often end the night alone in front of a synthesizer, teasing the crowd with instrumental riffs from raunchier songs including 'Erotic City' and Vanity 6's 'Nasty Girl.'

Replicating the success of the previous year's Las Vegas residency, Prince earned far more money from his 21 Nights In London than he would have done from a lengthier tour of different venues. Even the event's promoter, AEG's president of international touring, Rob Hallett, was amazed at its success, joking that he wished Prince had moved to a house numbered 9494, rather than 3121. Recalling initial negotiations for the residency, Hallett noted Prince's insistence that they stage 21 nights at the capital's largest venue. "We said: 'OK, let's do 21 nights in London,'" Hallet told the BBC, "'just as long as you're prepared for the last 10 days to be in Ronnie Scott's,'" a tiny jazz club in the center of town.[11] Prince, of course, knew better and "wouldn't even consider the possibility of anything else."[12]

During the high-profile launch parties for his *21 Nights* book the following year – at London's Dorchester Hotel, his place of residence during the 21 Nights stint, on October 1; and a two-concert performance New York's Ganesvoort Hotel on October 10, charging $1,000 and $300 a ticket for the latter's respective sets – Prince told reporters: "I couldn't have sold out 21 nights in London in the peak of my career, it would have been an impossibility."[13] Entering his 50th year, he seemed happy to trade on live performances of past classics rather than studio renditions of new songs. "His bands may seem more anonymous with every tour," said Alan Leeds, "but the general public probably couldn't care less as long as Prince remains capable of tearing up a stage."[14]

Despite the shows' unquestionable success – and what was essentially a heritage act selling out the 24,000-capacity O_2 for 21 nights to audiences consisting of largely fair-weather fans – the general public weren't entirely aware of the battle going on behind the scenes between Prince and his hardcore fans. Requests that no one take photos or videos of his London shows were heavily enforced by the O_2 staff. As ever, dedicated fans found a way of circumventing the rules, enraging Prince enough that he started to get litigious with the very people who follow his every move – and, eventually, with the whole of cyberspace.

The fall-out was reminiscent of events that had taken place earlier in the decade. In January 2004, Prince had forced guide2prince.org to close because it allowed online discussion of his bootlegs (the implication being that it also facilitated the sale of them). In October of the same year, he also went into battle with the owners of housequake.com, who subsequently came to an agreement with Prince's lawyers that allowed the site to continue running as long as its bootleg trading forum was closed and no 'illegal' photos from the Musicology tour were posted.

In December 2006, princefams.com was told to stop using images of the singer altogether. That particular matter was dealt with fairly quickly, but things took a turn for the worse the following summer when fans began posting photos and video clips from Prince's 21 Nights In London residency. The end result was the start of a full-scale war on the internet that threatened to rival Prince's battle with Warner Bros a decade earlier in terms of embarrassment.

Teaming up with Web Sheriff, an organization set up to help defend artists' intellectual-property rights, Prince set his sights squarely on some of the internet's most prominent sites. He challenged various BitTorrent portals to remove links to downloads of live recordings, YouTube to remove all videos containing his images and music, eBay to remove all auctions of counterfeit Prince material, and all other websites to remove his images, likenesses, and music.

Perhaps most damaging to his reputation was Universal Music Corp's insistence that Pennsylvanian mother Stephanie Lenz take down 29 seconds of footage of her 13-month-old baby dancing to 'Let's Go Crazy' in June 2007, just before the start of the London residency. Lenz in turn sued the company for acting in bad faith, invoking the same 1998 copyright law that Universal had cited. On August 28 2008, San Jose's District Judge Jeremy Fogel ruled that "copyright-holders can't order one of their songs removed from the web without first checking to see if the excerpt was so small and innocuous that it was legal."[15] Then, on February 25 2010, he voted in Lenz's favor, allowing her to recover legal fees incurred for fighting the takedown, while also paving the way for her to make a further claim to recoup the cost of seeking damages from Universal in her follow-up litigation.

"The Warner Bros battle left its scars, but it also made [Prince] a lot more savvy in terms of protecting his rights," Web Sheriff's John Giacobbi explained in an interview with *The Register*. "That dispute was about records and CDs, and now that we're into the digital age, he's fighting for his online rights."[16]

Unfortunately, Prince wasn't just targeting the likes of eBay and YouTube. In a replay of his actions of February 1999, he sent cease and desist letters to websites – including prince.org, princefams.com, and housequake.com – ordering them to remove all copyrighted images, including album sleeves and even fan tattoos of his 'love symbol.'

This time the fan sites grouped together, forming the Prince Fans United (PFU) coalition on November 5 and taking a stand against what they saw as an attempt not to "enforce valid copyright" (as Prince had claimed) but to "stifle all critical commentary." Negotiations between the two parties continued well into 2008, but a draft agreement drawn up between them was never signed. All images and music owned by Prince were removed from the sites, but anything that could be presented under the terms of 'fair usage' – including album sleeves – remained.

Further problems arose, however, and housequake.com sadly shut down on February 24 2009, during the run-up to the release of *LotusFlow3r*. Although no official reason was given, it appears that Prince may have objected to housequake.com's home-page banner. Despite celebrating – and indeed promoting – the forthcoming release, the imagery was presumably deemed too similar to Prince's official artwork. The site disappeared without a trace, leaving behind only a holding page reading "38:11," taken as a reference to either Job 38:11 – "And I said: 'Thus far you shall come, but no farther; And here shall your proud waves stop'" – or

Psalms 38:11: "For your arrows have pierced me, and you hand has come down upon me."

The proliferation of Prince media on the web, originally cultivated by the singer himself, had come back to haunt him. With all the mudslinging and litigation flying back and forth, it's no wonder that he wanted out. On December 23 2007, he took 3121.com and all of its multimedia content offline, followed by the rest of his web portfolio. By the end of the year his official web presence was nothing but a blank screen.

One good thing did come of the clash between Prince and the fan coalition. On November 8, three days after the formation of PFU, Prince sent out 'PFUnk,' a seven-minute funk extravaganza allegedly recorded in one night. "I hate to let you know that it's on," he sings, seemingly in reference to the tensions, before reminding his fans that "digital music disappears in a day ... I love all y'all / Don't you ever mess with me no more."

The song was greeted as one of his best recordings in years, apparently confirming some fans' assertions that Prince's best music is driven by aggression. Some felt that it was better than his three recent albums – *Musicology*, *3121*, and *Planet Earth* – put together. It was so good, in fact, that Prince renamed it 'F.U.N.K.' and released it as a digital-only single via iTunes later in the month.

After such an explosive end to 2007, Prince kept a low profile during the early part of the following year, during which time he took up residency in a rented Beverly Hills Park mansion, known as the 77. He stayed in Los Angeles for the rest of the year and made a series of low-key appearances around the city, turning up at various parties, guesting on stage at clubs with the likes of Blind Boys Of Alabama, and performing low-key early-hours concerts at the 77 and The Green Door.

By spring, however, the Prince machine had started to rumble once more. A one-off April 25 appearance on *The Tonight Show With Jay Leno* saw him unleash a new song, 'Turn Me Loose.' The song might merely have been a slice of the James Brown funk Prince could write in the time it took to perform, but it was notable for its return to more carnal matters. "Whatever's holding up this bed / Won't be here when I'm through," he sings to an unnamed woman who could also look forward to something that's "against the law in 13 states." It was the most straight-up funky Prince had sounded in years, but he ended up confining the recorded version to The Vault (perhaps having had second thoughts about the lyrics). It took LA's KJLH radio station to set the record loose after a resident DJ begged Prince for a copy on the promise that he wouldn't play it, only to fail to resist his own urges.

The Leno appearance was just a precursor to Prince's headlining performance at Coachella the following evening. Despite the rave reviews, a rumored $4.8

million fee, and onstage reunions with both Sheila E. and Morris Day, the high-point – an unexpected cover of Radiohead's 'Creep' – served only to reopen old wounds. Having forced all performance footage off of the internet, Prince then found his reasoning challenged once more when Radiohead's Thom Yorke questioned his right to do so. "Surely we should block it," Yorke said. "Tell him to unblock it. It's our ... song."[17]

A minor feud between artists was nothing compared to what Prince had coming in 2008. Despite being one of his quietest years, in terms of releases, since 2003, he would find himself on the rum end of three lawsuits before the year was out. An October 2007 case brought against him by video editor Ian C. Lewis resulted in the ruling on November 5 2008 that Prince should pay Lewis $58,000 in damages for unpaid work, unreturned equipment, and the breaking of a $25,000 computer (the judge's figure was a drop in the ocean for Prince, however, given that Lewis was seeking $1 million). Later that month, on November 17, Revelations Perfume & Cosmetics Inc sued both Prince and Universal for an alleged failure to promote their *3121*-branded perfume, claiming a loss of $2.5 million.

Even the live arena – which was usually where Prince raked in the dollars – gave him legal problems. Just ten days before he was due to perform, Prince cancelled a high-profile one-off performance at Dublin's Croke Park stadium (for which he was to receive $3 million). In turn, Promoters MCD sued the artist to the tune of €1.7 million, seeking to recoup the financial losses of promoting the show and having to refund 55,126 tickets. Despite Prince's lawyers' claim that "not one line" of an artist's contract had been drafted for the performance (a somewhat hypocritical defence from a man who once boasted of not needing a 'CONtract' when he signed Larry Graham to NPG), MCD countered that Prince's booking agents, William Morris Endeavor Entertainment, had made it clear via email that Prince was due to perform.

During the court case, which finally began on February 23 2010, it emerged that, when MCD's founder Denis Desmond grew alarmed at the lack of information coming from Paisley Park just weeks before the gig, Prince had ordered his WMEE contact Keith Sarkisian to "tell the cat to chill, I'll figure it out."[18] The warring parties eventually did just that, and the case was settled out of court for an undisclosed sum on February 26 2010. (That same day, Prince unveiled a new song, 'Cause And Effect,' with the lyrics "Leave no enemies / Leave no debt.")

In 2008, with such negativity surrounding him, it's no wonder that Prince sought to remind the world of his recent glories. On September 30, he released *21 Nights*, a hardback photo book chronicling his stay in London the previous year. Indeed, he rode the 2007 London residency's success into mid-April 2009, when he launched *The Prince Opus*, a leather-bound limited edition of *21 Nights* housed in a velvet box and boasting a Prince-branded iPod Touch featuring 40 minutes of 21

Nights live footage. If the $2,100 asking price seemed steep, the cost of the one-off 'Number One' edition, wrapped in alligator skin and sporting a platinum 'O{+>' symbol encrusted with 21 diamonds (five of them purple), is likely to have been astronomical. According to publishers, Opus Kraken, the book was due to "globally tour 12 major cities and be finally auctioned in late 2009," with the winner of the auction enjoying a private performance by Prince in LA for up to 50 guests, and receive the spray-painted '21' jacket he wore on the final London show. Its ultimate fate remains undocumented. Perhaps this had something to do with interest in the ridiculously expensive Kraken artifact only enjoying a short, early peak. Kraken's CEO and founder, Karl Fowler, boasted of having sold a third of the 950 standard editions in the first weekend, claiming: "We always knew that we would get to a sellout position within a few months."[19] (The *Opus* was, however, still being sold through Kraken's website a year later.)

Enjoying more longevity was the live recording *Indigo Nights*. Included with all editions of the book, it's a sizzling document of the after-show sets that Prince had played almost every night in London in the O_2's intimate IndigO$_2$ club. While many commented on the airbrushed, fashion catalog-feel of the photos (even down to the itemizing of every piece of clothing), photographer Randee St Nicholas was at pains to point out that this is how Prince's life really looks. "It may be glamorous to others," she said, "but that's his comfort zone. It's not like he changes to go out and be Prince. The guy looks amazing 24 hours a day."[20]

Despite the positive response to the book, Prince seemed determined to end 2008 on a down note. Ostensibly promoting *21 Nights*, he spoke to *The New Yorker*'s Claire Hoffman for an article published on November 24 as 'Soup With Prince.' He began by talking about spending his time in Los Angeles, so that he could "understand the hearts and minds of the music moguls ... to sit down with them, to understand the way they see things, how they read Scripture," before turning to the wider world. With the Presidential election on the horizon, Prince began drawing comparisons between the Republicans and Democrats; the former party "doing things and saying it comes from [The Bible], but it doesn't," the latter saying: "'You can do whatever you want.' Gay marriage, whatever." Although he quickly added that "neither of them is right," Prince had backed himself into a corner. According to Hoffman, whe Prince was "asked about his perspective on social issues – gay marriage, abortion," he tapped his Bible and said: "God came to the earth and saw people sticking it wherever and doing whatever, and he just cleared it all out. He was, like, 'Enough.'"[21]

Prince, the master of avoiding straight answers, had failed to give one at a crucial moment. His comments appeared on newsstands on November 17, with Hoffman herself interviewed for the magazine's website that day in anticipation of the main article appearing in print. Prince would later tell the *LA Times*'s Ann

Powers that he has gay friends, and that they "study the Bible together," but the damage was done.[22] California had held its state elections on November 4, with the controversial California Marriage Protection Act, known as Proposition 8, passed the same day. A new provision, Section 7.5 Of The Declaration Of Rights, was added to California's Constitution, declaring: "Only marriage between a man and a woman is valid or recognized in California." And while Prince had never openly said he was against gay marriage, for his gay fans – and everyone else who reveled in his 80s charge for sexual liberation – the singer's inability to unequivocally state that he was in favor of same-sex marriage came as a terrible blow.

Inevitably, the damage limitation operation began, but still without a direct clarification from the artist himself. As the comment (or lack of) spread across the world, Prince's insiders sent a message to the Los Angeles-based website – and leading Prince-watcher – Dr Funkenberry. Claiming that Claire Hoffman's piece was "chock full of misquotes," Funkeberry was told that "the parts about religion are especially misquoted."[23] (Rather undermining the force of the claims, however, was the admission that Prince had not allowed Hoffman to use a tape recorder.)

While living in Los Angeles seemed to have led to Prince becoming encased in a bigger bubble than ever, it's likely that, as a committed follower of the Jehovah's Witnesses (who "haven't voted for their whole inception"), he isn't worried about such earthly concerns as gay rights.[24] He lives his life as close to The Bible as possible; it is, for him, "a history book, a science book, a guidebook."[25] Oddly enough, despite Prince's uneasy relationship with the press, his most sympathetic supporter seemed to be Claire Hoffman. "For what it's worth, the way he said it wasn't hateful so much as sad and resigned," she told thenewyorker.com. "Prince is a true believer, and I think that's important to keep in mind in hearing his viewpoint."[26]

Perhaps surprisingly, in the immediate aftermath of the *New Yorker* article, Prince actively turned to the press, inviting a series of carefully vetted journalists to his Beverly Hills home for advance plays of his new work: a three-disc set featuring the Prince albums *LotusFlow3r* and *MPLSound*, plus *Elixer* by his latest protégé, Bria Valente. Prince would give the cream of LA journalists personal listening sessions of *MPLSound* while parked in his sports car (christened 'Miles Davis' for its dark black color), move to the bedroom to unveil *Elixer* (introduced as music which is "nasty, but not dirty"), and drive around Hollywood in his limo listening to *LotusFlow3r*.[27] The first the public got to hear of this new music was on December 17, when local rock radio station Indie 103 was given the honor of premiering *LotusFlow3r*'s 'Crimson & Clover' (a Tommy James & The Shondells cover), followed by 'Colonized Mind,' 'Wall Of Berlin,' and *MPLSound*'s '4Ever.'

After spending most of December 2008 shipping the album around Los Angeles and in attempt to find a satisfying method of distribution, it wasn't until early 2009 that Prince revealed the business model for this new venture. Despite his repeated claims that "the gatekeepers must change," it merely seemed that the emperor had put on new clothes.[28] Having decided that it was no longer "realistic to expect to put out new music and profit from it … and keep it from being [exploited]," Prince went straight to the distributors with the triple-album set.[29] Eschewing the major labels that he'd recently dealt with for *Musicology*, *3121*, and *Planet Earth*, Prince struck a deal with the Minneapolis-based national retailer Target. They sold the *LotusFlow3r/MPLSound/Elixer* set exclusively (and only in the USA), buying wholesale from Prince, presumably not returning unsold copies as part of the agreement. "The beautiful thing about the relationship," Prince told Tavis Smiley, noting that 30 million people went through Target's doors each week, "is that they're treating us like any other record company. They buy the same amount and they pay the same price, so we've done quite well already."[30] (The Smiley appearance was just one of several returns to some of the old promotional haunts that had previously helped Prince during *Musicology*. He also staged a three-night run on *The Tonight Show With Jay Leno* and stopped off at Ellen Degeneres's syndicated daytime show.)

Then came the inevitable launch of a new website. Having decided that the war was over, Prince envisioned a new 3D cyber playground for himself, where each of the three albums would have their own world. "Prince wanted LotusFlow3r to function like a videogame in its interactivity," Scott Addision Clay, the lotusflow3r.com designer, revealed shortly after its launch on March 24. He was quick to add that this didn't mean "you control Prince with jujitsu moves – that wouldn't be appropriate."[31]

Prince himself was so excited about the new website that he invited six journalists and three 'Purple Ticket' winners to the 77 for an intimate concert and personal tour of the site. (The ever-observant Emily Mackay of nme.com – the only British journalist present – seemed most amazed that, among the Tuscan designs, pink granite, and Turkish rugs, Prince's house was stocked with something as normal as Bounty kitchen paper.) But despite years of running his own label – and pioneering internet distribution – lotusflow3r.com's launch wasn't without its problems. Alarm bells must have rung for fans when Dr Funkenberry posted advance warnings from Prince's people just hours before the site was due to go live at the Princely time of 7:07pm. Among the advice given was: "If anyone has trouble downloading stuff, try later tonight and just listen to what is on the player … You may not get email confirmations for tickets until tomorrow."

It wasn't just confirmation emails that were missing. Most of the fans who paid the $77 membership fee appear not to have received the free *LotusFlow3r* T-shirt they were promised, in an echo of the *Crystal Ball* distribution problems of the mid 90s. (Unsurprisingly, communications with Paisley Park were still being ignored a year later, and the website eventually closed in March 2010.) As the year progressed, much of the promised catalog of unreleased concerts from The Vault seemed mostly to have been culled from footage of a handful of 2009 appearances. Even logging in to lotusflow3r.com was hard enough – and this was before fans had paid their fees. For all its 3D splendor, the site was initially inaccessible from Europe, and couldn't recognize underscores or other non-alphanumeric characters. Fans even had to crack a code, filling in the blanks in "Mar 07 _____," and "_____, California," before they could access the registration page. (The answers were "1986" and "Los Angeles.")

Those fans who finally found their way in – or simply waited for the three-CD set to be released through Target on March 29 – received a trio of albums that saw Prince asserting the various well-known aspects of his work. *LotusFlow3r* showed off his guitar chops; *MPLSound* returned to the electro-funk that launched the Minneapolis Sound over two decades before; and *Elixer* demonstrated his ability to pick largely characterless female singers to write unremarkable music for.

The albums' gestation stretched back to 2006, when Prince backed Támar on tour and fell in love with his guitar again, and continued until late September 2008. (An early take of 'Feel Good, Feel Better, Feel Wonderful' was emailed to NPGMC members on June 29 2006, while *MPLSound*'s 'U're Gonna C Me' first appeared on 2002's *One Nite … Alone*.) Much of *LotusFlow3r*'s organic feel can be credited to the fact that Prince enlisted long-term cohorts, including Michael Bland, Renato Neto, Greg Boyer, and Maceo Parker, to help record his most artistically questing release since *The Rainbow Children* (most of its psychedelic audio tricks can, however, be credited to Pro Tools).

Musically, when not invoking his jazz muse, Prince seemed keen to pay his dues to rock heroes such as Jimi Hendrix, as on 'Dreamer,' while also chucking a Hendrix-invoking 'Wild Thing' refrain into 'Crimson & Clover.' But while *The Rainbow Children* had a unifying vision – even if was somewhat heavy-handed – *LotusFlow3r*'s erratic flits from instrumental jazz to state-of-the-world commentaries and personal pleas such as 'Love Like Jazz''s wish to "feel like I've been hypnotized" fail to make it a thoroughly satisfying artistic statement. 'Wall Of Berlin' muddies the message further, with Prince using the politically charged image of the title as a springboard for a litany of playful double entendres such as "She went down … like the wall of Berlin." (Tantalizingly, Prince once alluded to a *LotusFlow3r* song called 'The Divine' that was so "mind-blowing" he doubted he would ever release it: the "harmonies hit" and Prince "put it away."[32])

The most heartfelt moment on the album (and the one for which Prince earned a Grammy nomination) is 'Dreamer,' which required a typically Prince-like 'explanation' for its message to disseminate. Speaking to Tavis Smiley in the first of two interviews to promote the albums, Prince revealed that it was inspired by comedian Dick Gregory's speech at Smiley's recent *State Of The Black Union* convention. "He said something that really hit home about the phenomena of chemtrails," he said. "When I was a kid, I used to see these trails in the sky all the time … and the next you know everybody in your neighborhood was fighting."[33] In referencing the conspiracy theory that chemtrails left in the wake of flying planes were actually biological agents sprayed across the earth at the government's behest, Gregory made Prince realize that he was living in a place that "feels just like a plantation" – in, as he sings, "The United States of the Red, White and Blue."[34]

Next, on *MPLSound*, Prince's overt adoption of Pro Tools-style digital recording results in a cold, distant feel. While the likes of '(There'll Never B) Another Like Me' and 'Chocolate Box' bounce along pleasantly enough (the latter perhaps featuring Prince's first wholly successful rap vocal interpolation, courtesy of Q-Tip), the overall effect is all too one-note. The likes of 'Ol' Skool Company' and 'No More Candy 4 U' – on which Prince bemoans two other modern day pet concerns: how much better music used to be crossed with some commentary on the recession; and the numbers of "haters on the internet" – sound like their creator is enjoying himself much more, in the studio, than any listener could via their stereo. He wasn't completely devoid of cheek, however. This 51-year-old one-time sexual omnivore uses 'Valentina' to send out a message to Salma Hayek's daughter: "Tell your mama she should give me a call."

If that showed there was juice in the old lemon yet, Bria Valente's *Elixer* was, as Prince himself noted, nasty – but not dirty. Valente wasn't "promoting promiscuity," he said, but singing about "her lover, who could be her partner for life."[35] But if the most Prince himself could say about the album was that it's "one of those sleeper records," recorded because they got tired of waiting for Sade to make a new album, it's difficult to know what he expected his fans to see in a singer who was better than Carmen Electra but still no Rosie Gaines.[36] Indeed, Prince seemed to be most interested in Valente because of "how rapidly she picked up understanding of scripture."[37] This hardly tallied with her being someone who could record a convincing steamy New Age soul album designed for "a whole lotta people [to] get pregnant off of."[38]

Tacked on at the end of two bona fide Prince releases, Bria Valente was never going to get much luck with the critics. Even Jon Bream, writing in her (and Prince's) hometown paper, the *Minneapolis Star-Tribune*, couldn't shake the feeling that it was "a throwaway, done as a favor for a friend."[39] (He probably wasn't far off, as Prince was introduced to the Minneapolis-born Valente by keyboardist Morris Hayes.) It's telling that the closest Valente ever got to performing live was when Tavis Smiley interviewed her immediately after speaking to her mentor. (Valente claimed that she and Prince were "just trying to make some stellar elevator music."[40])

Amazingly, the two Prince offerings seemed be the first for some time to unify reviewers, who generally accepted that he remained an adept musician even if there were no new tricks. The only real differences in opinion came over whether they preferred guitar-god Prince or electro-funk Prince. Most agreed with the *LAist*'s observation that *LotusFlow3r* is "faintly psychedelic with big gobs of distorted guitar thrown around liberally,"[41] while *MPLSound* was neatly summed up by *USA Today*, which noted that Prince was "revisiting the synth vibe of the 80s with his outsize ego intact."[42] A stand-out review by pitchfork.com's Jess Harvell graciously decided that assessing a new Prince album "all but demands forced objectivity and willfully ignoring his own first decade as a recording artist" – even if she conceded that *MPLSound* found Prince "pastiching his own 80s sound as a profitable parlor game."[43]

Despite a lack of radio play, and thanks no doubt to the fact that the triple-album package sold at Target for a recession-friendly $11.98, *LotusFlow3r* found itself peaking at Number Two on the *Billboard* chart in its first week on sale. Unsurprisingly, Prince refused to tour the album, especially as it was initially only available in America. Instead, he performed three full concerts in LA's Live Nokia Center, each at a different venue inside the complex, before making his first high-profile international appearance of the year when he played two sets at the Montreux Jazz festival on July 18. When *LotusFlow3r* eventually saw a European release in France, Prince undertook a mini-jaunt through Paris, performing another two sets in one day at the Grand Palais on October 11 (billed as 'All Day/All Night' and marking the first time that the historic venue had been used for a full-concert performance). He also recorded a mini-acoustic set for radio broadcasters RTL and made an appearance on Canal+'s *Le Grand Journal*.

Come the end of the year, with Prince's enthusiasm for *LotusFlow3r* presumably having wilted, he returned to try his luck in the hometown whose sound he had sought to reinvigorate on *MPLSound*. A Los Angeles-based court case followed when 3121 Rep Inc sued the owners of his $150,000-a-month Beverly Hills property for the return of a $300,000 security deposit, claiming that they had brokered the rental deal for Prince. (The owners of the property claimed that Prince made the payments himself, so the money should go to him; it was faintly reminiscent of the April lawsuit brought against the star by a literary agency seeking their 15 per cent fee for "the negotiations of a publishing deal" for *21 Nights*, in which the company alleged that he had finished the book behind its back to avoid paying.)

Back home, Prince seemed determined to make up for lost time: to give something back to Minneapolis, and ensure that it remained on the map. On October 24 he played his first concert at Paisley Park since 2004 in support of a Love 4 One Another coat drive. Then, in November, the longtime basketball fan was seen hanging out at Minnesota Vikings football games with Larry Graham – a new pastime, and one that would result in one of the oddest Prince releases yet.

CHAPTER 18

PRINCE IS ALIVE! (AND HE LIVES IN MINNEAPOLIS)

There's an incredible peace in
my life now and I'm trying to
share it with people.

PRINCE AT HOME IN PAISLEY PARK,
MINNEAPOLIS, 2010

ack in Minneapolis and openly engaging with the local community, Prince was clearly feeling invigorated. Having seen the Vikings beat the Dallas Cowboys 34-3 on January 17 2010 – a victory that enabled them to get through to the National Football Conference's championship game – Prince decided that he "saw the future"[2] in the Vikings' quarterback, Brett Favre. Rushing home with the sports team as his muse, he wrote 'Purple And Gold,' a new song designed to be roared from the terraces as fans cheered the home team on.

When it was unleashed via the Vikings' official website on January 21, however, Prince's "fight song" sounded little more than an out-take from Disney's *Enchanted*. With its thinly-veiled references to the Jehovah's Witness faith – "The veil of the sky draws open / The roar of the chariots touch down" – it's more high-school pledge than gritted-teeth cavalry call. The fans were dismayed; the song was quietly left alone. But Prince had succeeded in doing what the Vikings themselves hadn't: generating worldwide publicity. A week later, after spending much of his time in Minneapolis visiting the local clubs, Prince turned up at First Avenue – not to perform, but to attend the fifth birthday party for local public-access radio station 89.3 The Current.

As February 2010 drew to a close, Prince contacted the station again with another new song, 'Cause And Effect,' which premiered at 7:40am on February 26. It's a much more revealing – and enjoyable – affair than 'Purple And Gold.' While the music itself is still somewhat 'PFUnk'-lite, the message seems to be that Prince is back, and that he's happy with his lot. Given the chance to do it all again, he declares, he wouldn't change a thing. "If I could talk to myself back then right now / I'd say, 'Son, you might wanna stick around / Something amazing is about to go down.'" Touchingly, for a man who had spent much of the previous decade trying to eradicate the more outrageous side of his past, he seemed to have come to terms with his pre-conversion self. "If you stamp your passport full of regret," he sings, "You'll have nothing to remember but a lot to forget."

Typically, Prince's return home wasn't without its problems. Just a few months into the new year, the *Star-Tribune* reported that he owed "thousands of dollars in back taxes, interest, and fines on various properties" in the area, and that he was running the risk of forfeiting them if he didn't pay his bills on time.[3] Minnesota's Carver County authorities ran the news in a local newspaper, the *Chaska Herald*; it emerged that Paisley Park alone was $221,891.88 in arrears, while Prince's total debts were in excess of $500,000.

The news couldn't have broken at a worse time. On August 3, Prince – now almost perpetually court-bound – would find himself sued by his former lawyer, Ed McPherson, for an alleged failure to pay $49,987.74 in legal fees. Ironically, the fees were for services "in connection with a real estate transaction" for his old Beverly Park home – probably the return of the $300,000 deposit he put down on the 77 –

and for defending Prince's "alleged failure to pay agency commissions" for his *21 Nights* book deal. Even worse, however, was the fact that, as the one-year anniversary of lotusflow3r.com rolled around, there were alarming signs of fiscal mismanagement coming from within the Prince camp. (He had cleared his tax and legal debts by the end of September 2010.)

Since paying their $77 fee on March 24 2009, many subscribers to lotusflow3r.com were still chasing the site's customer support for the promised free T-shirt that never arrived. After looking into the situation, the prince.org fan site reported that lotusflow3r.com's telephone helpline had been disconnected, while emails sent to customer support were being ignored. Disgruntled fans began emailing lotusflow3r.com's team, stating that they did not want their subscription to be automatically renewed after the 12-month term ran out; on March 25 2010, however, many fans awoke to find that a further $77 had been deducted from their bank accounts.

An unsurprisingly speedy response from the website's development team claimed that this had only affected "the earliest adopters" of lotusflow3r.com – who were, of course, going to be refunded. The message also went out of its way to remind fans that "Prince had no hand in this ... the error was due to lack of thoroughness on our part." Speaking to the *Wall Street Journal* online shortly after the fiasco, Prince's lotusflow3r.com developer, Scott Addison Clay, admitted that "a few hundred" members had to be refunded. He also bemoaned his boss's lack of interest in the site once subscribers had signed up. Speculating that Prince had been disappointed by the number of sign-ups, Clay revealed that the web team only received fresh content "in dribs and drabs." After asking several times for the promised material from the Vault, Clay received a phone call from Prince, who told him to "cut it out."[4] Clay was sacked not long after the website's launch, and found himself in the position of having to hand over all the lotusflow3r.com files to his replacement.

What – if anything – Prince has in mind for the files remains to be seen. He has since shut the website down and once again erased his online presence. By the summer of 2010, despite attempts to send out positive signals, he seemed to be in need of some serious cash. Teaming up again with The Current, he celebrated his birthday publicly for the first time in years, giving the local radio station 'Hot Summer,' which had its debut on June 7, Prince's 52nd birthday. *Rolling Stone* guessed that the song was inspired by Minneapolis's record-breaking May heat wave; Prince told The Current's program director Jim McGuinn he thought it had "a B-52s feel to it." Such lowly ambitions would once have been out of the question. The disappointment was writ large in the review on stereogum.com, which concluded: "At least the lyrics are positive."[5]

Whatever his private situation, Prince was trying to remain upbeat in public. A week later, having been given a Lifetime Achievement award from BET, he could be seen in television coverage of the event. The star looked like a truly engaged member of the audience, enjoying every last minute of a tribute that saw Janelle Monae, Esperanza Spalding, Alicia Keys, and Patti LaBelle perform 'Let's Go Crazy,' 'If I Was Your Girlfriend,' 'Adore,' and 'Purple Rain' respectively. Inevitably, rumors began to circulate about a new album. Dr Funkenberry soon revealed that Prince's next release – the unashamedly backward-looking *20Ten* – would be given away by a selection of European print publications on July 10. But while Prince's representative, Kiran Sharma, boasted that the release marked "a world first of delivering the new album across multiple territories, through complimentary distribution channels," it was hard to escape the feeling of 'same but different.' More intriguing was Dr Funkenberry's claim that Prince had met with his old nemesis Warner Bros on June 22 – not only to discuss US distribution for the album but also to talk about "something else."[6]

Such a tantalizing – and mysterious – promise went all but ignored in the UK, however, where the media whipped itself into a bit of a Prince frenzy over the giveaway. Although it was not on the level of 2007's all-out-assault, the news that the *Daily Mirror* newspaper would include a copy of *20Ten* in its July 10 edition was greeted with a strong sense of anticipation. The following day, respected music journalist Paul Morley described how Prince's work "unfold[s] with fertile, otherworldly, Dylanesque consistency."[7] In Scotland, *20Ten* was released by the *Daily Mirror*'s sister newspaper, the *Daily Record*, before being unveiled by Belgium's *Het Nieuwsblad*, France's *Courier International*, and the Germany edition of *Rolling Stone*.

Equally consistent was the media campaign to accompany the album's release. The *Daily Mirror*, German *Rolling Stone*, and *Het Nieuwsblad* were all given access to Paisley Park in order to interview Prince – who pulled the strings as masterfully as ever in order to get what he needed. The published interviews had enough similarities to suggest that each paper's writers were treated to carbon copy experiences. (Sitting in on drums with Prince and the band, only to get fired for poor timekeeping, seemed to be a particular favorite for both musician and journalist alike.) It was the *Daily Mirror*, however, that received worldwide recognition for printing the inevitable controversial remark in the first of their weeklong run of features trailing the album's release.

Praising the *Daily Mirror* for allowing him to find new ways to release his music, Prince said: "The internet's completely over. I don't see why I should give my music to iTunes or anyone else. They won't pay me an advance for it and then they get angry when they can't get it."[8] Unsurprisingly, these comments shot around internet message boards and blogs by the end of the day, with most commentators decrying such a lack of vision – especially from a musician who had once pioneered internet distribution. But while in the 90s Prince had kicked against outmoded distribution models and replaced them with his groundbreaking cyber vision, denouncing the internet in order to strike deals with a print media whose very future has been left seriously challenged by technological advances seemed little short of madness. Furthermore, the idea of making a new album available for just one day in a newspaper seemed to go against Prince's ethos of ensuring his music reaches as many people as possible.

Prince found a number of staunch supporters among those who agreed with his concerns about Apple and iTunes (even if they questioned his overall logic). Writing online for *Forbes*, Quentin Hardy urged readers to cheer Prince for saying "outright what others are just acting on," noting that *Wired* magazine would run a cover story celebrating the internet's facilitation of free access to product before charging $4.99 for its own iPad application.[9] For Prince, however, perhaps more important was the fact that, for him, a newspaper advance would make much more money than an internet release, where the number of paying customers could not be guaranteed.

Being able to demand up-front payment for his work put Prince in a remarkable and enviable position. With *20Ten*, however, he failed to provide the product that ought to reward somebody else's advanced outlay and risk-taking. Unsurprisingly, the *Daily Mirror* trumpeted the work as Prince's "best album in 23 years" and put it "on a par with Elvis's 1968 comeback," singling out individual tracks as his "most soulful," "most spiritual," or "most romantic" for some time, for most listeners *20Ten* proved to be Prince's most disappointing record of the 21st century.

Whereas *1999* still sounds like a futuristic masterpiece, *20Ten* struggles even to sound relevant within the context of the year of its release. The production is slightly warmer and more organic than that of *MPLSound*, but the album still left listeners cold. 'Compassion' sounds like a watered-down version of 'Let's Pretend We're Married,' while the irritatingly breezy 'Everybody Loves Me' wholly fails to grasp what made 'All The Critics Love U In New York' such an enjoyable piece of tongue-in-cheek arrogance. There might be a nice 'quiet storm' ballad in 'Walk In Sand,' but Prince has been churning those out for years. And when he sings of taxes helping to build bomb-dropping planes "supposedly to keep us safe from Saddam" on 'Act Of God,' it's as if Prince is unaware that Saddam Hussein hasn't posed much of a threat since being hanged in December 2006, revealing an alarming level of disconnection in the process. Typically perverse, Prince buried the most interesting cut, 'Laydown,' on track 77 of the CD. The only *20Ten* offering to hint at past glories, it features murky, disconcerting guitar, complex synth lines, and a convincing rap in which Prince crowns himself "the Purple Yoda."

Despite the hype, the UK freebie only managed to shift an extra 379,000 copies of the *Mirror* and *Record* – a far cry from the *Mail On Sunday*'s claim that *Planet Earth* upped sales by 600,000 in 2007. On July 12, the *Mirror* began offering free copies of the album to anyone who ordered the newspaper online.

Prince himself seemed aware of the album's failings. He played only one *20Ten* track ('Future Soul Song') during the eight-date European tour he undertook to promote the record, and even then only as the penultimate song on the setlist of an after-show gig at the Viage in Brussels. Perhaps sensing the lackluster response to the album – even as he talked-up a planned deluxe edition for stores, with the disappointingly lukewarm addition of 'Rich Friends' – he began to drop hints that the copyright on his Warners albums was reverting back to him, and that he had already remastered a number of them.

Whether these remasters see the light of day – and whether Prince can resist tampering with them – remains to be seen, but he may well have something in the works. Never one to make live appearances unless he has some product to shift, he appeared at Harlem's Apollo Theater on October 14 – the day that 'Rich Friends' leaked online – to announce a new live residency, Welcome 2 America. Although the details were vague, he promised performances by the likes of Maceo Parker, Sheila E., and new young soul star Janelle Monae as part of a series of shows for which he urged fans to "come early and come often, because every time we play it's always something new." Just over three weeks later he was back on stage at the Viage, connecting with his live muse in a way that he hadn't all year: performing a three-and-a-half-hour after-show to close a second mini-tour of Europe.

Speaking to *Ebony* magazine in June 2010, in an interview conducted before the *20Ten* campaign had taken off, Prince was asked about the status of his relationship with Bria Valente. "Self-interest is on the back burner for now," he said. "There is too much at stake." Tellingly, he also mentioned a need "to get back to localized music distribution on all levels."[10] Meanwhile, his interview with the *Mirror* was peppered with quotes about how what he "always dreamed of [as] a young musician" was to play "in my basement. Music is my life. It's my trade. If I can't get it out of my head I can't function."[11]

Prince had first started to hint that he had mellowed and accepted his position in the world back in 2008, the year he turned 50. "How old are we really?" he asked. "It's all about ascension ... I look forward to these years when everything is just open sky. I wish this for every artist: freedom."[12]

From demanding that he produce his debut album himself to insisting that his Warners releases follow *his* business plan and ultimately working solely to his own models by pioneering internet distribution and even giving away entire albums for free, Prince has fought for freedom his entire career. Now, rather than argue with a label or distributor, Prince's main concern is "ask[ing] if they believe in God, then: 'What kind of business do you want to conduct: transparent or hide the ball?'"[13] He'll release albums and tour – and play the game – as long as the business is clean.

Approaching his mid fifties, Prince need never record another note of music; yet, as The Neptunes' Pharrell Williams noted during the videotaped introduction to Prince's induction into the UK Music Hall Of Fame, "He will continue to make great records for as long as he wants to. A man like that cannot be stopped." There will always be Paisley Park studios, and there will always be promoters willing to book him.

With such a celebrated back catalog behind him, Prince has, in his own words, pushed the envelope off the table. Having made at least five truly groundbreaking albums by the time he hit 30 – and recorded plenty more since then that lesser artists would struggle even to conceptualize – Prince has nothing left to prove. That the likes of The Neptunes and OutKast have found such widespread success with their updates of his stripped-down funk shows just how much the world still needs the sound Prince pioneered in the 80s. Even in 2010, hip-hop star turned pop-soul singer Cee Lo Green had a hit with 'Fuck You' – essentially a sunshine-funk-pop Prince song, right down to the screams on the bridge.

Alan Leeds believes that the only person Prince needs to prove anything to now is himself. "Maybe that's what keeps him passionate about his performing," he told Housequake in 2007. "He has cleverly carved out a niche for himself, using – even manipulating – the industry when it serves him, and ignoring it the rest of the time. And I don't think he cares one bit how it might look compared to anything else."

In his 52 years on planet earth, Prince has become one of those rare artists able to break the musical mold – and the business mold – more than once, not least with his high-profile battle for freedom from Warners and his early realization of the power of the internet. He can continue to turn out albums with one-off licensing deals as long as he can still fill live venues: the album proves he's still capable of writing songs, the tour makes money and reminds everyone why they still care.

In this respect, Prince might just be the most successful artist ever to walk the planet. He hasn't self-destructed or died, and he hasn't allowed himself to age disgracefully or descend into self-parody. Despite not having a genuine hit record in years, Prince can always claim that he's Number One at the bank. He shows no sign of stopping. Having changed the way music sounds and the industry operates, he can rightly claim to be the most prolific and inventive artist of modern times, without having lost sight of his first passion. After more then 30 years in the business he still maintains that "music to me is a life force. It's not what I do. It's what I am."[14]

TIMELINE

1958–1975

June 7 1958: Prince Rogers Nelson born to John L Nelson and Mattie Shaw at Mount Sinai Hospital, Minneapolis, Minnesota, USA.
1960: Mattie Shaw gives birth to a daughter, Tyka. She and Prince grow up with three siblings from John L Nelson's first marriage: Sharon, Lorna, and Johnny Nelson.
1963: Taken by his mother to see his father play the piano in the Prince Rogers Trio. Starts to play the instrument himself soon after.
1965: Enrolls at John Hay Elementary School and writes first song, 'Funkmachine.'
1968: John L Nelson and Mattie Shaw divorce. Prince sees Joni Mitchell in concert.
1970: Moves in with his father and attends Bryant Junior High.
1972: Enrolls at Central High School and is kicked out of his father's house. Stays for a while with his aunt, Olivia Nelson.
1973: Taken in by Bernadette Anderson, the mother of his friend André, with whom he forms his first band, Grand Central. The line-up is completed by Prince's cousin, Charles Smith, and later expanded to included André's sister Linda and a mutual friend, Terry Jackson.
1974: Charles Smith is kicked out of Grand Central and replaced by another school friend, Morris Day. The band changes its name to Grand Central Corporation, and is managed by Day's mother, LaVonne Daugherty. Later in the year, Pepé Willie, Prince's cousin by marriage, moves to Minneapolis from New York and starts to oversee the band's progress.
1975: Invited to play on recordings by Pepé Willie's group 94 East.

1976

Winter: Records first demo with Grand Central Corporation at ASI Studio, Minneapolis.
February 13: First interview published in the *Central High Pioneer*.
Spring: Grand Central Corporation becomes Champagne, partly to avoid confusion with Larry Graham's new group, Graham Central Station. Meanwhile, Prince is invited by Chris Moon, the owner of Moonsound Studios, to collaborate on some songs in return for free studio time.
June 7: Graduates from Central High School.
Summer: Continues to work on material at Moonsound, both in collaboration with Chris Moon and on his own.
Fall: Travels to New York in search of a record deal, but turns down an offer from Tiffany Entertainment to buy the publishing rights to the songs on his demo.
Late fall: Chris Moon plays Prince's demo to Owen Husney, the owner of a local advertising agency. Husney becomes Prince's manager, giving him an allowance that the singer uses to move into his own studio apartment.
December: Starts recording a new demo at Sound 80 Studios, Minneapolis.

1977

April: Owen Husney puts together a press kit and organizes meetings with five record labels: Warner Bros, CBS, ABC/Dunhill, A&M, and RSO.
April 8: Records 'Just As Long As We're Together' as part of an in-studio audition for CBS at Village Recorders Studios, Los Angeles.
June 25: Signs a recording contract with

Warners; celebrates by recording 'We Can Work It Out.'

July: Records 'Just As Long As We're Together' at Amigo Studios, Los Angeles, while being watched – without realizing it – by several Warners executives, who subsequently agree to let him produce his debut album himself (with the help of 'Executive Producer' Tommy Vicari).

September: Starts work on *For You* at Sound 80 Studio, Minneapolis.

October 1: Moves to the Record Plant, Sausalito, following technical difficulties at Sound 80.

Late fall: Work continues on *For You*, and on an unreleased collaboration with André Anderson.

1978

January 4: Starts overdubbing and mixing *For You* at Sound Labs, Los Angeles.

Late February: Finally completes work on *For You* after running up studio bills of $170,000.

February 28: Attends the Grammy Awards with producer Tommy Vicari.

April 7: *For You* released; reaches Number 21 on the Billboard R&B chart, but stalls at Number 163 on the main Pop chart.

June 7: 'Soft & Wet'/'So Blue' released; eventually reaches Number 12 on the R&B chart and Number 92 on the Pop chart.

June: Embarks on a brief promotional tour of record-store signings in support of *For You*.

Summer: Moves into his first home at 5215 France Avenue, Edina. Works on recordings with local singer Sue Ann Carwell and Pepé Willie. Holds auditions for a touring band at Del's Tire Mart, Minneapolis, eventually settling on a line-up of André Cymone (bass), Bobby Z Rivkin (drums), Gayle Chapman and Matt Fink (keyboards), and Dez Dickerson (guitar).

November: Moves rehearsals to Pepé Willie's basement after having equipment stolen from Del's Tire Mart.

November 21: 'Just As Long As We're Together'/'In Love' released; reaches Number 91 on the Billboard R&B chart but fails to reach the Pop 100.

December: Owen Husney resigns as Prince's manager.

1979

January 5: Plays first live show as a solo artist at the Capri Theater, Minneapolis.

January 7: Plays a showcase for Warners, after which the label decides that he's not yet ready to tour.

February 17: Records with Pepé Willie's friend Tony Sylvester in New York, where he cuts tentative versions of 'I Feel For You' and 'Do Me, Baby.'

Spring: Taken on by Hollywood-based management firm Cavallo & Ruffalo.

April: Starts work on *Prince* at Alpha Studio, Los Angeles.

May: Relocates to Hollywood Sound Recorders, where he will remain until June 13.

Mid June: Begins tour rehearsals in University Warehouse, Minneapolis.

July 10: Starts work on a side project with The Rebels (made up of members of his touring group) at Mountain Ears Studio, Boulder, Colorado. Sessions continue until July 21.

August: Plays several showcase gigs for Warners in Los Angeles.

August 24: 'I Wanna Be Your Lover'/'My Love Is Forever' released; reaches Number One on the Billboard R&B chart, and Number 11 on the Pop chart.

October 19: *Prince* released; reaches Number Three on the R&B chart, and Number 22 on the Pop chart.

November 20: Begins Prince tour at the Roxy Theater, Los Angeles.

December 2: Forced to cancel remaining tour dates after contracting pneumonia and almost losing his voice.

1980

January 23: 'Why You Wanna Treat Me So Bad'/'Baby' released; reaches Number 13 on the R&B chart.

January 26: Performs 'I Wanna Be Your Lover' and 'Why You Wanna Treat Me So Bad' on *American Bandstand*, but refuses to speak to Clark.

February 9: Resumes tour at the Orpheum Theater, Minneapolis.

February 21: Joins Rick James's Fire It Up Tour as support act in what is billed as the Battle Of Funk. Plays 40 shows in nine weeks, ending at the Municipal Auditorium in Nasville, Tennessee, on April 27.

May: Begins work on *Dirty Mind* at home on 16-track console, having recently replaced keyboardist Gayle Chapman with Lisa Coleman.

July: Completes post-production work on *Dirty Mind* at Hollywood Sound Recorders.

September 10: 'Uptown'/'Crazy You' released; reaches Number Five on the Billboard R&B chart.

October 8: *Dirty Mind* released; reaches Number One on the R&B chart, and Number 45 on the Pop chart.

November 26: 'Dirty Mind'/'When We're Dancing Close & Slow' released; reaches Number 65 on the R&B chart.

December 4: Plays first night of the Dirty Mind tour at Shea's, Buffalo, New York.

December 26: Completes first leg of the Dirty Mind tour at the Uptown Theater, Chicago, Illinois.

1981

January: Moves into a new home – which he paints purple – in Chanhassen, on the outskirts of Minneapolis.

February 19: *Rolling Stone*'s influential feature asks, 'Will The Little Girls Understand?'

March 9: Second leg of the Dirty Mind tour begins at Sam's, Minneapolis, with the focus now on more intimate club-sized venues.

April 6: Tour ends at the Saenger Theater in New Orleans, Louisiana.

April–May: Starts putting together a side project, The Time. Morris Day, author of *Dirty Mind*'s 'Partyup,' will be the focal point of the group.

May 29: The non-charting single 'Gotta Stop Messin' About'/'Uptown' is released in the UK on the same day that Prince begins a three-date European tour at the Paradiso club in Amsterdam.

June 4: Takes to the stage of Theatre Le Palace, Paris, at 2:30am after having to wait for equipment to arrive from London (where he had played two nights earlier at the Lyceum).

June: Starts work on his next album, *Controversy*, at home and in Los Angeles.

July: Replaces bassist André Cymone with Mark Brown (aka Brown Mark).

July 29: *The Time* by The Time released; reaches Number 50 on *Billboard*.

September 2: 'Controversy'/'When You Were Mine' released; reaches Number Three on the R&B chart, but stalls at Number 70 on the Pop chart.

October 5: Plays a one-off *Controversy* showcase at Sam's in Minneapolis.

October 9: Opens for The Rolling Stones, Memorial Coliseum, Los Angeles, but is booed off after 15 minutes. Flies straight home to Minneapolis.

October 11: Returns to Los Angeles after pleas from bandmates – and Mick Jagger – to play second show with the Stones. Crowd reaction is even worse than before, but Prince hangs on to complete a full set.

October 14: *Controversy* released; reaches Number Three on the R&B chart, and Number 21 on the Pop chart.

November 20: Plays first night of Controversy tour at the Stanley Theater, Pittsburgh, Pennsylvania.

December: Starts work on The Time's *What Time Is It?* during a break between tour dates.

1982

January 6: 'Let's Work'/'Ronnie, Talk To Russia' released; reaches Number Nine on the *Billboard* Soul chart.

January 14: Spends another week on *What Time Is It?* at Sunset Sound, Los Angeles.

January 25: Attends the American Music Awards at the Shrine Auditorium, Los Angeles. Meets Denise Matthews – who will soon become Vanity – at the after-show party.

March 14: Animosity between Prince and The Time spills over into a food fight after the final show of the Controversy tour at the Riverfront Coliseum, Cincinnati.

March: Shoots footage for *The Second Coming* at home in Minneapolis.

March 25: Begins work on a Vanity 6 album and his own *1999* at Sunset Sound, Los Angeles. Sessions continue until April 9.

April 20: Returns to Sunset Sound, where he remains until May 10.

May–July: Works at home on various songs that will subsequently appear either on *What Time Is It?* or on various solo projects, including *1999*, *Parade*, *Around The World In A Day*, *Sign "O" The Times*, and *Graffiti Bridge*.

July 16: 'Do Me, Baby'/'Private Joy' released, but fails to chart.

August 11: Vanity 6's eponymous debut released; reaches Number Six on the R&B chart and Number 45 on the Pop chart.

August 14: Completes work on *1999*.

August 25: The Time's *What Time Is It?* released; reaches Number Two on the R&B chart and Number 26 on the Pop chart.

September 24: '1999'/'How Come U Don't Call Me Anymore?' released; reaches Number Four on the Billboard R&B chart but initially stalls at Number 44 on the Pop chart, before climbing to Number 12 in April 1983 after re-promotion.

October 27: *1999* released; reaches Number Nine in the USA, and Number 30 in the UK.

November 11: 1999/Triple Threat tour begins at the Memorial Auditorium in Chattanooga, Tennessee.

November 21: The *Los Angeles Times* publishes what ends up being the last Prince interview for three years.

November 30: Plays the first of six shows in four days at the Masonic Temple in Detroit, Michigan – the city in which he is most popular.

December 16: '1999' promo video given its first airing on MTV; goes straight onto heavy rotation.

December 22: Photographed alongside Vanity for the cover of *Rolling Stone* but refuses to be interviewed – despite the fact that the cover shoot costs $10,000.

December 31: First leg of Triple Threat tour ends at the Reunion Arena, Dallas, Texas.

1983

January 14: Completes 12-inch mixes of his own 'Little Red Corvette' and Vanity 6's 'Drive Me Wild,' having started work on both a week earlier, while also helping Stevie Nicks with 'Stand Back.'

February 1: The second leg of the Triple Threat Tour begins at the Civic Center in Lakeland, Florida. Prince begins compiling ideas for *Purple Rain* in his purple notebook.

February 9: 'Little Red Corvette'/'All The Critics Love U In New York' is released, and eventually reaches Number Six on the *Billboard* chart, making it Prince's most successful single to date.

February 15: Screenwriter and director William Blinn flies out to see Prince perform in Minneapolis and discuss plans for *Purple Rain* (then known as *Dreams*).

March 3: Voted Critics' Artist Of 1982 by *Rolling Stone*.

Mid March: Alan Leeds is installed as Prince's road manager.

March 24: Jimmy Jam and Terry Lewis miss a concert in San Antonio after traveling to Atlanta to work with The SOS Band.

March 26: Prince, Jesse Johnson, and Morris Day spend the first of two days on the third album by The Time, *Ice Cream Castle*, at Sunset Studios in Los Angeles.

April 10: The Triple Threat Tour ends at the Pavilion, University Of Chicago, Illinois.

April 14: Resumes work on *Ice Cream Castle* with Jesse Johnson and Morris Day. Sessions continue until April 22.

April 18: Jimmy Jam and Terry Lewis are fired from The Time.

May: William Blinn moves to Minneapolis to begin work on a script for *Dreams*. Dez Dickerson leaves The Revolution to pursue a solo career, and is replaced by Wendy Melvoin. (Prince will soon begin an intense relationship with her twin sister, Susannah.)

Mid-May: Prince & The Revolution, The Time, and Vanity 6 begin rehearsals and acting classes in a warehouse in St Louis Park, Minneapolis.

May 16: Wins in six categories at the annual Minnesota Music Awards.

May 23: William Blinn completes first draft of *Dreams*, but leaves the project to work on the third season of the *Fame* TV show.

June 6: *The Wild Heart* by Stevie Nicks released. Prince plays keyboards on 'Stand Back.'

June 29: Voted Musician Of The Year at the second annual Black Music Awards.

August: Denise Matthews (Vanity) quits – or is asked to leave – the *Purple Rain* project.

August 3: Prince & The Revolution make their official debut at the First Avenue club in Minneapolis as part of a benefit for the Minnesota Dance Theater. Recordings of three songs from the show will be used on *Purple Rain*.

August 15: Recording sessions for *Purple Rain* begin at Sunset Sound studios, Los Angeles, continuing until September 21.

August 17: 'Delirious'/'Horny Toad' released; reaches Number Eight on *Billboard*.

September: Patricia Kotero – aka Apollonia – is hired to replace Vanity.

September 15: Albert Magnoli starts work on a new *Purple Rain* script.

October: New versions of 'Let's Go Crazy' and 'Computer Blue' are among the songs recorded in the rehearsal warehouse in St Louis Park, Minneapolis.

November 1: Shooting of *Purple Rain* begins in Minneapolis.

November 23: 'Let's Pretend We're Married'/'Irresistible Bitch' is released, but fails to match the success of Prince's other recent singles, stalling at Number 52.

December 22: Principal shooting of *Purple Rain* completed. While the wrap party takes place, Cavallo Ruffalo & Fargnoli convince Warners to finance the movie's distribution.

December 27: Extra scenes shot for *Purple Rain* in Los Angeles.

1984

January–April: Spends the first few months of the year at Sunset Sound working on The Time's *Ice Cream Castle* and *Apollonia 6*, as well as songs for *Around The World In A Day* and Sheila E.'s *The Glamorous Life*.

May 16: 'When Doves Cry'/'17 Days' released; goes on to become Prince's first US Number One, and biggest UK hit to date (Number Four).

June: Forms The Family with the surviving members of The Time and girlfriend Susannah Melvoin and begins work on an album with them.

June 4: *The Glamorous Life* by Sheila E. released; Number Seven R&B, Number 28 Pop.

June 25: *Purple Rain* released.

July–August: Work continues on The Family's album in Minneapolis. Prince meets Alan Leeds's saxophonist brother Eric Leeds, who plays on the album and joins the live incarnation of The Revolution. Meanwhile, engineer David Rivkin asks string arranger Clare Fischer to work on some Family songs. He will go on to work with Prince throughout his career, but the two will never meet.

July 4: *Ice Cream Castle* by The Time released; reaches Number 24 on the Pop chart and Number Three on the R&B chart.

July 18: 'Let's Go Crazy'/'Erotic City' released, becoming Prince's second US Number One hit.

July 26: *Purple Rain* receives its premiere at Grauman's Chinese Theater, Hollywood.

July 27: *Purple Rain* opens across the USA.

August 4: *Purple Rain* takes over from Bruce Springsteen's *Born In The USA* at Number One on the *Billboard* 200. It will remain there for 24 weeks.

September 7: *A Private Heaven* by Sheena Easton released, featuring the Prince composition 'Sugar Walls.'

September 26: 'Purple Rain'/'God' released; peaks at Number Two in the USA and Number Eight in Britain.

October: Rehearsals commence for the Purple Rain tour in Minneapolis. During this time Prince records 'Condition Of The Heart' for *Around The World In A Day*, finishes The Family's album, and records a longer version of 'I Would Die 4 U.'

October 1: Apollonia 6's Prince-penned eponymous debut is released; Number 24 R&B, Number 62 Pop.

November 4: The Purple Rain tour begins at Detroit's Joe Louis Arena, with support from Sheila E.

November 28: 'I Would Die 4 U'/'Another Lonely Christmas' released; peaks at Number Eight on *Billboard*.

December: Work begins on Sheila E.'s second album, *Romance 1600*. While touring, Prince continues to record songs for his own *Around The World In A Day* in studios across America.

1985

January–February: Continues to work on *Romance 1600* and *Around The World In A Day*.

January 28: Wins in three categories at the American Music Awards, but declines to participate in the post-awards studio session for 'We Are The World.'

February 2: Records '4 The Tears In Your Eyes' for the *We Are The World* album in a mobile recording truck in New Orleans.

February 9: *Purple Rain* is finally knocked off the top of the *Billboard* album chart by Madonna's *Like A Virgin*.

February 19: Wins in two categories at the British Phonograph Industry Awards in London.

February 21: *Around The World In A Day* is given its first airing at Warners' Los Angeles headquarters.

March 25: Wins an Academy Award for Best Original Song Score for 'Purple Rain.'

April: New version of '4 The Tears In Your Eyes' recorded at Los Angeles' SIR Studios. Later included on *The Hits/The B-Sides*. Elsewhere, the previously unknown scriptwriter Becky Johnston begins work on *Under The Cherry Moon*.

April 2: Cavallo Ruffalo & Fargnoli announce that Prince will retire from live performance after the end of the Purple Rain tour, which ends on April 7 at the Orange Bowl, Miami.

April 12: *We Are The World* charity album released, featuring the Prince composition '4 The Tears In Your Eyes.'

April 17: Work begins on *Parade* at Sunset Sound Studios, Los Angeles. Sessions continue until May 17. Prince also films the 'Raspberry Beret' promo video during his stay in LA.

April 22: *Around The World In A Day* released; reaches Number One in the USA and Number Five in the UK.

May: Only a few weeks after the release of one new album, Prince completes work on the first version of another one, *Parade*. Rehearsals begin in a new warehouse building on Washington Avenue, Minneapolis, Prince's old base in St Louis

Park having been torn down to make way for a recording complex.

May 7: *The National Enquirer* publishes an exposé, based on revelations by former bodyguard Chick Huntsberry, entitled 'The Real Prince: He's Trapped In A Bizarre Secret World Of Terror.'

May 15: 'Raspberry Beret'/'She's Always In My Hair' released; reaches Number Two on *Billboard*.

May 24: Returns to Sunset Sound to work on material for a Jill Jones solo album. Also records 'Hello,' which will become the B-side to his next US single ('Pop Life') as well as the UK release of 'Raspberry Beret' (which reaches Number 25). 'Paisley Park'/'She's Always In My Hair' released in the UK, where it reaches Number 18.

June 1: *Around The World In A Day* knocks *We Are The World* off the top of the *Billboard* 200.

June 7: Holds a 27th birthday concert at St Paul's Prom Center, Minneapolis.

June 18: Travels to France with Steve Fargnoli in search of locations and actors for *Under The Cherry Moon*. Returns to Minneapolis at the end of the month to begin casting, having hired Mary Lambert to direct the movie.

July 8: Work on *Parade* continues in another Minneapolis warehouse. Sessions continue into August, during which time Prince also records 'The Question Of U,' which will later crop up on *Graffiti Bridge*.

July 10: 'Pop Life'/'Hello' released; reaches Number Seven on *Billboard*.

August: Flies to Paris, where he is set to start work on *Under The Cherry Moon*, with Susannah Melvoin.

August 19: The Family released; reaches Number 62 on the Pop chart and Number 17 on the R&B chart.

August 26: Sheila E.'s *Romance 1600* released; reaches Number 50 on *Billboard*.

September 7: Becky Johnston completes the screenplay for *Under The Cherry Moon*.

September 16: Shooting of *Under The Cherry Moon* begins in the south of France, by which time Prince has moved into the Beach Regency Hotel in Nice, and is visited briefly by Susannah Melvoin.

October 2: 'America'/'Girl' released; reaches Number 35 on *Billboard*.

November: Paul Peterson quits The Family by phone. The remaining members of the group are subsequently invited to join The Revolution.

November 21: Shooting of *Under The Cherry Moon* completed.

November 26: Returns to Minneapolis and moves into a new house a mile away from Paisley Park.

November 30: 'Mountains' recorded live with The Revolution.

December: Post-production work on *Under The Cherry Moon* begins in San Francisco. Prince also starts work on an instrumental soundtrack for the movie and hangs out on occasion with Michael Jackson.

Late December: *Prince & The Revolution: Live*, a concert movie taped in Syracuse, New York, on March 30, released on VHS.

December 16: Returns to Sunset Sound, where he remains until January 22. His main focus is on *Parade*, but he also records 'Dream Factory' (intended for an album of the same name) and a series of live jams with The Revolution, as well as 'Can I Play With U?,' which forms the basis of an unreleased collaboration with Miles Davis.

1986

January: Shoots the 'Kiss' promo video with Wendy Melvoin. Meanwhile, work has begun on the construction of Paisley Park.

January 2: The Bangles' *Different Light* released, featuring Prince's 'Manic Monday.'

January 22: Completes work on an album entitled *The Flesh* culled from the Sunset Sound jams, but chooses not to release it.

February 3: Starts rehearsing at the Washington Avenue warehouse.

February 5: 'Kiss'/'♥ Or $' released. It becomes Prince's third US Number One, and reaches Number Six in the UK.

February 12: Pepé Willie releases an album of 94 East recordings entitled *Minneapolis Genius: The Historic 1977 Recordings.*

February 17: Work on Jill Jones's album resumes at Sunset Sound. Sessions continue until March 1.

March 3: The first of ten Hit & Run shows takes place at First Avenue, Minneapolis. As with each subsequent show, the venue details are only announced on the day.

March 4: Mazarati's *Mazarati* released on Paisley Park records, featuring Prince's '100 MPH.'

Mid-March: Starts work on *The Dream Factory* in his new home studio.

March 22: Starts work on Sheila E.'s third album at Sunset Sound. Initial sessions continue until March 26.

March 31: *Parade* released; reaches Number Three in the USA and Number Four in the UK.

April 15: Returns to America from Nice – where he had been shooting extra scenes for *Under The Cherry Moon* – after hearing about US air attacks on Libya.

Mid-April: Work continues on *Dream Factory.* At the end of the month Susannah Melvoin moves out of Prince's house, which she had been living in for the past few months.

May 7: 'Mountains'/'Alexa De Paris' released; reaches Number 23 on *Billboard.*

May 20: Wins Best Video ('Raspberry Beret'), Best Film Score (*Parade*), and Best Cover Artwork (*Around The World In A Day*) at the Minnesota Music Awards. Prince & The Revolution perform a short set to close the show.

May 26: Spends the first of four more days working on Sheila E.'s third album at Sunset Sound.

June 7: Celebrates his 28th birthday with a show at the Cobo Arena, Detroit.

June 17: Records material with The Revolution at the Washington Avenue warehouse, various bits of which become part of *The Dream Factory* and, in re-recorded versions, *Graffiti Bridge*, and The Time's *Pandemonium.*

July 1: *Under The Cherry Moon* receives its premiere in Sheridan, Wyoming, after a fan named Lisa Barber wins an MTV competition to have the launch in her hometown.

July 2: *Under The Cherry Moon* opens in cinemas across the USA. 'Anotherloverholenyohead'/'Girls & Boys' is released on the same day, and eventually reaches Number 16 on *Billboard.*

July 7: Resumes work on *The Dream Factory* in his home studio.

July 12: Relocates to Sunset Sound to complete work on the album. Sessions continue until July 18.

July 22: Prince & The Revolution spend the first of six days recording at the Washington Avenue warehouse.

Late July: Wendy Melvoin, Lisa Coleman, and Mark Brown all announce their intention to quit The Revolution, but are persuaded to stay.

August 3: The final Hit & Run show takes place at Madison Square Garden, New York.

Early August: Prince & The Revolution fly to London to begin rehearsals at Wembley Arena for the European Parade tour.

August 12: European Parade tour begins at Wembley Arena, London, and continues through August 31 at the Alsterdorfer Sporthalle in Hamburg, Germany.

September 5: Japanese Parade tour begins at Osaka's Festival Hall.

September 9: Plays final show with The Revolution at Yokohama Stadium, Yokohama, after which he returns to Minneapolis to work on songs for a musical (*The Dawn*) and a new jazz-funk project (Madhouse).

October 5: Returns to Sunset Sound, Los Angeles, where he will remain until December 26. Having scrapped *Dream Factory*, Prince turns his attention to two new projects: *Camille* and *Crystal Ball*, which will later be turned into *Sign "O" The Times* with re-recorded *Dream Factory* material. He also works on songs for other artists, including Sheila E., and records a set of songs for her birthday that later crop up on *The Black Album*.

October 7: Wendy Melvoin and Lisa Coleman are sacked from The Revolution after having dinner in Prince's rented Beverly Hills home. Prince then calls Bobby Z and fires him too. Mark Brown opts to leave of his own accord, but Matt Fink stays on to play in Prince's next band.

October 17: Prince's PR firm, The Howard Bloom Organization officially confirms that The Revolution have split up.

Early December: Warners rejects Prince's new album, a three-record set entitled *Crystal Ball*.

December 11: Throws a birthday party for Sheila E. at the Vertigo club in Los Angeles. The DJ plays an acetate of some songs that would later appear on *The Black Album*.

December 21: Records 'U Got The Look,' as featured on *Sign "O" The Times*.

December 28: Records 'Wally,' a song about breaking up with Susannah Melvoin, in his home studio, but then erases it (although he does reportedly record, and keep, a second version sometime later).

1987

January: Begins three months of rehearsals with his new band at the Washington Avenue warehouse.

January 10: Returns to Sunset Sound to complete work on *Sign "O" The Times* and Sheila E.'s third album, remaining there until January 15.

January 21: *8* by Madhouse released on Paisley Park Records; reaches Number 25 on the R&B chart.

February 18: 'Sign "O" The Times'/'La, La, La, He, He, Hee' released; reaches Number Three on the *Billboard* Pop chart and Number One on the R&B chart, and Number Ten in the UK.

February 19: Sheila E.'s eponymous third album released; reaches Number 56 on the Pop chart, and Number 24 on the R&B chart.

February 23: Begins rehearsals with Madhouse, who will provide support on the Sign "O" The Times tour.

March 21: Previews *Sign "O" The Times* material with a show at First Avenue, Minneapolis.

March 30: *Sign "O" The Times* released; reaches Number Six in the USA, and Number Four in the UK.

April 15: Travels to Europe for rehearsals ahead of the Sign "O" The Times tour.

May 6: 'If I Was Your Girlfriend'/ 'Shockadelica' released; reaches Number 20 in the UK but stalls at Number 67 on *Billboard*.

May 8: Launches Sign "O" The Times tour at the Isstadion, Stockholm, Sweden.

May 26: *Jill Jones*, written by Prince, released on Paisley Park Records.

Late June: Films Sign "O" The Times shows in the Netherlands with a view to releasing a concert movie in lieu of a US tour.

June 29: Sign "O" The Times tour ends at the Sportpaleis, Antwerp, Belgium.

July 6: Records at as-yet unfinished Paisley Park studio for the first time.

July 14: 'U Got The Look'/'Housequake' released; reaches Number Two in the USA and Number 11 in Britain.

July 18: Begins six days' worth of filming soundstage and dramatic footage for the *Sign "O" The Times* movie.

July 30: Starts work on second Madhouse album, *16*. Sessions continue until August 6.

September 11: Officially opens Paisley Park Studios.

September 19: Self-titled album by Taja Sevelle released on Paisley Park Records.

September: Tentatively finishes the script for his next film, *Graffiti Bridge*.

October: Starts work on *The Black Album*.

October 29: The *Sign "O" The Times* movie is screened for the press in Detroit.

November 3: 'I Could Never Take The Place Of Your Man'/'Hot Thing' released; reaches Number Ten in the USA and Number 29 in the UK.

November 18: Madhouse's *16* released, but fails to chart.

November 20: *Sign "O" The Times* opens across the USA.

December 1: Recalls *The Black Album* a week before its scheduled release.

December 10: Starts recording with Ingrid Chavez, before turning his attention later in the month to his own *Lovesexy*.

December 31: Holds a New Year's Eve benefit concert at Paisley Park for the Minnesota Coalition For The Homeless. Miles Davis guests with the band during the encore.

1988

January: Continues work on *Lovesexy* at Paisley Park.

February: Begins rehearsals at Paisley Park for upcoming Lovesexy tour.

March 8: *Lovesexy* listening party held at Warners' Los Angeles offices.

March 13: Records 'Love Song' with Madonna for her *Like A Prayer* album.

Late March: Makes video for 'Alphabet St,' despite having previously refused to do any promotional work for the album.

April 23: 'Alphabet St'/'Alphabet St (This Is Not Music, This Is A Trip)' released; reaches Number Eight in the USA and Number Nine in Britain.

May 10: *Lovesexy* released; stalls at Number 11 on the Billboard 200 but becomes Prince's first Number One album in the UK.

May 24: *Vermillion* by Three O'Clock

released, featuring Prince's 'Neon Telephone.'

June: Spends most of the month at Paisley Park working on a third (unreleased) Madhouse album, a Mavis Staples album, a new project entitled *Rave Unto The Joy Fantastic*, and music for the Lovesexy tour. Also records 'Pink Cashmere,' which is later released on *The Hits/The B-Sides*.

July 1: Fires publicist Howard Bloom, replacing him with senior Warners publicists Bob Merlis and Liz Rosenberg.

July 2: Travels to Paris to begin final *Lovesexy* rehearsals.

July 8: Starts Lovesexy tour at the Palais Omnisport De Paris-Bercy, Paris, France.

July 11: 'Glam Slam'/'Escape' released, despite Prince's attempts to block it. Reaches Number 29 in Britain but fails to chart on *Billboard*.

September 9: European Lovesexy tour ends at Westfalenhalle, Dortmund, Germany. US tour begins five days later at the Met Center, Minneapolis.

September 20: 'I Wish U Heaven'/'Scarlet Pussy' released in the UK, with the B-side credited to Camille; reaches Number 24.

Late September: Works on *Graffiti Bridge* songs at Paisley Park during a break in the Lovesexy tour.

Late October: Returns to Paisley Park to work on songs for *Rave Unto The Joy Fantastic* and *Graffiti Bridge*.

November 7: Sheena Easton's *The Lover In Me* released, featuring Prince's '101' and 'Cool Love.'

November 22: Chaka Kahn's *CK* released, featuring Prince's 'Sticky Wicked.'

November 29: US Lovesexy tour comes to a close at Reunion Arena, Dallas.

December 5: Resumes work on third Madhouse album, *24*. Sessions continue until December 15, around the time that Prince is asked to contribute a soundtrack to *Batman*.

December 31: Fires Cavallo Ruffalo & Fargnoli.

1989

January: Work continues on *Rave Unto The Joy Fantastic*.

January 20: Meets Tim Burton to discuss the *Batman* project.

February 1: Japanese Lovesexy tour opens at The Gym, Sendai; runs until February 13 at Oskajo Hall, Osaka.

Mid-February: Returns to Paisley Park to start work on the *Batman* soundtrack.

March 21: Madonna's *Like A Prayer* released, featuring a Prince co-write, 'Love Song.'

April 19: Two long-form videos taped in Dortmund on September 9 1988, *Livesexy 1* and *Livesexy 2*, released on VHS.

May 24: Mavis Staples's *Time Waits For No One*, which Prince produced and co-wrote much of, is released on Paisley Park Records, but fails to chart.

June: Starts work on a new album by The Time, *Corporate World*.

June 9: 'Batdance'/'200 Balloons' released; reaches Number One in the USA and Number Two in the UK.

June 19: *Batman* receives its premiere in Los Angeles.

June 20: *Batman* soundtrack released; eventually tops the charts on both sides of the Atlantic (the first Prince album to do so).

June 23: *Batman* opens across America.

June 26: *Be Yourself* by Patti LaBelle released, featuring Prince's 'Yo Mister' and 'Love 89.'

July: Works on a second Jill Jones album, but scraps plans for Madhouse's *24*. Meanwhile, Kim Basinger moves into Paisley Park and works with Prince on a second draft of the *Graffiti Bridge* script.

August 7: *The Cinderella Theory* by George Clinton released on Paisley Park Records.

September: *Corporate World*, intended as a new album by The Time, is completed.

September 15: 'Partyman'/'Feel U Up' released; reaches Number One in the USA

(Number Six on the R&B chart) and Number 14 in the UK.

Mid September: Starts work on a *Graffiti Bridge* album, reaching into The Vault for songs dating back as far as 1981.

October 1: Records an extended version of 'Scandalous,' dubbed 'The Scandalous Sex Suite,' with Basinger on vocals.

October 16: 'The Arms Of Orion'/'I Love U In Me' released; reaches Number 36 in the USA and Number 27 in the UK.

November: Meets Minneapolis club owner Ruth Bower to discuss plans to open a club together. Prince and Bower subsequently form a company, Heaven & Earth; Prince gives his 90 per cent share to bodyguard Gilbert Davison.

November: Albert Magnoli leaves his post as Prince's manager, and is replaced by Arnold Stiefel and Randy Phillips.

November 13: Records 'Funky,' which makes use of samples from material originally recorded for Miles Davis (probably 'Can I Play With U').

November 28: 'Scandalous'/'When 2 R In Love' released; reaches Number Five on the R&B chart, but fails to reach the Hot 100.

Mid December: Completes a new draft of the *Graffiti Bridge* script.

Late December: Begins rehearsals for upcoming Nude tour with a new line-up of Michael Bland (drums), Levi Seacer Jr (bass), Miko Weaver (guitar), Matt Fink and Rosie Gaines (keyboards), and the hip-hop dance trio The Game Boyz (Tony Mosley, Kirk Johnson, and Damon Dickerson).

Late December: Records 'Live 4 Love' and 'Diamonds And Pearls,' both of which will later feature on *Diamonds And Pearls*.

1990

January: Splits up with Kim Basinger, who promptly leaves the *Graffiti Bridge* project.

Early February: Reworks the *Graffiti Bridge* script for the last time.

February 11: Records 'Thieves In The Temple,' a last-minute addition to the *Graffiti Bridge* soundtrack.

February 12: Begins shooting *Graffiti Bridge* in Minneapolis (mostly on the Paisley Park Studios soundstage).

March 23: Completes principal shooting of *Graffiti Bridge*.

April: Postpones Nude tour and starts work instead on a new edit of *Graffiti Bridge* with Steve Rivkin after test audiences react poorly to an early print of the movie.

April 2: Chick Huntsberry dies of a heart attack.

April 30: Plays a benefit concert for Chick Huntsberry at Rupert's, Minneapolis, raising $60,000 for his former bodyguard's family.

May: Construction work begins on Prince's club, Glam Slam Minneapolis.

May 6: Warms up for the Nude tour at the St Paul Civic Center.

May 30: Cancels a press concert in Rotterdam to stay in Minneapolis and continue work on *Graffiti Bridge*.

June 2: Plays first date of the European Nude tour at Stadion Feijenoord, Rotterdam, The Netherlands.

June 19: Begins a record-breaking 16-night residency at Wembley Arena, London.

July 10: The Time's *Pandemonium* released; reaches Number 18 on *Billboard*.

July 17: 'Thieves In The Temple (Part I)'/'Thieves In The Temple (Part II)' released; reaches Number Six on the Billboard Hot 100 (Number One on the R&B chart) and Number Seven in the UK.

July 30: Spends the first of four more days editing *Graffiti Bridge* at home in Minneapolis.

August 4: Resumes Nude tour in Belgium.

August 20: *Graffiti Bridge* album released; reaches Number Six in the USA and Number One in the UK.

August 24: Completes European tour with a final show at London's Wembley Arena.

August 30: Begins Japanese leg of the Nude tour at the Tokyo Dome. Tour continues until September 10 at Yokohama Stadium.

September 11: Returns to the USA and immediately starts work on *Diamonds And Pearls*.

Mid September: Meets Tara Leigh Patrick, whom he will later rename Carmen Electra and record an album for, while shooting extra scenes for *Graffiti Bridge* in Hollywood.

September 18: *I Am* by Eliza Fiorillo released, featuring several Prince co-writes.

September 25: *Graffiti Bridge* album track 'Round & Round' by Tevin Campbell released as a single; reaches Number 12 on the *Billboard* Hot 100 (Number Three on the R&B chart).

Early October: Records 'Insatiable' for *Diamonds And Pearls* as well as an unreleased ten-track *New Power Generation* EP.

October 16: Rosie Gaines performs at the opening of Glam Slam Minneapolis.

October 23: 'New Power Generation (Part I)'/'New Power Generation (Part II)' released; reaches Number 27 on the Billboard R&B chart and Number 26 in the UK.

November 1: *Graffiti Bridge* receives its premiere at the Ziegfeld Theater, New York, before opening across America the following day.

December: Completes work on *Diamonds And Pearls* and promptly begins rehearsals for a tour in support of it, with Tommy Elm (later known as Tommy Barbarella) replacing Matt Fink on keyboards.

December 4: Another track from *Graffiti Bridge*, 'Melody Cool' by Mavis Staples, released as a single (b/w 'Time Waits For No One'); reaches Number 36 on the R&B chart.

December 20: Allows his 12-month contract with Stiefel & Phillips to expire and replaces them with former head of security Gilbert Davison, who also becomes the new president of Paisley Park; promotes press agent Jill Willis to the role of vice president.

1991

January 6: Warms up for an appearance at the Rock In Rio festival with a show at Glam Slam Minneapolis – the first at which his band is announced as The New Power Generation.

January 8: A third *Graffiti Bridge* single, 'Shake'/'The Latest Fashion' by The Time is released, but fails to chart.

January 18: Plays the first of three South American dates at the Rock In Rio festival, Rio de Janeiro, Brazil, followed by a one-off show at Estadio de River Plate, Buenos Aires, Argentina, on January 21, and a second night at Rock In Rio on January 24.

Late January: Sends tracks from the shelved Madhouse album *24* to Miles Davis as part of a renewed attempt at collaboration.

February 1: Sued for $600,000 by Cavallo Ruffalo & Fargnoli for breach of contract, fraud, and denial of contract in bad faith. Responds by suing his former lawyers for negotiating an unfavorable settlement with the management firm. (Both claims are eventually settled out of court.)

February 19: Two new albums featuring Prince collaborations released: *Contribution* by Mica Paris includes his 'If I Love U 2Nite'; *Times Squared* by Eric Leeds (issued on Paisley Park) features several co-writes and instrumental performances.

March: Meets with Warners in an attempt to convince them to release *Diamonds And Pearls* instead of a planned greatest hits set.

March 4: Starts work on solo projects by Ingrid Chavez and Carmen Electra at Larrabee Sound, Los Angeles, where he will remain until April 2. Also works on a long-distance collaboration with Kate Bush, 'Why Should I Love You?'

April 25: Records a new song with Rosie Gains for possible inclusion on her upcoming solo album.

Early May: Hires Lori Elle and Robia La Morte to play 'Diamond' and 'Pearl' for forthcoming live shows, videos, and photo shoots.

May 10: Records 'Gett Off,' which subsequently takes the place of 'Horny Pony' on *Diamonds And Pearls*.

May 14: Paula Abdul's *Spellbound* released, featuring Prince's 'U.'

May 28: T.C. Ellis's *True Confessions* released on Paisley Park Records, featuring three songs co-written by Prince.

Late May: Shoots a promo video for 'Gett Off.'

June 3: Plays two unscheduled concerts in Los Angeles: a lunchtime showcase at Warners, and an evening set at the China Club, Hollywood.

June 7: Marks his 33rd birthday by having a limited edition 12-inch pressing of 'Gett Off' sent out to club and radio DJs.

July 19: Performs at the opening of the Special Olympics at the Metrodome, Minneapolis.

July 29: 'Gett Off'/'Horny Pony' released; reaches Number 21 in the USA (Number Six on the R&B chart) and Number Four in the UK.

August 16: Plays a showcase set at the annual Warners convention.

August 19: Performs at MTV's tenth birthday celebrations at the Ritz, New York.

August 23: Cancels a one-off show at Blenheim Palace, England, after the production company, Diamond Productions, falls behind with contractual payments. (Unused tickets will be made valid for next year's tour.)

August 27: *Martika's Kitchen* by Markita released, featuring several Prince songs.

September 4: Performs on The Arsenio Hall Show.

September 5: Plays 'Gett Off' at the MTV Video Music Awards at the Universal Amphitheatre, Los Angeles, wearing his infamous 'assless' pants.

September 9: 'Cream'/'Horny Pony' released; reaches Number One in the USA and Number 15 in the UK.

September 10: 'Gett Off' video single released, containing five different promos.

September 18: Records 'My Name Is Prince,' for eventual inclusion on *Love Symbol*.

September 24: *May 19, 1992* by Ingrid Chavez released, featuring several songs co-written by Prince.

September 30: Records 'Letter 4 Miles' in response to Miles Davis's death two days earlier.

October 1: *Diamonds And Pearls* released; reaches Number Three in the USA and Number Two in the UK.

November 4: 'Insatiable'/'I Love U In Me' released; reaches Number Three on the *Billboard* R&B chart but stalls at Number 77 on the Hot 100.

November 8: Spends two weeks at Los Angeles' Record Plant working on 'Race,' as later featured on *Come*, and songs for Carmen Electra's forthcoming debut. Sessions continue until November 23.

November 25: 'Diamonds And Pearls' released; reaches Number Three in the USA (Number One on the R&B chart) and Number 25 in the UK.

December 1: Starts work on the follow-up to *Diamonds And Pearls*, which will eventually be identified only by his androgynous 'love symbol.'

December 15: Served with a $5-million lawsuit by Steve Fargnoli for defamation and breach of contract, in relation to the song 'Jughead.'

December 20: Opens a second Glam Slam club in Yokohama, Japan.

1992

January: Resumes work on the follow-up to *Diamonds And Pearls*.

January 11: Previews his upcoming Diamonds And Pearls tour at Glam Slam Minneapolis.

March 3: 'Money Don't Matter 2 Night'/'Call The Law' released; reaches Number 23 in the USA (Number 14 on the R&B chart) and Number 19 in the UK.

March 31: *Celine Dion* released, featuring Prince's 'With This Tear.'

April 3: Begins the Australasian leg of the Diamonds And Pearls tour at The Dome, Tokyo.

April 13: Plays first Australian show of the tour at the Entertainment Center, Brisbane.

April 25: Records 'Peach' and songs for The New Power Generation's *Goldnigga* at Studios 301, Sydney.

May 1: Alan Leeds resigns as Vice President of Paisley Park Records after ten years of working for Prince.

May 3: Concludes Australian tour at the Cricket Ground, Sydney.

Early May: Works with Mavis Staples on her album, *The Voice*.

May 25: Begins European leg of the Diamonds And Pearls tour at Flanders Expo, Ghent, Belgium.

June 15: 'Thunder'/'Violet The Organ Grinder'/'Gett Off (Thrust Dub)' 12-inch picture disc released in the UK, where it charts at Number 28.

June 30: 'Sexy MF'/'Strollin'' released; reaches Number 66 in the USA (Number 76 on the R&B chart) and Number Four in the UK.

July 12: Concludes European tour at the Palais Omnisport de Paris-Bercy, Paris, France.

July 14: *Night Calls* by Joe Cocker released, featuring a cover of Prince's '5 Women+.'

Mid-July: Records 'Eye Wanna Melt With U,' a last-minute addition to the forthcoming *Love Symbol* album.

August: Shoots promo videos for the *Love Symbol* singles while also working on songs for *Goldnigga*, a movie project called *Act I*, and a live show for ABC-TV, *The Ryde Dyvine*.

August 31: Signs new contract with Warners.

September: Helps out with the recording of Tevin Campbell's second album.

September 29: 'My Name Is Prince'/'Sexy Mutha' released; reaches Number 36 in the USA (Number 25 on the R&B chart) and Number Seven in the UK.

October 6: *Diamonds And Pearls Video Collection* released.

October 13: *Love Symbol* LP released; reaches Number Five in the USA and Number One in the UK.

November 17: Releases two new singles, one each for the pop and R&B markets: '7'/'7 (Acoustic Version)' reaches Number Six on the *Billboard* Hot 100 and Number 27 in the UK; 'Damn U'/'2 Whom It May Concern' reaches Number 32 on the US R&B chart.

December: Works on the soundtrack to the musical *I'll Do Anything*.

1993

January: Records material for the forthcoming *Glam Slam Ulysses* show, as well as songs that will later appear on *Come* and *The Gold Experience*.

January 20: Opens a third Glam Slam club in Los Angeles.

February 9: Carmen Electra's eponymous debut released on Paisley Park Records.

February 16: *Things Left Unsaid* by Eric Leeds released on Paisley Park Records.

February 18: Plays warm-up show at Glam Slam Minneapolis.

February 26: Plays another warm-up show at Glam Slam Los Angeles.

March 8: Begins the Act I tour at the Sunrise Musical Theater, Fort Lauderdale.

April 3: 'The Morning Papers'/'Live 4 Love' released; reaches Number 44 in the USA and Number 52 in the UK.

April 17: Concludes the Act I tour at the Universal Amphitheater, Los Angeles.

April 27: Announces his retirement from music to pursue "alternative media," adding that Warners will receive no further 'new'

material, only unreleased recordings plucked from The Vault.

May: Works on material for *Come* and the musical *Glam Slam Ulysses*.

June 7: Releases a statement confirming plans to change his name to the 'love symbol' that also provides the title of his new album.

June 14: Records a live jam at Paisley Park, footage from which will later form part of *The Undertaker*.

June: Completes work on *Goldnigga*.

Early July: Begins an unsuccessful attempt at recording a third Madhouse album.

July 26: The Act II tour begins at the National Indoor Arena, Birmingham, England.

August 3: Opens a New Power Generation store in Minneapolis, selling perfume, jewelry, and other merchandise, including records and posters.

August 21: *Glam Slam Ulysses* opens at Glam Slam Minneapolis, but closes after only a few weeks following bad reviews and poor attendance.

August 24: *The Voice* by Mavis Staples released on Paisley Park Records.

August 31: 'Peach'/'Soft & Wet' released; reaches Number 50 on the Hot 100, and Number 14 on the R&B chart.

September 7: Plays an early-hours show at the Act II after-show party at Bagley's Warehouse, London, for which tickets are sold to the public, after completing the tour at Wembley Arena. Footage of the after-show set will subsequently by issued on VHS as *The Sacrifice Of Victor*.

Mid-September: Starts work on an album with Mayte.

September 14: *The Hits/The B-sides* – credited to Prince, rather than his new name – released; reaches Number 19 in the USA, and Number Four in the UK.

September 17: Fires Paisley Park Vice President Jill Willis and replaces her with Gilbert Davison.

October: Records material for *Chaos And Disorder* and *The Gold Experience*.

October 5: *The Red Shoes* by Kate Bush released, featuring her collaboration with Prince, 'Why Should I Love You?'

October 12: *Hey Man... Smell My Finger* by George Clinton released on Paisley Park Records.

November 18: 'Peach'/'Nothing Compares 2 U' released; stalls at Number 62 on the R&B chart.

December: Places advertisements in British and American magazines looking for "the most beautiful girl in the world." Responses will be used as part of the promotion and packaging for the upcoming single of the same name. Meanwhile, *The Undertaker* VHS goes on sale at the NPG music store.

1994

Mid January: Works on material later included on *Exodus* and *The Gold Experience*.

February 1: Warners officially closes Paisley Park Records.

February 14: 'The Most Beautiful Girl In The World' released on NPG Records (with Warners' blessing) and distributed independently by Bellmark; reaches Number Two in the USA and Number One in the UK.

March: Starts recording *Kamasutra*, which he continues to work on through to the end of the year. It will later be played at his wedding to Mayte and released as a bonus disc with some versions of *Crystal Ball*, credited to the NPG Orchestra.

March 11: Presents *Come* to Warners. The label is not happy with it, and asks him to record additional, stronger material, which he does during the rest of March and April.

Mid April: Plays a series of one-off concerts at Glam Slam Minneapolis.

April 30: Attends the opening of a second NPG music store in Camden, London.

May 3: Plays the first of two early-morning sets at the Stars & Bars club in Monaco. The first is VIP-only; the second, on May 4, open to the public.

May 6: Plays another early-morning set, this time at Le Bataclan, while in Paris for a television appearance.

Mid May: Starts work on a second New Power Generation album, *Exodus*.

May 19: Presents a new version of *Come* to Warners. A week later, he gives the label *The Gold Experience* and requests that the two albums be released simultaneously, with one credited to Prince and the other to O{+>, in an attempt to see which of his personas is more popular.

May–June: Makes a series of late-night/early-morning appearances of varying length at Glam Slam Minneapolis.

Late June: Plays a series of one-off shows at Glam Slam Los Angeles.

July 14: Plays three shows at the Palladium, New York: one in the early hours of the morning, the second during the afternoon as part of a benefit for the Arthur Mitchell Dance Theater Of Harlem, and the third during the evening.

July 25: Plays the first show of a two-night stand at Glam Slam Minneapolis.

August 9: 'Letitgo'/'Solo' released; reaches Number 31 in the USA (Number Ten on the R&B chart) and Number 30 in the UK.

August 12: *1-800-NEW-FUNK*, a compilation of songs by upcoming NPG artists – as well as 'Love Sign,' Prince's duet with Nona Gaye – released on NPG Records.

August 16: *Come* released by Warners; reaches Number 15 in the USA and Number One in the UK. *3 Chains O' Gold* VHS also released.

Early October: Removes all memorabilia from Glam Slam Minneapolis after Gilbert Davison (whose name the club is in) resigns as head of Paisley Park Enterprises. Replaces Davison with his step-brother, Duane Nelson, who runs the company with Therese Stoulil and Julie Knapp-Winge, hiring and firing other staff seemingly at random in an effort to save money.

October 25: Agrees a reported $1-million deal to allow Warners to release *The Black Album*.

November 1: 'Space (Universal Love Remix)'/'Space' released; reaches Number 72 on the R&B chart.

November 22: *The Black Album* released; reaches Number 47 in the USA and Number 36 in the UK.

Late November: Levi Seacer Jr resigns as head of NPG Records – taking with him his girlfriend, publicist Karen Lee – while Prince is in Berlin for a scheduled performance at the MTV European Music Awards.

December: Films a series of promo videos for tracks planned for inclusion on *Chaos And Disorder*. (Not all of the songs end up on the album.)

1995

January: Starts work on *Emancipation*.

January–February: Plays a series of shows at Paisley Park and Glam Slam Los Angeles showcasing material from *The Gold Experience*.

March 3: Begins the Ultimate Live Experience tour of Europe at Wembley Arena, London.

March 6: *The Undertaker* and *Sacrifice Of Victor* given a wider VHS release by Warner Music Vision.

March 14: 'Purple Medley'/'Kirk J's B-Sides Remix' released; reaches Number 84 in the USA and Number 33 in the UK.

March 27: *Exodus* by The New Power Generation released on NPG Records.

March 30: Completes the Ultimate Live Experience tour at the Point, Dublin, Ireland.

April–June: Hosts a series of parties and plays a number of live shows at Paisley Park and Glam Slam Los Angeles.

August 1: Opens Paisley Park to the public,

with entrance fees varying depending on whether Prince will make a live appearance that day.

August–September: Plays a series of concerts at Paisley Park.

August 20: Glam Slam Los Angeles closes.

September 12: 'Eye Hate U'/'Eye Hate U (Quiet Night Mix)' released; reaches Number 12 in the USA (Number Three on the R&B chart) and Number 20 in the UK.

September 26: *The Gold Experience* released; reaches Number Six in the USA and Number Four in the UK.

November 27: *Child Of The Sun* by Mayte released on NPG Records.

November 30: 'Gold'/'Rock & Roll Is Alive! (And It Lives In Minneapolis)' released; stalls at Number 88 in the USA, but reaches Number Ten in the UK.

Late December: Officially announces his desire to terminate his contract with Warners and begin releasing his music himself on his own terms.

1996

January 6: Glam Slam Miami is shut down after a drugs raid. The New Power Generation music store in Minneapolis also closes down around the same time.

January 8: Begins a short Japanese tour at the Budokan, Tokyo.

January 20: Plays final Japanese date at Yokohama Arena.

Late January: Works on recording and compiling music for *Chaos And Disorder* and *The Vault … Old Friends 4 Sale*.

February 14: Marries Mayte at Park Avenue Methodist Church, Minneapolis, on the same day that he opens his first official website, which he calls The Dawn.

March 19: The *Girl 6* soundtrack, made up entirely of Prince songs, is released.

March 26: 'Girl 6' by The New Power Generation (b/w 'Nasty Girl' by Vanity 6) released; reaches Number 78 on the Billboard R&B chart.

April 1: Mayte's pregnancy is officially announced.
April 19: Paisley Park Studio closes its doors to outside acts.
April 21: Taken to Fairview Southdale Hospital's emergency room with chest palpitations after mixing aspirin and wine.
April 26: Renegotiates deal with Warners, with both parties agreeing to terminate his contract following the submission of two final albums, *Chaos And Disorder* and *The Vault ... Old Friends 4 Sale*.
May 20: Glam Slam Miami reopens for a week before shutting down for good.
June: Begins rehearsals with a new line-up of The New Power Generation.
June 21: 'Dinner With Delores'/'Right The Wrong' released as a promo single in the USA. In the UK – where it is given a proper release – it reaches Number 36.
July 9: *Chaos And Disorder* released, credited to O{+>; reaches Number 26 in the USA and Number 14 in the UK.
Late August/early September: Throws a series of parties at Paisley Park after it is reopened.
Mid September: Mayte is taken to hospital with sharp pains initially feared to be signs of a premature birth.
October 10: Plays *Emancipation* to EMI-Capitol prior to signing a manufacturing and distribution deal with the label.
October 16: Mayte gives birth to a son at Minneapolis's Northwestern Hospital. He is born with a rare genetic defect, Pfeiffer's syndrome, and dies a week later after being taken off life support following two unsuccessful operations.
October 26: Unveils the new NPG line-up during an early-hours show at Paisley Park.
Late October: Travels to Japan, where he will spend the next few days promoting *Emancipation*.
November 4: Tapes an interview with Oprah Winfrey at Paisley Park, to be aired on November 21.

Mid November: Gives a number of newspaper and magazine interviews in support of *Emancipation*.
November 13: 'Betcha By Golly Wow!'/'Right Back Here In My Arms' released; reaches Number 31 in the USA (Number Ten on the R&B chart) and Number 11 in the UK.
November 19: *Emancipation* released, credited to O{+>; reaches Number 11 in the USA and Number 18 in the UK.
December 23: Arlene and Erlene Mojica, Mayte's personal assistant and nanny, are fired from Paisley Park amid rumors that they were planning to sell their stories.
December 28: Performs two preview shows for his Love 4 One Another Charities tour at Paisley Park.

1997
January 7: Begins the Love 4 One Another Charities tour at Philadelphia's Tower Theater.
January 13: Sends two singles out to US radio: 'The Holy River' reaches Number 58 on the Hot 100 Airplay Chart, while 'Somebody's Somebody' hits Number 15 on the Hot R&B Airplay Chart. 'The Holy River' is also given a physical release in the UK, where it reaches Number 19.
February 14: *Kamasutra* by The NPG Orchestra released on cassette through NPG Records on the first anniversary of Prince's marriage to Mayte.
February–April: Makes a series of sporadic live and TV appearances in the USA and the UK.
April: EMI-Capitol shuts down, hampering distribution of *Emancipation*.
May: Starts work on The New Power Generation's *Newpower Soul* album and opens a new website, love4oneanother.com, through which he begins taking pre-orders for *Crystal Ball*.
May 17: Begins a second leg of the Love 4 One Another Charities tour at the CSU Convention Center in Cleveland, Ohio. The

tour continues until June 28 at the United Center, Chicago, Illinois.

July 21: Begins his second tour of the year, Jam Of The Year, at the Pine Knob Music Theater in Clarksdale, Mississippi.

August 23: Meets former Sly & The Family Stone bassist Larry Graham at an early-hours after-show performance at Nashville's Music City Mix Factory. Graham will subsequently become Prince's new spiritual guide and help convert him to the Jehovah's Witness faith. (Later the same day, Prince concludes the first leg of the Jam Of The Year tour at the Pyramid Arena, Memphis, Tennessee.)

Late August: Resumes work on *Newpower Soul*.

September 13: Begins a second leg of the Jam Of The Year tour at the Marine Midland Arena in Buffalo, New York.

Mid-to-late November: Takes a break from the Jam Of The Year tour to continue work on *Newpower Soul*.

December 8: Returns to live performance at the Fargodome in Fargo, North Dakota.

1998

January 22: Plays his final Jam Of The Year show at the New Arena, Oakland, California.

January 29: Initial shipments of *Crystal Ball* are sent out to fans.

February–April: Plays a series of concerts at Paisley Park, with Larry Graham often joining the NPG on stage.

April: Larry Graham moves to Minneapolis with his family.

April 20: 'The One' released as a promo single to radio stations as Prince begins the Newpower Soul tour at the Capitol Ballroom, Washington, DC. The tour continues until June 1 at the Convention Center, Indianapolis, Indiana, and includes several dates at Paisley Park.

June 30: *Newpower Soul* released; reaches Number 22 in the USA and Number 38 in the UK.

July: Plays several more shows at Paisley Park and makes a number of television appearances in support of *Newpower Soul*.

July 21: Makes 'The War' available for download at love4oneanother.com.

August 8: Begins a European Newpower Soul tour at Plaza de Toros, Marbella, Spain. The tour concludes on August 28 at London's Brixton Academy.

September 23: Begins another US tour, the Newpower Soul Festival, at the MCI Center, Washington, DC.

September 29: *Come 2 My House* by Chaka Khan released on Earth Song Records/NPG Records.

October 16: 'Come On' released in the UK with a number of remixes and 'The One' as B-sides; stalls at Number 65 on the singles chart.

October 24: Concludes the Newpower Soul Festival tour at Joe Louis Arena, Detroit, Michigan.

December 11: Holds a press conference in Madrid, announcing that he and Mayte plan to annul their wedding vows in order to renew them in a less traditional fashion.

December 15: Begins his second European tour of the year, Newpower Soul Music Festival Presents ... The Jam Of The Year, at the Pavilhão Atlântico in Lisbon, Portugal. The tour continues until December 28 at the Flanders Expo in Ghent, Belgium.

1999

January 2: Plays a one-off showcase set at Las Vegas' MGM Grand Studios.

February 2: *1999: The New Master* released; stalls at Number 150 on *Billboard*. *GCS2000* by Larry Graham/Grand Central Station is released on the same day by NPG Records.

Late February: Files lawsuits against fan magazines and websites, claiming they make money from bootlegging, passing themselves off as official organizations, and infringing upon his copyright. One of the magazines, *Uptown*, decides to fight his claims.

April: Meets with executives at several major labels in the hope of securing distribution for his next album.

April–May: Plays a series of concerts at Paisley Park (roughly one per week).

May: Signs a deal with Arista to release *Rave Un2 The Joy Fantastic* after bonding with label president Clive Davis.

July 3: Attends an Ani DiFranco concert in Minneapolis and asks both the singer and her sax player, Maceo Parker (a former James Brown sideman), to appear on his new album.

July: Signs an out-of-court settlement with *Uptown* magazine.

August–September: Continues work on *Rave Un2 The Joy Fantastic*.

August 24: *The Vault … Old Friends 4 Sale* released by Warners, credited to Prince rather than O{+>; reaches Number 85 in the USA and Number 47 in the UK.

September 6: Performs at the Mill City Festival, Minneapolis.

September–November: Begins promoting *Rave Un2 The Joy Fantastic*, playing a series of shows at Paisley Park, giving a number of interviews to magazines and television shows; spends two weeks in Europe in November making promotional appearances in the UK, France, Spain, Germany, and The Netherlands.

October 5: 'The Greatest Romance Ever Sold (Radio Edit)'/'The Greatest Romance Ever Sold (Adam & Eve Mix)' released; reaches Number 63 in the USA (Number 23 on the R&B chart) and Number 65 in the UK.

November 9: *Rave Un2 The Joy Fantastic* released; hits Number 18 in the USA but stalls at Number 145 in the UK.

December: Makes final promotional appearances in support of *Rave Un2 The Joy Fantastic* before blaming Arista for its failure to become a massive hit and

demanding the release of a second single. (The label refuses and drops the album from its priority list.)

December 17–18: Shoots a New Year's Eve pay-per-view special, *Rave Un2 The Year 2000*, at Paisley Park. The show features performances by Prince and The Time.

December 31: Allows his publishing deal with Warner/Chappell – the last contract he signed as 'Prince' – to expire.

2000

January–February: Hosts a series of early-hours DanceTilDawn parties at Paisley Park. The parties resume in April and early May, and between July and November.

March 4: Opens a new website, NPG Online, to replace love4oneanother.com.

April: Pays damages of $40,000 each to Tony Mosley and Levi Seacer Jr after claims that they had not received royalties owed to them for *Diamonds And Pearls* and *Love Symbol*.

April 29: Begins shipping the remix album, *Rave In2 The Joy Fantastic*, to NPG Music Club Members.

Mid May: Prince and Mayte divorce (exact date unknown).

May 16: Holds a press conference announcing that he will shortly return to using the name Prince, now that his Warner/Chappell publishing contract has expired.

June 5: *Rave Un2 The Year 2000* released on VHS and DVD.

June 7: Begins a weeklong event, Prince: A Celebration, at Paisley Park, which includes live performances by Prince and other artists, tours of Paisley Park, and the airing of various television appearances and unreleased songs.

July: Meets with the original line-up of The Revolution to discuss the possibility of making a reunion album, to be called *Roundhouse Garden*.

November 7: Begins the Hit N Run tour at the Palladium, Worcester, Massachusetts.

The tour continues until December 10 at the Aladdin Theater For The Performing Arts in Las Vegas, Nevada.
December: Starts recording *The Rainbow Children*.

2001

January–March: Completes work on *The Rainbow Children*, while also working on *One Nite Alone ....*
February 14: Opens another new, subscription-based website, NPG Music Club, designed to give fans full access to rare tracks and priority seating at live shows.
April 6: Makes 'The Work Pt. 1' available on Napster as a digital download.
April 10: 'U Make My Sun Shine'/'When Will We B Paid?' given a physical release; reaches Number 59 on the *Billboard* R&B chart.
April 14: Begins a second leg of the Hit N Run tour at the Civic Center, Atlanta, Georgia. Among the tour merchandise are three exclusive CD singles: 'Supercute'/'Underneath The Cream,' 'The Daisy Chain'/'Gamillah,' and 'Peace'/'2045: Radical Man.'
Late April: Begins shipping the remix album *Rave In2 The Joy Fantastic* to NPG Music Club members.
May 6: Completes the second leg of the Hit N Run tour at the Memorial Auditorium, Sacramento, California.
June 11: Opens a weeklong celebration, The Rainbow Children, at Paisley Park. The event includes listening and Q&A sessions and several live concerts. Much of it is filmed by noted movie director Kevin Smith but never released.
June 15: Begins the A Celebration tour at the Xcel Energy Center, St Paul, Minnesota. The tour continues until June 28 at the Marcus Amphitheater, Milwaukee, Wisconsin.
July 31: *The Very Best Of Prince* released by Warners; reaches Number 55 in the USA and Number Two in the UK.

August 25: Prince's father, John L. Nelson, dies aged 85.
November 20: *The Rainbow Children* is given a conventional release, having previously been made available as a download via NPG Music Club on October 16. It is the first major album to be credited to 'Prince' since 1994's *Come*, but stalls at Number 109 on *Billboard*.
December 31: Marries Manuela Testolini in Hawaii.

2002

February 22: Prince's mother, Mattie Shaw, dies aged 68.
March 1: Begins the US leg of his One Nite Alone ... tour at the Heritage Theater, Saginaw, Michigan. The tour continues until April 30 at the Arlene Schnitzer Concert Hall in Portland, Oregon.
Mid May: *One Nite Alone ...* is sent out to members of the NPG Music Club.
May 28: Begins a three-week Canadian tour at the Orpheum Theater, Vancouver.
June 21: Opens the third annual Paisley Park celebration, which this year is called Xenophobia. The event continues until June 28, and includes live performances by Prince and other associated acts.
June 30: 'Days Of Wild (Live)'/'1+1+1=3' released, but fails to chart.
October 3: Begins a month-long European tour at London's Hammersmith Apollo, finishing up at the Ahoy, in Rotterdam, The Netherlands, on November 2.
November 15: Arrives in Japan for the start of a two-week tour, which begins at the Kokusai Forum Hall in Tokyo.
December 10: *Electric Circus* by Common released, featuring Prince on 'Star *69 (PS With Love).'
December 15: Plays a one-off show at the Aladdin Theater For The Performing Arts, Las Vegas, later issued on DVD as *Live At The Aladdin Las Vegas*.
December 17: Having already been shipped

to NPG Music Club members in November, the three-disc *One Nite Alone ... Live!*, Prince's first official live album, is given a conventional release.

2003

January 1: Makes *Xpectation* available for download to NPG Music Club members, before adding *C-Note* to the site two days later.

February: Records *N.E.W.S.* with NPG musicians including a (briefly) returning Eric Leeds on saxophone.

July: Asks fans to send any unofficial releases they may own with a Warners logo on to Paisley Park. (The response is not good.)

July 29: *N.E.W.S.* is released, one month after appearing as a download on NPG Music Club.

August 19: *Live At The Aladdin Las Vegas* is released on DVD, one week after being made available to NPG Music Club members.

September 18: Announces an eight-date 'world tour,' which begins on October 17 at the Tamar Site in Hong Kong. The remaining dates include five concerts in Australia (in Melbourne, Sydney, and Brisbane) and two in Hawaii in December, at the Volcanoes Club in Honolulu and the Maui Arts & Cultural Center A&B Amphitheater in Kahuli.

2004

Late January: Begins a month-long series of live shows in Las Vegas, Los Angeles, and San Francisco in support of the forthcoming *Musicology*.

February 8: Duets with Beyoncé on a medley of *Purple Rain* songs and her 'Crazy In Love' at the Grammy Awards, sparking a resurgence of mainstream interest.

February 19: Gives a (pre-recorded) interview on *The Tavis Smiley Show*, and performs an acoustic version of 'Reflection'

with Wendy Melvoin – the pair's first public appearance together since 1986.

February 24: Holds a press conference to announce the forthcoming release of *Musicology*.

March 15: Plays lead guitar in an all-star tribute version of George Harrison's 'While My Guitar Gently Weeps' shortly after being inducted into the US Rock And Roll Hall Of Fame – in his first year of eligibility.

March 23: Signs a promotion and distribution deal with Columbia for the release of *Musicology*.

March 27: Plays a one-off pre-tour show at the Lawlor Events Center, Reno, Nevada.

March 29: Begins the Musicology tour at the Staples Center, Los Angeles, California, on the same day that he launches the NPG Music Club download store. Three new albums – *Musicology*, *The Chocolate Invasion*, and *The Slaughterhouse* – are made available for download, along with *The Rainbow Children*, *Xpectation*, *C-Note*, and *N.E.W.S.*

April 7: Sued by fan Anthony Fitzgerald after an incident in December 2003 during which Prince and his bodyguard are alleged to have assaulted Fitzgerald and stolen his camera after he tried to take a photograph of the singer.

April 20: *Musicology* goes on sale in record stores; reaches Number Three in the USA and Number Two in the UK.

May 3: 'Musicology'/'On The Couch' released, with an additional, download-only B-side, 'Magnificent'; stalls at Number 120 on *Billboard*.

May 13: *Rolling Stone* reports that Prince has been in talks with the Blue Note label about releasing a live instrumental album "in the near future."

May 28: Nielsen SoundScan and *Billboard* announce that CDs given away free with ticket purchases will no longer count toward the charts. (The move follows

Prince's successful exploitation of the loophole with *Musicology*.)

June: 'Call My Name' released as a promo single to radio stations. It will eventually peak at Number 27 on the *Billboard* R&B chart, and end up spending longer in the R&B charts than any previous Prince single.

July 2: Performs at the Essence music festival, shortly after appearing as his own support act in a wig, beard, and sunglasses.

Mid-July: Releases *Prince In Hawaii: An Intimate Portrait Of An Artist*, a book of photographs taken during the 2003 concerts in Hawaii.

August 12: Reopens Paisley Park as a movie-and-recording studio for hire. (It had been closed to everyone but Prince since the mid 90s.)

August 24: A double-disc 20th anniversary edition of *Purple Rain* is released on DVD, alongside single-disc versions of *Under The Cherry Moon* and *Graffiti Bridge*.

September 6: 'Cinnamon Girl' released in the UK with B-sides including 'United States Of Division' and audio and video tracks of 'Dear Mr Man (Live At Webster Hall)'; reaches Number 43.

September 11: Plays the final date of the Musicology tour at the HP Pavilion, San Jose, California.

Late September: Threatens prominent fansite housequake.com with legal action after taking a dislike to online discussion and trading of bootleg recordings.

October 2: Makes an agreement with housequake.com, the terms of which state that the website will close its bootleg-trading forums and remove all 'illegal' photos of the Musicology tour.

October 29: Rumors surface that Prince is working on a jazz album. He had previously invited bassist Matt Garrison and trumpeter Wallace Roney to Paisley Park to work on an album alongside former NPG drummer Michael Bland, but neither

musician actually met Prince and nothing came of the sessions.

November: A number of British and American television networks refuse to air the promo video for 'Cinnamon Girl' amid controversy over its depiction of a Muslim girl (played by an actress from New Zealand) who dreams of blowing up an airport.

November 2: First Avenue closes after its founder, Allan Fingerhut, files for bankruptcy.

November 5: Prince wins *Billboard*'s Digital Entertainment Award for Best Use Of Technology By An Artist.

November 12: First Avenue is given permission to reopen under new management.

2005

Late January: Rumors emerge claiming that an untitled acoustic/jazz album is set for release in March, but it never appears. Subsequent speculation suggests that Prince has recorded all-acoustic covers of a number of old songs.

February 13: Wins Grammy awards for Best Traditional R&B Vocal Performance ('Musicology') and Best Male R&B Vocal Performance ('Call My Name'); holds a 'secret' after-show party in the early hours of the following morning at his home in the Hollywood Hills.

February 28: Hosts another early-hours after-show party at his 3121 Hollywood Hills home, this time following the Academy Awards, and performs a short set for the 50 invited guests.

Early March: Sky TV in the UK reports that Prince has written a script for a film based on his life to "dispel the mystery that surrounds him." The same article also makes reference to several unreleased recordings made with Kylie Minogue in 1997.

March 19: Performs with Sheila E. at the

NAACP Image Awards after being given a Vanguard award.

July 12: 'So What The Fuss' by Stevie Wonder released, featuring Prince on guitar. The song also appears on Wonder's first new album in ten years, *A Time To Love* (released October 18).

Early August: The NPGMC asks club members to submit photos of themselves to be used on a dating website accessed in a promo video Prince is planning to make.

September 3: 'S.S.T.' released as a digital download, with proceeds going toward the Hurricane Katrina relief efforts. Prince reportedly wrote and recorded the song the previous day. It is subsequently issued on CD with 'Brand New Orleans' on the B-side, but stalls at Number 111 on *Billboard*.

September 22: The *Minneapolis Star-Tribune* reports that Prince needs a hip operation following health problems stemming from years of dancing in high heels. The story then appears in various other newspapers and magazines, including *The National Enquirer*, but is never confirmed.

November 2: The Songwriters Hall Of Fame announces that Prince is to be inducted at the organization's 37th annual ceremony in 2006.

December 9: *Billboard* reports that Prince has signed a deal with Universal for the release of *3121*.

December 13: Holds a press conference to confirm agreement with Universal, and releases 'Te Amo Corazón,' which reaches Number 67 on the *Billboard* R&B chart.

2006

January 17: Hosts a Golden Globes party in Los Angeles in the early hours of the morning.

January 19: Begins a short tour as a sideman to Támar, whose *Milk & Honey* is scheduled for release in the spring, at the Viper Rooms in Los Angeles.

February 4: Appears on *Saturday Night Live* for the first time in 17 years, performing 'Fury' and 'Beautiful, Loved And Blessed' with Támar.

February 7: 'Black Sweat'/'Beautiful, Loved And Blessed' released; reaches Number 60 in the USA and Number 43 in the UK.

February 15: Performs with the trio of Wendy Melvoin, Lisa Coleman, and Sheila E. for the first time since 1986 at the BRIT Awards in London, England.

February 27: Universal announces details of the *3121* 'Purple Ticket' campaign.

March 13: *How Late Do U Have 2 B B4 U R Absent* by George Clinton released, featuring Prince (as O{+>) on 'Paradigm.'

March 18: Plays final show with Támar at the Mansion Nightclub, Miami, Florida.

March 20: Newspaper reports reveal that Prince is being sued by his landlord over alterations he has made to his home in Los Angeles.

March 21: Appears at Tower Records on Sunset Boulevard at midnight to celebrate the release of *3121*. The album subsequently becomes his first to debut at Number One on the *Billboard* chart, and peaks at Number Nine in the UK.

May 6: Hosts An Evening With Prince: A Private Performance At Prince's House for the 24 winners of the 'Purple Ticket' competition.

May 25: Appears on the season finale of *American Idol*.

May 30: 'Fury'/'Te Amo Corazón (Live At The Brit Awards)'/'Fury (Live At The Brit Awards)' released in the UK, but stalls at Number 60.

June 12: Given a Lifetime Achievement Award at the 10th annual Webby Awards in recognition of his pioneering use of the internet.

June 16: Performs in Bryant Park, New York, as part of *Good Morning America*'s series of Friday morning concerts, and follows it with a late-night appearance for NPGMC members at the tiny Butter nightclub, beginning at 1am and playing for more than four hours.

June 28: Plays an early-hours set the morning after the BET Awards at the Beverley Hills Hotel.

July 4: Shuts down the NPG Music Club website, claiming in an email to members that it has gone "as far as it can go."

August 22: Another Warners best-of album, *Ultimate Prince* released; reaches Number 61 in the USA, and Number Six in the UK.

Early October: Moves into the Rio Hotel in Las Vegas, Nevada, in anticipation of his 3121 Jazz Cuisine residency.

October 31: The *Happy Feet* soundtrack goes on sale, featuring the Golden Globe-winning 'Song Of The Heart,' which Prince wrote specifically for the movie.

November 8: Holds a press conference announcing his 3121 residency at Las Vegas's Rio Hotel.

November 10: Begins a six-month residency in Las Vegas, playing most Friday and Saturday nights until April 28 2007 at the Rio Hotel's Club Rio, which is renamed Club 3121 for the duration. (Regular after-show events are held in the adjacent Jazz Cuisine Restaurant, with catering by Prince's personal chef, Lena Morgan.)

December 22: Reports suggest that Prince is in negotiations to launch a *3121* magazine, which ultimately becomes a new website, 3121.com.

2007

January 31: Plays one-off concert at Hard Rock Live, Hollywood, Florida.

February 1: Holds Super Bowl XLI press conference.

February 4: Performs the Super Bowl XLI halftime show at the Miami Garden stadium.

April 28: Plays the final show of his Club 3121 residency.

May 11: Plays a 'secret' gig at Koko in London, England, during the early hours of the morning, prior to another set at a charity fundraiser at Marlborough House.

June: Plays a series of concerts in and around Los Angeles, including a private gig at the Belmont Hotel on June 2 and four shows at the Roosevelt Hotel, on June 23–24 and 29–30.

May 19: Plays a one-off show at the Orpheum Theater, San Francisco.

June 1: Performs at the 9th annual ALMA Awards, Pasadena Civic Auditorium, Pasadena.

June 2: Performs small ALMA Awards aftershow concert at the Roosevelt Hotel, Hollywood, as part of a larger Grupo Fantasma show; later in the evening Prince joins Grupo Fantasma onstage at The Belmont, Austin, Texas.

June 15: Performs a one-off private function at the Grand Hôtel du Cap-Ferrat, St Jean-Cap-Ferrat, France.

June 24: Plays the first of two nights' concerts and aftershows at the Roosevelt Hotel, Hollywood. Performs a second two-night run at the venue on June 30.

July 7: Launches a line of 3121 perfume with three concerts in 24 hours, all in Minneapolis: at Macy's department store during the afternoon, the Target Center in the evening, and First Avenue during the early hours.

July 9: 'Guitar'/'Somewhere Here On Earth' is given a physical release, having previously been made available by the telecommunications networks Verizon in the USA and O$_2$ in the UK.

July 14: Stages a one-off performance at the Ross School Lawn, East Hampton, New York.

July 15: *Planet Earth* is given away free with copies of the *Mail On Sunday* in the UK.

July 16: Makes a surprise appearance at the Montreux Jazz Festival in Switzerland.

July 24: *Planet Earth* released in the USA, reaching Number Three on *Billboard*.

August 1: Begins his 21 Nights In London

residency at the O_2 Arena in Greenwich. Tickets are priced at £31.21 and include a copy of *Planet Earth*.

August 6: 'Chelsea Rogers'/'Mr Goodnight' released as promotional 12-inch single.

Early September: Teams up with 'internet policing specialist' Web Sheriff and begins cracking down on websites using his image, likeness, music, or videos.

September 19: Performs at the Matthew Williamson fashion show, held in a white tent on Eaton Square, London.

September 21: Plays final 21 Nights show.

September 29: Gives a private performance at Kolomenscoe Park in Moscow, Russia, for a rumored $2 million.

October 16: Hardware provider Ian Lewis sues Prince for $1 million, claiming that the singer took several hard drives worth $120,000 without paying for them, and returned a $25,000 computer in a state of disrepair.

November 5: Sends cease-and-desist letters to various fan websites insisting they remove all images, sleeves, lyrics, and likenesses of him. Three of the major sites – housequake.com, prince.org, and princefams.com – respond by forming Prince Fans United (PFU) and vow to fight the legal action.

November 8: Posts 'PFUnk' online in retaliation to the formation of the PFU coalition.

November 20: 'F.U.N.K.' (formerly 'PFUnk') is released on iTunes.

December 17: Plays at a private party for Jeffrey Soffer, the heir to the Turnberry corporation, for a reported fee of $2 million.

December 23: Shuts down 3121.com and seemingly begins the process of removing himself as much as possible from the internet.

2008

January 8: Nominated for NAACP's Outstanding Male Artist award.

January 10: Forces a taxi driver to remove videos from YouTube that feature Prince music playing on the radio.

January 25: Attends Benny Medina's 50th birthday party at Medina's West Doheny Hills mansion, Beverly Hills, Los Angeles. Prince allegedly insists that he be personally escorted in by the host; later that night, jeweler Pascal Mouawad presents Prince with a $375,000, 5.04-carat canary diamond ring.

January 31: Attends BlackBerry's Pearl 8130 launch party at the A&D Studio, Los Angeles, to watch singer Alice Smith perform.

February 10: Wins Best Male R&B Vocal Performance Grammy for 'Future Baby Mama,' and presents Alicia Keys with the Best Female R&B Vocal Performance award. *1999* is also inducted into the Grammy Hall Of Fame, while the original line-up of The Time reconvene for the first time in 18 years to perform 'Jungle Love' and back Rhianna on 'Umbrella' and 'Please Don't Stop The Music.'

February 25: Plays invite-only 1:30am concert at the 77, his Beverly Hills mansion, following the Academy Awards.

March 7: Joins The Blind Boys Of Alabama on stage at Los Angeles' Knitting Factory for 'Look Where He Brought Me From.'

March 29: Guests with The Escovedo Family at Harvelles, Redondo Beach, California.

April 6: Plays 1am concert at the 77 for about 100 invited friends and celebrities.

April 9: Plays one-off early-hours set at the Green Door, LA.

April 25: Performs unreleased song, 'Turn Me Loose,' on *The Tonight Show With Jay Leno* to promote Coachella appearance.

April 26: Headlines Coachella's Saturday night line-up for a reported $4.8 million.

May 31: Plays at early-hours BookExpo America party at the 77 to celebrate the launch of *21 Nights*.

June: *Entertainment Weekly* names *Purple

Rain the best album released between 1983 and 2008.

June 6: Cancels high-profile concert at Croke Park, Dublin; ticket-holders are notified on June 10, just six days before the concert is due to take place.

June 22: Plays another early-hours show at the 77.

June 25: Plays at invite-only early-hours afterparty concert at his Beverly Hills home, following the June 24 BET Awards.

August 8: Turns up at Las Vegas venues, Planet Hollywood Resort's Privé and Hard Rock Hotel's The Joint, to hang out and watch live music.

August 12: Blocks dentist Andrew Bain's release of 'Purple Rain' on his debut album. Bain's rendition got him signed to Sony for £1 million in July.

August 20: San Jose District Judge Jeremy Fogel rules that "copyright-holders cannot order one of their songs removed from the web without first checking to see if the excerpt was so small and innocuous that it was legal" under fair use. Stephanie Lenz had sued Universal Music Corp for acting in bad faith in removing a 29-second YouTube clip of her 13-month-old son dancing to 'Let's Go Crazy' in June 2007.

August 23: Sits in with Stereofox at the Green Door, Los Angeles, playing guitar on one song.

September 22: Plays another one-off early-hours gig at the 77.

September 30: Releases the *21 Nights* photo book and the attendant *Indigo Nights* live album.

October 1: *21 Nights* is launched at the Dorchester Hotel, London. 'Purple Ticket' winners are invited, but Prince does not attend.

October 10: Performs two concerts at the Ganesvoort Hotel, New York City, as part of the *21 Nights* launch. Proceeds from the $1,000 and $300 tickets for each show are given to the Love 4 One Another and Urban Farming charities.

October 23: Presents Donatella Versace with the Superstar Award at Fashion Group International's 25th annual Night Of The Stars at Cipriani Wall Street, New York City, alongside Jennifer Lopez.

November 5: Is ordered to pay video editor Ian C. Lewis $58,000 in damages after being sued for failure to pay for Lewis's editing work, breaking a $25,000 computer, and not returning other computer equipment.

November 11: Invites Big Boy and the morning crew from LA radio station Power 106 to his house for dinner and to listen to new songs.

November 16: Joins Q-Tip onstage at the House Of Blues, Las Vegas, to play guitar on 'Vibrant Thang.'

November 17: Revelations Perfume & Cosmetics Inc sues Prince and Universal for alleged failure to promote the 3121 perfume, claiming a loss of $2.5 million.

November 24: The *New Yorker* publishes Claire Hoffman's controversial piece 'Soup With Prince.'

December: Prince starts shipping the albums *LotusFlow3r*, *MPLSound*, and *Elixer* to radio stations and selected media, looking for a suitable deal.

December 15: Concert promoter MCD sues Prince following the Croke Park cancellation, claiming €1.7 million in financial loss and damage to its reputation.

December 19: LA radio station Indie 103 premieres 'Crimson & Clover,' 'Colonized Mind,' 'Wall Of Berlin,' and '4Ever' during *Jonesy's Jukebox*.

December 21: Warner Music Group orders that all of its videos be removed from YouTube.

2009

January 6: Guests on stage with Lafayette & Trumbul at Hollywood's Bardot venue.

January 12: Performs an early-hours concert at the 77.

January 29: BET list Prince at Number Three in their Top 25 most influential artists.

January 30: Shoots a *LotusFlow3r* commercial for Target at Universal Studios, Los Angeles.

February 1: Hosts an early-hours lotusflow3r.com celebration party and performs an intimate show at his Beverly Hills mansion, inviting six members of the press and three 'Purple Ticket'-winning fans to "a journey though the galaxy."

February 9: Stages post-Grammys concert at his Beverly Hills mansion in the early hours of the morning.

February 20: Attends *Vanity Fair*'s Hollywood Domino party at Andaz hotel, West Hollywood, Los Angeles, but stays for only five minutes.

February 23: Plays an early-hours Oscars after-party concert at the Avalon, Hollywood. The event is rumored to have been filmed for lotusflow3r.com. The 500 $100 tickets were sold to fans on a first come, first served basis.

February 24: Leading Prince website housequake.com shuts down.

February 28: Stages a benefit concert for Tavis Smiley's Annual State Of The Black Union Symposium at LA Live Nokia Center's Conga Room, Los Angeles.

March 19: Holds a press listening session for *LotusFlow3r*, *MPLSound*, and Bria Valente's *Elixer* at The Crown Bar, Los Angeles, on the same day that the *Minneapolis Star-Tribune* puts at Number 10 in its list of the top 15 greatest Minnesotans.

March 24: *LotusFlow3r*, *MPLSound*, and *Elixer* are made available for download from lotusflow3r.com

March 25: Performs 'Ol' Skool Company' on *The Tonight Show With Jay Leno*.

March 26: Performs 'Dreamer' on *The Tonight Show With Jay Leno*.

March 27: Performs 'Feel Good, Feel Better, Feel Wonderful' on *The Tonight Show With Jay Leno*.

March 28: Plays three shows at the LA Live Nokia Center, Los Angeles, in three venues – the Nokia Theater, the Conga Room, and, in the early hours of March 29, Club Nokia – with three different bands.

March 29: *LotusFlow3r/MPLSound/Elixer* released as a three-CD package in Target stores.

Mid-April: Launches the $2,100 *21 Nights: Prince Opus* in a limited run of 950 copies in conjunction with Kraken Opus.

April 21: Is sued by a literary agency claiming to be his "exclusive agent with respect to the negotiations of a publishing deal" for *21 Nights*.

April 22: Pre-records 'Crimson & Clover' for *The Ellen Degeneres Show*, which airs the following day.

April 27: *Tavis Smiley* airs the first half of a two-part interview with Prince.

April 28: *Tavis Smiley* airs the second part of its Prince interview, along with an interview with Bria Valente.

May 28: Performs 'Somewhere Here On Earth' on the final *Tonight Show With Jay Leno*.

June: 3121 Rep Inc sues the owners of Prince's $150,000-a-month Beverley Hills mansion for the return of a $300,000 security deposit, claiming to have brokered the rental deal for Prince. The property's owners claim that Prince made the payments himself, so the money should go direct to him. Prince, meanwhile, returns back to Minneapolis and begins hanging out at the local clubs, notably Envy.

June 8: Attends Apollo Theater's 75th Anniversary Gala in New York.

July 18: Performs two concerts at the Montreux Jazz Festival.

July 31: Uploads 2009 Montreux Jazz Festival performances of 'Little Red Corvette' and 'When Eye Lay My Hands On U' to lotusflow3r.com.

August 13: Performs two concerts at the Salle Garnier, Monte-Carlo.

August 16: Plays a one-off show at the Sporting Monte-Carlo – Salle des Étoiles, Monte-Carlo.

October 4: Attends the first show by Thom Yorke's new band, Atoms For Piece, at the Orpheum Theater, Los Angeles.

October 5: Attends the Yves Saint Laurent fashion show at the Palais de Tokyo, Paris.

October 6: Attends the Chanel fashion show at the Grand Palais, Paris.

October 7: Attends the Galiano fashion show at Halle Freyssinet, Paris.

October 11: Performs two shows at the Grand Palais, Paris, at 5pm and 10pm. The shows, promoted as 'All Day/All Night,' mark the first time the historic venue has been used for a full concert performance.

October 12: Gives press conference to French journalists at the Hôtel Costes before recording an interview and three-song acoustic set for French station RTL (aired on October 17) and staging a one-off concert at Le Cigale.

October 14: Performs a 15-minute live set for Canal+'s *Le Grand Journal*.

October 17: Uploads RTL performances of 'Feel Good, Feel Better, Feel Wonderful,' 'Mountains/Shake Your Body,' and 'Why You Wanna Treat Me So Bad?' to lotusflow3r.com, along with video recordings from the Montreux Jazz Festival of 'Peach' and 'Eye Love U But Eye Don't Trust U Anymore.'

October 19: Guests on stage with Dr Mambo's Combo at Bunker's, Minneapolis.

October 24: Plays a charity concert at Paisley Park – his first performance there since 2004 – with a Love 4 One Another coat drive.

Early November: The primary Prince bootleg discography site, thedatabank.org, closes down.

November 29: Attends the NFL match between the Minnesota Vikings and the Chicago Bears at the Vikings' Mall Of America Field stadium with Larry Graham.

December 2: Earns a Best Solo Rock Vocal Performance Grammy nomination for 'Dreamer.'

December 9: Art Of Prince opens for the press at the San Francisco Art Exchange, with the public opening following on December 11. The exhibition features work by lotusflow3r.com designer Anthony Malzone.

December 27: *Minneapolis Star-Tribune* gives Prince two spots in its 'Ten Lasting Impressions Of The 00s' feature: for returning to the name 'Prince' and launching the NPGMC in May 2001; and for staging three concerts in his hometown on July 7 2007.

December 31: Attends Black Eyed Peas' New Year's Eve party at the Luxor hotel, Las Vegas.

2010

January 21: Prince's "fight song," 'Purple And Gold,' is uploaded to the Minnesota Vikings' website.

January 29: Makes an appearance at Minneapolis public radio station 89.3 FM The Current's fifth anniversary party at First Avenue.

February 23: Concert promoter MCD's case against Prince begins in Ireland's Commercial Court.

February 25: A California court rules in favor of Stephanie Lenz's right to keep a YouTube posting of her son dancing to 'Let's Go Crazy' online.

February 26: Prince agrees an out-of-court settlement with MCD. Minneapolis radio station 89.3 The Current debuts his new song, 'Cause And Effect.'

March 24: *Minneapolis Star-Tribune* reports that Prince owes "hundreds of thousands" of dollars in back taxes to "the state, the Chaska School District, and a host of other government bodies." (Prince settles the debt on September 13 2010.)

March 31: Attends Janelle Monae's concert at The Varsity, Minneapolis.

May 3: Sits in with Dr Mambo's Combo onstage at Bunker's, Minneapolis, along with several members of the NPG.

May 4: Performs at the Time 100 Gala at Lincoln Center, New York, to celebrate *Time* magazine's '100 Most Influential People Of The Year.'

May 5: Plays a short, unannounced early hours after-show at Village Underground, New York City, backed by the band booked to play that night and NPG singers Shelby J, Liv Warfield, and Elisa Dease.

May 14: Attends the album launch for Gayngs' *Relayted* at First Avenue, Minneapolis. Prince is later captured in a snippet of their promo video for 'The Last Prom On Earth.'

June 7: 'Hot Summer' premieres on 89.3 The Current. It does not appear on any album or single.

June 16: Guests with Larry Graham & GCS at B.B. King Blues Club And Grill, New York City.

June 22: Meets with Warners to discuss a possible US distribution deal for *20Ten* prior to attending a Cassandra Wilson concert at the Cataline Bar & Grill in Hollywood.

June 27: Receives a Lifetime Achievement Award at the tenth BET ceremony, held this year at the Shrine Auditorium, Los Angeles. A tribute performance sees Janelle Monae, Esperanza Spalding, Alicia Keys, and Patti LaBelle perform 'Let's Go Crazy,' 'If I Was Your Girlfriend,' 'Adore,' and 'Purple Rain' respectively.

June 28: Performs a one-off early-hours show at SoHo House, West Hollywood.

July 1: Guests – along with Sheila E. and NPG harmonica player Frédéric Yonnet – on 'Superstition' at Stevie Wonder's concert at Palais Omnisports de Paris-Bercy, Paris.

July 4: Begins a seven-night 20Ten European tour at the Roskilde Festival, Denmark.

July 10: *20Ten* is given away with copies of the UK's *Mirror* newspaper. Similar deals follow with a range of other European publications, including Scotland's *Daily Record*, Belgian newspaper *Het Nieuwblad*, the German editon of *Rolling Stone*, and the French *Courier International*.

July 11: Plays the first of three after-show events during the tour, offering up the only live performance to date of a *20Ten* song, 'Future Soul Song.'

July 25: The European 20Ten tour ends at Espace Nikaïa festival in Nice, France.

August 3: Prince's former lawyer, Ed McPherson, files papers with the Los Angeles court, claiming unpaid legal fees of up to $49,987.74. The case is later settled out of court.

Mid-August: Sheila E. sells the *From E 2 U* EP, featuring a new Prince song, 'Leader Of The Band,' at gigs and online.

October 14: Holds a press conference to announce a new live residency, Welcome 2 America, at the Apollo Theater, Harlem, New York, on the day that 'Rich Friends' leaks online.

October 18: Begins a mini-tour of Northern Europe at Vestlandshallen, Bergen, Norway.

November 7: Plays a three-and-a-half-hour after-show at Viage, Brussels, Belgium.

November 14: Headlines the Yasalam After-Race Concerts closing night at Yas Arena, Yas Island, Abu Dhabi, an exclusive event for attendees of the Abu Dhabi Grand Prix.

November 18: Plays the final night of his mini-tour of Northern Europe at GelreDome, Arnhem, The Netherlands.

December 14: Opens the Welcome 2 America residency with the first of three nights at Izod Center, East Rutherford, New Jersey.

December 18: Plays the first of several Welcome 2 America shows at Madison Square Garden, New York, with a second to follow on December 29.

ENDNOTES

INTRODUCTION
1   *Details* (1991)

CHAPTER 1
1   Liz Jones *Slave To The Rhythm*
2   *A Current Affair* (1991)
3   MTV (1985)
4   *Guitar World* (1998)
5   Liz Jones *Slave To The Rhythm*
6   *Larry King* (1999)
7   Liz Jones *Slave To The Rhythm*
8   *Musician* (1981)
9   *Icon* (1998)
10   *Los Angeles Times* (1981)
11   *Rolling Stone* (1981)
12   *Rolling Stone* (1985)
13   *Prince: The Glory Years*
14   *Liquid Assets: Prince's Millions* (BBC 3 2003)
15   *Prince: The Glory Years*
16   *Central High Pioneer* (February 13 1976)

CHAPTER 2
1   *Prince: The Glory Years*
2   *Rolling Stone* (1990)
3   *Prince: The Glory Years*
4   Alex Hahn *Possessed*
5   *New York Times* (1996)
6   *New York Times* (1996)
7   *New York Times* (1996)
8   Liz Jones *Slave To The Rhythm*
9   Alex Hahn *Possessed*
10   *St Paul Dispatch* (1978)
11   Liz Jones *Slave To The Rhythm*
12   *Prince: The Glory Years*
13   *Prince: The Glory Years*
14   Alex Hahn *Possessed*
15   Dez Dickerson *My Time With Prince*
16   Dez Dickerson *My Time With Prince*
17   Alex Hahn *Possessed*
18   Liz Jones *Slave To The Rhythm*
19   Dez Dickerson *My Time With Prince*

20   *Rolling Stone* (1979)
21   *Observer Music Monthly* (2007)
22   housequake.com (2006)
23   *Keyboard* (1991)
24   Dez Dickerson *My Time With Prince*
25   Alex Hahn *Possessed*
26   Rick James *The Confessions Of Rick James*
27   *Prince: The Glory Years*
28   Dez Dickerson *My Time With Prince*

CHAPTER 3
1   MTV (1985)
2   *Rolling Stone* (1981)
3   *Rolling Stone* (1981)
4   Dez Dickerson *My Time With Prince*
5   Liz Jones *Slave To The Rhythm*
6   housequake.com (2007)
7   Alex Hahn *Possessed*
8   *Rolling Stone* (1981)
9   *Rolling Stone* (1983)
10   *Rolling Stone* (1985)
11   *NME* (November 29 1980)
12   *Prince: The Glory Years*
13   *Rolling Stone* (1981)
14   *Minneapolis Tribune*
15   Liz Jones *Slave To The Rhythm*
16   *Rolling Stone* (1985)
17   *Bass Player* (1999)
18   *Performing Songwriter* (2002)
19   *NME* (November 14 1981)
20   Alex Hahn *Possessed*
21   *Details* (1991)
22   *Sweet Potato* (1981)
23   Dez Dickerson *My Time With Prince*
24   Alex Hahn *Possessed*
25   Dez Dickerson *My Time With Prince*
26   thewavemag.com (2003)

CHAPTER 4
1   *Prince: The Glory Years*

2   Liz Jones *Slave To The Rhythm*
3   Liz Jones *Slave To The Rhythm*
4   *Los Angeles Times* (1983)
5   *Bass Player* (1999)
6   *Rolling Stone* (1990)
7   thelastmiles.com (2005)
8   Alex Hahn *Possessed*
9   *Top 10 80s Soul* (Channel 4 2001)
10   *Musician* (1997)
11   *Prince: The Glory Years*
12   *Rolling Stone* (December 9 1982)
13   Miles Davis with Quincy Troupe *Miles: The Autobiography*
14   *NME* (November 20 1982)
15   *Philadelphia Enquirer* (November 21 1982)
16   Liz Jones *Slave To The Rhythm*
17   thewavemag.com (August 2003)
18   Liz Jones *Slave To The Rhythm*
19   Alex Hahn *Possessed*
20   Alex Hahn *Possessed*
21   Dez Dickerson *My Time With Prince*

CHAPTER 5
1   *Purple Rain: Backstage Pass*
2   Miles Davis with Quincy Troupe *Miles: The Autobiography*
3   *NME* (1995)
4   Liz Jones *Slave To The Rhythm*
5   *Purple Rain: Backstage Pass*
6   *Purple Rain: Backstage Pass*
7   Barney Hoskyns *Imp Of The Perverse*
8   Barney Hoskyns *Imp Of The Perverse*
9   Barney Hoskyns *Imp Of The Perverse*
10   Liz Jones *Slave To The Rhythm*
11   Liz Jones *Slave To The Rhythm*
12   Liz Jones *Slave To The Rhythm*
13   Alex Hahn *Possessed*
14   Alex Hahn *Possessed*
15   Nikki Sixx *The Heroin Diaries*

16 Nikki Sixx *The Heroin Diaries*
17 *Purple Rain: Backstage Pass*
18 MTV (1985)
19 *The Oprah Winfrey Show* (November 21 1996)
20 *Rolling Stone* (1984)
21 *New York Post* (1984)
22 *Miami Herald* (July 27 1984)
23 *Philadelphia Daily News* (July 31 1984)
24 *Detroit Free Press* (July 27 1984)
25 Alex Hahn *Possessed*
26 Alex Hahn *Possessed*
27 Liz Jones *Slave To The Rhythm*
28 Alex Hahn *Possessed*
29 Liz Jones *Slave To The Rhythm*
30 *Rolling Stone* (1985)
31 Dez Dickerson *My Time With Prince*

CHAPTER 6
1 *Liquid Assets: Prince's Millions* (BBC 3 2003)
2 *Rolling Stone* (1985)
3 *Rolling Stone* (1985)
4 *National Enquirer* (May 1985)
5 *Rolling Stone* (1985)
6 *Rolling Stone* (1985)
7 Alex Hahn *Possessed*
8 *Icon* (1998)
9 thelastmiles.com (2005)
10 Liz Jones *Slave To The Rhythm*
11 Liz Jones *Slave To The Rhythm*
12 MTV (1985)
13 Liz Jones *Slave To The Rhythm*
14 WHYT Radio (June 6 1985)
15 *Entertainment Weekly* (1999)
16 MTV (1985)
17 *Rolling Stone* (1985)
18 *Rolling Stone* (1990)
19 *Prince: The Glory Years*
20 *New York Times* (April 22 1985)
21 *NME* (May 4 1985)
22 *New York Times* (April 22 1985)
23 *Detroit Free Press* (April 28 1985)
24 *Rolling Stone* (1985)
25 *Rolling Stone* (1985)
26 *Rolling Stone* (1985)
27 *Rolling Stone* (1985)

28 *Rolling Stone* (1985)
29 *Rolling Stone* (1985)
30 WHYT Radio (June 6 1985)
31 *Liquid Assets: Prince's Millions* (BBC 3 2003)
32 housequake.com (2007)
33 WHYT Radio (June 6 1985)
34 *San Jose Mercury News* (July 3 1986)
35 AOL web chat (July 22 1997)
36 *Philadelphia Daily News* (July 3 1986)
37 *Rolling Stone* (1990)
38 *Prince: The Glory Years*
39 thelastmiles.com (2005)
40 *Detroit Free Press* (March 30 1986)
41 *St Paul Pioneer Press* (1992)
42 *Prince: The Glory Years*

CHAPTER 7
1 *I Love The 80s* (BBC TV 2001)
2 Liz Jones *Slave To The Rhythm*
3 *Mirror* (June 8 2007)
4 AOL web chat (July 22 1997)
5 *Rolling Stone* (1985)
6 prince.org (2005)
7 prince.org (2005)
8 *Rolling Stone* (1990)
9 housequake.com (2007)
10 Alex Hahn *Possessed*
11 *I Love The 80s* (BBC TV 2001)
12 *The Hits/The B-sides* liner notes (Warners 1993)
13 *Rolling Stone* (1990)

CHAPTER 8
1 *Prince: The Glory Years*
2 Yahoo! Internet Live (1997)
3 housequake.com (2006)
4 *Rolling Stone* (1990)
5 Alex Hahn *Possessed*
6 MSN Music Central (1996)
7 *Top 10 80s Soul* (Channel 4 2001)
8 *Rolling Stone* (April 23 1987)
9 *New York Times* (April 12 1987)
10 *NME* (June 4 1987)
11 *Rolling Stone* (1990)
12 Liz Jones *Slave To The Rhythm*
13 Liz Jones *Slave To The Rhythm*

14 prince.org (2005)
15 housequake.com (2007)
16 *Liquid Assets: Prince's Millions* (BBC 3 2003)
17 *Details* (1998)
18 *Rolling Stone* (1985)
19 Miles Davis with Quincy Troupe *Miles: The Autobiography*
20 *Liquid Assets: Prince's Millions* (BBC 3 2003)
21 *Ebony* (2004)
22 *El Pais* (1996)
23 *Rolling Stone* (December 3 1987)
24 *Philadelphia Daily News* (November 20 1987)
25 Alex Hahn *Possessed*
26 thelastmiles.com (2005)
27 *Musician* (1997)
28 Miles Davis with Quincy Troupe *Miles: The Autobiography*
29 Miles Davis with Quincy Troupe *Miles: The Autobiography*
30 thelastmiles.com (2005)
31 thelastmiles.com (2005)
32 *Guitar World* (1998)

CHAPTER 9
1 *Rolling Stone* (1990)
2 Liz Jones *Slave To The Rhythm*
3 Liz Jones *Slave To The Rhythm*
4 Alex Hahn *Possessed*
5 *Rolling Stone* (1990)
6 *NME* (March 11 1995)
7 *Rolling Stone* (1990)
8 Alex Hahn *Possessed*
9 *Rolling Stone* (1990)
10 prince.org (2005)
11 *St Paul Pioneer Press* (May 15 1988)
12 *Rolling Stone* (June 16 1988)
13 *Detroit Free Press* (May 9 1988)
14 prince.org (2005)
15 *Rolling Stone* (1990)
16 *Prince: The Glory Years*
17 Liz Jones *Slave To The Rhythm*
18 *Philadelphia Daily News* (June 20 1989)
19 *Rolling Stone* (August 24 1989)
20 *Detroit Free Press* (June 19 1989)

21 *Rolling Stone* (August 24 1989)
22 *Liquid Assets: Prince's Millions* (BBC 3 2003)
23 *Los Angeles Times* (August 1989)
24 Liz Jones *Slave To The Rhythm*
25 Alex Hahn *Possessed*
26 housequake.com (2007)
27 Liz Jones *Slave To The Rhythm*
28 billboard.com (June 7 2010)
29 *Rolling Stone* (1990)
30 *Rolling Stone* (1990)
31 *Rolling Stone* (1990)
32 *Rolling Stone* (1990)
33 *Entertainment Weekly* (November 1990)
34 *St Paul Pioneer Press* (November 2 1990)
35 *Washington Post* (November 9 1990)
36 *USA Today* (1990)
37 Liz Jones *Slave To The Rhythm*
38 *Rolling Stone* (1990)
39 *Time* (September 17 1990)
40 *Q* (1990)
41 *New York Times* (August 19 1990)
42 *Rolling Stone* (1990)
43 *Village Voice* (1990)

CHAPTER 10
1 prince.org (2005)
2 As told to Charles Waring (2004)
3 *Rolling Stone* (1990)
5 *Liquid Assets: Prince's Millions* (BBC 3 2003)
6 *Details* (1991)
7 housequake.com (2006)
8 *Details* (1991)
9 prince.org (2005)
10 MTV (1995)
11 *Entertainment Weekly* 1990
12 *NME* (October 5 1991)
13 Alex Hahn *Possessed*
14 As told to Charles Waring (2004)
15 fiyamag.com (2005)
16 fiyamag.com (2005)
17 As told to Charles Waring (2004)

18 *Liquid Assets: Prince's Millions* (BBC 3 2003)
19 *Rolling Stone* (November 26 1992)
20 *Interview* (1997)
21 *Spin* (November 1992)
22 *Minneapolis Star-Tribune* (October 11 1992)
23 As told to Charles Waring (2005)
24 As told to Charles Waring (2005)
25 *Details* (1991)
26 As told to Charles Waring (2004)

CHAPTER 11
1 *Rolling Stone* (1996)
2 *USA Today* (1996)
3 *Rolling Stone* (October 14 1993)
4 *Q* (1993)
5 *Entertainment Weekly* (1993)
6 *Liquid Assets: Prince's Millions* (BBC 3 2003)
7 prince.org (2005)
8 As told to Charles Waring (2004)
9 As told to Charles Waring (2005)
10 *Los Angeles Times* (1996)
11 housequake.com (2007)
12 housequake.com (2007)
13 housequake.com (2007)
14 Liz Jones *Slave To The Rhythm*
15 *Interview* (1997)
16 *Time Out* (1995)
17 *The Oprah Winfrey Show* (November 21 1996)
18 *Vibe* (1994)
19 *Rolling Stone* (September 8 1994)
20 *Detroit Free Press* (1994)
21 *St Paul Pioneer Press* (August 16 1994)
22 *Detroit Free Press* (November 29 1994)
23 *Time* (December 12 1994)
24 *LA Times* (1996)

CHAPTER 12
1 *El País* (1996)

2 WHYT Radio (June 6 1985)
3 *Rolling Stone* (1985)
4 *Liquid Assets: Prince's Millions* (BBC 3 2003)
5 *St Paul Pioneer Press* (January 15 1995)
6 *Liquid Assets: Prince's Millions* (BBC 3 2003)
7 *St Paul Pioneer Press* (1995)
8 *An Evening With Kevin Smith*
9 Liz Jones *Slave To The Rhythm*
10 *Liquid Assets: Prince's Millions* (BBC 3 2003)
11 prince.org (December 2005)
12 *Rolling Stone* (1996)
13 MSN Music Central (1996)
14 *The Oprah Winfrey Show* (November 21 1996)
15 *St Paul Pioneer Press* (1996)
16 Liz Jones *Slave To The Rhythm*
17 *St Paul Pioneer Press* (September 24 1995)
18 *Vibe* (1994)
19 *Interview* (1997)
20 *Los Angeles Times* (1996)
21 *USA Today* (1996)
22 *Times* (UK) (July 6 1996)
23 *Los Angeles Times* (1996)
24 *Forbes* (1996)
25 *USA Today* (1996)
26 *USA Today* (1996)
27 *St Paul Pioneer Press* (1996)
28 *El País* (1997)
29 *El País* (1997)
30 *El País* (1997)

CHAPTER 13
1 *Forbes* (1996)
2 *Interview* (1997)
3 *Harper's Bazaar* (1997)
4 *Hello!* (1996)
5 *The Oprah Winfrey Show* (November 21 1996)
6 MSN Music Central (1996)
7 *Guitar World* (1998)
8 *El País* (1996)
9 fiyamag.com (2005)
10 *Los Angeles Times* (1996)
11 *Billboard* (1996)
12 *Chicago Sun-Times* (June 21 1996)

13 nme.com (1996)
14 *New York Times* (1996)
15 *The Oprah Winfrey Show* (November 21 1996)
16 *Interview* (1997)
17 *The Oprah Winfrey Show* (November 21 1996)
18 *Interview* (1997)
19 fiyamag.com (2005)
20 *Interview* (1997)
21 *USA Today* (1996)
22 *Rolling Stone* (1996)
23 *New York Times* (1996)
24 *USA Today* (1996)
25 *New York Daily News* (November 19 1996)
26 *The Oprah Winfrey Show* (November 21 1996)
27 Liz Jones *Slave To The Rhythm*
28 *Muppets Tonight* (ABC September 13 1997)
29 *City Pages* (April 2 1997)
30 *City Pages* (April 2 1997)
31 fiyamag.com (2005)
32 *Paper* (1999)
33 *Minneapolis Star-Tribune* (1999)
34 *Minneapolis Star-Tribune* (1999)
35 fiyamag.com (2005)
36 fiyamag.com (2005)

CHAPTER 14
1 *New York Times* (1999)
2 *NME* (1995)
3 housequake.com (2007)
4 *Guitar World* (1998)
5 *Minneapolis Star-Tribune* (February 24 1998)
6 *NME* (1998)
7 *Vibe* (1994)
8 AOL webcast (1997)
9 *Interview* (1997)
10 *Purple Doves* (2004)
11 *BET Tonight: Talk Back With Tavis Smiley* (October 27 1998)
12 *Good Morning America* (1998)
13 *Guitar World* (1998)
14 *BET Tonight: Talk Back With Tavis Smiley* (October 27 1998)
15 *BET Tonight: Talk Back With Tavis Smiley* (October 27 1998)
16 *USA Today* (1999)

17 *Paper* (1999)
18 *BET Tonight: Talk Back With Tavis Smiley* (October 27 1998)
19 *Details* (1998)
20 prince.org (2005)
21 *Shift* (November 1999)
22 *Paper* (1999)
23 *Minneapolis Star-Tribune* (1999)
24 *USA Today* (1999)
25 *Bass Player* (1999)
26 *Minneapolis Star-Tribune* (1999)
27 *NME* (1999)
28 *Guardian* (1999)
29 *New York Times* (1999)
30 *New York Times* (1999)
31 *USA Today* (1999)
32 *NME* (1999)
33 *Entertainment Weekly* (1999)
34 *Interview* (1997)

CHAPTER 15
1 *An Evening With Kevin Smith*
2 MTV (1985)
3 MTV (1985)
4 *NME* (1995)
5 *Guitar World* (1998)
6 *Guitar World* (1998)
7 *Entertainment Weekly* (2004)
8 *Giant* (2006)
9 *Humo* (May 18 2007)
10 *USA Today* (September 27 2008)
11 *LA Times* (January 8 2008)
12 *USA Today* (2001)
13 *Boston Globe* (November 27 2001)
14 *Rolling Stone* (January 17 2002)
15 *Wired* (2004)
16 housequake.com (2006)
17 Yahoo! Internet Live (2001)
18 *Vibe* (1994)
19 *An Evening With Kevin Smith*
20 *An Evening With Kevin Smith 2*

CHAPTER 16
1 *USA Today* (June 23 2004)
2 *Canadian Press* (2004)
3 *Gallery Of Sound* (September 2004)
4 *Business 2 Magazine* (December 2004)
5 *Forbes* (1996)

6 sfexaminer.com (March 29 2004)
7 *Wired* (September 2004)
8 *Rolling Stone* (2004)
9 *Time* (April 12 2004)
10 *Billboard* (April 15 2004)
11 *Rolling Stone* (April 19 2004)
12 *New York Times* (April 19 2004)
13 *NME* (May 7 2004)
14 sfexaminer.com (March 29 2004)
15 *Los Angeles Times* (April 26 2004)
16 *Billboard* (May 8 2004)
17 *Billboard* (May 8 2004)
18 *Billboard* (May 8 2004)
19 *Newsweek* (2004)
20 MTV.com (April 28 2004)
21 *Newsweek* (April 2004)
22 *Newsweek* (April 2004)
23 *Billboard* (March 17 2006)
24 *Music Week* (February 25 2006)
25 *Minneapolis Star-Tribune* (February 25 2006)
26 *Washington Post* (March 2006)
27 *Chicago Sun-Times* (March 1 2006)
28 *Billboard* (March 2006)
29 *Times* (UK) (March 2006)
30 *Entertainment Weekly* (March 2006)
31 *Billboard* (March 2006)
32 *Minneapolis Star-Tribune* (March 21 2006)
33 housequake.com (April 1 2005)
34 housequake.com (April 1 2005)
35 clubplanet.com (January 4 2007)

CHAPTER 17
1 *USA Today* (September 27 2008)
2 *Entertainment Weekly* (2004)
3 housequake.com (April 2007)
4 Yahoo! News (June 29 2007)
5 *USA Today* (September 27 2008)
6 *Billboard* (July 30 2007)
7 *Telegraph* (July 10 2007)
8 *Guardian* (July 2007)
9 *Rolling Stone* (July 2007)
10 *Tavis Smiley* (April 28 2009)
11 BBC News (November 27 2008)

12   BBC News (November 27 2008)
13   New York Associated Press (October 23 2008)
14   housequake.com (2007)
15   sfgate.com (August 20 2008)
16   theregister.co.uk (September 13 2007)
17   Associated Press (May 30 2008)
18   *Irish Independent* (February 25 2010)
19   *Wall Street Journal* (April 16 2009)
20   *USA Today* (September 27 2008)
21   *New Yorker* (November 24 2008)
22   *LA Times* (January 8 2009)
23   drfunkenberry.com (November 17 2008)
24   *LA Times* (January 8 2009)
25   *LA Times* (January 8 2009)
26   newyorker.com (November 17 2008)
27   latimes.com (December 31 2008)
28   *LA Times* (January 8 2009)
29   New York Associated Press (October 23 2008)
30   *Tavis Smiley* (April 28 2009)
31   *Variety* (April 20 2009)
32   *USA Today* (September 25 2008)
33   *Tavis Smiley* (April 27 2009)
34   *Tavis Smiley* (April 27 2009)
35   latimes.com (December 31 2009)
36   *Tavis Smiley* (April 28 2009)
37   *Tavis Smiley* (April 28 2009)
38   *LA Times* (January 8 2009)
39   *Minneapolis Star-Tribune* (March 25 2009)
40   *Tavis Smiley* (April 28 2009)
41   laist.com (March 21 2009)
42   *USA Today* (March 24 2009)
43   *USA Today* (March 24 2009)

CHAPTER 18
1   *Daily Mail* (July 6 2010)
2   Fox9 (January 21 2010)
3   *Star-Tribune* (March 24 2010)
4   *Star-Tribune* (March 24 2010)
5   stereogum.com
6   drfunkenberry.com (June 24 2010)
7   guardian.co.uk (July 11 2010)
8   *Daily Mirror* (July 5 2010)
9   *Forbes* (July 9 2010)
10   *Ebony* (July 2010)
11   *Daily Mirror* (July 5 2010)
12   New York Associated Press (October 23 2008)
13   *USA Today* (September 27 2008)
14   *USA Today* (September 27 2008)

INDEX

Words In Italics indicate album titles unless specified as something else. 'Words In Quotes' indicate song titles. Page references in **bold** refer to illustrations.

A

A&M (record label), 15
ABC/Dunhill (record label), 15
'Aces,' 14
Ad Company, The, 14
'Adore,' 85
'All My Dreams,' 78
'Alphabet St,' 97
Amendolins, Don, 48
'America,' 63
American Artists Inc, 14
American Idol (TV), 208
American Bandstand (TV), 22
American Music Awards, 36, 59

Anderson, André (aka André Cymone), 11, 18, 21, 29–30, 187
Anderson, Bernadette, 11, 163
Anderson, Linda, 11–12
'Anne Stesia,' 99
'Annie Christian,' 30, 31
'Another Lovely Christmas,' 124
'Anotherloverholenyohead,' 70
Apollonia *see* Kotero, Patricia
Apollonia 6, 51–2, 56
Apollonia 6, 51, 55
Arista, 137, 180–1, 184
Around The World In A Day, 62–5, 70
'Around The World In A Day,' 62
'Avalanche,' 192

B

'Baby,' 14
'Baby I'm A Star,' 49, 54, 100

'Baby Knows,' 183
Baker, Hayward, 10
'Ballad of Dorothy Parker, The,' 73, 85
'Bambi,' 21, 22, 122
Bangles, The, 51, 70
Barber, Lisa, 68
Basinger, Kim, 100–1, 103, 104–5, 124
'Batdance,' 101
Batman (movie), 100
Batman (soundtrack album), 100–3, 124, 135
Beatles, The, 9, 45, 64, 66
'Beautiful, Loved And Blessed,' 205
'Beautiful Ones, The,' 54, 74
'Beautiful Strange,' 184
Bennett, Brenda, 36, 51
Bennett, Roy, 32, 56, 98
Benton, Jerome, 28, 40–1, 52, 67, 74, 77, 103

Beyoncé, 199
Big Chick *see* Charles Huntsberry
'Big Tall Wall,' 74
'Billy Jack Bitch,' 129, 142
Black Album, The, 94–8, 101–3, 133
'Black Sweat,' 205, 207
Blackshire, Kip, 186
Blackwell, John, 186, 192
Bland, Michael, 90, 106, 221
Blinn, William, 47–9
Bliss, Atlanta (aka Atlanta Bliss), 77, 87
Blondie, 25
'Blue Light,' 117
'Bob George,' 94–5
Bobby Z *see* Rivkin, Bobby
Borm, Rob, 112, 136
Bowie, David, 46, 180
Boyer, Boni, 87
Boyer, Greg, 191, 221
Brandt, Gary, 20–2
Bright Lights, Big City (movie), 82
BRIT Awards, 33, 80, 140, 206
Brooks, Greg, 77, 87
Brown, James, 9, 17, 26
Brown, Mark, 30, 57, 69–71, 77, 79,
Burton, Tim, 100–1

C

C–Note, 196
C.O.E.D., 106
Camille, 82–3
Camille (character), 78, 82–3, 92, 95, 102, 191
Campbell, Tevin, 107
'Can I Play With U?,' 91–2
'Can't Stop The Feeling I Got,' 108
Cardenez, Mark, 50
Carmen Electra, 119
Carwell, Sue Ann, 20–1
Castle-Hughes, Keisha, 202
Cavallo & Ruffalo, 20
Cavallo, Ruffalo & Fargnoni, 20, 43, 47, 49, 76, 99, 100, 102, 111, 113, 125, 139

Cavallo, Bob, 20, 23, 25, 38, 47, 49, 51, 54, 66, 88, 99, 102, 135
CBS (record label), 15–16
Champagne, 12, 28, 48, 52
Chaos And Disorder, 143, 164, 165, 167, 174, 181
Chapman, Gayle, 19, 23, 43
Chavez, Ingrid, 95, 96, 105, 119
'Chelsea Rodgers,' 213
Child Of The Sun, 163
'Chocolate Box' 222
Chocolate Invasion, The, 194, 200
'Christ, The,' 188
'Christopher Tracy's Parade,' 69
Clark, Dick, 22
Clinton, George, 17, 65, 76–7, 105, 118, 132, 175, 176, 177
'Cloreen Baconskin,' 174
Coleman, David, 62
Coleman, Gary, 28
Coleman, Lisa, 26, 38, 41, 42, 60–2, 69, 73, 77–9, **146**, 168, 178, 194, 206
Columbia (record label), 91, 137, 192, 201, 211–12
Come, 130, 132–3, 140, 142, 186
'Come On,' 176
Come 2 My House, 176–7
'Comeback,' 166
Command, John, 49
'Computer Blue,' 54
Concrete Jungle, 119–20
'Condition Of The Heart,' 63, 65
Controversy, 29–31, 37
'Controversy,' 31, 38
Controversy tour, 32–4, 36, 40, 47, 56, 98
Corporate World, 103
Cortés, Joaquin, 170
'Crazy You,' 18
'Cream,' 112
'Cross, The,' 85, 188
Crystal Ball, 83–4, 90, 127, 137, 173–4, 179, 181, 192, 194, 220
'Crystal Ball,' 77, 78
Cymone, André *see* Anderson, André

D

D'Arby, Terence Trent, 71, 144
'D.M.S.R.,' 39
'Dance, The,' 200, 207
'Dance On,' 97
'Darling Nikki,' 54–5, 63–4, 204
Daugherty, LaVonne, 12
Davis, Clive, 180–2, 184
Davis, Miles, 37, 39, 45, 69, 87–8, 92
Davis, Támar, 204–6, 221
Davison, Gilbert, 110, 136–7
Dawn, The, 194
Dawson, Rosario, 178
Day, Morris, 11–12, 28, 33–4, 41, 48–50, 52, 53, 55, 103–4, 107, 108, 174, 217
'Dead On It,' 94
'Delirious,' 39, 169
Diamonds And Pearls, 111–3, 117, 122, 124, 126, 135, 183
'Diamonds and Pearls,' 112
Diamonds And Pearls tour, 110, 112–117, 119–20
Dickerson, Damon, 106, **153**
Dickerson, Dez, 19–21, 23, 25, 27, 32–3, 38, 39, 42–3, 48, 57, 66, **145**, 178
'Dinner With Delores,' 143, 165
Dirty Mind, 23, 25–30, 40, 94, 96, 125
'Dirty Mind,' 26, 38, 99
Dirty Mind tour, 26–7, 29
'Do It All Night,' 26
'Do Me, Baby,' 29, 31, 32
Doell, Peter, 37
'Dolphin,' 122–3, 142
'Don't Play Me,' 174
'Don't Talk 2 Strangers,' 162
'Dopamine Rush Suite,' 90
Dream Factory, 73–80, 82–3, 110, 124, 174
'Dream Factory,' 82
Dulfer, Candy, 191
Dylan, Bob, 27, 59, 96
Dyson, Kat, 164, 176

E

Easton, Sheena, 45, 84
Earth Wind & Fire, 15–16, 20
8, 86–7, 90
Electra, Carmen (aka Tara Lee
    Patrick), 119, 127, 136, 222
'Electric Chair,' 101
'Elephants & Flowers,' 108
Elevate Hope Foundation, 106
Elfman, Danny, 101
Elle, Lori, 112
Ellis, T. C., 118
Elm, Tommy, 110
Emancipation, 38, 137, 165–9, 173,
    184, 188, 202
EMI-Capitol (record label), 166, 168
'Empty Room,' 196
'Endorphinmachine,' 132, 141
'Erotic City,' 82, 124, 162, 191, 213
Escovedo, Pete, 55
Escovedo, Sheila *see* Sheila E.
Exodus, 130, 138–9, 175
'Extraordinary,' 182, 192
'Eye No,' 97, 111
'Eye Wanna Melt With U,' 117

F

Family, The, 50, 67, 69, 74, 76, 163
The Family, 74
'Family Name,' 190, 192
Fargnoli, Steve, 20, 25, 32, 38–9,
    51, 61, 65–6, 83, 102, 113,
    135
Fink, Matt, 19, 22–3, 63, 79, 86, 90,
    106, 110–11
Fire It Up tour, 23
First Avenue (club), 49, 52, 54, 57,
    225
Fischer, Clare, 69–70, 73, 74
'5 Women +,' 182
Flesh, The, 73, 86
Flyte Time, 28, 52
Flyte Time Productions, 41
Foley, James, 49
For You, 8, 14, 16–22, 98, 164, 183
'4 The Tears In Your Eyes,' 60, 124

'Forever In My Life,' 75, 85
'Free,' 39
Fresh, Doug E., 178
'Friend, Lover, Sister, Mother/Wife,'
    168
'Funkmachine,' 9
'Fury,' 207
'Future, The,' 101, 106

G

Gaines, Rosie, 110–11, 114,
    119–20, 124, 127, **152**, 164,
    178, 205, 222
Game Boyz, The, 113, 114, 126
Garcia, Anna, 105
Garcia, Mayte, 75, 114–15, 117,
    131, 132, **156**, 162–6, 169–71,
    188, 189, 190
Gasparoli, Tom, 170
Gaye, Nona, 122, 132
Geneva, 186
'Get On The Boat,' 207
'Gett Off,' 112, 136
Girl 6, 162
'Girl 6,' 162
'Girls & Boys,' 68, 70, 162
Glam Slam (clubs), 92, 116, 136,
    140
Glam Slam Ulysses, 119
Glamorous Life, The, 45, 56
'Glamorous Life, The,' 51
Glover, Cat, 87, 94, 96, 98
'Gold,' 142
Gold Experience, The, 122–4,
    129–33, 138–44
Golden Raspberry Awards, 69
Goldnigga, 123, 126–7, 130, 138–9
Gore, Tipper, 55, 57
'(Got 2) Give It Up,' 90
Graffiti Bridge (album), 107–8, 111
Graffiti Bridge (movie), 45, 73, 88,
    99–100, 102–8, 110, 118, 135
Graham, Larry, 12, 29, 128, 171,
    176-9, 186, 223
Grammy Awards, 41, 82, 104, 199
Grand Central, 11–12, 28
Grand Central Corporation, 12

'Greatest Romance Ever Sold, The,'
    182–3
Grumpy Old Men (movie), 136
'Guitar,' 213

H

Hahn, Alex, 179
Hammond, John, 192
Harris, Jimmy *see* Jimmy Jam
'Have A Heart,' 192
Hayes, Isaac, 12
Hayes, Morris, 114, 186, 222
'Head,' 23, 26, 32, 54
'Hello,' 60
High, 194, 200
Hit & Run tour, 76
Hits/The B-Sides, The, 78, 102,
    124–5, 128, 162
Hoffs, Susanna, 51
'Holy River, The,' 168
Hookers, The, 36
'Hot Thing,' 85, 87
'Housequake,' 82, 85–7,
'How Come U Don't Call Me
    Anymore,' 124, 162
Hubbard, Jerry, 50
Huntsberry, Charles 'Chick' (aka Big
    Chick), 33, 41–2, 59–60, 88,
    92, 181
Husney, Britt, 17
Husney, Owen, 10, 14–17, 19, 21,
    142

I

Ice Cream Castle, 45, 50, 55
'I Could Never Take The Place Of
    Your Man,' 85, 165
'I Feel For You,' 22, 45, 177
'I Love U But I Don't Trust U
    Anymore,' 170, 183
'I Love U In Me,' 102, 124, 140
'I Rock Therefore I Am,' 165
'I Wanna Be Your Lover,' 21, 22
'I Want U (Purple Version),' 120
'I Wonder U,' 70, 77
'I Would Die 4 U,' 49, 54

I'll Do Anything (movie), 118, 162, 182
'I'm Yours,' 19, 21
'If Eye Love U 2Night,' 132
'If Eye Was The Man In Ur Life,' 203–4
'If I Was Your Girlfriend,' 85–6, 124,
'In This Bed Eye Scream,' 79, 168
'Insatiable,' 112
'Interactive,' 132, 174
'International Lover,' 39, 40
'It's Gonna Be A Beautiful Night,' 85, 87

J

'Jack U Off,' 31, 39, 108
Jackson, Janet, 41, 71, 211
Jackson, Michael, 42, 45–6, 59, 100, 116, 138, 202
Jagger, Mick, 27, 32
Jam, Jimmy, 28–9, 40–1, 46, 50, 56, 71, 104, 110
'Jam Of The Year,' 120, 176
Jam Of The Year tour, 168–9, 173
James, Rick, 23, 33
Jason, Terry, 11
Jay And Silent Bob Strike Back, 104
Jehovah's Witnesses, 79, 170–1, 178, 186, 188–90, 195, 199, 219, 225
Johnson, Alphonso, 56
Johnson, Becky, 65
Johnson, Cheryl, 129, 142, 189, 199
Johnson, Jellybean, 28, 74
Johnson, Jesse, 28, 33, 34, 40, 41, 55, 61, 82, 104
Johnson, Kirk, 106, 114, **153**, 164
Jones, Jill, 41–2, 67, 76
Jones, Quincy, 46, 59
'Joy In Repetition,' 108
'Judas Smile,' 200
'Jughead,' 113, 126
'Junk Music,' 73
'Just As Long As We're Together,' 15, 16

K

Kamasutra, 90, 175
Kartalos, Olga, 53
Khan, Chaka, 22, 45, 69, 176, 177, 179
King, Marva, 176
'Kiss,' 70–1, 182
Knapp-Winge, Julie, 137
Kotero, Patricia (aka Apollonia), 51, 55
Krattinger, Karen, 56

L

La Morte, Robia, 112
'Ladder, The,' 62, 63, 64
'Lady Cab Driver,' 11, 39
Lambert, Mary, 66–7
Last December, 194
'Last December,' 191
'Le Grind,' 94
Lee, Karen, 137
Lee, Spike, 95, 162
Lee, Tommy, 50
Leeds, Alan, 41, 42, 48, 56, 76, 89, 90, 92, 97, 137, 199
Leeds, Eric, 69, 73–4, 77, 87, 90, 94, 115, 119, 196
'Let's Go Crazy,' 54, 64, 82, 199, 215, 227
'Let's Have A Baby,' 168
'Let's Pretend We're Married,' 55, 187, 228
'Let's Work,' 33
'Letter 4 Miles,' 92
Levinson, Gary, 14
Lewis, John, 90
Lewis, Terry, 28, 40, 50, 56, 71, 104, 110
'Life Can Be So Nice,' 70
'Lion Of Judah,' 80
'Little Red Corvette,' 38–9, 42, 45, 53, 178, 201
'Live 4 Love,' 113
Livesexy 1 (movie), 99
Livesexy 2 (movie), 99
'Loose!,' 133

M

Mabry, Lynn, 106
'Mad Sex,' 176
Madhouse, 76, 79, 86–7, 90, 92, 119, 195, 196
Madonna, 66, 69, 102, 116, 213
Madrid 2 Chicago, 194
Mae, Vanessa, 195–6
Magnoli, Albert, 49, 51–3, 66, 99–100, 103, 104
Mail On Sunday, 138, 212
'Manic Monday,' 51, 70
Marcil, Vanessa, 122
Matthews, Denise (aka Vanity), 36, 41, 43, 49–51, 69, 86,
Mazarati, 69, 71
McClean, Maya, 209
McCreary, Peggy, 37
McMillan, L. Londell, 143, 180
Melvoin, Jonathan,
Melvoin, Susannah, 54, 66, 67, 70, 73–5, 77, 79, 82, 83, 85, 92, 114, 163
Melvoin, Wendy, 43, 48–9, 57, 60, 61, 62, 66, 69, 70, 73, 77, 79, 80, 85, 92, 168, 194, 206
Minneapolis Dance Theater Company, 49
Minneapolis Sound, 28, 41, 57
Minnesota Coalition For The Homeless, 92
Mitchell, Joni, 26, 30, 50, 192
Modernaires, The, 43
Moir, Monte, 28, 50

Love 4 One Another Charities tour, 168, 223
Love4OneAnother, 189
'Love Is Forever,' 14
'Love Sign,' 132
Love Symbol, 116–17, 122–3, 126, 191
Lovesexy, 88, 96–9, 101, 108, 119, 186, 187
'Lovesexy,' 97
Lovesexy tour, 87, 95, 99–102, 135, 201

Mojica, Erlene and Arlene, 170
Mondino, Jean Baptiste, 66, 96
'Money Don't Matter 2 Night,'
    112–13
Montreux Jazz Festival, 223
Moon, Chris, 12, 14, 16
Moonsie, Susan, 30, 36, 41, 51
Morgan, Lena, 209
Mosley, Tony (aka Tony M), 95, 106,
    113, 117, 123, 126, 139, **153**
'Most Beautiful Girl In The World,
    The,' 130–2, 163, 183
'Mountains,' 70, 113
'Movie Star,' 77, 78, 92
MPLS, 132
MPLSoUND, 67, 219–23, 228
MTV, 42, 43, 45, 52, 68
MTV Video Music Awards, 112,
Muppets Tonight (TV), 169
'Muse 2 The Pharaoh,' 190
Musicology, 80, 137, 189, 197,
    199–204, 207, 208
Musicology tour, 104, 201–3, 214
'My Little Pill,' 182
'My Name Is Prince,' 116–17, 126
'My Tender Heart,' 120

N

'Nasty Girl,' 36, 189
National Enquirer (magazine), 46,
    60, 88, 181
N.E.W.S., 196
Nelson, Duane (stepbrother), 10–11,
    89, 137
Nelson, John L. (father), 6, 9–11,
    26, 53, 62, 63, 100, 101, **145**,
    163
Nelson, Olivia (aunt), 11
Nelson, Sharon (half-sister), 14, 26
Nelson, Tyka (sister), 11
Neto, Renato, 175, 191, 196
New Power Generation, The (aka
    NPG), 90, 97, 111, 113,
    115–17, 123, 126, 130, 144,
    162, 166, 175, 186
'New Power Generation, The' (song),
    108

Newpower Soul, 133, 175–7, 179,
    182, 191, 200
1999, 30, 31, 37–40, 45, 49, 65,
    70, 84, 125, 228
'1999,' 6, 38, 42, 78, 100, 178–9
1999/Triple Threat tour, 40–3, 47, 53
1999: The New Master, 120, 178–9,
    184
94 East, 12, 14
'Nothing Compares 2 U,' 74, 75,
    124
'Now's The Time,' 87, 209
NPG Music Club (aka NPGMC), 173,
    184, 186, 191–5, 199, 200–1,
    208, 221
NPG Orchestra, 175
NPG Records (label), 128, 130, 131,
    138–9, 143, 168, 176–8, 179
Nude tour, 106, 110–11, 113, 114,
    119–20, 141
NWA, 94

O

O'Connor, Sinead, 75
O'Neal, Alexander, 28
'Old Friends 4 Sale,' 60, 182
1-800-NEW-FUNK, 90, 131–2
'100 MPH,' 71
One Nite Alone …, 192–4, 221
One Nite Alone … Live, 193
One Nite Alone … tour, 191–3,
    195–6
'1+1+1=3,' 191
'One U Wanna C, The,' 80
Ostin, Mo, 25, 39, 47, 51, 63, 75,
    83, 95, 103, 130

P

'P Control,' 142
'Paisley Park,' 63–4
Paisley Park Records (label), 74–6,
    105, 118–19, 127–8, 137, 175,
    177, 205
Paisley Park (home/studio), 11, 73,
    88, 89, 92, 101, 102, 104, 114,
    122–3, 135–6, 141, 144, 163,

    166, 169, 184, 186, 190, 195,
    209, 223, 225, 227
Pandemonium, 103
'Papa,' 10, 133
Parade, 62, 65, 69–71, 73–4, 76,
    78, 85, 195
Parade tour, 77–80
Parents' Music Resource Center, 55
Paris, Mica, 132
Parker, Charlie, 87
Parker, Maceo, 175, 191, 221
'Partyman,' 101
'Partyup,' 26, 28
Patrick, Tara Lee *see* Electra, Carmen
'Pearls B4 The Swine,' 192
'Peach,' 105, 123, 124
Peterson, Paul, 50, 74
'PFUnk,' 216
'Pheromone,' 133
Phillips, Randy, 103, 110, 136
'Pink Cashmere,' 124, 162
'Place in Heaven, A,' 73
'Plan, The,' 168
Planet Earth, 80, 137, 138, 174,
    211–13, 216, 229
'Play In The Sunshine,' 85
'Pop Life,' 60
'Pope,' 124
'Positivity,' 97
Power, Robin, 45
'Power Fantastic,' 78, 124
Presnail, Heidi, 137
'Prettyman,' 186
Prince Rogers Trio, 9
Prince, 20–22, 25, 27
Prince & The Revolution: Live
    (video), 61
Prince With 94 East: One Man Jam,
    12
'Private Joy,' 30
Purple Rain (album), 11, 33, 45,
    54–6, 61, 63–4, 65, 66, 75, 96,
    103–4, 135, 199, 203
Purple Rain (movie), 10, 28, 43, 45,
    47–53, 56, 66, 67, 69, 103–4,
    203
'Purple Rain' (song), 49, 59, 99,
    227

Purple Rain tour, 55–7, 59, 60–1, 63, 168
'Push It Up,' 176

Q

'Question of U, The,' 108

R

'Race,' 133
Radiohead, 144, 217
Rainbow Children, The, 125, 186–7, 189–92, 195, 196
'Rainbow Children, The,' 191
Raitt, Bonnie, 76
Rasheed, Jerome Najee, 186
'Raspberry Beret,' 63–4, 65, 201
Rave Un2 The Joy Fantastic, 137, 182–4, 186, 200, 202
'Rave Unto The Joy Fantastic,' 101
Rave Un2 The Year 2000 (TV), 184
Rebels, The, 21
'Rebirth Of The Flesh,' 82
'Reflections,' 204
Revolution, The, 48–9, 52, 53, 57, 61–2, 66, 68, 69–70, 71, 73–4, 77–9, 82, 83, 92, 111, 113, 162, 178
Rihanna, 104
Rivkin, Bobby (aka Bobby Z), 18, 19, 23, 40, 47, 49, 70–1, 77, 79, **146**, 194
Rivkin, David, 14, 17, 69
Rivkin, Steve, 105
Rock And Roll Hall Of Fame, 201
Rodgers, Chelsea, 190
Rogers, Susan, 10, 62, 69–70, 75, 82, 86, 95
Rolling Stones, The, 31–2, 75, 211
Romance 1600, 56, 62
'Ronnie, Talk to Russia,' 30, 38
Roundhouse Garden, 79, 194
RSO (record label), 15
Ruffalo, Joe, 20

S

'S&M Groove,' 200
Sacrifice Of Victor, The (video), 123
'Sacrifice of Victor,' 133
Safford, Wally, 75, 87
Sallet, Emmanuelle, 67
Santana, 18, 55
Santana, Carlos, 17, 180, 182
'Satisfied,' 207
'Scandalous,' 100, 101, 104, 112
Scientology, 189
Scott, Mike, 164
Scott Thomas, Kristin, 67–8
'Screams Of Passion, The,' 74
Seacer, Levi Jr, 73, 87, 90, 110–11, 119, 137
Second Coming, The (film project), 34, 47, 89
Seger, Bob, 53
Sevelle, Taja, 76
'7,' 116–17, 136, 140
'17,' 132
'17 Days,' 51
'Sex In The Summer,' 166
'Sexual Suicide,' 77
'Sexuality,' 188
'Sexy MF,' 116–17, 126
Shaw, Mattie (mother), 9, 10, **145**, 163
'She Spoke 2 Me,' 162
'She's Always In My Hair,' 124
'She Gave Her Angels,' 169, 174
Sheila E., 45, 51, 55–7, 62, 70, 73, 74, 77, 87, 91, 92, 94, 98, 106, 206, 217
Sheila E., 56
Shlain, Tiffany, 208
'Shockadelica,' 61, 82
Shoop, Jamie, 36
'Shy,' 142
Sign "O" The Times (album), 74, 77–9, 82–7, 92, 94, 113, 162
Sign "O" The Times (movie), 47, 88–90, 94
'Sign "O" The Times' (song), 84–5, 213

Sign "O" The Times tour, 87–8, 98, 99
Sisco, Rob, 203
'Sister,' 26, 54
'Six,' 87, 92
16, 90
Sixx, Nikki, 50
Slaughterhouse, The, 200
Sly & The Family Stone, 12, 18, 38, 85, 171, 176, 188
Smith, Charles (cousin), 11–12, 20
Smith, Kevin, 138, 194–5
Smith, Rhonda, 106, 164, 175, 196
'Soft & Wet,' 14, 16, 18, 22, 25
'Solo,' 133
'Sometimes It Snows In April,' 70, 79
'Somewhere Here On Earth,' 213
'Song Of The Heart,' 208
Sonny T. *see* Thompson, Sonny
SOS Band, 40, 56
'Space,' 133
Sparks, Billy, 52
Spector, Phil, 16, 38
'Spirituality,' 188
'S.S.T./Brand New Orleans,' 204
Stamp, Terence, 67
Staples, Mavis, 76, 105, 118, 123, 127, 177, 189
'Starfish & Coffee,' 73, 169
Starr, Jamie (alter ego), 28–9, 36–7, 50
Statler, Chuck, 34
Steeles, The, 123
Stefani, Gwen, 182, 183
Stern, Howard, 129
Stiefel, Arnold, 103, 110, 136
Stiffleman, Gary, 143
Stoulil, Therese, 137
'Strange Relationship,' 78, 85
'Sugar Walls,' 45, 55
Superbowl XLI, 211
'Sweet Baby,' 117

T

'Take Me With U,' 51
Támar *see* Davis, Támar

'Tambourine,' 64
'Te Amo Corazón,' 204
'Teacher, Teacher,' 77
'Temptation,' 62, 63
'Ten,' 90
Testolini, Manuela, 170, 189–90
'There Is Lonely,' 182
'Thieves In The Temple,' 107–8, 114
Thompson, Sonny (aka Sonny T), 122, 139
3 Chains O' Gold (video), 117
'3 Chains O' Gold,' 117
3121, 125, 137, 189, 194, 204–8, 221
3121 (fragrance), 217
3121 residency, 104, 208–9
'Thunder,' 112
Thyret, Russ, 15, 142
'Tick, Tick, Bang,' 107–8
Tiffany Entertainment (publishing company), 14
Time, The, 11, 21, 23, 28–9, 32–4, 36–7, 38, 40–1, 43, 46, 49–50, 52, 55–6, 67, 73, 74, 75, 86, 103–4, 107, 110, 118, 194, 208
Time, The, 29
Tony M. see Mosley, Tony
Toys, 79
'Trust,' 101
Truth, The, 173–4, 192
Tutu, 91
21 Nights in London, 46, 75, 137, 138, 189, 190, 213–14, 217
21 Nights In London (book), 217–18, 223, 226
Twinz, The, 190
'200 Balloons,' 101, 102
'2 Nigs United 4 West Compton,' 94

U

'U Got The Look,' 83–4, 87, 183
Ultimate Live Experience tour, 140–1, 144
Ultimate Prince, 125
Under The Cherry Moon (movie), 46, 66–70, 73–5, 96, 107

'Under The Cherry Moon,' 70
Undertaker, The (video), 88, 122–3
Universal (record label), 125, 204–5, 215, 217
'Uptown,' 26, 30, 37, 63
USA For Africa, 59–60

V

Valente, Bria, 178, 190, 219, 222, 229
Vandross, Luther, 41
Vanity see Matthews, Denise
Vanity 6, 36–7, 40, 48, 49, 56, 75, 162, 213
Vanity 6, 36–7, 50
Vault, The, 89, 108, 120, 124, 128–9, 138, 174, 183, 193, 216, 220
Vault, The ... Old Friends 4 Sale, 60, 143, 181–2, 192
'Venus De Milo,' 70, 192
Very Best Of Prince, The, 125
Vicari, Tommy, 17, 20
'Vicki Waiting,' 101
'Visions,' 73, 78

W

'Wally,' 75
Warner Bros (record label), 15–16, 17, 20, 25, 26, 30, 39, 47, 54, 62, 71, 75–6, 83, 90, 91, 95–6, 100, 102–3, 105, 107, 115, 116, 119, 120, 122–133, 135–8, 142–4, 164, 169, 178–9, 181, 227
Warner Bros Pictures, 51–2, 65–6, 69, 75
Waronker, Lenny, 130
'Wasted Kisses,' 176
'We Are The World,' 45, 59
'We Can Work It Out,' 15
Weaver, Miko, 74, 77, 87, 111
Webby Awards, 208
Wendy & Lisa, 79
What Time is It?, 36–7
'When 2 R In Love,' 94, 95

'When Doves Cry,' 45, 52, 54, 59, 125
'When Eye Lay My Hands On U,' 200
White, Maurice, 16, 25
White, Verdine, 15, 16
'Why You Wanna Treat Me So Bad?,' 22, 32
Williams, Clarence III, 53
Willie, Pepé, 12, 14, 19
Willis, Jill, 110, 136
Womack, Bobby, 45
Wonder, Stevie, 15, 25, 38, 59
'Work, Pt. 1, The,' 186
'Wouldn't You Love to Love Me?,' 46
Wyman, Bill, 32

X

'Xenophobia,' 192, 196
Xpectation, 195–6

Y

Yorke, Thom, 217
Young, Angus, 33

Z

Zahradka, Suzy and Gary, 136

AUTHOR'S THANKS

To Darling Nicky and Chota, who have had to put up with more Prince blather than they ever agreed to. If I was anything else, I'd be the water in your bath.

It's taken a lot of work to get here, and I would like to thank: The Jawbone Family: Nigel, Tom (just as well you forgave me my Homer moment), and Jon, for trusting me in the first place, being supportive, and helping me through. Jono Scott, for his ever-vigilant eyes, encouragement, and excellent suggestions. Mum and Dad for putting up with endless phone calls about Prince and other unrelated nonsense that they probably didn't need. Mum also for playing *Diamonds And Pearls* in the car when I was a kid – who knows what effect that might have had? And dad for coming up from Plymouth so that I'd not be alone for one of the 21 Nights In London. Thanks also to Matt for indulging me at the third of six O_2 concerts, and then going out and buying more Prince CDs to confirm that people are still interested. The rest of the family for various things, some related, some not. And everyone else in alphabetical order: Jamie Atkins; Keith Badman, for his ever-upbeat emails and introducing me to the Jawbone team in the first place – if not for you, we'd not be here, and that's pretty, pretty, pretty, pretty good; Joe Harman, who lent me his dad's *Sign "O" The Times* video, which made me spend my last bit of money on the *Purple Rain* and *SOTT* albums the next day; Tim Holmes; Jake and Keri Kennedy, for looking after me and allowing me to descend upon the coast whenever; Alan Lewis; Emily Mackay; Joel McIver; Kris Needs; Simon Oliver and his beady eyes; Sophie Portas – if not for your suggestion all those years back, I wouldn't have considered being a music journalist in the first place; Richard Sugg. Finally … Per Nilsen for his tireless work as a Prince archivist. Without *The Vault*, this book would not be half of what it is.

And, of course, thanks to Prince himself for creating the music and living such a fascinating life.

BIBLIOGRAPHY

Jon Bream *Prince: Inside The Purple Reign* (Collier 1984)
Miles Davis with Quincy Troupe, *Miles: The Autobiography* (Simon And Schuster 1989)
Dez Dickerson *My Time With Prince: Confessions Of A Former Revolutionary* (Pavilion 2003)
Alex Hahn *Possessed: The Ride And Fall Of Prince* (Billboard 2003)
Dave Hill *Prince: A Pop Life* (Faber 1990)
Barney Hoskyns *Prince: Imp Of The Perverse* (Virgin 1988)
Jel D. Lewis (Jones) *Prince – Is Back On Top, The Man, The Artist: In His Own Words* (Xlibris 2006)
Rick James *The Confessions Of Rick James: Memoirs Of A Super Freak* (Amber Communications 2007)
Liz Jones *Slave To The Rhythm* (Warner 1998)
Michaelangelo Matos *Sign 'O' The Times* (Continuum 33⅓ 2004)
Brian Morton *Prince: A Thief In The Temple* (Canongate 2007)
Per Nilsen *Dancemusicsexromance – Prince: The First Decade* (Firefly 1999)
Nikki Sixx *The Heroin Diaries: A Year In The Life Of A Shattered Rock Star* (Pocket Books 2007)
Uptown *The Vault: The Definitive Guide To The Musical World Of Prince* (Uptown 2004)

Plus the following publications, broadcasts, and resources: 3121.com, AOL Online, *An Evening With Kevin Smith*, *An Evening With Kevin Smith 2: Evening Harder*, Associated Press, BBC Magazine online, bbcnews.co.uk, *BET Tonight: Talk Back With Tavis Smiley*, *Bass Player*, *Boston Globe*, *Business 2 Magazine*, *The Canadian Press*, *Central High Pioneer*, *City Pages*, ClubPlanet.com, *A Current Affair*, *Daily Mail*, *Daily Mirror*, *Details*, *Detroit Free Press*, drfunkenberry.com, *Ebony*, *El Pais*, *Entertainment Weekly*, FiyaMag.com, *Forbes*, Fox9, *Gallery Of Sound*, *Giant*, *The Guardian*, *Guitar World*, *Harper's Bazaar*, *Hello*, housequake.com, *Humo*, *I Love The 80s*, *Icon*, *Interview Magazine*, *Irish Independent*, *Keyboard*, laist.com, thelastmiles.com, *Liquid Assets: Prince's Millions*, *Los Angeles Times*, lotusflow3r.com, MSN Music Central, mtv.com, *Minneapolis Star-Tribune*, *Musician*, npgmusicclub.com, *New York Times*, *The New Yorker*, *Paper*, *People Weekly*, *Performing Songwriter*, *Philadelphia Daily News*, *Philadelphia Enquirer*, pitchfork.com prince.org, prince-live.com, *Oprah*, *Prince: The Glory Years*, *Q*, *Record Collector*, theregister.co.uk, *Rocky Mountain News*, *Rolling Stone*, *San Hose Mercury News*, *Shift*, sfexaminer.com, sfgate.com, *Spin*, *St Paul Dispatch*, *St Paul Pioneer Press*, stereogum.com, *Sunday Times*, *Sweet Potato*, *Tavis Smiley*, *The Telegraph*, *Time*, *Time Out*, *Top 10 80s Soul*, *USA Today*, *Variety*, *Vibe*, *Village Voice*, *Wall Street Journal*, *Washington Post*, *Wired*, Yahoo! Internet Live, Yahoo! News.

PICTURE CREDITS

The pictures used in this book were provided by the following copyright holders, and we are grateful for their help. **Jacket front** Brian Rasic/Rex Features; **4** Richard E. Aaron/Redferns/Getty Images; **145** Rex Features; Richard E. Aaron/Redferns/Getty Images; **146–7** Richard E. Aaron/Redferns/Getty Images (2); **148** Brian Rasic/Rex Features; **149** Ebet Roberts/Redferns/Getty Images; **150–1** Nils Jorgensen/Rex Features; Ebet Roberts/Redferns/Getty Images (inset); **152–3** Araldo Di Crollanza/Rex Features (2); **154** Mick Hutson/Redferns/Getty Images; **155** Araldo Di Crollanza/Rex Features; Brian Rasic/Rex Features; **156–7** Paul Bergen/Redferns/Getty Images; Brian Rasic/Rex Features (inset); **158** Kieran Doherty/Redferns/Getty Images; **159** Frank Micellota/Getty Images; **160** JW International/Redferns/Getty Images.

"The problem is getting it all out before another idea comes along." **Prince to *Rolling Stone* (1985)**